DYING FOR RIGHTS

CONTEMPORARY ASIA IN THE WORLD

CONTEMPORARY ASIA IN THE WORLD

David C. Kang and Victor D. Cha, Editors

This series aims to address a gap in the public-policy and scholarly discussion of Asia. It seeks to promote books and studies that are on the cutting edge of their disciplines or promote multidisciplinary or interdisciplinary research but are also accessible to a wider readership. The editors seek to showcase the best scholarly and public-policy arguments on Asia from any field, including politics, history, economics, and cultural studies.

For a complete list of books in the series, see page 375.

DYING FOR RIGHTS

*Putting North Korea's Human
Rights Abuses on the Record*

———

SANDRA FAHY

Columbia University Press
New York

Columbia University Press
Publishers Since 1893
New York   Chichester, West Sussex
cup.columbia.edu

Copyright © 2019 Columbia University Press

Library of Congress Cataloging-in-Publication Data
Names: Fahy, Sandra.
Title: Dying for rights : putting North Korea's human rights abuses
    on the record / Sandra Fahy.
Description: New York : Columbia University Press, [2019] | Includes
    bibliographical references and index. |
Identifiers: LCCN 2018057893 (print) | LCCN 2019012874 (ebook) |
    ISBN 9780231548991 (electronic) | ISBN 9780231176347 (cloth : alk. paper)
Subjects: LCSH: Human rights—Korea (North) | Human rights—Korea
    (North)—International cooperation.
Classification: LCC JC599.K7 (ebook) | LCC JC599.K7 F34 2019 (print) |
    DDC 323/.04409513—dc23
LC record available at https://lccn.loc.gov/2018057893

Columbia University Press books are printed
on permanent and durable acid-free paper.
Printed in the United States of America

Cover image: Getty Images © Christian Petersen-Clausen

This book is dedicated to those who live and die under the system it describes. ∽

Normal men do not know that everything is possible.

—David Rousset

CONTENTS

x Contents

ACKNOWLEDGMENTS

I am grateful to David C. Kang, Victor D. Cha, and Anne Routon for their inspiration to write this book. Two scholars provided superb feedback on the proposal in 2015, which steered the scope of the book in a manageable direction. I am honored to work with Caelyn Cobb in the process of editing, refining, and slimming down this manuscript, while retaining its core importance. I am grateful to Patricia Bower for her excellent copyedit of this book. Two anonymous reviewers read and gave expert feedback on the entire book in a timely, respectful, and detailed manner. I was struck by the sensitivity and care with which they responded to the material.

Among scholars and friends, I wish to thank Jieun Baek, Aleesa Cohene, Danielle Chubb, Carol Dusseer, James Farrer, Anna Fifield, Valérie Gelézeau, Stephan Haggard, Chris Hess, Joon Grane Hetland, Keith Howard, Joanna Hosaniak, Faith Geraghty, Teodora Gyupchanova, Edward Howel, Gwangil Jung, Jean Lee, Seayoun Lee, Anne McKnight, Kathy Moon, Johan Pottier, Leela Rnlt, Jordan A. Y. Smith, Hyun S. Song, David Wank, and Andrew Yeo. Many people cannot be named here as doing so would curtail their access to North Korea in the future.

I am grateful to my parents and my family for encouraging me as I worked through this manuscript. Mary Anna Hawkshaw, thank you for providing necessary mental escapes, fun, and comfort; Pat and Erin, thank you for giving me a quiet, secluded place in which to work on the last phase of the publication. Erin, thanks for asking, "Are you done yet?" as a method of greeting, which made me hide from you and finish. I am grateful to my sisters for providing legal and medical expertise on matters in the book. I am also grateful to my little ones, I.F. and the two who came along in the process, S.P.F. and R.D.A.

My research assistant for this book was Yeonji Ghim, a brilliant, capable, and impressive young scholar—thank you, Yeonji, for the quick turnaround on materials, for your intuition, and for your dedication. Anyone would be lucky to have you as a research assistant, and I am grateful to have had you on board. Yeonji also provided help checking my Korean to English translations, transcribed many of the North Korean documentaries, and "drank the Kool-Aid" with me as we pored over North Korea's state media together. She also translated materials from Chinese and Japanese.

Some of the news articles in this text are from Russian, Chinese, Czech, and Swahili language sources. I am grateful to translation assistance from Evgeniya Kawai, Lenka, NaVylete, and Kinyua L. Kithinji.

I am deeply grateful to my colleagues in the Faculty of Liberal Arts at Sophia University for selecting this manuscript for two grants that helped in the research and preparation of the manuscript. The Academy of Korean Studies provided a grant that helped research into military civilian relations in the Democratic People's Republic of Korea (Grant number: AKS-2014-R04). During the writing of this book, portions of chapters were presented at universities in the United States and Japan. I am grateful to the gathering of faculty and students at these institutes where ideas for this book could be road-tested prior to publication: Wellesley College, the University of Oregon, Yale University's Council on East Asia Relations, and Hitotsubashi University.

DYING FOR RIGHTS

INTRODUCTION

Descent

A line of poetry kept surfacing in my mind as I wrote this book. It's by the poet and novelist Rainer Maria Rilke. Rilke is popular among South Korean readers; I suspect, if they could, North Koreans would love him too. The line, from *Sonnets to Orpheus*, originally was written as a grave marker: "among these winters there is one so endlessly winter / that only by wintering through it will your heart survive."[1]

Researching North Korea's rights situation, as I have for nearly two decades, is like wintering through an endless winter. Those who join in this practice—former North Koreans, activists, scholars—know the grief that comes with it, though we don't often agree on who is entitled to it. I once shared about this grief with a North Korean activist friend. "That was our life," he chided me. "You only have to research it." Laughing, he reminded me, "We *lived* that."

Those of us with ordinary lives, as the epigraph to this book states, hardly know that everything is possible. The best and worst of us is that we can get used to anything. But getting used to everything-that-is-possible is not the same as putting violations on the record and looking for a way out of them.

Only a day before this ribbing, I was chatting with Jeong Kwang Il, a former North Korean political prisoner, a man whose story appears in these pages.[2] I asked him a question I often ask North Koreans:

"When you dream, which Korea are you in?"

"I don't," he answered. "Dream? I don't even sleep."

We were in a traditional Korean coffee shop, in a small town outside of Seoul. It was early 2018. Snow sat on the mountains and ice floated on the Yellow Sea in heavy chunks. The coffee shop was empty except for Jeong, his bodyguard (defectors who are outspoken about the North Korean regime in South Korea are given guards for protection), and a fellow activist friend. Though Jeong had lived for over a decade in South Korea and his bodyguard thought he knew Jeong the whole time, the bodyguard was surprised to learn about the nature of his sleep. "You don't sleep?"

Jeong answered, "I don't sleep. If I sleep, I wake in the prison camp. Every time."

We sat in silence, powerless to remedy this theft, one of so many the regime committed against him. All of us knew his story, the kind of torture he survived in the camp. A pained expression gripped his face, and though we sat in a banal setting, I could see he was back there. I glimpsed that part of him that would always be in the North Korean camp dying for rights.

Later my activist friend, usually based in the United States, said, "Yeah, he never sleeps. He calls me at night because he can't sleep." With or without medication, no sleep without torture. Three o'clock. Four o'clock. Five o'clock in the morning. Sleep brings the prison camp. When he left North Korea (DPRK), the camp came too. Sleep, that indulgent necessity the body and mind crave, even that indulgence is void of pleasure.

Rights violations can be world destroying for those who experience them. The world of wakefulness and the world of sleep—nothing is untouched. Survivors are resilient, of course, but the perpetrator's reach is like a gas seeping into everything, reaching across geopolitical borders, the borders of wakefulness and sleep alike.

Human Rights Violations: The Use of Categories

How did Jeong find himself in the political prison camp to begin with? Each person's story of how they experienced rights violations differs at the level of detail, but there are clear patterns that fall into distinct categories. In order to grasp the spectrum of forces leading to rights abuses in North Korea, it is useful to categorize the types of violations under investigation. When examining rights throughout this study, I categorize them as relating to socioeconomic and political rights, on the one hand, and physical integrity rights, on the other. In other words, violations that emerge from structural factors and those that result from direct physical force. For example, the inability to access food is a structural matter connected to social, economic, and political rights, whereas the state's use of torture is a violation of a person's physical integrity.

Grouping rights in this way serves three purposes. First, the subject of human rights is vast and the array of issues involved gets confusing unless they are categorized. Approaching rights thus categorized is in keeping with traditional framing. It is also in keeping with how things are experienced on the ground, which leads to the second reason.

When social, economic, and political rights are violated, the culprit is difficult to identify. With violations to physical integrity, the perpetrator is right there, willfully causing harm. An apt example comes from when I conducted research with North Korean famine survivors, who had defected to Seoul and Tokyo, for my book *Marching Through Suffering: Loss and Survival in North Korea*. When asked about who or what they saw as responsible for the famine, almost none of the survivors traced culpabilities back to how the country was governed when they lived in the North. Rights violations that are structural manifest in the violation of social, economic, and political rights, and as such, the perpetrator is unseen, diffuse, and at times even assumed not to exist.

Rights violations of the socioeconomic and political variety differ from those of physical integrity violations in how they are perpetrated and experienced. Here I am primarily referring to how these violations are, or are not, understood as connected to state power. For example, an individual's inability to access sufficient food is a qualitatively different human experience than an individual's experience of arbitrary imprisonment, torture, or forced abortion. Thus, categorizing violations enables an assessment of these very different types of human experience.

The third reason is that respect for rights, and their violation, occurs as a plurality. Within this plurality, certain rights bear relation to each other: the failure to uphold one means the other will also fail. Rights are symbiotic; they are mutually supportive. The same occurs when they are violated. Grouping rights according to socioeconomic and physical integrity categories is not arbitrary. There is liaison between these; the violation of socioeconomic and political rights in North Korea often leads to violations of physical integrity rights.

Violations Continue

The details of Jeong's case illustrate the liaison between the failure to uphold socioeconomic and political rights and the violation of his physical integrity. Having no bone to pick with the North Korean government, Jeong led a normal life. He began, in the late 1990s, to conduct cross-border trading in China, an action driven by the desire to improve his family's financial situation. Unable to self-advocate for a different form of political economy in his country, not even thinking such a thing *should* be possible, he conducted his work illegally. Reported to state authorities, he was detained and tortured for nine months, during which they accused him of being a spy for the South Koreans.

In his public testimony to the United Nations Jeong said it would have been better for him to die than to continue to try to convince them of the truth. So he gave a false confession, trading certain death for a life changed by imprisonment and torture. Many North Koreans live unaware of the fact that they trade some rights for others in an effort to stay alive. Many reach the point where they die for lack of rights. Jeong was sent to a political prison camp for three years.[3] His release from the prison, which was unusual, came when it was determined that he was in fact only trading; he was not a spy. Once out of the prison, he left North Korea.

The evidence in this book shows that the North Korean state doesn't give up pursuit of those who defy it. The state's memory is long, and its reach is global. When Jeong defected and spoke out about the state, his fate was sealed. Now it isn't enough to torture Jeong, to turn his sleep into a prison. So long as he speaks about violations internationally to those with power—nongovernmental organizations (NGOs), government officials, readers—North Korea isn't finished with him. The same goes for any defector. Wherever and whenever possible, North Korea is listening, watching, recording. Not to improve human rights and make life better for its citizens but to target those who speak too loudly and gather too large an audience. The state's intention is to threaten and shame them into silence.

Yet many former North Koreans continue to speak about abuses *because* those same abuses continue for friends, family, and neighbor alike, unabated back in North Korea. It is not only of themselves that North Koreans speak; their testimony is often focused on their community of fellows back home. Defectors have no value for the North, but defectors' ability to tell about the life of the North Korean collective to the international community is what the state seeks to silence. Defectors and those who help them—writers, publishers, or even reviewers who identify the faults of the state—are targeted.[4]

Aim, Argument, and Findings of the Book

The aim of this book is to provide an overview of rights violations committed by the North Korean state—domestically and globally, against citizens and noncitizens—from its earliest history up to contemporary times. The book examines North Korea's response to allegations leveled since the 1970s up through the years following the United Nations' groundbreaking Commission of Inquiry report of 2014. The book places emphasis of analysis on violations committed in the contemporary while mapping the historical precedents of rights violations. Since its founding, North Korea has never granted political rights to its people, and though it claimed to provide socioeconomic rights, these went unfulfilled. These earliest of violations are outlined, but my analysis focuses on the last four decades for several reasons: more information is available about contemporary violations; there is global pressure for North

Korea to correct these failings; North Korea is making concerted domestic and international efforts to deny these allegations; and, finally, these violations are ongoing. The past is present. The book aims to be as comprehensive as possible, but it would run into many volumes and thousands of pages if it examined all documented violations. Though gaps may exist, the overall picture is clear, sobering, and disturbing.

The argument presented by the evidence is a sorrowful one: rights violations committed by the North Korean state were in place at the start. In other words, the rights violations are intrinsic to the state and ongoing. The evidence shows that these violations occur as a matter of course in everyday life, domestically and abroad, for citizens. But the story doesn't end there. From the evidence supporting this argument, a laundry list of troubling findings follows.

North Korea violates the rights of its citizens abroad, those who defect, and those who raise a loud voice of critique internationally. The reach of the state is global and its memory no respecter of time. North Korea makes use of foreign nationals as sympathizers, operationalizing them to discount human rights allegations. North Korea makes use of foreign nationals as pawns, using their nation's respect for international human rights norms to angle for North Korean state interests. North Korea produces media for domestic and international consumption aimed at denouncing standard, globally accepted legal human rights norms. It denounces foreign citizens who aim to protect and fight for the rights of North Koreans. The state co-opts foreign media to legitimize and distribute its message globally. Finally, North Korea's international engagement on the subject of rights indicates that it is taking few practical steps to improve conditions while making elaborate efforts to seem as though it is accepting responsibility, even while dodging it.

Despite this, North Korea's rights situation is not a hopeless case. At the close of analysis, the book offers evidence for hope despite the exceptionally complex nature of the case. North Koreans are suffering and dying for lack of rights. This book puts the horrendous case of these crimes against humanity on the record for the general public, into the market of ideas. The testimonies of survivors are before the world, the accounts they relay of atrocities are ongoing, and the violations they speak about remain unanswered by the international community.

Korea's Division and Human Rights

To appreciate why human rights violations are so starkly different in the two Koreas today, it is necessary to go back in time. Korea wasn't always divided into North and South. For more than five centuries the Korean Peninsula was a dynasty called Chosun, with diplomatic relations with China and Japan.[5] In

1910, as Japan expanded its empire into East Asia, the Korean Peninsula was annexed. In 1945 Japan surrendered to the Allies and pulled out of Korea. The occupation lasted thirty-five years, but the resentment—for both Koreans and Japanese—lasts to this day.

On the official level, a political vacuum was left behind after the Japanese surrendered. Many people across the peninsula were politically minded nationalists and communists. The struggle for what kind of government Korea should have had been under way abroad since the annexation, in the form of Korean Provisional Governments in exile. However, a new period of struggle would emerge. As one historical phase of misery under foreign control ended for Koreans, another was to begin.

Two zones of occupation were created: the United States occupied the South, and the Soviet Union occupied the North. They were divided by the 38th parallel. The peninsula was critical geopolitical turf for these global powers, and each side worried that the other would claim the entire peninsula, uprooting a fragile power balance in East Asia.

The Cold War between the United States and the Soviet Union led each to install their choice of leader, one north and one south of the parallel. In 1948 two separate governments were established. In Pyongyang, Kim Il Sung was installed. He had been a guerrilla fighter against the Japanese, fighting with the Chinese and the Russians for a liberated Korea. In the South, the United States installed Syngman Rhee in Seoul. Rhee was educated in the United States, at Princeton, during Korea's occupation, and he was known as an anticommunist.

Two years later, in June 1950, with the help of the Soviet Union, Kim Il Sung invaded South Korea (ROK), sparking the Korean War. The United States and South Korea, backed by the United Nations, fought the invasion. The North Koreans, with the help of the People's Republic of China, nearly captured the entire southern part of peninsula. The United States, ROK, and United Nations fought back and nearly claimed the entire northern part of the peninsula. The global powers turned Korea into their battlefield at the price of millions of soldiers, but by far the greatest cost was borne by the Korean people, a cost that continues to this day. No life was untouched by this war. The peninsula was a battlefield where millions were injured and brutalized, where families were separated and children orphaned, a chaotic graveyard where millions died. In 1953 hostilities were halted with an armistice agreement. And for what? The two powers were back where they began, at the 38th parallel, the initial dividing line.[6] What the Korean War gave to those who survived was a personalized story of agony for every family and generation on down the line, North and South.

Over the generations of division, changes—economic, social, and political—took shape in both Koreas. At first blush, North Korea made the better impression of the two as the economy was stronger in the first few decades. However, in time South Korea emerged from its authoritarian dictatorship to become a democracy. With much blood lost, the citizens of South Korea fought for their right to democratic governance. The North struggled to batten down the hatches against the revolutions that shattered the Soviet satellites. When the Soviet Bloc collapsed, the financial aid dried up and humanitarian disasters eroded the already anemic economy. The social, economic, and political differences between the two countries continued to grow in contrast. Today, in every area of life the two Koreas represent the material manifestation of how politics shapes culture and, most profoundly, how politics shapes rights.

You can find the effects of the division in the bones of people born on either side of the 38th parallel. In 2011 researchers measured height differences in Koreans born prior to and after the division of the Korean Peninsula. When they examined the height of 6,512 defectors in South Korea, they found that North Koreans born before the division of the Korean Peninsula were taller than their South Korean peers. Combined with this, and more damning still, they found that all "North Korean cohorts born thereafter were shorter than their South Korean counterparts."[7] What could possibly be more nutritious in the South? Politics.

Stunting is the body's way of sacrificing linear growth in order to survive. Stunting doesn't happen from a few missed meals. It is the long-term result of protracted malnutrition at critical growth periods. The border between North and South Korea, arguably more than any other border in the region or world, demonstrates how political demarcations—how political rights—materialize in the flesh and bones of citizens. This is not metaphor. The spread of contagious diseases such as tuberculosis and multidrug-resistant tuberculosis in North Korea can hardly be compared with South Korea. The 38th parallel is found in mortality rates either side of the border. It is counted in births and the weights of newborns. It is demonstrated again and again in the number of people who gamble their lives crossing the border from one kind of life to find another.

The armistice agreement established the cessation of armed conflict on the Korean Peninsula, but the war continues by other means. Preparation for war continues in the form of regular military exercises and the conscription of citizens—males for two years in South Korea; men and women for ten and seven years, respectively, in the North. National security laws in both Koreas restrict access to information about the other side. South Korea's security laws have grown laxer over time and are now nowhere near the level of censorship found in the North, which is among the most severe in the world. Human rights in South Korea are not perfect—no state's are. But the types of rights that South Koreans fight for are on par with those sought in democracies worldwide. Yet only a step over a thin line to the North, people of the same heritage are dying for lack of basic rights.

The North Korean government is at a fatal impasse. Decades of subtle and coercive authoritarian control have kept the current political structure in place, but advances in media technology and the flow of information are challenging that hermetic structure. The global success of South Korean soft power has seeped into the pores of the North. Meanwhile, the North's economy is limping along as it faces increasing global isolation and sanctions. If the North Korean government were to even marginally liberalize access to information or freedom of movement for its people, its political structure couldn't withstand the impact such revelations would bring. Indeed, bits of international non-state-sanctioned information are seeping in—just as information about the situation on the ground is seeping out—at great risk to the people and the state itself.

North Korea targets those who publicly critique it because the Korean War continues by other means. North Korea's abuse of defectors is indicative of unresolved issues on the Korean Peninsula as a whole, which stem from Korea's occupation by Japan, the occupying forces after World War II, and the Korean War. North Korea and its sympathizers evoke this history—which is abundant with brutalities and crimes against humanity—to justify contemporary violations and ongoing atrocities. The historic experiences on the Korean Peninsula (occupation, division, war, division again) are cast as the nation's founding traumas. In North Korea, they serve the ideological function of authorizing and justifying current restrictions on freedoms. It is possible to consider how mitigating factors of historical context shape the formation of rights in North Korea, but infinite regression can only go so far. It is illogical to infinitely regress historically to attribute blame for violations that continue in the contemporary moment. Accountability is squarely and solely on the North Korean state for the violations it commits.

Throughout the text I refer to the North Korean government, regime, state, and leadership interchangeably. I recognize that these are not the same, and yet—particularly under Kim Jong Un's leadership—they are so synchronized overall that I have chosen to refer to them interchangeably for ease of reading. This study is not aimed at identifying which governmental bodies are culpable for which specific rights violations. Future truth and reconciliation tribunals will uncover that. It is sufficient at this stage, as the evidence shows, to see the government system itself as enmeshed with culpability. Kim Jong Un, his family, the Korean People's Army, the Korean Workers Party, and those soldiers "big and small" who abide orders are complicit and accountable for abuses committed domestically and abroad in the name of North Korea.

The Commission of Inquiry

When the United Nations Human Rights Council (UNHRC)—the world's highest body for examining human rights—decided to form the Commission of Inquiry (COI) on North Korea in 2013, it wasn't a bolt out of the blue. For those in the activist community, it was a long time coming. Decades of human rights work in South Korea, in Japan, and internationally finally pushed the United Nations to form the commission. Prior to the decision, the United Nations had tried other approaches. There had been a special rapporteur, but he received no information from North Korea. Over the decades, evidence was mounting that North Korea's human rights violations were widespread, systematic, and ongoing. If the allegations were proven true, this meant the North Korean state was committing crimes against humanity, among the most serious allegations of rights violations a state can commit, since its earliest history.[8]

The formation of a COI signaled that the Human Rights Council was taking the allegations seriously and stepping up its investigation.[9] As an indication of the seriousness of the case among the Human Rights Council, the severity of the allegations, and the reliability of existing evidence, the decision to conduct the inquiry was carried without need for a vote. The United Nations established a commission of experts mandated with inquiring into allegations of rights abuses. Their main task was to determine whether the allegations of atrocities in North Korea were true and if they amounted to crimes against humanity. If the violations were found to be deliberate, part of a systematic campaign, and the cause of human suffering or death on a large scale, they would be classified as crimes against humanity.

On May 7, 2013, the president of the Human Rights Council, then ambassador Remigiusz A. Henczel of Poland, announced that Michael Kirby, former justice of Australia; Sonja Biserko of Serbia; and Marzuki Darusman of Indonesia, the aforementioned special rapporteur on the situation of human rights in North Korea at the time, would serve as members of the COI. This team of three was given the support of nine experienced human rights officials to help in the process of delving into the allegations.[10] As is customary with the UN COIs, the country under investigation is invited to participate. North Korea was repeatedly welcomed to collaborate with the commissioners, but these invitations were ignored.

By ignoring the United Nations' invitations to participate in the inquiry, North Korea created a self-fulfilling condemnation of the report. When it was published, North Korea accused the commissioners of bias for not conducting an in-country investigation. As Justice Michael Kirby explained, the UN commissioners had been saying, "Let us come in, if any mistakes [in allegations] have been made we will acknowledge this. If not us, then let some other international trusted inspectors access the country."[11] North Korea's response to the invitation was to ignore it, believing this would undermine the findings. However, North Korea could not hide the wave of migration out of the country over the past thirty years. In countries where these individuals have settled, such as South Korea and Japan, it is possible to speak with them. It was to this disparate community, and others affected by DPRK's violations, that the commission sought to carry out testimonial hearings.

Published in early 2014 and based on extensive research, including public and private interviews with nearly two hundred experts and defectors, the nearly four hundred pages of detailed findings leave little unacknowledged.[12] There were so many individuals who wanted to give testimony about their experience of rights violations that the commission couldn't possibly hear them all. The commission held private, off-the-record hearings, but for those willing to go public, it conducted hearings in Seoul, Tokyo, Bangkok, London, and Washington, D.C. Unlike other commissions, the public hearings were accessible to everyone.[13]

Listening to the oral testimonies adds dimension. What exists between words, between conceptual misunderstandings, in the silences and grief-stricken crying, reveals as much as the words themselves. Survivors were putting their lives on the line by putting their stories on the record. For many, their desperation was palpable. Grief spread out from their stories. Professional translators struggled against their own emotive responses, throats choked with anguish, as they relayed the stories of survivors. A momentous event was unfolding: North Koreans en masse were holding their government to account, and the world's most powerful human rights body was listening. The case was clear: rights violations are intrinsic to the state, profoundly cruel, and ongoing in nature.

The report contextualizes the case of North Korea, explaining that "the gravity, scale and nature of these violations reveal a state that does not have any parallel in the contemporary world."[14] The commission found the state responsible at the highest levels for crimes against humanity.[15] As an indication of the severity of the matter, North Korea's human rights violations were put permanently on the UN Security Council agenda, and several rounds of national and international sanctions followed. North Korea began to respond, and then another cruel twist unfolded.

North Korea's Response

North Korea submitted its own human rights report to the United Nations on September 15, 2014, seven months after the COI report was published. The *Report of the DPRK Association for Human Rights Studies* explains that North Korea's history vis-à-vis American imperialism is not recognized as the contributing factor for current socioeconomic and geopolitical isolation. But the COI commissioners had included details—quite reasonably—of the historic context for rights violations in North Korea: experiences of colonization, the liberation of Korea from the Japanese, the early formation of the two Koreas, the Korean War, and the development of North Korea up to the present are all recognized. This means the report included everything from punishment of colonial collaborators, to prisoners of war and abductions—whether Japanese, Korean, or other nationalities—to refoulement, or forced repatriation, from China and other countries, to forced abortions in detention facilities, to torture-induced false confessions in political prison camps, and so on. It also identified the role of China in thwarting North Koreans' access to refugee rights. The COI report consolidates this misery of findings and makes for a disquieting read.

North Korea's report, by contrast, is indifferent to the plight of its citizens and instead focuses on the criminality of enemy states (the United States, South Korea, Japan), with an emphasis on U.S. aggression during the Korean War. Wrongs committed against the state—namely, the violation of state sovereignty—are erroneously highlighted as *the* primary human rights violation.

The UN report was instrumental in compelling this response from North Korea, albeit rhetorical, on the topic of human rights domestically and internationally. As the commission was conducting its investigation, North Korea prepared its response. Since the report's publication in 2014, North Korea has disseminated the state's take on human rights through the production of an array of news articles, broadcasts, documentaries, and international public events. This book examines a snapshot of the print media output from 2014 and 2015 and audiovisual output from 2014 through to 2018. Screenshots of North Korean media were recovered from internet archives and are thus of limited quality and resolution when reproduced in this book. Due to YouTube security practices, some of North Korea's channels and videos have been taken down. This highlights the difficulties of conducting research on a hard case like North Korea. It also points to the need to preserve North Korean state media products for what they can tell us, albeit inadvertently, about conditions in the country. Since the COI, on the topic of human rights North Korea has never been this voluble.[16] A savvy aspect of this response takes the form of using foreign media. By granting CNN International, a U.S.-based international cable channel, access to its citizens, North Korea endeavors to spread its state rhetoric through reputable cable news outlets. Through the voices of selected North Korean citizens, whom foreign journalists have been permitted to interview, North Korea enlivens its state rhetoric. As this book goes to press, North Korea continues to invite foreign media to Pyongyang to conduct interviews with citizens who claim their family members were abducted by South Korea from China while working at North Korean restaurants.[17] More recently, North Korea's own media has conducted interviews with return defectors—people who defected to South Korea, saw the error of their ways, and were permitted back into North Korea. These individuals share stories not with CNN but with state media journalists, narrating about the rights violations in South Korea. The impact of these audiovisual materials is difficult to assess, but the intent is to cast doubt on rights claims.

"It's rough in a lot of places, by the way."

In his 2018 State of the Union address, U.S. president Donald Trump referred to the stories of North Korean defector Je Seong Ho and American citizen Otto Warmbier to highlight the horrific brutality of the North Korean regime. Je Seong Ho survived discrimination, torture, and severe hunger after suffering a brutal accident with a railway car at the age of thirteen. He hobbled out of North Korea on wooden crutches made by his now-deceased father. As Trump recounted Je's story in his speech, he paused for effect and the young Je stood to audience applause, holding his crutches aloft. The Warmbier family wept as Trump recounted the detention of their son, Otto, by the regime. The young Warmbier, healthy and full of life, left them for the adventure of a lifetime in North Korea. Not foreseeing the deadly seriousness of the state, he took a propaganda poster hanging in the personnel-only section of the hotel where he stayed. In a media-staged kangaroo court, he wept as he read his confession and was sentenced to fifteen years' hard labor. Only the North Korean regime knows the details of what transpired during Otto's detention, which led to him being returned to his homeland with a severe brain injury.

Then the U.S. president did an about-face. At the Singapore Summit in June 2018 between Trump and North Korean president Kim Jong Un, Trump received a pointed question at the end of his press conference. "You said North Korea has more brutally oppressed its people than any other regime on Earth. Do you still believe that is the case having sat down with Kim Jong Un? Does he need to change that?"[18] Trump's answer was a desecration: "I believe it is a rough situation over there. No question about it. We did discuss it today strongly. Knowing what the main purpose of what we are doing is here denuking [sic]. Discussed at good length. We will be doing something on it. It's rough. It's rough in a lot of places, by the way. We will continue that and I think ultimately agree to something. It was discussed at length outside of the nuclear situation. One of the primary topics."[19]

The answer—if not the ham-fisted wording—could have been predicted. Leading up to this artfully stage-crafted event, the road was littered with nuclear-grade melodrama between the two neotenous leaders. This downplaying of rights rhetoric by North Korea's primary rival was exactly what the regime wanted. To have discussion of rights completely eliminated, a boon. And yet as Trump answered the journalist, he did worse still. He gave credence to an illogical claim much loved by North Korea: that the existence of rights violations in any part of the world means we cannot critique rights violations anywhere.

While Trump acknowledged "it's rough" he followed this up with "it's rough in a lot of places, by the way." In doing this, he wasn't answering the question, he was changing the subject. The joint statement between the two countries carried no mention of human rights.[20] This throws into question his claim that rights were discussed "strongly" and "at length," and that they were one of "the primary topics" between himself and Kim Jong Un.

The UN special rapporteur on North Korea, Tomás Ojea Quintana, was quick to point out that the only reference to human rights in the joint statement—and this is a stretch—was the mention of promoting prosperity on the peninsula. Other than that, Ojea Quintana said, any "reference to human rights . . . was absent."[21] The summit focused on North Korea's nuclear weapons program and nuclear provocations, but it was remiss of the United States to not mention human rights in the joint statement, particularly because the United States had been so critical up to that point. Distracting from the rights issue is a strategy of the DPRK, and the nuclear issue is perfect for this. Another strategy of the DPRK is to conceptualize human rights as only achievable through peace on the peninsula, and this cannot be resolved amid nuclear weapons development. Thus the catch-22.

A few years prior to the Singapore Summit, the year the COI report was published, a North Korean state representative stood up at the United Nations and, speaking to a gathering on the topic of human rights, said: mind your own business. But when a country fails to respect the rights of its people, responsibility shifts to the world community. We must hold that country to account because these violations are crimes against humanity. North Korea's rights abuses are the business of humanity. To think otherwise is to deem North Koreans as not part of the world community. The violations are ongoing and intrinsic to the regime, and there is no internal mechanism whereby the government is accountable to the people—this alone is a flagrant violation of human rights law.

The risk that comes with ignoring this won't be borne by Koreans alone. North Korea's ongoing development of nuclear weapons is an existential danger to the world as we know it.[22] North Korea is not only a threat to its own people but to the world. The state is able to produce nuclear weapons and nuclear delivery systems, yet it refuses to fulfill the most basic of rights such as access to food, medicine, and free media while entirely suppressing political and religious freedoms. For a relatively small country with 23 million people, it has the third-largest standing army in the world. The provision of resources and security are directed toward the regime, not the people. Since the UN COI report, after a short-lived interest in rights, there has been a shift from a focus on rights to a focus on nukes. Denuclearizing the Korean Peninsula is not the only issue, nor the most pressing. The findings of the United Nations in 2014, which found the North Korean state responsible at the highest level for crimes against humanity, is still before the world, and it remains unanswered.[23]

Studying Public Testimony

Much of this book, and the secondary material it subsequently draws upon, is based on the testimonies of defectors speaking—often publicly—at the United Nations and other venues. Unlike my first book, which examined defector testimonies that I personally and privately recorded, my use of public testimonies in this book injects additional complexity to my study of the scope of human rights violations in North Korea. Several factors conspire to impact the source material in ways that were frustratingly beyond my control: the public nature of the testimonies, the interviewers' use of translators to communicate with North Koreans, the types of questions asked and not asked, the fact that witnesses were sometimes misunderstood and these misunderstandings were not clarified, people were spoken over, and insightful gaps in mutual understanding were not more rigorously pursued. However, I don't wish to suggest that private one-on-one interviewing is easier or ideal. As I elaborated in the introduction to *Marching Through Suffering*, there are countless issues related to personality, gender, age, and the positionality of myself as a white, Korean-speaking, U.K.-educated woman that impacted on my interlocutor's desire to speak about some details and withhold others. North Korea studies scholars have acknowledged these difficulties.[24]

The testimonies delivered at the United Nations were investigated through the profession of law, not the discipline and methodologies of anthropology in which I am trained. The commission was making a *legal* assessment of evidence, not a theoretical or ideological one. Constraints on time, language proficiency, and the public nature of the forum meant the subtle lived experiences of violations, and the recollection of them, could not be probed. The commission was primarily focused on documenting atrocities—appropriately so—and less able to extend itself to an additional examination of how these violations were understood, coped with, or remembered—aspects that I find particularly insightful to the overall psychosocial space of North Korea.

The COI's final report relies heavily on testimonies of former defectors, experts, and non-national witnesses to present a sophisticated, readable, and comprehensive analysis of North Korea's crimes against humanity. However, to get closer to the testimonial experience of North Korea's violations, I listened to all of the original public testimonies made available by the UN commission.[25] I focused my analysis on the emotive indicators as I listened and watched: speed of vocal delivery, silences, changes in voice tone, crying, hesitation, display of body injury, and so on—and I also focused on points in testimony where these affects and demonstrations emerged. Testimony is a dialectic. As such, I was compelled to examine the affective response of the commission investigators (usually modulated) and the translators (usually unmodulated). I also read through the English and Korean transcripts of the oral testimonies made available by the UN commission as I watched the video testimony. Combined with the audiovisual, I applied discourse analysis to these materials. Employing these technologies enabled me to slow things down and check expressions carefully. The pages that follow demonstrate where this method of engaging the material was used for multilayered insights into the lived experience of these rights violations.

Access (or Lack Thereof) to North Korea

When the UN's commission was established, it publicly appealed to anyone with direct personal experience of alleged rights violations in North Korea to make contact, clearly indicating a point of contact and a deadline. As is typical with Commissions of Inquiry, the commission sought to conduct on-the-ground investigations within the country. They repeatedly requested permission from the state to do this, and they were repeatedly ignored. North Korea's refusal to grant entry to the commission hampered its efforts at information gathering and necessitated the use of testimonials from defectors as opposed to adding to those insights with testimonials from North Korean citizens in-country. Clearly it was in the interest of the commission to further round out their investigation into alleged crimes against humanity by conducting interviews with citizens in North Korea, to inspect criminal and political prisons, to investigate sites of torture and execution, and to hear from government officials. The commission was unable to access any of these.

In an artful gesture, North Korean representatives said that Special Rapporteur on Human Rights Marzuki Darusman was welcome to visit Pyongyang on condition he come as an ordinary person, not in his capacity as the UN special rapporteur. The invitation is confounding. How could he visit North Korea *without* being the special rapporteur? The stripped-down, depoliticized person of Darusman was being welcomed, but his expertise and the organizational power that he represents was denied. I describe this gesture as artful because it illustrates a phenomenon observable in almost any rhetoric emerging from North Korea: the phenomena of access without access, telling without telling, truth without truth, information without information, and so on. Other scholars, referencing North Korea's own literature, have described this mind muddying rhetoric as "the fog."

In parallel with the commissioners' denial of access, I too sought to visit North Korea to research disability rights, among other issues for this book, but was denied a visa even though I hold a passport from a country that has diplomatic relations with the North. As is typical, no reason was given for the denied visa. Literature from North Korea's Association for Human Rights Studies states that anyone interested in studying about human rights in North Korea is welcome to do so, but they should first accept North Korea's view on rights.[26] In other words, they provide access without real access.

There are indeed some signs of progress regarding access in the wake of the UN COI report—and I argue that even access without access provides increasingly more information about the situation despite limitations. North Korea ratified the Convention on the Rights of Persons with Disabilities in 2016. Following this, North Korea welcomed the UN expert on the rights of people with disabilities, Catalina Devandas Aguilar, to visit the country in 2017. This was an exceptional development. Her end-of-mission statement indicates that she was granted access to many of the representatives and places of interest she requested. Critically, however, she was denied meetings with the Central Court, the Ministry of Labor, the Ministry of City Management, the Ministry of State Construction Control, the Central Bureau of Statistics, and any mental health facility.[27] The latter issue of mental health was a priority issue for her mandate. Indeed, even on the level of metaphor, restricted access to those with mental disabilities speaks to a larger trend of restricting access to the private internality of North Korea.

Devandas Aguilar was granted access to Pyongyang and the city of Pongchon in South Hwanghae Province. In her preliminary findings, presented to a closed meeting of journalists in North Korea, she acknowledged the efforts North Korea is trying to make in improving the lives of the disabled. More telling and illustrative was her observation on stigma and disability in North Korea. In expressing her concerns on stigma, critically, she elaborated on who she didn't get access to and those who were absented from her visit:

> I was also informed that families are reluctant to expose children and adults with disabilities in the community. . . . During my visit, I noted that efforts are focused primarily on deaf and blind people. I only interacted with one wheelchair user, and although I have encountered a few autistic children and children with intellectual disabilities, and one little person (i.e. a child with achondroplasia), I could not obtain information from them on their particular situation. Moreover, I did not meet any person with psychosocial, multiple or severe disabilities.[28]

Unable to meet people with mental illness or visit their location, the UN expert could not assess their rights situation. So too of those with psychosocial, multiple, or severe disabilities. Yet, even with this abridged view, Ms. Devandas Aguilar could still make assessments. She noted that the "majority of infrastructure" is not accessible to disabled persons, including new builds from February 2017, after North Korea ratified the disabilities convention.

This pattern of access without access complicates investigators' claims, and it facilitates speculation about the veracity of findings. Speculation is injected into findings because experts primarily rely on at-a-distance sources (defector testimony, satellite images, underground journalism, activists, and North Korea's representatives and publications). Not surprisingly, that is the principal critique that North Korea and its sympathizers level at the UN COI report itself. Of course, the critique needs to be leveled at North Korea's prohibition on access. The UN commissioners appealed for access and were denied. As such, the investigation weighed heavily on information-gathering methods that offered the most access possible: defector testimonies.

Money and Memory: Information Corruptors?

When dealing with defector testimony, the specter of possible misinformation lingers. When I conducted research for my first book, I didn't pay my interviewees. Many interlocutors were the family and friends of individuals I worked with in the defector community. At the time, I was a PhD student with little funding who wouldn't have been able to afford to conduct interviews if cash had to be exchanged. I did bring small gifts as a gesture of thanks and took people out for lunch. What I also exchanged, albeit indirectly, was my labor, over the years I conducted the research, as a translator and writer for grant applications at defector-run NGOs. None of the defectors ever requested payment, and no mention was made of it.

However, political scientist Jiyoung Song identifies the giving of a fee as a "standard practice" in place for years.[29] She clarifies that initially in the 1990s defectors would be compensated for transport and meals, approximately $30 at that time. By 2014, the fee was $200 per hour. It is reasonable that someone would be compensated for their time recounting experiences about life in North Korea. However, the issue Jiyoung Song identifies is that financial compensation raises difficulties in terms of the effect it has on the relationship between interviewer and interviewee and on the content of testimony. A government official from the South Korean Ministry of Unification relayed to Jiyoung Song that fees could range from $50–$500 per hour, "depending on the quality of information." As Song explains, this practice "drives the demand for 'salable stories': the more exclusive, shocking or emotional, the higher the fee."

Paying for stories could encourage a bleed-to-lead tendency among our interviewees, and this is where we find the concern that paying for testimonies could lead to deception. This creates at least two consequences. First, the defector might distort her story, adding misery here and cutting banality there.

Second, the stories that reach the larger public will be those that are most horrific. Defectors with experiences that are difficult but ordinary may self-select to remain silent.

Some defectors are paid for their testimony whether by organizations, universities, or researchers. Publicly delivered testimonies are often paid. This was not the case with testimony delivered to the United Nation's COI, which forms the bulk of my research for this book, though some of those who did give testimony are "famous" defectors who have been paid in the past, such as Shin Dong Hyuk. The story of Shin's testimony is illustrative of how social, economic, and geopolitical issues coalesce to compromise advocacy, documentation, and improvement of rights. These issues coalesce in the argumentation put forward by deniers, such as North Korea and North Korea sympathizers.

Shin's life story captured the world's attention due to the horrific nature of his experiences and his age when they happened. His book, *Escape from Camp 14*, was published in English in 2012 with the help of journalist Blaine Harden; the Korean version (*Out into the World*) had been published in South Korea in 2007. When I met Harden and inquired about the book's royalties, he told me they split it 50/50 between them.

Shin's horrific testimony was one of hundreds that galvanized the UN to establish the COI in the first place. His story was indeed one of the most severe, and some of its details appear in the pages that follow in my examination of North Korea's documentaries about him. As the commission was making its way through the public hearings in Japan, South Korea, England, and the United States in 2013, North Korea—familiar with Shin's published memoir and aware of his increasing "victim-fame"—was preparing a very public dressing-down. In 2014 a documentary appeared on YouTube and other social media outlets. The two-part video titled "Lie and Truth"—examined in the pages that follow—presents Shin's father, stepmother, coworkers, and neighbors as they tell the "true story" of Shin's life. Around this time Harden got a phone call from Shin. He needed to clarify some parts of his narrative. Later editions of the book now carry a preface that identifies these corrections, and Blaine Harden's author website explains his experience of this deception as an author. Within the North Korean activist, defector, and human rights scholarly community, the story of Shin's testimony continues to be divisive. Allies who wish to remain anonymous have told me they think the entire story is bunk, that he is resented for causing widespread doubt over accurate testimonies; others say his testimony is mostly true (and more harrowing, given his clarifications) while some small details of place and time remain inaccurate.

To be clear, I am *not* suggesting Shin deceived his readers or Harden in order to make money. What is critical here is that testimonies can be interpreted as bound to issues of money because these memoirs—being brutal personal accounts of life in a part of the world so rarely understood—often sell very well. They sell well, and thus they both raise awareness and make money.

In another two-part documentary that North Korea made to traduce Shin Dong Hyuk, they accuse him—and other prominent defectors—of being paid by the United States to make up horrible stories about their former homeland.[30] They claim that money is a tool of chicanery used by the United States to conduct war by other means, tempting defectors (genetic plutomaniacs) to fabricate horrendous stories. According to North Korea, defector testimonies, money, and deceit are knotted together. Not surprisingly, a similar critique is leveled at another defector, Yeonmi Park. Ms. Park's appalling testimony is of events that took place in North Korea and China, and the unique horrors of China lasted nearly a decade; she was a young teen at the time she witnessed the worst aspects. Relaying her testimony in passable English, a third language she learned late in life, standing on a large stage, wearing a beautiful Hanbok that accentuated her beauty and diminutiveness, the young, tearful Ms. Park melted hearts. The world wept. Her fame grew.

North Korea learned of her, and her forthcoming memoir, too. Her public speeches that itemized personal suffering would now circulate in the media sphere along with the North Korea's personalized defamation. Forever wielding the tool of rhetoric, North Korean state media titled the documentary about her *A Poisonous Mushroom*. The conclusion is unmistakable: no good can come of something grown in shit. The camera captured a gathering of former neighbors who diagnosed her and her family as stricken with pleonexia: the sick compulsion that drove her to lie for profit. The video was uploaded to YouTube. While some aspects of Yeonmi Park's narrative were inaccurate—which she later corrected—these inaccuracies are minor and do not undercut the message of her story: that rights violations in North Korea are numerous and real.

Inconsistencies across a single defector's narrative can be attributed to a number of factors, often in combination. Memory can be fickle, and trauma is known to impact the recall of events. Individuals who give public testimony, whether in print or speech, often do so with the needs, desires, and fears of the audience consciously or unconsciously in mind.[31] Testimony is a performative act because it moves between the mute witness (the dead, the one who remains inside North Korea), the person who witnessed and experienced (the survivor), and the witness to the survivor (the UN, the NGO, the North Korean state).[32] It is clear that factors such as memory, trauma, and the context of delivery shape testimonies. Another factor is time. Trauma, whether felt, imagined, vocalized, or dreamed, is characterized by reoccurrence. This loopedness of trauma weaves a kind of inescapable unendedness to the events recounted. Time is particularly critical in the sense that its passage plays on memory and that trauma plays with time but also in the sense that the things testified to are at once over and ongoing.

Consider how collective suffering that is both historic and ongoing manifests from the Korean War. The division of the Korean Peninsula continues to guarantee the separation of families, their punishment for connection with the "wrong" side, and their highly public mourning when the two states agree to rare family reunion meetings. Consider further: if a person manages to escape from a North Korean political prison or to survive the famine, this brings freedom but also the traumatic awareness that those left behind continue to suffer.

Testimony from North Korea is about both past and present conditions. This continuity of the past in the present adds complexity because the witness speaks of her own past but also about the collective suffering that is ongoing in the country. Because she testifies for those who continue to live in suffering but who cannot speak, both speaker and listener are implicated in culpability. We are listening to history that is also present.[33]

If it were only one man's story and a story that happened in one home, perhaps inaccuracies would concern us less. This leads to the question: When listening to defectors, do I imagine this person to speak for a collective? We are listening to a personal story that is also a story of the collective. In telling stories publicly, the private loses distinction. Testimonies emerging from the closed space of North Korea intensify the sense that they speak for public and private both: the individual, the personal, and the specific for the collective universal.

Structure of the Book

This book is divided into two parts. Part I examines rights violations related to social, economic, and political rights as well as to physical integrity rights. The chapters in this part survey rights violations as they emerge in day-to-day life within North Korea. This portion of the book demonstrates that rights are violated in core areas of daily life in North Korea; thus, life itself is threaded through with a guaranteed vulnerability. Further, it demonstrates that rights violations related to social, economic, and political rights lead to violations of physical integrity. This keeps violations locked in place and ensures the state remains incontrovertible. Violations in these areas of life are virtually unavoidable for anyone (Kim Jong Un being the only exception), and as North Koreans brush up against these each day, they come into contact with increased vulnerability for rights violations that cascade into worsening situations.

Part I also examines how the North Korean state exports and imports its coercive control over citizens and noncitizens through overseas labor and the circulation of drugs and weapons abroad. The violations emerge within North Korea but also travel beyond its borders, migrating into China, Russia, parts of Africa, the Middle East and Europe as North Korean citizens are exported abroad for labor. The violations travel as North Korean citizens migrate, legally and illegally, into these territories. In this respect North Koreans are inherently vulnerable to rights violations because of their country of origin, which has predisposed them to be at differential risk to illness, lack of access to information, and social inequality. North Koreans are also vulnerable if they move with the permission of their state because the state enforces limits on their freedoms beyond its borders. It is as if the state travels with them when they move.

Part II examines how the North Korean state attempts to put forward a public image that is about protecting human rights, domestically and abroad. It demonstrates how the denial of rights violations occurs at the highest level of the state, and this denial is spread far and wide. This part of the book identifies how the state manipulates foreign citizens in-state and abroad toward the ends of the state. It demonstrates that the coercive reach of the state is vast and profoundly sovereign-centric at the cost of human life domestically and internationally. The North Korean state abuses the rights of foreign nationals through abductions from South Korea and Japan and through the capture and detention of U.S. citizens. North Korea's manipulation of other states and their respect for human rights via these foreign nationals is highlighted.

Manipulation occurs at the level of the body, but it also manifests in rhetoric. North Korea's state media endeavors to appear multidimensional on the topic of rights, using savvy technology to do so, particularly in the last five years, all the while masking abuses at home and abroad. By forensically examining video footage and rhetoric from North Korea's state media, part II traces the sophisticated tools of manipulation that are intended to confuse and disorient audiences, whether domestic or international. What seems multidimensional is rather a charade. Movement along the surface of the text, much like a Mobius strip, flips the traveler upside down and disorients: it seems plural, but is eerily one-sided.

The conclusion marks an ascent out of the study. It gives the reader an omniscient view of the rights violations heretofore under consideration and makes recommendations for ways forward, indicating reasons for hope. Despite the bleakness of the stories featured in this book, improvement of human rights is possible in North Korea.

PART I

THE CRIMES

CHAPTER 1

THE HISTORY OF HUMAN RIGHTS VIOLATIONS IN NORTH KOREA

Our people, who took power into their own hands, have come to enjoy democratic rights and liberties never known at any period in the history of our country. This can be seen from the fact that the entire people take an active part in political life, and it is also graphically shown in the social composition of the people's committees.

—Kim Il Sung, 1946

From its founding years, North Korea promoted the idea that its regime respected rights.[1] This rhetoric of rights—which was actually antithetical to established international human rights norms—has continued across the Kim family dynasty. Present conditions could be seen in the past, according to historian Andrei Lankov. Through North Korea's political transition from Stalinism to Kim Il Sungism, its earliest years had "peculiarities" in play.[2] While there are many particularities to the North Korean state, from its earliest history there are clear violations of rights. The bulk of this book examines contemporary violations that each of the Kims subsequently oversaw during their individual reigns. Yet the historical context of present-day violations was seeded in the state's founding years. Throughout the early history, the state failed to uphold socioeconomic and political rights, though it always claimed to protect these. The early history shows that the state violated physical integrity rights—and wasn't afraid to admit as much. The latter violations were acknowledged as necessary for the protection of the state.

Colonial Legacies of Order and Disorder

In 2018 the celebration of North Korea's seventieth founding anniversary took place in Pyongyang Square. The passage of time might seem to mark that North Koreans have had no experience with any type of democratic process for seventy years. However, it has been much longer than that. Koreans were not, strictly speaking, citizens under the Japanese occupation, when many were peasants for whom the notion of political participation was truly unusual. The conditions in which North Koreans found themselves, politically, at the founding of the DPRK, were oppressive and harsh, but at least they were under their own Korean people, not foreign hands.[3] Meanwhile, in South Korea, conditions at the time of the partition were arguably much the same in terms of harsh treatment toward political opposition.[4]

Korea's liberation was achieved through Soviet and American occupation of the peninsula, which ended Japanese rule in 1945. For North Korean nationalists, this was a frustrating fact. Kim Il Sung determined that Korean society was corrupted by colonialism, a feature that could only be undone through cultural purification.[5] This objective would create a bloodbath over the years leading up to the Korean War, through it, and after. Most Koreans had some connection with the Japanese, according to historian Balazs Szalontai;[6] there were more collaborators than active resisters between 1937 and 1945. The impact of Japanese colonialism was something that had to be thoroughly cleansed from North Korea. Kim Il Sung went about doing this and yet kept other features of colonialism in place. As the Japanese retreated, they damaged economic enterprises, but Soviet soldiers were also out of order. Even contemporary accounts from the period by those sympathetic to the Soviets reported looting and rape carried out by Soviet soldiers until they were brought under the control of commanders.[7] The first "real supreme ruler" from 1945 to 1948 was Colonel-General Terentii Fomich Shtykov, and in 1947 the Soviet military was the primary management, with oversight from Moscow. After enduring thirty-five years of occupation, North Korea faced a new era of foreign presence. The desire to consolidate the nation under one Korean nationalism was strong.

Eliminating Political Plurality

Early North Korean history shows there was friction between North Korea and the post-Stalinist Soviet Union, but North Korea still modeled much of its sociopolitical features upon this template.[8] On paper, early political life looked diverse. There were many democratic institutions, such as an elected parliament. Local councils were elected, but these were never contested elections. There was only ever one candidate for one seat, and he was handpicked by the party mandarins.[9] Decision making occurred via the top ranks of committees, whether the Korean Workers Party committees, the committee in school or work, or the Central Committee.

The early political landscape of North Korea was complex. There were communists from the Domestic faction and from the Yan'an pro-China faction, and there were former guerrillas. The former two had little in common with the latter, and the three often spoke different languages. The Soviet Koreans spoke Russian. The Yan'an spoke Chinese, and even the guerrillas had been overseas during the occupation. The Domestic communists were mostly from the South.[10] Lankov notes that Kim Il Sung was "among equals" in his first decade of rule, but through the Korean War and after he managed to eliminate or weaken factions that opposed him.

The only time that the Kim leadership was challenged, that we know of, was in August of 1956. Efforts to openly resist Kim Il Sung were made possible by a few features of the times: there was a "thaw" in communist capitals in the mid-1950s that created an atmosphere of possibility. Kim Il Sung interpreted the unfolding de-Stalinization process sweeping through the Soviet Union and other communist states as a threat to his leadership. Within North Korea the Yan'an faction shared its plans to angle for influence over Kim Il Sung with the Soviet embassy. Kim Il Sung was on an overseas trip at the time, which might have given the group time to make its plan. The attempt to change the disastrous leadership failed, and Kim Il Sung further cemented his grip. The Kim family dynasty was fixed in place and—to date—has had the longest rule in communist history.[11] After the August incident, basic human rights in North Korea were further curtailed as the country became more militarized and worship of Kim Il Sung took hold.

Kim Il Sung held show trials in 1953 and 1955 where associates from political factions were accused and executed for ridiculous crimes such as being a spy for the Japanese secret police or the United States or South Korean government.[12] The trials were followed by the elimination of communists with connections to these factions. Kim Il Sung blamed the disaster of the Korean War on leading individuals in the factions. The Korean War destroyed the country economically, but it was a political boon for Kim Il Sung.

The Korean War led to greater intensification of political repression in North Korea. In December 1950 Kim Il Sung attributed setbacks of the Korean People's Army and the occupation of North Korea by U.S. and South Korean forces to the failures of his subordinates. They were expelled from the party. Whereas in 1948 there had been a demotion of Domestic communist leaders, after the Korean War the purge involved groups of party leaders from both the Soviet and Domestic communist factions.[13] Top-level members were purged as well as ordinary Korean Workers Party members who were identified as behaving passively under enemy occupation—up to five hundred thousand party members were disciplined between 1950 and 1951.[14] Szalontai observes that this tendency to question the loyalty of subjects is not unique to North Korea.[15] The Japanese military viewed soldiers captured by the enemy as traitors; Stalin sent 23 percent of returned Soviet prisoners of war and citizens deported by the Nazis to the gulag or to battalions for reeducation.[16]

After the Korean War, South Korean communists who had gone north were purged from the leadership—the whole faction destroyed. The 1953 trial of South Korean Workers Party members resembled the show trials of the Soviet Union and East Europe.[17] Southerners were deemed second-class citizens in North Korea—though they had gone north to enjoy communism, they were part of the South Korean communist movement that didn't survive Syngman Rhee. Kim Il Sung noted to a Hungarian delegation in May of 1959 that one hundred thousand South Koreans in North Korea were receiving reeducation.[18]

North Korean politics from 1945 to 1948 saw some support for the indigenous religious Chondogyo Party and the Democratic Party. However, by the 1950s these were co-opted into use by the regime to present a sense of diverse political participation for overseas propaganda.[19] On August 27, 1957, the first postwar elections to North Korea's Supreme People's Assembly took place. The elections had little meaning. Lankov reports that "the predictable result was 99.92 percent support for the party" and the same participation rate. The subsequent election in 1962 resulted in 100 percent participation and support for Kim Il Sung.[20] The opposition's demands were published in party propaganda material in early 1958. "Some factionalists who had managed to sneak into the law enforcement and judiciary bodies even used deceptively good-looking pretexts of 'human rights protection' to release [from prisons] not a small number of hostile elements." The same collection of propaganda material stated that the "antiparty counterrevolutionary factionalist elements . . . created unprincipled slogans of 'democracy' and 'freedom' in order to break the steel-like unity of our party."[21]

The first wave of defections from North Korea occurred from 1945 to 1951 and was largely made up of those who supported opposition to Kim Il Sung—privileged individuals such as former landowners, business owners, traders, and former petty officers in colonial office under the Japanese. Also among this wave of refugees were Christian activists. Estimates place the number at 580,000 people, and another million during the war itself.[22]

By 1964, in addition to obvious targets like merchants or collaborators with the Japanese, North Korea viewed those of South Korean origin as politically unreliable.[23] After the Korean War, North Korea also wanted to eliminate anyone who might have been injected into North Korea by U.S. intelligence or

South Korean forces. Interior Minister Pang Hak Se issued a decree that spies would be given amnesty if they gave themselves up. Additionally, anyone who helped capture spies would be rewarded with the personal property and real estate of the culprit. Security forces were not paid, so it is likely this decree led to abuses.[24]

Kim's Personality Cult

North Korean government representatives shared their frustration about Kim Il Sung's dictatorship over country and party with foreign allies. Yan'an faction member Yi P'il-gyu wrote: "Kim Il Song's personality cult has become quite intolerable. Kim Il Song's word is law. He is intolerant and does not seek advice. He has gathered sycophants and lackeys all around him in the Central Committee and the cabinet."[25] Concern over Kim Il Sung's personality cult and the poor living standards of the ordinary people were the main critiques that opposition members shared every time they met with their foreign counterparts. These areas of critique connected with the failure of the state to grant basic socioeconomic and political rights as promised. In 1957 the North Korean government passed Resolution 102, which prohibited the selling of cereals. Cooperatives could only sell surplus grain to the state, not through private commerce. By 1958 private selling ceased to exist, and vendors were compelled to join cooperatives or they would not be entitled to ration coupons for food and other necessities.[26]

Starting around 1959 state-sanctioned history books contributed to a sense of North Korean historical self-sufficiency through reduced reference to the participation of the Soviet Army and the Chinese People's Liberation Army in the liberation of Korea. This era also saw the widespread distribution of the book *Memoirs of the Anti-Japanese Guerrillas*, a book that, to this day, must be read by all adults so they are able to discuss it at indoctrination sessions. Between 1957 and 1960, 95.8 million copies of this book were printed.[27] This contributed to the sense that, from the 1930s, Kim Il Sung led his guerrillas, as the only true communists, toward salvation of the country. The state constructed special rooms dedicated to the study of Kim Il Sung's work, for which they claimed that all North Koreans should be grateful.

The cult of personality surrounding Kim Il Sung bears some resemblance to Japan's emperor worship, but it is also unique. Kim Il Sung was hyperactive, while the Japanese *tenno* was passive; Kim Il Sung used purges to remove those who threatened to oppose him, whereas the Japanese military regime did not. The leadership cult emerged rapidly in North Korea. In 1946 the first university was established and named after Kim Il Sung. To this day it is deemed the most prestigious. The following year schools were erected for orphans of revolutionary martyrs in Kim Il Sung's home village of Man'gyongdae.

Szalontai observes that in Eastern Europe only Josip Broz Tito's Yugoslavia saw cult leadership emerge as quickly.[28] However, even at this early stage of cult leadership, Kim didn't have absolute power. The top leadership was not monolithic, states Szalontai, and the guerrillas formed only a minority in the Korean Workers Party. Even by 1948, the Political Committee and the Central Committee were divided equally between Soviet-style communists (of whom Kim Il Sung was one) and Domestic communists (who were not trusted by Kim Il Sung).[29]

Isolation from Foreigners, Criticism, and Thought Reform

North Korea began to eliminate from universities and occupations anyone who had a connection to foreign allies such as the Soviet Union, out of fear that spies were seeking to undermine the country. The result of these actions led to isolation from allied foreigners and a fear of anything different, while criticism sessions, of self and other, created isolation from fellow nationals. By the 1960s criticism sessions became a feature of daily life for all citizens. These weekly sessions require people to critique how they have lately failed to adhere to state ideological values. Criticism of how others have failed is also expected. These sessions are one of the powerful means by which North Korea maintains a system of surveillance and indoctrination.[30]

During its occupation by Japan, Korea endured an assimilation policy that involved the use of Japanese language. North Korean writers relayed to Hungarian foreign diplomats that the Japanese language was a dangerous tool in Japanese imperialist expansion.[31] Teaching Korean youths Japanese at school was the principle means by which young Koreans were influenced by the empire's propaganda. Naturally, the Korean language also absorbed many Japanese loan words. The legacy of this "linguistic occupation" can be seen in the early treatment of North Koreans who had contact with foreigners or who spoke foreign languages.

The earliest reference to restrictions on contact with foreigners inside the country is found in a record of communication between the North Korean ambassador to East Germany, Pak Kil-yon, and a Soviet diplomat in May 1956. The new restriction called for officials who wanted to meet a non-national to first seek permission from their supervisor. Bear in mind, these rules applied to officials, not ordinary people, and these officials were typically only seeking relations with fellow communists from Russia and China. As a further sign that connections with the wider world were shrinking, the local branches of the Korean Society for International Cultural Exchange—whose work was to spread Soviet culture—were forced to close. The Korean Workers Party Central Committee put an end to the performance of Soviet plays in the spring of 1956, and the College of Foreign Languages—where most students were studying Russian—was closed.[32]

Students who returned from Hungary, fleeing a revolution there, were regarded with suspicion once they got back to Kim Il Sung University. Some were minded by fellow students because they were deemed difficult for teachers to manage. Others were removed to reeducation centers. Teachers were also replaced, for reasons of ideology, despite a teacher shortage. Examinations in ideology and personal criticism were useful in identifying who needed removal.[33] Public executions of purged individuals and groups, without trial, was the norm. The fact that North Korea didn't hold trials but did conduct ongoing criticism, which sometimes lasted weeks on end, was a departure from Soviet legal norms.[34] Andrei Lankov notes that these long public sessions of humiliation were also acceptable spaces to physically abuse victims.[35]

As part of its political cleansing campaign, authorities disappeared anyone who had exposure to foreign influences, such as foreign-language interpreters, out of concern that there could be spies among these people. The concern wasn't that these people could be spies for the Japanese or South Koreans—but rather the Soviets! Abroad, North Koreans students asked for asylum in Moscow and were granted it. Even at this early time in its history, North Korea engaged in efforts to recapture these dissidents and return them home for punishment. The North Korean secret service succeeded in abducting a particularly outspoken student, Yi Sang Gu, during the day in the center of Moscow.[36]

Lack of press freedom emerged just as quickly as newspapers were established. This was possible because all newspapers in North Korea are organs of the party and the cabinet, continuously monitored and supervised by the party's Propaganda and Agitation Department. Broadcasts are similarly controlled, with additional direction from the United Front Department.[37] North Korea removed any writer with ties to the Japanese. The result was a depletion in the number of writers and a low number of films produced. The vast majority of writing available was translated from the Soviet Union. North Korean films didn't exceed 10 percent of what was available; 60 percent were of Soviet origin.[38] Cut off from Western scientific journals due to Kim Il Sung's isolationist policies, science scholars had to rely on Soviet sources. The notion of instilling thought reform through reeducation was not particular to East Asia, as Szalontai reminds us that Yugoslavia, Romania, and the right-wing dictatorship in Greece also wished to reeducate prisoners.[39] However, North Korea has taken reeducation, self-criticism, and thought reform to a new level.

Population Control

To mobilize and control the population, North Korea made use of organizations such as Save the Nation Labor Corps and the Patriotic Neighborhood Association, which had been set up by the Japanese colonial authorities. The type of political reeducation that North Korea used early in its history resembles Japan's thought-reform methods. The Chinese Communist Party also used similar methods of population control.[40] As early as the late 1950s and early 1960s, the elite in Pyongyang took on the position as masters of the country.[41] The separation between the citizens in the capital, and those beyond it, began to take form.

The government nationalized large and medium industries by 1946. Until the late 1950s people were able to engage in small private retail trade. Even after the Korean War, a little over 32 percent of all retail throughout the country occurred through private business.[42] However, the collectivization of agriculture from 1954 to 1955 ensured that nearly 50 percent of peasants were pressed into cooperatives.

From what was left of the population after the Korean War, the government forcefully relocated whomever it deemed unreliable to the mountainous northern parts of the country.[43] From 1958 to 1959 North Korea conducted an "unending nightmare" of purges—these large-scale removals of people that the government deemed questionable is considered the greatest elimination of people in North Korean history.[44] North Korea's minister of the interior relayed to a Soviet diplomat that during a six-month period between 1958 and 1959, the police found one hundred thousand "hostile and reactionary" individuals. The same number of people were sent into exile for reeducation between 1945 and 1948.

As a further level of control, the Korean Workers Party put forward a document that would henceforth stratify the entire North Korean population. "On Transforming the Struggle Against Counterrevolutionary Elements into an All-Party, All-People's Movement" was issued on May 30, 1957. People were placed into categories that determined their present and future socioeconomic and political life. The classification was determined by the background of a person's family, their political behavior, and the perception of their political loyalty.[45] This would eventually be the Songbun system, which took over a decade to complete and would play a central role in North Korean politics and society from then on.

In 1958 a system was implemented that enabled microlevel control within a "five household responsibility system"—what would later become the *inminban* (neighbor group). This ensured that every single North Korean was connected to a neighbor unit, which ensured ideological education and political reliability.[46] Naturally, this facilitated surveillance and a system of informing on people who deviated from the strict standard of political life.

Early Food Crises

In 1955 North Korea suffered a decline in urban food supply. Kim Il Sung was most concerned with ensuring that food supply to the urban population was not in peril, although the rural areas were also suffering. However, the policies that the leader put in place not only failed to resolve the situation, they made it worse. The state limited the sale of rice in state shops and suppressed private grain trade—these steps led to food shortage, which knocked the prices up on the black markets.[47] People from the northern provinces headed south in search of food, and many died on the way. According to Hungarian diplomatic reports between April and May of 1955, the Hungarian-run hospital in Sariwon conducted autopsies on twenty people and determined they died from starvation. The famine hit not only the northern provinces but also the southern ones. Children and adults in Pyongyang were collecting buds and leaves as substitute food.[48] The Polish hospital in Hamhung reported illnesses due to people eating poisonous grasses. Numbers of homeless and orphans increased, restaurants shut down, larceny and robbery increased. Those working at the fringes of the state, such as street vendors, were most severely affected. But even state workers received severely reduced rations of only three hundred grams of rice per day.[49]

In April 1956 the state news organ, the *Rodong Shinmun*, carried an editorial that mentioned the food crisis. The editorial was in no way apologetic or self-critical; rather, the author directed responsibility for the crisis onto the population itself. People should conserve food, the piece suggested, and supplement their diet with foraged items such as bark and grasses.[50] The paper was withdrawn from circulation after half an hour. Szalontai speculates that the admission of a food crisis—though hardly sympathetic to the people—was too much. North Korea's aid donor at that time, the Soviet Bloc, was frustrated and insisted on intervention. Soviet and East European diplomats informed North Korea that prohibiting private grain trade would result reduced production by the peasantry. Meanwhile, the Romanian ambassador questioned North Korea's rapid collectivization. The Hungarian diplomat at the time held North Korea responsible for the economic situation. He further noted that the press was covering up the food crisis.[51]

North Korea wanted to overtake South Korea in terms of economic development; such goals would be a hugely uphill battle for North Korea's much smaller population, yet the North would continue to try. In the 1960s, as South Korea's economy began to improve, the North's efforts to compete in industrial and military development continued to negatively impact the everyday living standards of its people. Szalontai argues that this tension to outgun South Korea militarily and economically created the justification to rule North Korea with an iron hand.[52] While there was popular discontent in 1955 and 1959, which the Korean government and the Korean Workers Party acknowledged, this was attributed to economic and social problems, not political discontent.[53]

Farmers made up 80 percent of the population, and they were poor. Yet the government taxed their income at more than 50 percent. If farmers did not hand over these extortionate taxes, physical violence, detention, and murder were the consequences. "Violence, not persuasion," was the method of the party and the cooperatives.[54] Representatives criticized the violation of physical integrity rights, complaining that "distortions of socialist legality" were taking place. Andrei Lankov explains that, in "post-Stalinist Soviet political jargon," this meant people were being arrested arbitrarily, executed en masse, and tortured.[55]

Since the late 1980s, if farmers had inadequate food production, the government did not compensate for this with overseas purchase, nor did the government facilitate peoples' ability to legally provide for themselves. By the late 1980s, North Korea continued to adhere to their existing ideology, fearing that opening up would send North Korea in the direction of other failed Socialist states. The government did not institute reforms to structural aspects of the economy and agriculture because doing so would free up the population, who might then demand different governance.[56] According to the standards of international human rights, governments are obliged to make maximum use of available resources to feed hungry populations. Even in times of emergency or crisis, states are responsible for preparing to meet the needs of people for "transitory and emergency food requirements in ways that encourage recovery, rehabilitation, development and a capacity to satisfy future needs."[57] North Korea made decisions in terms of food security that were about avoiding the possibility of social unrest, which could lead to governmental change.

Killing Faith

There were Protestant missions in Pyongyang, considered the "Jerusalem of the East" by foreign missionaries, and Sunchon.[58] In 1907 the Pyongyang Great Revival led to thousands of Christian converts.[59] However, as the scholar Hazel Smith notes, even prior to communism in the north, Christian influence on Korean culture was not particularly well received. Indigenous religion such as Chondo (heavenly way) emerged as a response to foreign religious influence, whether from China, Japan, or further afield.[60] North Korea's government upheld this indigenous religion while identifying Christianity as a tool used by foreign missionaries to repress Koreans during the colonial era. As Smith observes, religions are used instrumentally in North Korea, whether indigenous or foreign.[61] Kim Il Sung's family on both sides was active in the religious community, and he was raised in a Protestant Christian family. His maternal grandfather was a minister. Kim Il Sung's father went to missionary school.[62] Further, many of the religious communities were linked to anticolonial resistance against the Chinese and Japanese.[63]

Prior to the Korean War, a group of Christians held a protest in Sinuiju to express political views. They were fired upon by police, and twenty-three people were killed. After the incident Kim Il Sung visited the city to ameliorate tensions between communists and Christian nationalists. During 1945–1948 religious freedom was restricted (for example, the land and property of religious organizations was confiscated). Religious groups had ties throughout all levels of society at this point in North Korean history. For this reason, and because Kim Il Sung had yet to fully establish and solidify the regime, persecution of religious groups was delayed. Thus, to limit and weaken religious groups, their property was confiscated without compensation. Revenue was cut off through prohibitions against religious organizations possessing cash; they could only withdraw money from the bank if given prior approval. They were not permitted to accept donations from congregants. Anyone appealing for donations could be sentenced up to two years in prison, and anyone carrying out religious activities could be subjected to one year of reform labor training.

Up to the Korean War, Christian churches remained open, and worship was permitted. However, Christian political activities subsequently were "ruthlessly stamped out."[64] Suppression of religious freedom was critical to the military campaign during the Korean War. Prior to the Incheon landing, when North Korean forces were in Seoul, they captured and shot to death—as instructed— fifty priests and sixty pastors.[65] Approximately forty thousand Christians fled to South Korea when UN forces reached as far as the Amnok River during the Korean War—a historic mass defection to South Korea from the North. After the Korean War, Kim Il Sung's policies changed. Prior to the war, the seminary was tolerated by Kim Il Sung. After 1953 there were no ordained priests or organized Christian churches in the North.[66] Kim Il Sung held that communist society could not move forward with religious people. In a 1962 speech to the People's Safety Agency (the North Korean secret political police) Kim Il Sung explained the elimination of religious believers for the sake of communism: "We cannot move towards a communist society with religious people. This is why we had to put on trial and punish those who held positions of deacons or higher in Protestant and Catholic churches. Other undesirables . . . were also put on trial. Those who did not [give up religion] were sent to prison camps."[67]

This anti-Christian atmosphere was heavy with propaganda, and policies aimed at eliminating Christians after the Korean War. Religious freedom was suppressed between 1949 and 1953. For example, monasteries were closed. A period of religious obliteration then occurred from 1954 to 1971, facilitated through mutual surveillance and the banning of religious activities. All religious followers were classed as counterrevolutionary.

The countrywide classification system, Songbun, was used to identify and eliminate religious believers, particularly from 1966 to 1971. Residents were reregistered, which enabled the authorities to determine classes of people and subdivide them as "basic" and "complex." Later, the Ministry of Public Security, guided by the Central Party, classified people into fifty-one different groups, each falling into one of three broader class divisions—core, wavering, and hostile. As part of identification within these fifty-one classes, individuals of religious leaning were given the number 37 for Protestants, 38 for Buddhists, and 39 for Catholics. These three, among others of politically questionable identity, were deemed hostile and were subjected to severe surveillance and punishment.[68]

* * *

In the regime's early years, the systematic and deliberate nature of North Korea's rights violations were not fully known to the international public. This changed in the 1970s. Amnesty International published a report on North Korea's arbitrary imprisonment and torture of two foreign nationals, Venezuelan communist Ali Lameda and French left-wing activist Jacques Sedillot.[69] The two went to North Korea in the 1960s, relocated there more or less permanently due to communist sympathies, and worked for the foreign propaganda office. They were tasked with spreading the usefulness of Juche and Kim Il Sungism abroad. After a few years of work, each separately raised doubts that the hyperbole of North Korea propaganda would be convincingly received abroad. These doubts earned them each a place in prison, where they were tortured.[70] The treatment of these two men brought some international attention to North Korea's rights violations, but the reports were individual cases. Neither Sedillot nor Lameda spoke publicly about the experience. They did tell Amnesty International about the condition of other prisoners; although they were kept separate from them, they were able to hear other prisoners being tortured and knew something of their poor living conditions.

The full extent of North Korea's system of political prison camps, and thus the systematic nature of violations amounting to crimes against humanity, would burst into international attention in the late 1990s. By that time there were thousands of North Koreans resettled in South Korea, the vast majority due to famine. These individuals reported experience and knowledge of prison camps to South Korean intelligence upon customary arrival debriefing and to NGOs after settling in South Korea. Within a few years some survivors of prison camps began working together in an NGO they established called NK Gulag. That group recorded the names of prisoners and guards, the locations and layout of camps, conditions of prisoners, and types of torture. Thus, the famine was, ironically, beneficial for human rights in North Korea because without it, the extent of violations within the country would not have been exposed as it has now been. It is quite plausible that had it not been for the famine of the

1990s, which compelled so many North Koreans to leave their country—a country few had contemplated leaving before—North Korea's gravest atrocities might never have come to light.

While North Korea claimed to uphold protection of social, economic, and political rights, it staunchly defended violation of people's physical integrity rights as necessary for national survival. The leading state newspaper, *Rodong Shinmun*, explained the process in a 1995 article: "We do not conceal or lie about our partiality, we do not obscure our class-consciousness in the context of human rights. Socialist human rights are not class-transcending human rights to grant freedom and human rights to hostile enemies who oppose socialism, or to disobedient traitors who stand against the People's interests. Our human rights are the rights that legitimise the persecution of enemies of the class, violating human rights of the People, workers, peasants, or intellectuals."[71]

Removal of national enemies is, for the regime, about survival. The present is viewed through a veil that ghosts it with the past. And the past was horrendous. There were tremendous rights violations and war crimes committed during the Korean War, for which the United States and other countries are accountable and have yet to be redressed. Indeed, the same can be said of Japan's treatment of Korea during occupation. Abuses committed by the United States and the Japanese are a standard feature in North Korean media, literature, and history books. It instills a sense of victimhood and persecution and the necessity for violent protectionism. The atrocities committed against Koreans since the early twentieth century—not only by the United States and Japan but also by powerful nation-states that turned a blind eye to the Japanese occupation of Korea—is crucial knowledge for any dignified approach to the study of the Koreas because it explains the very legitimate struggle for recognition and legitimacy across decades.[72] It also makes the actions of North Korea, domestically and internationally, more comprehensible. It helps us to understand how the United States and Japan are perceived as enemies by the domestic population. They are enemies past and the present: the current prime minister of Japan, Shinzo Abe, is, after all, the grandson of the class-A war criminal and postwar prime minister Nobusuke Kishi.[73] Remember, North Korea interprets politics as a mode of inheritance. As such, the situation of Japanese politics is viewed as a toxic continuation of past wrongs. And yet infinite historical regression can only go so far, particularly when the actions of the North Korean state at present are without parallel in the contemporary world for the extent of ongoing, widespread, and arbitrary persecution. The North Korean state is accountable at the highest levels for rights violations that date back to the formation of the country and up to the present.

CHAPTER 2

FAMINE AND HUNGER

I was one of the oldest kids so I could at least pick up food that had fallen to the ground. Those who were very young, they had no idea how to beg or steal food from other houses, that's why they ended up dead.

Twenty-four out of seventy-five orphans passed away of starvation. They reported the children died of diseases, but the children aged seven and onwards died of malnourishment. These children were not able to walk because they were too weak. The bodies of the children were buried in the backyard of the orphanage. It was in the summer of 1997 that this happened.

No, no, there was nothing to eat in the orphanage. In 1996 and 1997, the orphanages tried to release as many children as possible because they didn't have anything to give the kids. They thought the kids were better off begging in the streets. It would be better than starving to death sitting in the orphanage.[1]

M r. Kim Hyuk, the speaker in the account at the start of this chapter, was born in 1982. He lost his mother when he was four, and his father died in the famine. At age thirteen, as the famine years mounted, he was sent to an orphanage. As the famine worsened, the orphans scattered like leaves. And they continue to scatter. Video recorded by North Korean citizens operating secretly from the state shows that as recently as 2016, North Korean children were wandering the streets of illegal markets starving, begging, and dying for food.[2] Australia Broadcasting News footage reveals children starving in orphanages in 2011, with local administrators blaming harvests and weather.[3] Aid workers interviewed by the Associated Press reported the words of North Koreans themselves: They are a proud people. They don't complain; they retreat into their homes and die of hunger. The Associated Press video reported the famine conditions worsening in 2015.[4] According to some survivor accounts, the so-called March of Suffering famine of the 1990s actually began in the late 1980s. For some regions of North Korea, citizens are heading into thirty years living with hunger.

The famine of the 1990s was a disaster for North Koreans, a disaster that evolved slowly over a period of years that complicated day-to-day lives, often with increasing severity. The famine pressed people into behavior that compromised their adherence to the ideology of their country. The assumption that food problems cause people to be less loyal to the government seems logical, but it should be cautiously considered. The famine compelled many people to behave in ways that the state would characterize as less loyal, but there are strong indications that the majority of North Koreans did not see their government as primarily culpable for the food crisis. Some experts claim that people blamed the government for their predicament, but such blaming usually came after North Koreans defected and had exposure to the international community.[5] More often than not, at the time of the famine people were too misinformed and too distracted by the complex demands of making do with so little to identify the cause of the calamity. People's interpretation of cause and effect was— and continues to be—confused due to the nature of censorship in North Korea, due to the complexity of the famine itself, and due to the high degree of misinformation about the famine spread through state media.[6] This chapter illustrates rights violations that predated the 1990s famine, the role that the famine has played in tipping the balance of rights violations toward the unbearable, and the current famine conditions that still endure in North Korea.

As the world has seen, the famine was not the death knell of the North Korean state, but it did change the country and the people in many ways. The famine of the 1990s created the most troubling period for North Koreans' day-to-day survival since the Korean War. Survivors of the famine frequently referred to that time as being like the Korean War not only for how haggard and beaten people were by the experience but also because the famine was something that had to be endured, an ill that couldn't be avoided because the salvation of the nation-state was at stake.[7] Hunger, illness, and the uncertainty of things ever improving were aspects of daily life that required endurance. The state ideology stressed the importance of national survival over individual survival. Human death was a real possibility, but the Korean nation would not perish. To ensure that disgruntled citizens could not change the social fabric, the government sought to control people's natural impulses in times of crisis through misinformation and harsh punishment of transgressions.[8] Given the mounting difficulties of life, people transgressed in areas of sociopolitical life that would have been unthinkable or simply unnecessary before, and this effectively increased rights violations. Survival coping strategies were risks that opened the possibility for survival but also new worlds of suffering.

Famine and the Right to Food

"Few human rights have been endorsed with such frequency, unanimity or urgency as the right to food, yet probably no other human right has been as comprehensively and systematically violated on such a wide scale in recent decades."[9] In 1999 the Committee on Economic, Social and Cultural Rights recognized that the right to adequate food is achieved when a person, alone or in community, has the "physical and economic access at all times to adequate food *or means for its procurement.*"[10] Further highlighting the critical feature of access and means, the current UN special rapporteur on the right to food, Hilal Elver, states: "The right to food is the right to have regular, permanent and unrestricted access, either directly or by means of financial purchases, to quantitatively and qualitatively adequate and sufficient food corresponding to the cultural traditions of the people to which the consumer belongs, and which ensure a physical and mental, individual and collective, fulfilling and dignified life free of fear."[11] Precipitated by the ongoing famine, untold numbers of North Koreans are living lives as prisoners, stateless children, and unrecognized refugees because of the failure of the government to make reasonable changes that it is obliged to make as a signatory to the Universal Declaration of Human Rights. Article 25 of the Universal Declaration of Human Rights states, "Everyone has the right to a standard of living adequate for the health and well-being of himself and of his family, including food, clothing, housing and medical care and necessary social services, and the right to security in the event of unemployment, sickness, disability, widowhood, old age or other lack of livelihood in circumstances beyond his control."[12] Other international norms further enshrine the right to food. The International Covenant on Economic, Social and Cultural Rights, Article 11, which North Korea ratified in 1981, is a binding covenant on North Korea, yet the DPRK fails to provide safe access to enough food or safe means for its procurement.

Globally, prior to the 1970s, overpopulation and geographic climactic vulnerability were thought to be the main causes of famine. Though these views were erroneous, they still persist today as people draw correlations between hunger and food supply. In its earliest theoretical formulations, famine was perceived to be caused by overpopulation; most notably, Robert Malthus propagated this notion.[13] The twin ideas that overpopulation or insufficient food leads to famine are still misunderstood as a principal factor leading to famine. Indeed, prior to the twentieth century, national disasters or conflicts that left communities without enough food to survive often triggered famines.[14] In the late 1970s analysts stopped designating some regions of the world as natural famine zones or "famine belts" because they began to see that famine was caused by factors other than climate conditions.[15] With advances in technology and infrastructure, climate alone does not give rise to famine, regardless of where it occurs. Multiple causal factors contribute to famine. Yet the types of famine we see emerging and the ways people die during famine have changed.[16] By the early 1980s analysts could fully appreciate the complex dynamics of famine. Thus, social, political, and economic conditions, in addition to geography, climate, disaster, and conflict, are all now commonly understood factors in understanding famine.[17] In addition to these causal factors, scholars began to understand how famine impacts different people differently. Socioeconomic, political, gender, and other demographic features form "baseline" features that shape who survives, thrives, or dies during famine.[18] The progression of famine through an area is determined by baseline variables.[19]

In the case of famine, a person's access to labor and resources profoundly shapes their survival outcomes. Experts call these variables "entitlements." When looking at a famine, the entitlement approach enables the analyst to holistically examine the sociopolitical and economic factors that lead people to be at differential risk to famine. A person can obtain goods and services through entitlements that are bound by cultural and legal norms—beliefs about who ought to get what, and under which conditions, and legal and economic norms about how these beliefs are put into practice.[20] If, by the bonds of law or culture, your access to entitlements is limited, then you are at increased risk unless you engage in illicit survival strategies. However, illegal efforts can also contribute to, sustain, or exacerbate conditions of famine.

Famines result from the inability of an individual to acquire enough food—not from there being insufficient food. Famines can emerge within active markets and economies. The theory that a decline in available food causes famines is not useful because it does not account for the dynamics of exchange economies and preexisting social inequalities.[21] We might presume there is a shortage of food when in fact there is a problem of allocation or entitlement linked to unequal power relations. Causal factors may not necessarily be the same factors that sustain the famine. Triggering factors, such as lack of open market access to food, create an environment where coping strategies such as buying food at illegal markets inadvertently become sustaining causes of the famine: prices are prohibitively high, driven up by high demand and shortage.

Famine is not inevitable but within human rational control; it is linked to relations of power.[22] Famine highlights preexisting weaknesses in a society, and because it is a process, rather than an event, famine usually spreads easily within these weaknesses, exacerbating them and sharpening lines of inequality. Lines of inequality are exacerbated by systematic depravation of basic capabilities within a population where parts are defenseless against economic shocks not linked to production and agriculture activities. This is what Amartya Sen calls "capability poverty."[23] Research on disaster shows that stresses are distributed unequally to different parts of society, and this unequal distribution is likely to mirror preexisting social inequalities. Similarly, famine is rarely general to an entire country or region but more likely appears in areas that are economically and politically marginalized. Because famine is specific to particular areas, large numbers of a population can be affected—as much as 5–10 percent—while the social system will survive without serious consequences.[24] Throughout history, places that have experienced famine are consistently those countries and populations that are politically marginalized and economically impoverished.[25]

A decline in food availability from international sources, combined with a supply of external economic aid, is a new kind of entitlement problem.[26] Commercial imports of food in North Korea fell as humanitarian assistance arrived. The savings created by this were allocated to other resources instead of fixing the cause of food unavailability. The famine cannot be attributed to decline in domestic food availability alone; rather, it developed and worsened because of a failure to adjust imports and military expenditures according to the needs of the population.

North Korea's Famine as Catalyst

Famine manifests socially in ways that make it hard to track back to how it links to rights violations. This is often particularly the case for famine victims. The insights of survivors of North Korea's famine shed new light on famine experience and explain why famine is not often seen—even by survivors themselves—as resulting from those in power or the government. Unlike physical integrity rights violations such as mass arbitrary incarceration, torture, or public execution, famine is not a sudden event. Rather, it moves slowly and unevenly throughout a community or country. It is a process that creeps into a territory. Resources diminish, and gradually people make do with less and less. People who are responsible for the famine, those in political power, are so removed from the individuals affected that the famine, on the ground, seems to be at once an act of some demonic design or the fault of those nearest who are also trying to make ends meet in an unfair situation. The absence of free and open information, as seen in North Korea throughout its history, confounds the disastrous situation further. The causal forces of famine, the injustices that undergird it, are often multiple and complex. Inquiry into famine reveals a mix of rights violations such that, if those rights had been respected, suffering and death could have been avoided.

North Koreans in the 1990s saw any changes to ordinary social life as detrimental and as signifying the depth of an individual's moral degradation—that is, for average people but not the government or leadership. North Koreans cited divorce, prostitution, and the abandonment of children as examples of this. The effort to maintain the state's preferred lifestyle—specifically, socialist life—was a major theme in the oral histories I collected during the writing of my first book on the North Korean famine. There was a strong reluctance to change former ways of living or engage in behavior antithetical to socialist ideology, even when doing so would alleviate suffering in situations like famine. The maintenance of lifestyles was not only an individual enterprise. The government also had an interest in maintaining a socialist lifestyle and at the very least maintaining adherence to, if not also belief in, Juche socialist ideology. "Juche" is a North Korean term said to encapsulate the idea of national self-reliance. Invented by Hwang Jang Yop, an elite party secretary of North Korea during the reign of Kim Il Sung, Juche was meant to improve North Korea's image abroad.[27] Discrepancies between reality and ideology have generated a lack of confidence in the ideological apparatus but not a collapse of the ideology and subsequent destabilization of the locus of power.[28] Authors Kongdan Oh and Ralph Hassig point out that North Koreans are politically disengaged and lack the necessary energy to get politically engaged.[29] It could also be the case that the population sees no viable or safe opportunity for political engagement and thus finds it devoid of interest apart from what is required to live without running afoul of the state.

Political engagement takes a scripted form in North Korea. How people are encouraged to interpret their given situation shapes the form of political thinking and activity. Significantly, the famine of the 1990s was never referred to as a famine by the North Korean government. Instead it was termed the March of Suffering by the state. In Korean, *konanui haenggun* refers to the difficult march of suffering undertaken by Kim Il Sung as he fought against the Japanese in Manchuria to liberate Korea in the 1930s. Political engagement during the famine thus meant behaving in a likewise fashion to Kim Il Sung and struggling against the difficulties so that the nation survives.

Famine typically does not occur in a society where there is a functioning democracy and the free exchange of information.[30] More recently it has been pointed out that democracy and free access to information are not necessarily the panacea for all famines, and this makes sense when we consider that not all famines are alike.[31] However, the notion of media and information as a means by which to alleviate famine is significant in the North Korean case. Some scholars argue that increased contact with the international community means

North Koreans will begin to question their government and demand better living standards.[32]

The famine compelled many North Koreans to seek resources outside of their home country in China, South Korea, and beyond. Although there were rights violations, few felt compelled to leave the country on that basis. These North Koreans were not fleeing from ideology, politics, or overly controlling government per se. Even with the famine, few defectors identified the food crisis as a political or human rights issue.[33] Rather the vast majority of these people were fleeing hunger, which in turn was a material manifestation of a failed ideology, politics, and economics steered into the ground by their government. They were moving *toward* food, medicine, and other resources they needed to survive. Few people defected from North Korea prior to the 1990s. The decision to defect is often taken with great reluctance, an act said to be unthinkable prior to the food crisis. Since the 1990s, over a period now nearing thirty years, in small groups and alone, tens of thousands have crossed the Sino-Korean border.

The movement of North Koreans into China, precipitated by the famine, was the point of no return for growing international awareness of North Korea's rights violations. Once in China, many North Koreans continued toward South Korea. They in turn helped others to defect and resettle. The numbers began to swell (see figure 2.1). As more and more people defected, the true extent of the violations became known to the international community. North Koreans came to know the true extent of abuses occurring throughout their own country, which formerly they may only have suspected.

Today, parts of North Korea remain vulnerable to famine. Large segments of the northern-most population were then and still are capability-poor—a fact that is determined by government decree over political reliability, whether through connections with the South during the Korean War, or connections with the Japanese during colonialism, or the suspicion of these. Such economic, political, and social factors determined dynamics of undernourishment,

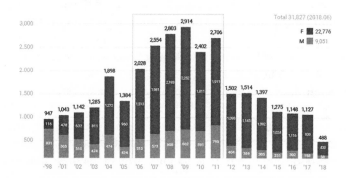

2.1 Number of North Korean defectors entering South Korea

Ministry of Unification, 2018, https://www.unikorea.go.kr/eng_unikorea/relations/statistics/defectors/

starvation, and famine and restricted the means to alter entitlements. Attempts to alter one's entitlements to food, whether through theft, defection, or the somewhat less dangerous acts of selling in the market, were dealt with severely in North Korea because these were considered capitalist in nature and therefore treasonous. Such acts resulted in disappearances, imprisonments, torture, or public executions. There is virtually no opportunity for an individual to safely participate in decisions or public debate about entitlements in North Korea.

Dependency on entitlements to food and material goods through the Public Distribution System, illegal markets, and farmers' markets remains strong in North Korea; consequently, vulnerability to famine and undernourishment remains great. Entitlements are highly complex in North Korea in that they are narrowly circumscribed, making it impossible to survive unless you are deemed deserving within entitlement structures. Rule bending and breaking is common but hidden and rife with danger. For instance, those in contact with friends and relatives in China often drew upon these networks to survive. Similarly, those North Koreans with ties to descendants in Japan, though disadvantaged in terms of government distributions, could survive on gifts sent from Japan (though receiving these items required a series of bribes to local authorities). None of these entitlements was legal, and, if caught, the punishment was extreme. In North Korea, the degree of freedom an individual or family has to "establish ownership over an adequate amount of food" directly impacts the severity of hunger.[34] For North Korea to reach nutrition security, fundamental changes are needed in the economy and politics of the country.

The Increase of Rights Violations After Famine

Within North Korea, the famine of the 1990s created a situation where more and more people were engaged in behavior deemed transgressive by the state. The promise of the state to provide economic, social, and cultural rights—the so-called second-generation rights much lauded by North Korea—continued to go unfulfilled. What we know now about the famine, and the government's failure to prevent it, is that it created a situation where more and more people moved from facing socioeconomic and political rights violations into facing violations of physical integrity. The famine complicated life, as people were more likely to be engaged in activity that ran afoul of the state's profoundly restrictive laws, simply to survive. With the famine, categories of wrongdoing became broad and opaque. Individuals who had never run afoul of the state before found themselves in compromised situations with difficult ideological choices between personal survival and loyal behavior to the state. The famine compelled people to live differently; in some cases this also caused people to think differently about their lives. For some, this manifested in the decision to leave their country. However, some who left the North and crossed into China still planned to return home. Learning how harshly they would be punished for defecting in the first place led them to continue living in China or to migrate onward to South Korea.[35]

The famine tipped the balance against law- and ideology-abiding ordinary North Koreans. Survival meant being elite or turning toward criminality. Prior to the famine it was possible to live a reasonable life in North Korea without the immediate threat of rights violations so long as you were of the right family background and obeyed political expectations. The famine changed that because it made living day-to-day more volatile. With the famine, formerly benign things such as complaining about hunger, questioning where food was coming from, or traveling to get food or medicine became dangerously politicized as antigovernment behavior. In this respect the famine can be identified as the inflection point of North Korea's widening disregard for rights.

In an effort to get access to adequate food, hungry populations in North Korea sought alternative foraging methods. It was hard to find substitute foods in the mountains because so many people were looking. Fields and mountains were denuded of anything edible. But finding something to eat was not the end of the matter. The items had to be carefully prepared to ensure they were edible and not dangerous. Often this required pounding, boiling, and fermenting. With few trees for firewood, it was difficult to keep fires hot enough to boil water. If the preparation was successful, then it was possible to enjoy the substitute foods, but even this enjoyment might not last, as digestion problems from such items often lead to constipation or diarrhea.

The North Korean government thought the famine could be managed through ideology, social control, and triage of resources. They were wrong. To this day North Korea is food insecure. Up until the late 1980s North Korea benefited from the assistance of the Soviet Union through friendly pricing and trade. With the collapse of the Soviet Bloc in the late 1980s and early 1990s, North Korea lost financial support. Yet, as the economy worsened, the government took no action to change policy. The country was using old and outdated farming equipment in addition to unsustainable farming practices that relied on Juche ideological guidance of self-sufficiency. There were a few reform options for North Korea to take; many of them would have been good for the people, and none of them would have benefited the government's interests. It is estimated that 600,000 to 1 million individuals died in the 1990s famine. "This was a man-made preventable tragedy. These people died needlessly, and the government is deeply culpable in this outcome," explains Andrew Natsios.[36] In addition to those who died, tens of thousands had their lives upended by the famine, the ongoing postfamine issues related to food access, and the state's attempt to control behavior by cracking down further. The existing scholarship on famine robustly demonstrates the causal linkages between famine and the absence of, or failure to respect, basic political and economic rights. However, even while denying political and economic rights, the state could have made policy decisions that would have averted the famine. Kim Il Sung and his son Kim Jong Il decided against such policy changes in the full knowledge that failure to do so would lead to the deaths of hundreds of thousands. North Korea's current leader, Kim Jong Un, continues to avoid changes that could ensure nutritional security for the people.

Government Culpability in Famine

North Korea's 1990s famine, like those of the mid-1980s in Ethiopia, Sudan, Malawi, Madagascar, Iraq, and Bosnia, came about through deliberate acts of commission by the state and were not prevented, though they could have been.[37] North Korea had what is called a "priority regime famine" in the 1990s because ideological programs and government policies were placed above feeding and providing for hungry people. Priority regime famines are characterized by a weak local economy and a lack of political will or capacity to intervene.[38] The culpability of government systems in the emergence of famine has highlighted the role of local, national, and international responsibility. The worst famines in the last century have occurred under some of the most corrupt governments: Joseph Stalin's Holodomor, Mao Zedong's Great Leap, Pol Pot's Khmer Rouge famine, Mengistu Haile Mariam's famine in Ethiopia, and Kim Jong Il's March of Suffering.[39]

While the North Korean government claimed that the famine was an act of nature, they also claimed it was due to international sanctions and embargos, not a result of domestic policy. Famine scholarship shows that this is highly improbable. Developments in infrastructure and technology particularly in the last half of the twenty-first century mean that North Korea could have redirected its resources and policies toward ensuring the right to adequate food, but the government chose otherwise. The famine resulted from the state's failure to prioritize the needs of its people over political policy. The famine was a material manifestation of rights violations kept in place by the highest levels of state governance.

Political economists Stephan Haggard and Marcus Noland argue that the North Korean famine was similar to others in the twentieth century in that it was created in a totalitarian state. The famine was the cumulative effect of two generations of economic mismanagement and social engineering, emerging in a context where the population had no mechanism to push the government to protect the people's right to food. The government could have improved food availability through freeing up resources devoted to the military.[40] North Korea claimed then, and now, that it needs to strengthen its military to defend itself against U.S. aggression. However, resources were prioritized not only for the military but also for the elite. It was necessary to appease this social class so they would not waver from state loyalty. Former state poet Jang Jin-Sung describes receiving additional rations such as imported food every week and other resources such as clothing and even items for infants that came from the United Nations and other NGOs' humanitarian donations.[41]

Globally, famine and food crisis are rooted in decisions that leaders in power make. The famine in North Korea, then and now, highlights tensions between individual human rights and national sovereignty where arguments around failure to uphold the former are justified as the necessary price to pay in securing the latter. Sometimes the curtailment of rights, the derogation of rights, is justified as due to a national emergency. Some rights may be derogated, according to the United Nations, "during times of war or public emergency."[42] However "the emergency must be *actual*, affect the whole population and the threat must be to the very existence of the nation."[43] Further, these derogations must be of "last resort" and "temporary."

Due to the armistice, the Koreas are still technically at war. As a result, North Korea invokes this rationale to explain poor conditions in its country. In the North's human rights report to the United Nations, it writes:

> Maintenance of [the] armistice situation is the main obstacle in [the] creation of [a] peaceful atmosphere for the promotion of Human rights. Due to the persistent manoeuvres of the United States, which escalates tension on [the] Korean peninsula taking DPRK as [the] enemy and violating the armistice agreement, rights of the people for peace and development have been seriously jeopardized and [the] Korean people have been living in constant danger of war.

North and South Korea are still at war, but the armistice clarifies that the Korean War is not *actual* but notional. States of emergency must be actual rather than notional. Further, the state of emergency must be something that threatens the existence of the nation, not a threat to the government of the nation or its social fabric. If the armistice is the main obstacle to a peaceful atmosphere for human rights, how is it that South Korea doesn't suffer the same degree of egregious crimes against humanity? North Korean state media claims that watching movies or similar influences from foreign countries is a ruse of psychological warfare from enemy states aimed at altering the socialist fabric of the country. When North Korea derogates citizen rights, it does so not as a temporary measure or as a last resort but pervasively, systematically, extensively, and egregiously. Furthermore, certain kinds of rights must *never* be derogated under any circumstance. These are rights such as the right to life, the right to be free from torture, the right to not face inhumane or degrading treatment or punishment, the right to be free from slavery and servitude, and the right to be free from retroactive application of punishment. People were denied the basic right to life when the state failed to prevent the famine, when the state failed to permit migration within and out of the country, and when the state failed to permit people to engage in free economic activity. Thus, the "state of emergency" claim put forward by North Korea does not hold. Rather, the use of such language shows North Korea's tendency to wield the language of international rights norms to justify the aims of the government.

North Korean state media, along with their other publications, use arguments of cultural relativism to defend their version of human rights.[44] Within this framework, the notion of "universal" human rights is interpreted as a tool of Western imperialism; thus, resistance to Western constructs of human rights is linked with resistance to Western imperialism and Western hegemony. Difficulties suffered by the North Korean people are attributed to enemy nation states. The United States and Japan have some of the strongest global economies, and since they have isolated North Korea, the North is not able to develop its economy. Thus, according to North Korea's logic, the 1990s famine resulted from natural disaster and international economic embargo rather than from North Korea's failure to liberalize its economy; to permit people to sell freely; to permit people to alter entitlements to employment, movement, and resources; and to deprioritize the military.

The North Korean government could have diverted financial resources from the military to the people, but it opted otherwise. Even while the government put military spending first, soldiers went hungry. Significant portions of state resources, including those directly under the control of the supreme leader, were put toward the purchase of luxury goods and the lauding of the Kim family's personality cult even while people starved.[45] North Korea claims that such triage of resources was necessary, and continues to be necessary, for national defense. Nevertheless, the fact that a famine occurred and that food security continues to be an issue is "an indictment of the ethics of the country."[46] In international law, state food crimes are explicitly identified as crimes against humanity. Deprivation of access to food is included in the Rome Statute of the International Criminal Court as the crime of extermination.[47] North Korea is not a signatory to the Rome Statute, but if people are deliberately deprived of food or if a country neglects to ensure the right to food to a population, this is an international food crime.[48] Many states claim that war can be a complicating factor in food crimes, as observed by human rights scholar Rhoda E. Howard-Hassmann, but experts have described North Korea as a country where war is not a "complicating variable."[49] North Korea continues to argue otherwise. If domestic human rights are aligned within international rights norms, citizens can be protected from state food crimes. Consider: in North Korea there is no accountability or transparency, and state decision-making is entirely top-down. Because there is no freedom of expression and opinion, of information or press, or of assembly or association, North Koreans are not able to gather and safely discuss, debate, and share ideas about how they may improve their lives.[50] Without these freedoms, the sociopolitical environment for discussing access to food and the right to alter access to food is dangerous and too risky. Thus, it becomes clear why huge numbers have opted to take individual clandestine methods of survival, including through migration. This is the option the vast majority of North Koreans selected.

Mismanaging Aid

The North Korean government had a few options to solve its food problem. They could make economic reforms, like those of China, which would have included stimulus permissions such as private investment and economic freedom. The North chose not to do this. They could have cut military spending, in terms of weapons system development and investment. The North didn't choose this either. They could permit international humanitarian aid. This they did, but with severe restrictions on surveillance and control of aid workers.[51]

The famine of the 1990s brought the international community's attention to North Korea through the seemingly apolitical lens of humanitarian disaster. Of course, famine *is* a human rights issue, but, framed as a humanitarian issue, the international humanitarian aid workers could address the needs of some of the neediest with permission of the North Korean government while not raising the provocative specter of international rights norms. Unable to shake leaders into respecting the rights of their citizens, humanitarian agencies put their energies where they can to save as many lives as possible despite the underlying problems that persist. North Korea claimed the famine was an act of nature, which enabled the state to save face domestically, but few famine experts outside of North Korea could in good conscience agree with such a claim. The international community responded to requests for aid, but by the time aid workers were on the ground assessing malnourishment, they found that the famine had been well under way years prior to their arrival. Aid workers knew the famine had been under way for years because children and young adults were stunted, a phenomenon that indicates malnourishment early in life. In 1998 eighteen nutritionists from the United Nations Children's Fund, the World Food Programme (WFP), and the Humanitarian Aid department of the European Commission, in collaboration with the North Korean government, measured the heights and weights of more than 1,500 children from six months to seven years of age. The report indicates that 62 percent of the children suffered from chronic malnutrition (based on height-for-age) and 16 percent were acutely malnourished (based on weight-for-height). In a joint press release, the agencies underlined that "this puts North Korea among the top 10 countries with the highest malnutrition rates in the world"[52] This suggests that the problems had been many years in the making, as assessments on stunting retroactively assess conditions of famine. Already too much time had passed during which North Korea could and should have avoided the catastrophe.

Even after the WFP was permitted entry into North Korea, the government did not grant access to the worst affected areas: the three northeastern provinces of Hamgyong-Bukdo, Hamgyong-Namdo, and Yanggangdo. Not only the WFP but other humanitarian organizations such as the International Committee of the Red Cross were not permitted entry to those areas. The northeastern provinces are areas where less politically desirable citizens live, people who are of lower Songbun, who receive 200–300 percent less food on the Public Distribution System, when it was running, than those of higher Songbun. Tun Myat, one of the senior officers with the WFP at the time, told the North Koreans that if the WFP was not permitted entry to those areas, they would shut down the program.[53] North Korea relented to some extent, but not entirely, and granted some access to those regions. When Tun Myat gained access, he said that the local officials in those areas didn't try to hide details. Officials in other counties hid the famine by delivering programmed answers and not sharing statistics.[54]

The famine could not be accurately assessed by international aid agencies because the North Korean government limited operations and information about conditions within the country. One of the reasons restrictions were placed on them was because relief efforts in the country were viewed as potential imperialist weapons, waiting to strike.[55] Humanitarian workers inside North Korea provide a good example of the country's social control in operation. In order to limit the threat of influence posed by these individuals, constraints were put on international humanitarian workers. The main goal of these constraints was to ensure control of the flow of information, people, and goods within the country. Aid workers were denied access to about 25 percent of the country, representing about 15 percent of the population. Aid workers had no way to assess the needs of people in inaccessible areas, although suspicion was that things couldn't be better in inaccessible parts.[56] Areas that were once accessible became inaccessible, and vice versa, for "no clear reason."[57]

It was also difficult for aid workers to know if their efforts were having any positive impact because official information and data were difficult to access and of questionable reliability. Former UN humanitarian coordinator in the DPRK David Morton described the situation as follows:

> Agencies were not permitted to conduct random monitoring of programmes or spot checks, which are the normal means to determine that aid is properly used. National security overrides every other consideration in the DPRK. If there was a choice between external aid and national security, there was

no contest: national security would automatically prevail. . . . Even giving us a list of beneficiary institutions was perceived to have national security implications.[58]

Communications were also strictly controlled for reasons of national security: long-distance radio communications or satellite phones as well as normal communication equipment for UN agencies and NGOs were not permitted. In addition, the use of an emergency international air ambulance service, which would provide emergency medical evacuation, was not guaranteed permission to land in Pyongyang.[59] NGO and UN staff were monitored all the time by a minder provided by the government. "Some 80,000 nurseries, kindergartens and schools were believed to receive food aid for children who were WFP's beneficiaries. A list of beneficiary institutions was always promised but never provided, because, the Koreans said, they were having difficulty assembling all the names of the institutions and translating them into English."[60]

There were problems with roads, energy supplies, and basic resources for the delivery of aid, so it is not a surprise that there would be delays and added confusion with language and translation, particularly as it would all be on the North Korean side since they did not permit Korean-speaking foreign workers.[61] The linguistic helplessness of aid workers in North Korea, both past and present, has resulted in their maintenance and delivery of North Korea's systemic inequality. The society has no means of interacting with the international community on a direct level, and any interaction is mediated through interpreters and strictly supervised. The linguistic powerlessness of aid workers in North Korea was part of an obvious, deliberate, and sustained effort at control. The international community and aid workers can be duped by informants who are "vulnerable to manipulation and deception."[62] It is argued that foreign aid must meet the needs of the people as they themselves define those needs; however, the North Korean government stipulates needs and how they are to be met rather than letting the people themselves decide. Expecting this kind of government to be an amiable force in the lives of the most disadvantaged members of its population is wishful thinking.

These and other contradictions are some of the factors that resulted in NGOs such as Care International, Oxfam, Action Against Hunger, Doctors Without Borders, and Doctors of the World ceasing operations in North Korea. Doctors Without Borders operated a considerable program in North Korea between 1995 and 1998. They supplied drugs and medical training to over a thousand health centers in addition to sixty feeding centers for malnourished children in three provinces. Throughout that time, the NGO became convinced that aid wasn't reaching those most in need, and thus they withdrew in the fall of 1998.[63] Hugo Slim, senior research fellow at the Oxford Institute of Ethics, Law and Armed Conflict, writes that these motivations may not have been uncommon given the conditions of powerlessness, frustration, anger, and fear under which many humanitarian workers and NGOs work in North Korea.[64] The WFP in North Korea was and is the leading UN agency in the country as well as the main body for food aid. North Korea was also the UN agency's biggest single operation worldwide. In North Korea, WFP works with the government's Public Distribution System to deliver aid. The bulk of the food is delivered to institutions and nurseries because there is a focus on the most vulnerable and because this form of aid is the easiest to track and monitor. The main type of aid given to North Korea is in the form of food and medical aid. Sometimes the aid has taken the form of food production, such as technical assistance with agricultural projects related to food production.[65] In addition to food production, food distribution is also a concern. Grain shipments have been triaged, in the sense that stocks were sent out to some areas but not others. The east coast was particularly limited in terms of food distribution, especially late in 1995. From the start of the relief effort, the government focused relief and monitoring on the west coast, insisting that food be delivered through the main west coast port of Nampŏ despite the fact that the transportation system linking the west and the east had broken down.[66] Prominent North Korean defectors in South Korea have remarked on the issue of food distribution, explaining that basic faults in infrastructure handicap the whole system. Defector Kang Chol-Hwan writes:

> There is one aspect of the current famine that doesn't attract enough attention. Besides the production problems that arise from inadequate work incentives, fertilizers and working tractors, there is also the problem of distribution. The Yodŭk canton, for example, was still running surpluses as late as 1990, but no trains were available for transport. The only alternative transportation was the country's aging fleet of run-down trucks which kept breaking down on the unpaved roads. Rice that was needed in the city sat rotting in the countryside, while manufactured goods the country people needed never left the city.[67]

Contributions in the form of fertilizers, improved irrigation systems, reliable electricity, and expanded use of agricultural facilities and equipment have helped to bolster agricultural output. Among international donors, South Korea still gives massive amounts of food aid to North Korea. However, during the mid-1990s the North Korean government stipulated that aid from South Korea would only be accepted if it came in unmarked bags, ensuring that international aid would not bring with it an awareness of the international community among regular North Koreans. Between 1995 and 2003 South Korea provided $904.5 million worth of aid.[68]

Military grain stockpiles were from 400,000 metric tons to as high as 1.5 million metric tons. That is said to be 5 percent to 20 percent of normal annual demand.[69] The government could have drawn on these, but those I interviewed said that they were not drawn on, which suggests that shortages were a function of distribution more than aggregate supply. In May 1997 the North Korean government agreed to permit direct shipments to the east coast from Chongjin. In July the first delivery to Chongjin was made, but even then the east coast received only one-third of a 25,000-ton shipment.[70] Natsios's analysis of shipping manifests comes to the conclusion that during all of 1997–1998, only 18 percent of all WFP aid was shipped to eastern ports despite the fact that those provinces constituted approximately a third of the prefamine population and had a high overall dependence on the Public Distribution System.[71]

Nearly a decade after the famine began to take shape, aid agencies were still not given full and independent access to the population, and there was little systematic information about the famine.[72] For instance, the WFP in 2008 and 2009 still had access to only 131 counties.[73] There are still entire areas about which aid agencies have no knowledge whatsoever. At the time of the 1990s famine and during food security issues today, the information that North Korean authorities grant to aid agencies and the mode of distribution that the government regulates are biased, opaque, and compromise the mission of aid agencies providing care to those most in need. Scott Snyder, senior fellow for Korea Studies and director of the Program on U.S.-Korea Policy at the Council on Foreign Relations, explains that the "amount of food distributed through the PDS [Public Distribution System] is no longer an indicator of imminent distress within the North Korean system, yet it has remained the WFP's primary indicator of distress."[74] A staff member of Doctors Without Borders wrote in the *Guardian* that by distributing food through North Korea's Public Distribution System, their relief operations had become part of the system of oppression.[75]

Famine Then, Nutritional Insecurity Now

The most basic of human rights, the right to be free from hunger and have access to adequate food, was violated by the North Korean state during the 1990s. Condemningly, one of the main findings of the UN Commission of Inquiry states that the problem of access to food continues today. The government continues to prioritize population groups, and it distributes food and facilitates access to resources according to political loyalty.[76] The North Korean government "deliberately deprived" and "neglected to ensure" food to the population.[77] The DPRK has long maintained that its domestic nutritional concerns are the result of natural disasters such as drought and flooding, but this is not the case. Domestic nutrition deficits are a consequence of government policy, inaction, and criminalization of coping strategies. Regime stability was prioritized over human rights. People were dispossessed of food and the means of getting food. Following existing patterns of social discrimination within the country, known as Songbun, North Korea privileged certain geographic areas and people deemed loyal, according to this politically inherited classification system.

The two shocks that followed the famine of the 1990s worsened economic, social, and cultural rights for North Koreans. In July 2002 the government implemented economic reforms in agricultural, food, and industrial sectors. The aim of these reforms was to "eliminate the incentive for farmers to divert the harvest each year to sell on the farmers' markets."[78] The reforms had a disastrous effect, with inflation and grain prices rising 300 percent.[79] Since the establishment of the country in 1948, North Korea's tendency has always been to allow "ideology to trump rational economics"; this tendency, expressed by the scholar Victor Cha at the UN Commission of Inquiry public hearings in Washington, D.C., has been observed by countless other scholars in the fields of history and political economy.[80] The biggest problem, Cha clarifies, is that the North Korean government officials fear that economic reform would mean the loss of political control, so they are trapped in a "classic closed political system reform dilemma."[81] If they open up the economy, an essential reform to salvage the country, the country as they currently know it will be changed forever. To paraphrase Cha's testimony to the commission, the only thing keeping the North from being like the South is politics. The politics of the North is having a hugely detrimental effect on the people and society. The people are entirely unable to make demands of their government or to hold their government to account. As such, in the last four decades, North Korea has struggled with widespread economic failure that has manifested materially in terms of famine, food insecurity, and shortages of fuel, electricity, medicine, and other essentials for ensuring basic minimums for socioeconomic rights.

The UN Food and Agriculture Organization defines food security as existing when "all people, at all times, have physical, social and economic access to sufficient, safe and nutritious food to meet their dietary needs and food preferences for an active and healthy life."[82] However, George Kent, author of *Freedom from Want: The Human Right to Adequate Food*, explains that it is more useful to identify the nutrition status of people because this tells us about suitable food, basic health services, and care of the elderly and children. He writes, "Malnutrition generally results not from lack of food in the community but from the skewed distribution of the food that is available." The skewing in distribution arises because some people are too poor or too powerless "to make an adequate claim on the food that is available."[83] A more accurate term of assessment is "nutrition security," which identifies the importance of food quantities in addition to other inputs, such as health services, "at all times for all people."[84]

A study of the heights of 6,512 defectors to South Korea made the critical finding that those North Koreans born before the division of the Korean Peninsula were taller than that of their South Korean peers. It made the further finding that all "North Korean cohorts born thereafter were shorter than their South Korean counterparts."[85] Stunting occurs when the body sacrifices linear growth in order to survive. These findings make clear that North Koreans have struggled to achieve adequate nutrition from the formation of the country until the present day. There are also regional deviations in nutritional assessments. An assessment of nutrition conducted by the DPRK government, published in 2012, found that stunting prevalence was highest in Kyanggangdo (at 43 percent in 2004 and 39.6 percent in 2012). Pyongyang had the lowest rate of stunting (at 24 percent in 2014 and 15.6 percent in 2012).[86] However, the height assessments in the study strongly point to widespread undernutrition throughout North Korea.

The issue of nutrition in North Korea has widespread and long-term consequences for the socioeconomic and political well-being of the country and the region. Malnutrition has significant consequences for overall health and mortality. If malnutrition occurs in childhood, it has long-term impacts that effect the individual's lifelong health, the health of any children they may have, and even their grandchildren.[87] There are strong links between malnutrition and disease, even after malnourishment has passed. With children and infants, the consequences can be significant for brain function and development throughout the lifespan. Stunting is a common consequence of malnutrition in children. In the long term, children who suffer malnutrition are at increased risk of chronic diseases such as type-1 diabetes and adult cancers.[88] School-age children with prior experience of undernutrition show altered stress response, indicated by elevated cortisol levels, heart rates, and urine epinephrine.[89] Children malnourished severely enough to result in stunting have cognitive deficits during school years; it is associated with undermining their developmental potential.[90] Infant mortality is most immediately caused by diarrhea or pneumonia, but malnutrition makes the risk of death from these extremely likely. The infant mortality rate in North Korea for 2017 was 22.13 deaths per 1,000 births; for children under age five, the mortality rate was 27.17.[91]

A malnourished person is more likely to contract tuberculosis, one of the leading contagious diseases in North Korea, which is then more likely to develop into serious infection. Poor nutrition impacts negatively on the neuropsychological development of children. Malnourished children are more likely to perform poorly compared with children who have not suffered. Medical studies have found "long-lasting deficits in intelligence and school performance."[92] Exposure to malnutrition decreases the ability of children to benefit later from an enriched helpful environment.[93] The social, economic, and political environment where children live also has a direct impact on their nutritional status. Nutritional problems have a political dimension. Since there is no space for public or private debate in North Korea, there are no political opportunities to demand that leaders transform existing unequal access to food and health resources.

CHAPTER 3

DISCRIMINATION AND
RELIGIOUS PERSECUTION

*My younger sibling wanted to enter the party in 2007, but was turned
down because we have cousins in China and that is considered as a sign
of bad foundation (Songbun).*

—Defector Lee, Interview (no date given) in Database Center for
North Korean Human Rights

*One day, one of her children told the guests that they had an interesting
book and took out the bible to show them. This story spread around and
the family was completely ruined.*

—Defector Koh, Interview in June 2011, Database Center for
North Korean Human Rights

After the Korean War, North Korea set up people's court trials to
deal with farmers and their families who had been involved with
the UN Command peace units. The peace units had been set up
by the UN Command and South Korea to maintain public order. As such, they
were connected to the enemy. In the people's courts of early North Korea, many
farmers were executed and their family members sent to remote areas of the
North. These were among the earliest people categorized as being hostile to the

North Korean state by virtue of family-linked Songbun.[1] There were many millions of Koreans who fled south during the Korean War. In the southern part of North Korea, in provinces such as Hwanghae and Kangwon, families left behind by those who fled were treated as traitors. Having family in the South automatically established a person as hostile to North Korea. This is not a phenomenon of yesteryear, though the Korean War halted decades ago. Anyone found to have family who willingly left North Korea is automatically categorized as hostile to the state. The state's antagonism toward these groups is visible in media rhetoric, which summarily denounces people who leave North Korea, past and present, as "human scum." In this chapter, I elaborate the forms of profound discrimination inherent in North Korean society. While North Korea claims to be a country without class or discrimination, the generational discrimination under Songbun as well as religious persecution and other forms of social control show otherwise.

The system of hereditary discrimination is kept in place, top-down, by the Suryeong (the leader, the Korean Workers Party general-secretary), the Korean Workers Party, the local party secretaries, and the North Korean legal system. The Ministry of Public Security conducts investigations into every citizen's Songbun. Other agencies that carry out investigations related to social classification are the prosecutor's office, the State Security Department—counter intelligence forces separated from national police forces in 1973 to better serve the regime and leadership—the Korean People's Army, and the Military Security Department.[2] This network of security, formed from the national police, the state secret police, and the military security, ensures that Songbun is enforced.

Postliberation North Korea disavowed former security structures put in place during the Japanese colonial period (1910–1945) through a process of sweeping old power out through purges. The "techniques of social discipline and control" that the Japanese had in place in North Korea were still in use, however, but were "internalized and transferred" to the new state.[3] The newly formed police force had expansive duties that resembled that of police in Japan and former colonial Korea. The police were the authority on what was right, good, and proper. They guided society in morally correct thought and behavior, and they enforced state policy.[4] Each day police were expected to read ten rules designed to train them in a disciplined social life, improved self-awareness, and the spirit of sacrifice. In addition to these police were "thought police" and secret police modeled after the Soviet secret police, tasked with detaining groups of more than four persons.[5] This all sounds deeply troubling, but historian Charles Armstrong explains that the surveillance project of postliberation North Korea was actually uncoordinated and sloppy.

There were no genuine distinctions between the police and the military. Individuals who had been locked up by the Japanese, Korean nationalists in colonial political prisons, were free the day after liberation. These individuals were valued by the people's committees as "graduates" of colonial prison because their survival in such places ensured their devotion, dedication, and loyalty to Korean nationalism.[6] Armstrong writes that the colonial prison experience likely taught North Korean leadership the value of prison as a means to control the population.[7] Methods of torture used by Japanese soldiers are identical to those experienced by former political prisoners from North Korea. For example, forcing prisoners to kneel with a broomstick inside the knee joints is identical to the torture used in political prison camps.[8] This suggests that methods of torture and punishment learned in these prisons were used by prison guards in North Korean prisons.[9]

At various times in the early history of North Korea there were waves of purges in an attempt to deal with opposition, faction, and detraction groups. Kim Il Sung conducted purges for two years starting in August of 1956, eliminating factions from the USSR, China, those with ties to the southern part of the Korean peninsula, and anyone who questioned his dictatorship. A group led by Choe Chang-ik and Park Chan-ok was set to fight the dictatorship of Kim Il Sung at the Third Congress of the Workers Party in April 1956. A report examining the repository of disclosed documentations from the Russian State Archive by James F. Person shows conversations between the North Korean party leaders and the Soviet Ambassador and other officials before the third Party Congress of 1956.[10] Kim Il Sung's political position was under threat, the cult of personality was "intolerable," but the removal of Kim was seen as a last resort. With a disturbing contemporary resonance, North Korean opposition group Yan'an member and minister Yi P'il-gyu said of Kim Il Sung in 1956, "The personality cult of Kim Il Sung has acquired an intolerable character. He does not tolerate any criticism or self-criticism. The world of Kim Il Sung is law."[11] By May 31, 1957, nine thousand people had been sentenced to death for counterrevolutionary crimes.[12] The dictatorship of Kim Il Sung was further entrenched between 1957 and 1960, where enemy and ally were systematically identified throughout the country as friendly, neutral, and enemy.[13] From its early history to the present, North Korea has sought to weed out counterrevolutionary elements. They continue to be tracked down and controlled either through forced imprisonment or forced residence in remote special districts of the country. The various categories of hostile classes are placed in remote and inhospitable areas of the country and never in Pyongyang. Although there are areas where only loyal classes may live, such as in Pyongyang, the removal of hostile groups to remote areas does not mean that the remote areas are entirely populated by hostile classes, however.

To ensure state security, not only must some individuals be weeded out, but others must be provided with privileges and thus dominance. This is why resources are allocated as the state prioritizes for its survival. The military and security agencies must be provided for as part of their work, which involves controlling the so-called hostile class. Because the North Korean state perceives itself to be under threat from hostile groups domestically and internationally, it is always on a war footing with these groups and must allocate resources accordingly.

Songbun

"Songbun" is an official North Korean term for a system that has operated throughout North Korea since the earliest purges. Songbun refers to a person's genetically inherited political destiny, with all of North Korean society stratified into three basic groups: core, wavering, or hostile. The fact of social stratification finds itself in varied expressions. Class groups are as distinct as tomatoes, apples, and grapes. Tomatoes are red through and through. Tomatoes make good communists. Apples are only red on the outside. Apples are wavering and need political education. Grapes are not red at all and are "unredeemable."[14] When sociopolitical dynamics alter the slang and patterns of language as demonstrated in the example above, this reveals truths both pervasive and powerful. Although some defectors report being unsure of their class, which suggests there is great room for ambiguity, all are aware of limitations on education, profession, marriage, and residence due to their position in society. Even though a student may achieve the best grades, medical colleges will refuse entry on the basis of the student having bad Songbun.[15] The Korean Bar Association conducted a study with refugees, finding significant awareness of class stratification in North Korean society. The Songbun classification system shows "considerable coincidence" with the nutritional conditions found within the population in research conducted by the World Food Programme, UNICEF, Save the Children, and the European Union that gives the percentages of children with no evidence of malnutrition, moderate malnutrition, and severe acute malnutrition. The ration system in North Korea is linked to Songbun.[16] The nutritional data of the three broad classes strongly suggest the state distributes quantity and quality of food along lines of classification through the Public Distribution System, North Korea's centralized means of distributing food, clothing, and other goods throughout the country.[17] For an individual to receive their allotment, they must pick up their distribution at the center where they are registered. Thus, the system facilitates regular checks on movement throughout the country. It is not possible to get distributions in areas where one does not live.

The research of Robert M. Collins, a retired political analyst with thirty-seven years of experience at the U.S. Department of Defense, highlights the evidentiary link between domestic resource allocation within North Korea and the state's attempt to survive by dividing resources according to categories of perceived political loyalty. Keeping Songbun in place and stratifying people according to their loyalty and usefulness to the state is a means of national survival. Songbun stratification plays a role in determining who is more vulnerable to rights abuses. One-third of North Korea's population is effectively positioned as indentured labor to the remainder of the population through this system. In discriminating against people because of their alleged links to South Korea, the Japanese, or related historic offenses, North Korea violates article 2 of the UN Universal Declaration of Human Rights, which states that every person is entitled to rights "without distinction" of race, social origin, or birth. In discriminating against its population in this stratified way, North Korea also violates several conventions.[18]

Moreover, North Korea's state publications and artistic creations indicate prescriptive treatment of people according to Songbun. In 1987 North Korea produced a movie called *Guarantee*, which portrayed a worker who is poor because members of his family were living in South Korea; he had poor Songbun.[19] Elsewhere, and with arguably far greater impact, the Ministry of Public Security—the national police force—uses a manual to educate officers on how to treat people according to Songbun. The manual is called the "Resident Registration Project Reference Manual." Throughout the text, the reader is instructed by quotations heading each chapter from Kim Il Sung and Kim Jong Il on the crucial task of differentiating people according to their political classification. This indicates the thorough institutionalization of determining people's loyalty to the state.[20]

The leaked Ministry of Public Security manual from 1993 states: "Songbun and social stratum regulations must conform to the party's class and mass doctrine, and in doing so, *must isolate hostile elements* and serve the majority of the people."[21] The manual instructs officers that everyone's family history must be investigated. All investigations must uphold the security of the Kim family. The manual contains pages that describe at length and with examples the various classification of individuals. Categories are allocated for both families and descendants. Seven options are described for the core class, fifteen for wavering, and twelve for hostile.

Following from the logic of North Korea's Songbun classification, it is not difficult to imagine the state's justification for linking criminal liability among family. A person may have done nothing more than be related to someone who has committed an offense. Crime by association (*yongchwajae*) is the criminal act of being related to someone who has committed a crime. *Yongchwajae* captures the idea that someone can be both bodily and mentally criminal and that criminality cannot be expunged from them but is passed on through their family, their social connections, and any interaction others have with the individual.

The state record continues to demonstrate a stratified society. An electronic document with data on Pyongyang residents was leaked to the South Korean magazine *Weekly Chosun*. The file provides extensive details on residents' names, ages, birthplaces, residences, employment, spouses' names, and political party affiliations. In total, over two million residents are mentioned on the list. The highest Songbun were omitted from the list, as were children under age seventeen.[22] A massive hold of personal information documents is kept underground in the Ministry of Public Security (Inmin Boanseong) underground document storage facility at Manpo City, in Chagang Province. Each person over age seventeen in North Korea has an individual file and a household file. These are held at the city- or county-level police headquarters. Every citizen in North Korea is given a "Songbun number" at birth, which is decided by a collective recommendation from local resident registration officers, related to Ministry of Public Security section chiefs. The final determination on an individual's Songbun comes from the local party secretary. Songbun numbers are "legible" to those in-the-know in that certain numbers correspond with different regions and organizations. For example, 12398 identifies Anju city, whereas 2892 identifies the State Security Department.[23] Files detail all essential information on the person, such as place and time of birth, family members, political background, occupation, relevant physical features, and so on.

Elsewhere in publicly available North Korean state media, the state explains explicitly that it cannot value all people equally. In a news article published in *Rodong Shinmun* titled "For the Protection of True Human Rights," the text states that hostile and impure elements (read: people) that oppose socialism and violate the interests of the people cannot be granted freedom and rights.[24] Other North Korean publications indicate the recognition of "human rights" while also identifying the importance of treating people according to their loyalty. In a 1970s North Korean dictionary, human rights are defined as the "means to execute the dictatorship against the enemies of the working class."[25] Later definitions of human rights incorporate the idea of class and duty. Rights are something that are enjoyed according to one's social status in society and according to how well one fulfills their duty. Rights are granted by the Suryeong (the leader) for loyalty that is demonstrated to him. This ideological structure clearly indicates that normative international concepts of human rights are incompatible with North Korean state ideology. As Kim Soo-Am's analysis shows, detailed human rights policy consistent with international human rights standards or procedures of implementation and practice are inherently limited in this theory.[26] Because of how human rights are conceptualized in North Korea, the state has set up a frame of thinking where, as long as people are loyal to the leadership, a good life is theoretically possible, if you are of the right political background, through the ideology of the Ten Principles (*yu-il sasang sibdae wonchick*). These are investigated in chapter 7.

Songbun can be imagined as a political ethnos, people who are grouped according to their perceived loyalty to the leadership. Hostile elements are on the lowest end of this political-ethnos spectrum, and one of the tasks of loyal North Koreans is to weed out the hostile elements. In such a frame, human rights may be viewed by lower Songbun individuals as something preserved for the elite. The elite may view the internationally community's desire to bring "western Imperialist" rights as an effort to grant rights to undeserving political criminals.[27] Even to have inclusion within the DPRK's constitution is beyond possibility for the class of individuals deemed "wavering." Rights are only granted to those who fulfill the idealized role of citizen within the socialist system of North Korea. However, as legal scholar Patricia Goedde observes, even for the most privileged in North Korea, "The Constitution cannot be viewed as a permanent, protective covenant of individual rights," such as we might be familiar with in Western democratic states. Despite this, changes to the document over time reveal policy development in the North Korean government.[28]

Since the 1990s, with the widespread collapse of the Public Distribution System, the development of markets enabled North Koreans from different classes more opportunities than in the past. It would be wrong to assume that the markets removed the binds of class stratification. Eking out survival is sometimes possible through these channels, but the markets have not upturned class stratification. Corruption, widespread in North Korea, has also not eliminated Songbun. Certainly, with enough money, things such as medicine, housing, food, and even college education can be bought, but the political ethnos of state decree cannot be undone. The ability of a few to personally alter their plight through corruption does not equal the total restructure of the problems that disenfranchised them. Bribes typically move up the chain of human social value, not down.

Has Songbun changed over time? Robert Collins finds that technology has facilitated quick, integrated data for the North Korean state to classify its entire population, enmeshing Songbun with "social, legal, criminal and political data."[29] With the slight relaxation of the market in North Korea, more corruption has spilled into the system. It is possible, but very uncommon, for bribery to occur during Songbun investigations. At higher levels this is less likely as investigators must be particularly thorough. Even if Songbun could be altered, such alterations bring a network of traces that can be tracked back to the fraud in certain future investigations.[30] In December of 2003 North Korea's Ministry of Public Security began using a computer program to digitize data on resident registration as a way to track people based on Songbun, address, occupation, and so on. This computer program, called Chungbok 2.0 (Faithful servant

2.0) is used to systematize human rights exploitation, and it is available to authorities throughout the country.

Religious Faith as Political Crime

State-led opposition to religious belief in North Korea dates back to the liberation of Korea from the Japanese in 1945. North Korea sought to disempower religious organizations further by stripping property and land from religious groups through legal reforms without compensating them.[31] The religious community suffered severe financial reverses, with currency reforms in December of 1947 that regulated religious organizations' possession of cash.

It wasn't enough to bankrupt spaces of religious practice. Faith also had to go. In 1946 the elimination of superstition became a national movement that was shortly transformed into "The Campaign of Thought for State-Building," which encompassed religion and superstition in one blow. Sunday was transformed into a day of work and Monday a day of rest. Curfews were in place to eliminate the possibility for evening worship. To encourage distrust and dislike for clergy, their membership was accused of being landowning capitalists.[32] As the years passed North Korea took bishops and abbots into custody. Religious relics and sacred objects were blasphemed and destroyed. Buddhist temples were kept as cultural assets but hollowed out of religious purpose. By the 1950s North Korean criminal law had a provision against religious bodies requesting donations.[33] Leading up to and during the Korean War, North Korea killed religious believers en masse.[34] After the Korean War a further period of "obliterating" religious freedom occurred, although it was largely phrased as a struggle against antirevolutionary forces.

Faith is hard to destroy. North Koreans continued to believe in Buddha, Jesus, and Mary. Those who continued to practice secretly or defiantly were found and killed. Arguably, decades of religious-political purges swept through North Korea until the 1970s. With the new classification system, as many as half a million people were "dangerous" to the Kim Il Sung government. This was a system for the entire population, fifty-one classifications in all. Those with religious connections were given numbers: 37, 38, and 39 for Protestants, Buddhists, and Catholics, respectively. All of these were deemed "hostile" to the state and as such should be surveilled and punished.

If you read the North Korean constitution, article 68 provides for freedom of religion. North Korea's own human rights report submitted to the United Nations in 2014 also outlines the state's purported commitment to religious freedom. That text states: "In the DPRK, everybody is fully provided with the rights to choose and follow their religion and thought according to their own free will. Every citizen has chosen to follow the Juche Idea."[35] However, the indications are clear that North Korea does not tolerate citizens who have chosen non-Juche belief. In June 2011 a defector named Koh told the Database Center for North Korean Human Rights the following story.

> [The woman] had crossed the border to China and came back with a bible. She apparently hid the bible in the house. Her husband was a promising man so the man had many visitors. One day, one of her children told the guests that they had an interesting book and took out the bible to show them. This story spread around and the family was completely ruined. That same year, [she] was taken to Onseong State Security Department for interrogation where she was severely beaten and tortured. She became paralyzed from the waist down, so the Department released her. She was almost dead when she got released but recovered her health enough to pass medical checkup for imprisonment. She was sent to Hamheung Oro Prison where she died. I heard her husband also died in 2009.[36]

The connection with China leads to a spread of abuses into that territory. In 2016 a Korean-Chinese pastor named Han Choong-ryeol was found dead. He was the pastor of a three-hundred-member church in the province of Jilin, which borders North Korea close to the Korean city of Hyesan. Pastor Han was found with wounds to his neck that appeared to be from a knife or axe. Local activists and journalists claim his death was due to North Korean agents.[37]

North Korea has adopted a parallel policy toward religion. Through this, the government can claim to the international community that they respect and guarantee freedom of religion, but in practice religion is suppressed.[38] Visitors to North Korea have attended Christian mass and toured Buddhist temples, but these spaces are for the performative acts of religion that are designed to evade criticism from the international community. The South Korean government estimates that there are now 121 religious facilities in North Korea. The parallel policy toward religion wasn't in place from the start of North Korea's founding. According to the Database Center for North Korean Human Rights, the leadership has adapted policy to religion, with increasing severity and nuance.

In tandem with continued religious persecution, North Korea began reaching out to the international religious community in the 1970s. Through these international religious groups North Korea promotes the idea of "peace" on the peninsula and seeks the support of international groups toward this end. While skirting genuinely religious topics and promoting the amorphous signifier of "peace," North Korea is able to shape South Korean and U.S. political practices on the peninsula as inherently hostile and generally antagonistic to humanity. This type of messaging continues as this book goes to press.

How do we make sense of the fact that North Korea claims to respect religious freedom but then detains and tortures individuals who leave Bibles in hotel rooms? North Korea began reaching out to the international religious community beginning in the 1970s. Then and today, the gesture is primarily aimed at obtaining aid from foreign religious organizations rather than about building and spreading religious faith. Foreign nationals accused of trying to bring religion to North Korea have faced severe punishments. This alone indicates that promotion of religious practice is not acceptable and that the celebration of religious belief is not the point of North Korea's international religious engagement. North Korean state-led religious organizations are a front for getting access to resources. Kenneth Bae, a missionary from the United States, was detained in November 2012 in North Korea. U.S. citizen Jeffrey Edward Powell was detained for leaving a Bible in his hotel room in April 2014. Canadian pastor Hyeon Soo Lim was detained on charges of conspiracy. As North Korea turned to the international religious community to make use of the international religious community's resources, there has been an increase in punishments toward those foreigners, or any citizen, who actually practices religious faith.

The movement of North Korean citizens across the Sino-Korean border has led to an increase in religious materials flowing back into North Korea. Research by the Database Center for North Korean Human Rights shows that the 2000s saw the highest records of religious persecution. The sharp increase in border crossings that occurred during the famine years resulted in increased contact with religious believers and religious materials in China, as many groups within the activist community are religion-based. This in turn led to an increase in contact with foreign believers and religious material. After Kim Jong Un came to power, he increased border control, leading to a drop in successful migration attempts and thus a drop in reports of religious persecution, which may or may not mean a drop in actual religious persecution. The northernmost province of North Hamgyong has the highest persecution rates; this is also the province from which the most people out-migrate. Protestants constitute the greatest number of persecuted individuals, followed closely by a group of similar size of "unknown" religious belief.[39] Persecution results from individuals being accused of participating in religious activities, possessing religious items, propagating religion, or having contact with religious people.[40] The Database Center for Human Rights gathered the information for these findings from victims, who form the largest group of subjects; witnesses; those who heard through hearsay; and perpetrators (the smallest group). North Korea sought relations with international religious organizations as early as 1963.[41] The 2000s were a period when the North Korean government opened churches to establish relations with foreign churches and religious NGOs.[42] Open Doors, a U.S.-based organization serving persecuted Christians worldwide, reports that the churches are a sham, mostly empty when foreigners visit, and locals who do attend are "fake" petitioners.[43] The principle aim of North Korea's religious organizations is to garner support in the form of education, training, and aid from international religious groups.[44] North Korea's religious organizations are government organized, and spokespersons use their positions to operationalize the government's political aims. For instance, rather than speaking about religious topics, they identify the need for the removal of U.S. forces from South Korea. Religious activities within the country are suppressed, but government-led international engagements are instrumental for garnering foreign currency and humanitarian aid and for an improved image of the DPRK internationally. The insincerity of North Korea's respect for religious belief is further evidenced by the country's treatment of foreign nationals accused of proselytism, a crime easily committed by leaving a Bible behind in a hotel room, for instance, as Jeffrey Powell did in April 2014, for which he served six months in prison.

* * *

It has become banal and quotidian, since North Korea's earliest history, to uncover, identify, remove, and eliminate anyone deemed threatening to the state. The Songbun practice of inherited inequality is kept in place, top-down, and may not be questioned through any forum at all: to do so would transform the self from one political category into one far worse. Political loyalty is a genetic feature of existence that determines how well one lives, where one lives, and what work one does. This systematic social stratification generates fear and maintains strict control over the entire population. Songbun ensures the distribution of resources, opportunities, and aspiration according to inherited political loyalty to the Kim family. By extension, the denial of religious freedoms achieves similar results: it ensures that the heart and mind are not captive to anything but the Kim family. Persecuting religious believers while pretending to value religions with Potemkin churches and international engagement blatantly indicates that the North Korean state seeks advantages for the regime above the spiritual well-being of its people.

CHAPTER 4

INFORMATION CONTROL

Once I made a mistake. I slipped. . . . I misspelled the name of Kim Il Sung. I skipped the Sung and people on top found out about it when they were inspecting at the state level. The state censorship institution summoned me and they asked me what the name of the Supreme Leader was. . . . I begged for forgiveness. I admitted that I had made a mistake, but because of that I was in the training camp for six months. . . . It was an innocent mistake but sometimes we are sent to a three to six month sentence in labor camps.

—Defector Jang Hae Sung at the UN Commission of Inquiry

Jang Hae Sung served a six-month sentence in a reeducation labor camp for a typo; this was not shameful, he clarified during the public hearings for the Commission of Inquiry in Seoul. Journalists write so much they are bound to make a mistake here and there. He begged forgiveness, but the North Korean regime felt that reeducation was still necessary.

The ability to speak publicly and openly, to hold discussions and debates, to scrutinize leaders and local officials, to read media that is uncensored, to write and speak freely—these daily practices are essential to accessing, demanding, and protecting human rights. They are also fundamental to enjoying life. If people have access to free and open media, they then have the possibility to create alternative arrangements, individually and institutionally, for protective security in areas of basic human rights.[1] Access to information, particularly in the form of open media, undergirds protective security for rights. Censored media undergirds protection of the state and disenfranchises the population from information that could assist them in making critical life decisions. Arguably, more than any country, at any time in history, North Korea represents a state of near total control over media, opinion, and self-expression unlike anything we have seen. This failure to protect basic rights to freedom of expression by the North Korean state is truly "without parallel" in the contemporary world.[2]

North Korea has no free media.[3] The international organization Committee to Protect Journalists lists North Korea as one of the world's most censored countries.[4] Media studies experts have observed it as the "most closed media environment in the world."[5] A study by Reporters Without Borders that looked at surveillance, censorship, imprisonment, and disinformation identified three state-run agencies in North Korea as "enemies of the internet" for their control over the domestic intranet system, their crackdown on the distribution of foreign media, and their monitoring of cellphones and radio broadcasts.[6] Of the twelve main newspapers, twenty periodicals, and the single national broadcaster, all content comes from the official state media agency, the Korean Central News Agency (KCNA), which is the mouthpiece of the government. All radio and television broadcasts, music, dance, theater, literature, newspapers, and periodicals are a product of state propaganda organs. Defectors who worked professionally in North Korean media report that the style and messaging is virtually unchanged with the passage of time.[7]

Too much of the wrong kind of information, such as state-sanctioned media, causes complications in daily life. Knowing too much, as gleaned through foreign media or reading between the lines of state media, is dangerous. Thinking and speaking through contradictions, paradoxes, and riddles is a feature of life for North Koreans.[8] This chapter explores the trouble that comes with information: the trouble with gaining access to it, the trouble with relaying it (such as having the proper tone of voice), and the trouble it creates in the practice of critical thinking on the ground.[9] Too much information of the wrong kind has the power to shape life in profound ways. What kinds of knowledge limits are placed on DPRK citizens? Why is information controlled? What gets controlled, and how? Is information control total? Are there any clandestine methods of communication? North Korea criminalizes access to information from the international community, believing that it threatens control of the social fabric, which might then threaten government control.[10] The presence of information as well as its absence creates a range of critically troublesome issues for North Koreans.

Both the Universal Declaration of Human Rights and the International Covenant on Civil and Political Rights guarantee the right to freedom of expression.[11] Article 19 of the UDHR states: "Everyone has the right to freedom of opinion and expression; this right includes freedom to hold opinions without interference and to seek, receive and impart information and ideas through any media and regardless of frontiers."[12] In June 2016 the United Nations made a further resolution to protect freedom of opinion and expression online, extending to the virtual realm the same rights that people should have in the world.[13]

At the plenary meeting of the Central Committee of the Korean Workers Party on March 31, 2013, Kim Jong Un delivered a speech of about twenty minutes, reading directly from a prepared script, about the new intention or "Byungjin line" of developing the economy and nuclear armed forces simultaneously. After the speech, Kim delivered a few unscripted remarks. According to high-ranking defector Thae Yong Ho, present at the meeting, these comments were of critical importance. Speaking at the Center for Strategic and International Studies in 2017, Thae, formerly a diplomat to the DPRK embassy in London, held up his index finger to highlight the point to his Washington-based audience. Reading from his own notes, he quoted Kim Jong Un's comments given in 2013 to the gathering of the Central Committee of the Workers Party: "[The] forthcoming war will not be the war between DPRK and USA but it will be the *war of idea and will* among ourselves."[14] Kim's comments were not tangential to his reference to the Byungjin policy. The new Byungjin line is about simultaneously developing the economy and nuclear weapons so as to ensure that people, domestic or international, don't seek to change the country.

The "war of idea and will" is a war the state is fighting against attempts to undermine the North Korean state through methods of psychological war, which it sees as coming from imperial powers. North Korea sees the inflow of information as the continuation of the Korean War by other means. This war is chiefly fought against the inflow of international media and illicit DVDs, USBs, foreign broadcasts, and the like. Exposure to these, North Korea rightly believes, will change the minds and hearts of its people, perhaps leading them to demand a different state of affairs.

With technological advances and the shrinking size of items used to transmit foreign information, North Korea knows it has a difficult task in terms of information control. Thus, the development of nuclear weapons serves a dual purpose. With nuclear weapons at his disposal, Kim Jong Un can crack down on any protests, whether inspired by access to foreign information or otherwise, without fear that the international community would risk the consequences of humanitarian intervention on a nuclear state. North Korea learned this lesson from Iran, Libya, and Syria.[15] To round out control, Kim Jong Un placed increased pressure on elites after he took office. After his speech to the Workers Party in 2013, the "war within" began with sweeping purges throughout the country, with an emphasis on the elite. The international community saw the impact of this in increased defections from this population group.[16]

State-Sanctioned Information

Distorted. Incomplete. Hypnotic. Hyperbolic. In my assessment these are the best words to describe information that is permitted in North Korea. This information is *always* pro-state. The resulting misinformation inhibits people's ability to make personal decisions through reliable insights on economic, social, and political conditions. A tiny bit of truth may exist in the media, but that tiny kernel is smothered. Read through carefully, the media does have a method. For instance, in 2008 North Korea published information about a global food crisis in its newspaper the *Rodong Shinmun*. Indeed, there was a global food *pricing* crisis. The issue was not shortage, as North Korean readers were led to believe, but rather one of *cost*. Because it was useful for North Korea to distort the information as an issue of supply, the tiny kernel of truth concerning "food" and "crisis" was excised from the critical information concerning cost. Shortage resonates with ordinary Koreans' experience of day-to-day life, but the crisis was not one of shortage, as readers were led to believe. Rather it was one of cost and, thus, access to food by those most vulnerable.

The case of misinformation concerning food availability is typical of how North Korean state media severely curtails and shapes citizen knowledge about issues critical to their existence. When the famine of the 1990s occurred, the North Korean government told citizens that it was caused by natural disasters and economic sanctions from enemy states. This information was inaccurate and misleading. While there were floods and then droughts, and while there were countries that couldn't trade with North Korea, such things could never lead to a famine on their own. Rather, it came about through a combination of factors related to agricultural policies, loss of socialist trade partners, reliance on Juche ideology for domestic and international affairs, criminalization of entrepreneur practices that were actually coping strategies, and most of all because the government prioritized military spending and defense of state socialism over liberalizing the economy. It was much easier and resistance less likely to emerge if the government could encourage people to believe that responsibility for the famine was due to nature and other nation-states.

Distortion of information adds a complex feature to life in North Korea and to the human rights situation in particular. Information distortion is a tool used by the state and citizen alike. In my previous book *Marching Through Suffering*, I examine how a range of groups of people understood the famine. In the oral accounts I recorded with survivors, I found that people adopted and manipulated state discourse as a means to convey clandestine information or to express dissatisfaction.[17] The camouflage of information was necessary and useful, but it also meant that ambiguity, misinformation, and confusion reigned supreme.

North Korea's social censorship, often in the form of self-criticism sessions and tight control over media, is deliberate. Through censorship, North Korea controls what is known about the country and how that knowledge should be understood. History has abundantly shown that the absence of free media creates conditions in which socioeconomic disasters such as famines and crimes against humanity thrive. North Korean studies scholar Yong Sub Choi explains that North Korea rules through force, but force is not enough. There is a "consent mechanism" that holds control in place; this consent is fostered through life review meetings, *saenghwal chonghwa*, such as self-criticism sessions and mutual-criticism sessions, where ideology becomes indoctrination.[18] These meetings are held in factories, schools, farms, and all manner of work places where people (over the age of fourteen) evaluate themselves and others publicly in relation to the state ideology.[19] People are expected to give a "brief report about their personal misdeeds and unsound actions." However, according to Korean studies expert Andrei Lankov, "in real life these sessions are akin to theatrical performances," where individuals will admit things that are not too damning; "nonetheless," he elaborates, "these sessions help to keep the population in line and in some rare cases even lead to the exposure of significant ideological deviations."[20] Compelling people to participate in ritualized behavior about being loyal is one of North Korea's "most efficient governing strateg[ies]."[21]

The North Korean government also uses collective criticism sessions and surveillance to maintain a society of paranoia, watchfulness, and blame. The ritualized critique of self and others is an intrinsic part of life enforced by the North Korean state, although some individuals may occasionally use strategies of self-protection to circumvent state control by making up things done wrong and agreeing among friends to lay blame on marginal indiscretions.[22] Criticism sessions are public events typically held weekly. They take on a performative aspect, with blame directed at self and others along with a professed willingness to do better in future. Criticism sessions are not only about the self; they are also about the other, and in this respect they inculcate a sense of duty for the well-being of the group onto the individual. If the individual does wrong, it is burdensome and dangerous for the whole. The practice travels with North Koreans when they work abroad or at sea, whether as forced laborers or diplomats. It is expected of all North Koreans. Most recently, even the leader, Kim Jong Un, expressed self-blame related to his inability to control flooding in the country (a confession that neatly captures his misdirected governing skills).[23]

Surveillance works in tandem with criticism sessions. It is assumed to be always operational, but subtle. Each neighborhood block will have a few designated *inminban*, individuals charged with watching fellow citizens and working in conjunction with local police. However, individuals are also expected to surveil family members and spouses.[24] Surveillance and criticism sessions are tools within the social control apparatus of North Korea. The police can step in to use these tools at any time.

North Korea's human rights report, which it submitted to the United Nations on September 15, 2014, declares that citizens have the right to "freedom of speech, of the press, of assembly, demonstration and association (article 67)."[25] The text later clarifies, saying, "All kinds of advocacy of war of aggression, discrimination and violence, acts of instilling national, racial and religious antagonism and propaganda to threaten or harm the *security of the state and social order* are absolutely prohibited."[26] Such a quotation might bring to mind bomb-making manuals, but in practice Bibles are deemed eruptive. Access to sanctioned information in North Korea is shaped by factors of social ranking, also known as Songbun, which places people geographically throughout the country but also determines what kind of occupation they can have and who they can marry. However, *all* people in North Korea, regardless of Songbun, are subjected to extremely limited access to information. After the famine and the disastrous currency reform, the *Rodong Shinmun* even directed its censorship toward the uncanny realms of the occult by including stories that discouraged the circulation of superstition and the use of fortunetellers and healers.[27]

Regarding freedom of assembly and protest, North Korea's own human rights report claims that citizens "are fully provided" with this right. After the United Nations released its Commission of Inquiry report in March of 2014, a huge public protest was held in Pyongyang. It was an anti–human rights report demonstration. Throughout its own report, North Korea appeals to existing international human rights norms but misinterprets the meaning of these and thus relegates the matter to a semiotic debate. A group wishing to assemble and protest must notify the People's Committee and the People's Security Organ of the corresponding area three days prior. Notification of the intention to protest is not unheard of in democratic states either. However, in the North's report, it clarifies gatherings that "harm the security of the State, violate social stability, order, soundness of society and morality and encroach upon other people's rights and freedom are prohibited." The report continues, self-consciously, "It is also regulated in the Article 21 of the International Covenant on Civil and Political Rights."[28] Thus, it is hard to imagine what could possibly be protested under such conditions. Article 21 of the International Covenant on Civil and Political Rights states: "The right of peaceful assembly shall be recognized. No restrictions may be placed on the exercise of this right *other than those imposed in conformity with the law and which are necessary in a democratic society* in the interests of national security or public safety, public order (ordre public), the protection of public health or morals or the protection of the rights and freedoms of others."[29] The reader should note that North Korea sees itself as a democratic state, yet expressing dissent, for example, toward Kim Jong Un is a contravention of law in North Korea, and it would be a contravention of national security law as identified therein.

North Korea's human rights report clarifies that "everybody is fully provided with the rights to choose and follow their own religion and thought according to their own free will."[30] However, the following paragraph suggests that every North Korean has quite miraculously chosen Juche. "*Every citizen* has chosen to follow the Juche Idea. . . . This is not forced by the state or anybody else. It is the faith and will of *all* DPRK citizens."[31] And yet, if you ask someone who has left the country, they will tell you: "Ninety-nine percent of people would rather take a nap than listen to the political propaganda."[32]

Authors Ralph Hassig and Kongdan Oh observe that North Korea is "propaganda-rich, information-poor."[33] Political scientist Joo Hyung-min studied North Korea's *Rodong Shinmun* between 1991 until 2011 and found that there were more than 1,500 articles covering the topic of antirevolutionary thought. Over a twenty-year period, campaigns against antirevolutionary thought reappear in relation to economic difficulties such as the collapse of the Soviet Bloc, the 1990s famine, and other internal crises. This is important because people do question difficulties in day-to-day life when in times of crisis. Joo found that despite the twenty-year period covering antirevolutionary thought instruction, the articles bear an uncanny similarity across four themes: infiltration, hidden agenda, danger, and solution.[34] The overriding message of the news describes a situation where North Korean people are vulnerable to infiltration from hostile states' hidden agendas, which are dangerous to the fabric of North Korean society and must be remedied through the solution of Juche and Songbun politics.[35] Reading North Korea's *Rodong Shinmun* newspaper in "reverse," as suggested by Joo Hyung-min, is a method of finding out what ordinary people might be doing or thinking on the ground because the state is prescribing what *not* to do.[36]

The Korean Central News Agency and the War Against Will

One of the key things North Korean media does is try to imagine what people may be feeling or thinking and then preempt any desire to change the country. This is achieved by stating what might be desired and then showing how pointless or dangerous it is for you and those around you. The best example of this is the DPRK's reportage of the military trial of Jang Song-thaek. This high-profile case was covered in television and print media in North Korea. Portions of the KCNA's article are reproduced here at length to capture the state's narrative of Jang's desire and his downfall. At first glance, it may seem curious that North Korea would report the details of Jang's case and his alleged plot to overthrow the regime, real or imagined. It seems risky for the state to report the alleged antiregime activities of Jang because we might assume his actions could inspire others. Yet, intriguingly, the KCNA identifies Jang's alleged critiques of the state in some detail. Consider the following sections, with italics for my emphasis, lifted from North Korea's media: "He fully revealed his despicable true colors as a traitor for all ages in the course of questioning by uttering as follows: 'I attempted to trigger off discontent among service personnel and people when *the present regime does not take any measure despite the fact that the economy of the country and people's living are driven into catastrophe.* Comrade supreme leader is the target of the coup.'"

In this text, the KCNA identifies an irrefutable fact of life and a common observation among North Koreans—that the economy is not doing well and hasn't been for several decades now. This observation is made antirevolutionary by linking it with discontent and the desire to trigger more discontent among peers because the government doesn't take any measures against the economic difficulties. Jang's attempt to "trigger off discontent" about the fact of economic "catastrophe" is what leads to his downfall. It is permissible to recognize that there are economic difficulties, but it is criminal to attribute this to the government and then take your thoughts and spark discontent among an aggregate of like-minded fellows. Jang is held up as the antagonist; the government is protagonist. The narrative walks the reader through Jang's alleged plan. The narrative moves from the thoughts of Jang to his attempt to create an aggregate of like-minded peers, particularly in the armed forces.

> As regards the means and methods for staging the coup, Jang said: "*I was going to stage the coup by using army officers who had close ties with me or by mobilizing armed forces under the control of my confidants.* I don't know well about recently appointed army officers but have some acquaintances with those appointed in the past period. I thought the army might join in the coup if the living of the people and service personnel further deteriorate in the future. And *I calculated that my confidants in my department including Ri Ryong Ha and Jang Su Gil would surely follow me* and had a plan to use the one in charge of the people's security organ as my confidant. It was my calculation that I might use several others besides them."

The KCNA narrative links Jang's plan for a coup with his alleged plan to gather personnel in the armed forces. The text is careful to detail that Jang doesn't know the recently appointed comrades but has acquaintances among those appointed in the past. We can only speculate if Jang really did attempt a coup. Real or alleged, what the North Korean leadership fears is a citizenry that has a combination of well-informed discontent about the government's role in the country's economic difficulties along with enough armed force to overthrow the leader for decades of government inaction. Putting this image forward through the narrative enables the state media to narrate its result as inevitable failure. The coup is doomed to fail not because it is impossible—no, the leadership must be protected—but rather because Jang's intent is selfish and mercantile.

> Asked about the timing of the coup and his plan after staging the coup, Jang answered: "I didn't fix the definite time for the coup. But it was my intention to concentrate my department and all economic organs on the Cabinet and become premier when the economy goes totally bankrupt and the state is on the verge of collapse in a certain period. *I thought that if I solve the problem of people's living at a certain level by spending an enormous amount of funds I have accumulated under various names after becoming premier, the people and service personnel will shout 'hurrah' for me and I will succeed in the coup in a smooth way."*

This portion of the KCNA article claims that Jang tried to use the differences existing in the cabinet for his individual gain. The notion of differences within the North Korean government itself may sound unusual; however, the research of political scientist Patrick McEachern demonstrates that government organs are not a monolith of strategy but that there are fissions between them over how to approach problems in the country.[37] It is normal that there would be disagreements in how the country should resolve its problems. Contrary to how it may look, McEachern finds that North Korea is not a "one-man rule" state. He explains, "While Kim is certainly the most important political player in North Korea, he still must rule a complex political system and should not be understood as the system."[38] McEachern describes North Korean politics as "a type of highly centralized monarchy with some court politics at the top."[39] Drawing on North Korean media, elite speeches, and commentaries available through federal deposit libraries in the United States, McEachern shows that the party, military, and cabinet contend for specific institutional interests within North Korea.[40] However, in the case of the KCNA article about Jang, the state media twists his agenda to be about seizing power from the supreme leader rather than about trying to work with his colleagues in the cabinet to develop positive change in the government that might improve things for the people. "Jang *dreamed such a foolish dream* that once he seizes power by a base method, his despicable true colors as 'reformist' known to the outside world would help his 'new government' get 'recognized' by foreign countries in a short span of time."[41]

As this example shows, North Korea tries to preempt what might be the will of the people or of those in government and plays through the scenario using

Jang as an example of the fate on offer, should they dare. Of course, this is one of the highly publicized cases. Former North Korean diplomat Thae Yong Ho revealed that Kim Jong Un engaged in widespread purges of elites after he took control of the country. Following the execution of Jang Song-thaek, there were sweeping purges. The former North Korean ambassadors to Sweden and UNESCO, along with the deputy ambassadors, were forced to return to Pyongyang and expelled from the Foreign Ministry. The former North Korean ambassadors to Cuba and Malaysia were sent to prison camps. It is unknown if these individuals are living or dead.[42]

Emotional Messaging and False Truths

The state-sanctioned media conveys its message, relayed through the radio, television, or in print media, in a fashion that demonstrates emotion-laden affect. The media accomplishes this with pitch or tone of voice in audiovisual material or with bolded text and strong adjectives in print. Emotional messaging is always present in written text and is particularly linked with nation-states with which North Korea disagrees. Defectors who formerly worked as television broadcasters and newsprint reporters provide insight into what is required from those behind the scenes of state media.

If people who work in the press make mistakes, their errors are treated as "political mistakes." Jeong Jin Hwa worked as a TV announcer in North Korea for ten years from 1989 to 1999. Because her grandfather fought against the Japanese during colonial rule, her family was treated with privilege and thus she was entitled to such a public and powerful job. Later, at her public hearing at the UN Commission of Inquiry in Seoul after she defected, she explained her job in North Korea: "This [the media report] is an ideology we're trying to convey and that ideology, our ideology, it's the ideology of the North Korean government. And people like me, we always have known that what we say, the mistakes we make in terms of what we say, could lead to death for us."[43]

None of the radio or television broadcasts produced by North Korea are conducted live. They are always prerecorded with plenty of practice beforehand. Mistakes are not tolerated because by their nature they deviate from the state's rhetoric. All broadcasts in North Korea are strongly inflected with affective emphasis that guides interpretation. Not only *what* is said but *how* it is said is of critical importance. This is true for anyone working in the media as well as for ordinary people on the street. In informal settings, learning what not to say is both subtle and overt.[44] This mirroring of standard-broadcast affect appears in interviews conducted with the "man on the street" that the news media conducts with "random" passersby in Pyongyang. This phenomenon is examined in detail later in this book.

When speaking the names of Kim Il Sung, Kim Jong Il, or the current leader, Kim Jong Un, announcers must convey emotion and seriousness in their tone of voice. The rule announcers must abide when speaking the name of the leader is "one tone higher, and one rhythm slower."[45] When countries such as South Korea or the United States are mentioned, announcers are instructed to insert "the most hatred, the most hostility" they can into their voice.[46] Neutrality of voice, affectless tone, is not possible. Instead, affect-laden tones and emphasis are a requirement. It is not enough just to speak words. The words must be transmitted through an aural emotional frame so that the feeling they evoke, rather more than the meaning, can be understood. Jeong, the former broadcaster, explained, "There would be different intonation for each word. So we would say [it] as if we were trying to chew each word. So we would say, 'These monsters of the Anti-Revolutionary Korea and the United States . . .' we would be emphasizing, putting special emphasis and trying to put in different feelings . . . we would enunciate so that our feelings toward these countries could be more clearly conveyed."[47]

Along with the proper emotional tone, media in North Korea always makes use of a "hostile modifier" to describe the country being discussed. A country defined as hostile toward North Korea cannot be mentioned by name only. Language relating to nation-states always appears as a pairing: South Korea is rendered the "antirevolutionary Korea"; the United States is rendered as the "warmongering United States." As such, South Korea and the United States become "more than a country" for North Korea.[48] The hostile modifier that couples nation-states with negative adjectives is a national ideological grammar. The hostile modifier ensures that geopolitical alliances are clearly delineated for listeners.

Jang Hae Sung, the man whose story opened this chapter, worked as a reporter for KCNA from 1976 until 1996. When he began his job, he was not aware of North Korea's domestic difficulties. Like Jeong, Jang was also the grandchild of a man who had fought against the Japanese. As such, Jang was eligible for an occupation of privilege in the media. However, having been born in China, he was excluded from occupations such as security police or safety police. He was still not in the "core" class, but he was far better than workers or farmers. During the course of his career, as part of his job, he did a lot of research. He was collecting information on what Kim Il Sung had done well. Jang Hae Sung was aware of the standards of his job. He expressed the application of the Ten Principles as the basis of his job as a reporter. In particular, he singled out the fourth principle, which expects North Koreans to make Kim Il Sung's ideology and instruction their own personal belief and opinion. "We must make Great Leader comrade Kim Il Sung's revolutionary ideology our faith and make his instructions our creed." Jang elaborated, "When you talk, when you publish, we are always to quote the instruction and the word of Kim

Il Sung and Kim Jong Il and we should not write anything that goes against Kim Il Sung and Kim Jong Il. This was something that was above the constitution. If you are going to report, if you are going to lecture, if you are going to publish, we are only to quote the instructions, the words of Kim Il Sung, and that has to be the basis."[49] Failure to do this is criminal.

Because he was a journalist, Jang Hae Sung's job enabled him to research and travel throughout North Korea. This mobility and access to information, he says, made him realize there were a lot of problems with the regime. His personal opinion began to slip from the confines of the fourth principle. Being a member of the media, he had access to information and comparative contexts in ways that other portions of the population simply do not. He was able to get a travel permit, something difficult to obtain in North Korea. He was able to compare what he had been taught with what he was learning. In addition, he drew comparisons between North Korea and what he was learning about South Korea. "I developed contempt for North Korea. But all the thoughts I had, I could not write them down. I wrote about the greatness of Kim Il Sung and his regime, but my thought was completely opposite of what I was writing."[50]

Jang Hae Sung's writing, like that of other reporters, was checked and rechecked to ensure it fell in line with the ideology and instructions of the leadership. This checking is achieved through the guidance of the ministry charged with party propaganda, which controls all media. The newspaper division is in charge of television, radio, and newspapers. They come up with a plan, which is then sent up the chain to be approved. If approved, it is distributed to each division to be sent out to the public. Everything is controlled and inspected by the ministry. Doing anything beyond what is instructed results in trouble. Jang's newsprint articles were checked by three different people at three different levels within the media organ. They were checking to ensure his writing was consistent with the ideology of the state. A few months after publication, news articles are checked again retroactively. Checking past newspaper articles ensures consistency of language style and messaging across time. Readers familiar with North Korean media will acknowledge these efforts have been a total success. North Korean state-sanctioned media and state communication domestically and internationally is remarkably consistent in tone, voice, and message. It reads as if a single individual composed the entire opus. It is not surprising to learn from Jang, then, that "everything is written according to the instruction, word for word, and if anything is different, in the worst case you are sent to prison." If human error occurs, as it surely must through a typo or misspelling, the punishment may be slightly more lenient, such as a few months of reform through labor.[51]

Jang Hae Sung served six months in a reeducation camp for a typo. He had missed typing the final syllable in Kim Il Sung's name. When the people above him were inspecting his writing, they naturally spotted the omission. Begging forgiveness, Jang was sent to reform through labor. This was not a shameful experience, he clarified, because writers write, and they can make mistakes in this process. If a journalist makes mistakes repeatedly, that would ensure his expulsion from the media. Journalists are routinely screened so patterns of mistakes will be spotted. He continued in his job, following along with the ideology of North Korea. He was promoted to a higher position as a reporter. This gave him access to more important issues and events. But further incongruities between state rhetoric and reality were revealed, such as Kim Il Sung's true birthplace and the North's provocations to the South precipitant to the Korean War.[52] Having learned of these incongruities, he spoke to a few close friends; as he did, "these things just came out of my mouth." And the expected result followed. His words were relayed to the security police, compelling him to flee North Korea or face brutal punishment.[53]

In describing her job as an announcer, Jeong explained that she and others in her position were conduits circulating fake truths. "The only truth in North Korea is what is said and what is told by Kim Il Sung, and Kim Jong Il. If Kim Il Sung or Kim Jong Il said something is white, even if it is black, we have to accept it as the truth, as white. . . . Even if what we read was not the truth, we were more than prepared to say it was the truth."[54] Unlike Jang, who had access to more information and could research and travel, Jeong stated that she did not know that what she was reading to the public was not the truth. When asked by Commissioner Marzuki Darusman if she could differentiate what she was broadcasting from the truth, she replied, "I don't think I knew." What is curious about this exchange is that Jeong had just finished saying, a moment before, that reporters were expected to read whatever was in front of them "even if what we read was not the truth." This suggests there were moments when she was aware of the disconnect between what she read and what she knew to be false. Her earlier comment "even if it was black" indicates that she was aware she was broadcasting the state's version of truth.

Commissioner Darusman asked again if she had been able to differentiate the true from the false. Again, curiously, she answers that she doesn't think she knew. Her answer is neither that she didn't know nor that she did. What her answer discloses is the looped paradoxes of information in North Korea and the impossibility of freely expressing as much. Information is so thoroughly controlled in North Korea that even acknowledging that information is controlled is a truth that must be twisted into communication without too much directness. To speak about the fact that the media is controlled is controlled. To acknowledge the reality of the regime as an apparatus of control is justification for the removal of that individual from society for speaking too accurately.

Making a mistake, misspeaking, particularly if you are working in the media, is a political issue. Jeong explained, "People in the media, if they slip just once, they can disappear overnight, and their family can be gone overnight and sometimes the three generations are wiped [out]."[55] Slipping in error or slipping out of the myth into a spoken reality is a dangerous act not necessarily met with sympathy from fellow citizens. On the punishment for slipping, Jeong said, "People think that they deserve it because they turned their backs on the regime."

Information that is misconstrued, decontextualized, and false is used by North Korea to psychologically shape the inner world of its citizens and to proscribe correct behavior. If they do not believe or if they harbor doubt, the state ensures that they know to behave as if they do believe. By controlling knowledge that people have access to, the state preemptively makes a strike against its citizenry imagining anything other than the current state of affairs. Accurate, truthful, and critical information carries within it the *certain* possibility to destroy the North Korean state in its current manifestation.[56] Accurate, truthful, and critical information, identified by some defectors as akin to a nuclear bomb, would obliterate the Potemkin structures built by the North Korean state.

Freedom of Expression in Arts and Education

Not only daily media but also the arts are explicitly political in North Korea. Writers are not permitted to write personal opinions or make accurate observations of the world they experience, and of course not just anyone can be a writer. Writers, should they have talent, are selected from elite Songbun families.[57] Hyung Sung-Ga was a writer who once spoke his mind while drunk. He merely observed the fact that writers were not permitted to write their own ideas. For speaking this truth, he was sent to Number 15 political prison camp, Yodok. In prison with Hyung was another writer by the name of Choi Ak-Soo. Both were very talented writers and bent their skill to accommodate the state's demand to capture the fictional accomplishments of Kim Il Sung. The two men committed suicide by hanging in the camp. It is easy for a writer or broadcaster to slip into a political prison camp.

As part of political education, ordinary citizens are expected to learn from state-sanctioned films. Kim Jong Il was fond of cinema and saw it as an excellent method for spreading propaganda. On November 6, 2005, the Korean Documentary and Scientific Film Studio produced a documentary called *Inerasable War Crimes of Japan*, which anatomizes Japan's atrocities in Korea, Japan's worship of war criminals, and the complicity of the United States in Japan's Imperialism.[58] A monthly magazine established by Kim Jong Il, *Recollections of the Anti-Japanese Fighters*, was mandatory reading nationwide.[59] The magazine glorifies the guerrilla activities of Kim Il Sung and his comrades. Theater, film, and self-criticism sessions are not only entertainment but are an "ideological matrix that ... organizes and mobilizes society."[60] In a culture that remains rooted in Confucian ethics of collectivity, family, and hierarchy, such ethics extend to the state and its place in the world. Thus, the ideas of kinship, community, inheritance, and place within a society are part of how North Korea represents nationhood to its citizens.[61]

Professor Kim Suk-Young notes that the survival of socialism in North Korea can be attributed to the strength of "family rhetoric" that appears throughout sociocultural performances in the country.[62] The citizenry are singularized through the rhetoric of family, which operates as a synonym for the nation-state. State propaganda is the site of the state's "ideal self" promotion. Naturally, it would be wrong to assume that the state's intention with propaganda is always effective all the time with everyone. However, the population is compelled to engage with state media. Part of education in North Korea requires that revolutionary operas, films, and other dominant cultural forms are discussed and emulated in daily study sessions, at workplaces, and at schools.[63] Kim Suk-Young identifies this as the "contagious power" of North Korea's "official culture."[64]

Korean literature scholars Alzo David-West and Dafna Zur observe that literature is an extension of politics.[65] North Korean authors instruct that, when writing for children, characters with negative traits should be presented in ways that are unambiguously negative.[66] "Politically minded citizens" are molded through literature, and children's literature does not escape this process but rather is a "direct channel for conveying hegemonic political discourse."[67] The Korean War is a subject regenerated again and again in North Korean children's literature and magazines, appearing hundreds of times since 1953.[68] Zur's careful analysis of the texts shows the significant roles that both storyline and illustration play in evoking emotions. The child subject is "unequivocally innocent," which highlights the vulnerability of the subject vis-à-vis war, but paradoxically the child is also willing to "sacrifice itself" when necessary, against the enemy.[69] Comparative literature scholar Immanuel Kim shows how carefully media professionals examine the political meaning behind different plot lines in TV, novels, and movies.[70]

Echoing a point made by Koen De Ceuster and others, North Korea is not a land of "no art"; indeed, there is continuity with the Korean tradition, and aesthetics exist alongside politics that are subsumed under the state.[71] However, former North Korean state poet Jang Jin Song—who wrote "There was no poetry in hunger. North Korea is a nation without poetry"—might disagree.[72] Former members of the Chosun Writers Association have said as much: "We cannot regard [North Korean] literature as literature. . . . It's a long time since the purity of literature disappeared from the [North Korean] literary world."[73] Scholar Brian Myers argues that, beyond the role of Juche ideology and Songbun, North Korea's official culture is also deeply ethnonationalist. This, he suggests, is the prevailing ideological thrust of the state.[74] Writers who do not conform to the strict official literary policy face punishment through reeducation, imprisonment, or death.[75] "Literature is the Party's thought weapon," the International Publishers Association writes.[76]

Art in North Korea teaches its children to fulfill filial piety toward the geopolitical aspirations of their ancestors. This also strongly echoes Songbun, the inheritance of parental and ancestral behavior in the child. As a children's poem from North Korea instructs: "Even when you aim your rifle, / You know you can hear / Faint whispers in your ear: / You are aiming the bullet that your father and mother / Could not fire."[77] The child is a revolutionary figure and fighter, battling imperial powers of decades past, guided by her ancestor's national fight. According to international rights norms, the right to freedom of expression and opinion extends to children's right to learn, play, and create. Although North Korea's rights report acknowledges the rights of the child, their own state-sanctioned literature and, indeed, the testimony of defector children confirm the state's failure to respect these rights. Some state-sanctioned publications, available domestically and internationally, valorize children's acts of self-sacrifice for the salvation of state ideological objects.

In 2006 North Korea's English magazine *Democratic People's Republic of Korea* published an article about Yu Hyang Rim with the title, "She was nine years old."[78] Yu, a student in Pyongyang Misan Primary School, had a news article dedicated to her because of her self-sacrifice for portraits of Kim Il Sung and Kim Jong Il. She saved them from a house fire by carefully wrapping the portraits in a blanket. Soldiers found her in the burned-out house, asphyxiated on top of them. North Korea posthumously awarded her the Kim Il Sung Children's Honor prize. Her former school was renamed after her to reflect her heroism. The magazine indicates that this child was commended for her loyalty to the leadership. Several years later, the Group for the Production of Films for School Youth and Children of Pyongyang University of Dramatic and Cinematic Arts produced a documentary about her called *Immortal Flowers That Blossomed at Campus.* By the time the documentary was made, somehow in her posthumous state, Yu Hyang Rim had managed to save "three generals of Mt. Paektu."[79] It is impossible to know if this story is true or not, or if there is some kernel of truth that state media has borrowed to persuade readers. My goal here is not to struggle with the truth of this story. Where children's rights are concerned, it is more useful to consider what kind of press and publication environment is revealed through this type of story.

Other children have also been lauded for their self-sacrifice for portraits of the leadership, an embodied metaphor of their loyalty. Contemporary gestures like these are linked to past heroism such as the children's guerrilla corps of the Fatherland Liberation War (the North Korean name for the Korean War). North Korean children learn of historic "juvenile revolutionaries" such as Kim Kum Sun, Jon Ki Ok, and Mok Un Sik. They learn math through the prism of geopolitics to calculate how many "bastard Americans" can be killed.[80] A KCNA article clarifies that the role of children in the postwar period rests in the field of sociopolitical activities, such as risking their lives to evacuate portraits "under unexpected circumstances."[81]

In 2012, during floods and resulting landslides, fourth-year student Han Hyon Gyong risked her life for the portraits of Kim Il Sung and Kim Jong Il. Her sacrifice shows the "noble *mental world* of the Youth League," the KCNA reported.[82] As a sort of consolation for the girl's death, Kim Jong Un sent his autograph to the officials, worker units, and children of Han's town, stating that he hoped the noble spirit she displayed would live on and help the country.[83] One can only imagine some in the town wished the autograph would be sealed in a fireproof box and placed on the mountaintop, free from flood, fire, explosion, and the desperate hands of loyal children.

Word Revolution

UN Commissioner Sonja Biserko asked Kim Soo-Am of Korea Institute for National Unification if he could make an assessment whether there would at some point be civil disobedience or rebellion within state structures. She asked, "What is your feeling according to sentiments of people that you have interviewed so far?" He answered, "Explicitly, people cannot talk about complaints about the regime. When we do in-depth interviews we are trying to find out what is underneath, or below what they are saying. Those who have escaped from North Korea, they have some discontent."[84] He then distinguishes between daily difficulties and discontent and those looking for freedom. He confirms that there are people who have left because of discontent toward the regime.

Jee Heon A, from the city of Chongjin, North Hamgyeon Province, lived in Yun Sun area on the border between China and North Korea. She had an ordinary life in North Korea. After her defection, at the UN public hearing and in preparation for the Commission of Inquiry report, she was asked if there was anything else that was not covered in her testimony. She stated, "In the very inner part of North Korea, I just want to say that, people are fighting against the regime in North Korea." There are indications of tiny, private utterances of change. While the overall media apparatus still speaks with the same voice, tone, and message, on the ground and among trusted interlocutors brief syllabic revolutions are spoken. Kim Jong Un becomes the "small guy" or the "little man"—"What does the little guy know about politics?" Of course, these are not yet a demonstration of what Commissioner Sonja Biserko was asking, which concerned activates within state structures.

Storytelling is strictly forbidden. Yet, despite the dangers, turns of phrase and dark humor exist in North Korea. Clandestine expressions borrow the state rhetoric in part and rephrase a word or syllable to turn the meaning sharply against the claims of the state. These linguistic jabs emerge and circulate because a significant portion of the community shares similar thinking over the issues embedded in the expressions. If significant portions of the community did not find resonance with the ideas couched in the expressions, such turns of phrase would not be popularized or circulated. Yet they do. Countless numbers of defectors in South Korea, if asked, will recall sly turns of phrase and jokes that eviscerated "some chubby guy" or critiqued social inequality.

The leader is said to be like the sun. "If you get too close to him, you burn to death, if you go too far from him, you freeze to death." When a task is clearly accomplished without the help of the leadership, "all thanks to the leader" will be referenced as a way of indicating how little help actually comes from the leader. A joke that has circulated in Pyongyang concerns a teacher covering the delicate topic of evolution. A student asks, amazed, "Are we all really descended from apes?" "Yes," the teacher answers. Not quite satisfied, the student seeks clarification, "Even Kim Jong Un?" Noting the explosiveness of this, the teacher answers, "Everyone except Kim Jong Un." North Korean jokes also identify the stark differences between North and South Korea in terms of social inequality, hypermaterialism, and hypermasculinity. To paraphrase: in North Korea if you become a party officer, "it's as if you have gained an extra testicle." In South Korea, the joke continues, with enough money, "even a woman can have testicles."

The institutional bureaucracy of North Korea can be subtly criticized by altering a syllable here or there in a process that identifies the institutional factors leading to inequality. For example, the People's Armed Forces take things by force. The secret police take things secretly. The security police take things securely. The planning committee takes through planning. And the party takes like they are having a party. Since North Korea's Military First Policy, the military have carried out abuses on the population. This has not escaped linguistic jabs. Corps commanders steal without saying much, the division commander steals divisively, a regimental commander steals in a regimented way, a battalion commander steals a battalion of stuff, a middle-man company commander steals from the middle, and a platoon leader steals without a sound.

When she lived in North Korea, defector Mina Yoon visited the countryside where her uncle lived. She was surprised to find him alone, not tending his pig and goat as he usually did. "My goat and pig decided to join the army," he explained. In her online article, she writes: "The situation was like this: A few days back, a couple of soldiers sneaked into his barn and stole his animals. Searching for the animals, he found a note near the area where his goat used to be that said, 'Protecting one's country is the most sacred vocation on earth. Believing what the pig chose to do was a right thing, I am following him.— Sincerely, your Goat.'"[85]

When her relation told her what happened, she didn't know whether to laugh or cry. The military were in need, yet so too was her uncle, she reasoned. Later, when people asked about the absence of the goat and pig, her uncle explained that it was thanks to his consistent political education that his pig and goat both volunteered to join the army. Such expressions highlight the coerced situation of individuals. Other phrases indicate the magical way intractable situations can be altered. A common joke in North Korea is that Newton was wrong, there are not three laws of motion, but four—the fourth being cash money since it can make anything move in North Korea.

Serbian democracy activist Srđa Popović's insightful term "laughtivism" identifies the critical role humor and mockery play in social dissent. Popović observes that humor can undermine authority, shake off apathy, and create allegiances.[86] Laughter is not in the toolkit of the dictator, where everything is deadly serious. This is reminiscent of the words of Audre Lorde, who observed that "the master's tools will never dismantle the master's house."[87] To paraphrase Kim Suk-Young, writing on laughter in North Korea: laughter traces how reality and illusion blend, and rather than hiding trauma, it reveals it and facilitates survival.[88]

The presence of alternative speech in North Korea certainly confirms that North Koreans are aware of the inequalities among them. It also shows that linguistically there are fleeting moments of resistance. The ability of word resistance to mobilize into sustained, aggregate, sociopolitical change can only occur if such like-minded people are able to meet regularly and safely without risk of being killed. As yet, this reality hasn't proved to exist. As Joo Hyung-min observes, without "independent unions, autonomous intellectuals, North Korean versions of samizdat," there is little chance for major social revolution. Furthermore, Joo observes, the word revolutions do not point to a set of values or ideologies to shore up a new ideological direction for a rebellious group.[89] Word rebellion at this stage seems stuck on observation and critique. Trust is a factor that is essential for group counterpolitical mobilization, and defectors readily admit that it is hard to trust anyone in North Korea. Indeed, the market, the location where information flows a little more freely, may also be what is keeping the regime afloat as it absorbs the shocks of society's economic stresses. Clandestine speech in North Korea shows that not everyone agrees with the mythic reality put forward in the state media.

CHAPTER 5

FORBIDDING THE FOREIGN

The regime has murder, deception and nuclear bombs in its arsenal, the weapon I wield is truth.

—Jang Jin-Sung, *Dear Leader*

Jang Jin-Sung, former state poet to Kim Jong Il, knows firsthand how much the regime fears information. If significant portions of the population gain knowledge of how much better life could be, he explains, such empowerment would spell the end of the state in its current manifestation. To the North Korean government, information is like a nuclear bomb. As such, it has to be delicately and expertly assembled. It requires strict control and strategic deployment. This analogy is not overdrawn. North Korea is profoundly concerned with what kind of information enters, circulates, and exits its borders. When border crossers are refouled from China, among the first questions of interrogation are Who did you meet? What media did you see? Who did you speak with? In 1997 Kim Jong Il issued an internal party declaration stating, "The Sino-DPRK border is an ideological border, just like the 38th parallel."[1] The ideology of the North must be kept free from outside tampering. The regime's rhetoric identifies information as a weapon of psychological war used by hostile nations to undermine the social fabric of North Korea.

Information, particularly foreign information, is carefully surveilled and embargoed. The state cracks down on foreign information in the form of books, magazines, and the like but also immaterial information flows such as radio and television broadcasts and the internet, although internet, radio, and television broadcasts are sometimes accessible along the Sino-Korean border. Forbidden are foreign books, magazines, movies, music, and digital formats of these that are transferrable via USBs, cellular phones, DVDs, or cassette tapes. Any leaflets or materials sent into the DPRK via helium balloons, such as those from South Korea–based rights activists, are also illegal. By censuring these types of information, North Korea is in violation of several human rights norms such as the right of opinion, the right of assembly, and the right to dignity. This chapter examines the state's tight control over foreign media entering the country and its attempts to prevent information about North Korea leaking to foreign media. However, this form of censorship has backfired; it has led to the creation of illicit networks to consume foreign media as well secret modes of communication among the North Korean people to share what they know.

Foreign Information

Gossip, rumor, and jokes that criticize the government are dangerous for their potential criminality. Article 222 of North Korea's criminal code identifies concocting rumors that cause mistrust of the state and social disruption as an offense punishable by several years of reform through labor. A person is also in violation of the legal code—public regulation Article 226—if they spread illegal media, electronic or otherwise. Socialist culture in North Korea is violated through Article 193 if a person imports, distributes, makes, or keeps media that "reflects decadent, carnal or foul contents." Such a person will be accused of being decadent if they watch, listen to, dance along with, or read media that is "decadent, carnal or foul"—in other words, non–North Korean.

Legal restrictions on foreign media have increased since the mid-2000s, while at the same time there have been increases in foreign radio broadcasts into North Korea since the mid-2000s. (While radio jamming does occur, it is not widespread. Foreign stations can be heard if the radio can pick up the broadcast.) There are people accessing illegal media in North Korea. Researchers Nat Kretchun and Jane Kim wrote an insightful report about North Korea's "quiet" information changes; they report widespread use of illegal media such as movies, music, and radio broadcasts among those they interviewed.[2] They rightly identify that North Korea no longer has complete control over information inside the country. However, the state still has a huge monopoly on it. Foreign radio broadcasts enable North Koreans to get access to "real-time" information, while movies and television shows from South

Korea and elsewhere provide engaging plot stories that capture audiences. Kretchun and Kim argue that as more and more people get access to illegal media, they are increasingly sharing the material with trusted networks. They also found that although there are strict punishments for accessing such items, the possibility to avoid punishment does exist through bribes and the irregular enforcement of punishment. It is heartening to learn from the report that, as information flows in, North Koreans are able to create space between themselves and the leadership—the people are able to make greater sense of the gap between the myth and sanitized image put forward by the state and reality on the ground. Rather than the vertical, top-down structure of North Korean state media, which is still in place and powerful, the inflow of foreign media permits horizontal information flows between people. It is through their individual acts of defiance, along with improvements in technology, that North Koreans now have more access to outside information than they did twenty years ago.

Beyond word of mouth, some North Koreans have access to other information sources such as DVDs and radio broadcasts. However, the use of media is not equally accessible across the country or across social groups. Elites with money and those who live on the border with China are more likely to use DVDs and listen to radio broadcasts. Among those groups, the timeline of foreign media use has been plotted roughly as follows:

Radio (shortwave), circa 1997
Television (not satellite), circa 2000[3]
DVD and mobile telephones (not necessarily smartphones), circa 2004
Laptop computers, circa 2008
USBs, circa 2011

Significantly, it is elites and border residents who are largely accessing these devices and non-DPRK media, when these are accessed at all. Defectors frequently report that it is those with money who are significantly more likely to use, circulate, and enjoy foreign media. Given this, it is more important still that media be circulated to the wealthy, those on the border, and those with access to power, not only because they can purchase it but because they can also potentially avoid punishment through paying bribes.[4] In short, those who are most disenfranchised by the North Korean government are among the least likely to gain access to foreign media. Nevertheless, foreign media is making inroads into North Korea, and the domestic audience finds it interesting, informative, and enjoyable. The motivation for using outside media varies across the user spectrum. The Kretchun and Kim study found that some people used the media for fun while others used it to collect business information or to prepare for defection.[5]

Foreign media users in North Korea consume in secret because of the dangers posed by getting caught. Because the foreign media is used secretly, it is difficult for North Koreans to know for sure who else is doing the same. While some defectors expressed the belief that fellow citizens might have been doing so, they couldn't be certain. It is not something that could be discussed publicly. This sustains an atmosphere of opacity in North Korea, maintaining the idea that the majority agrees with the state's status quo.

Unlike radio or television consumers, DVD viewers appear less secretive of their behavior. Those who watch DVDs reported viewing them with trusted friends and family.[6] A radio or television with a dial that is tunable to foreign media is an illegal device in North Korea, whereas DVD players are not illegal, nor are domestic-content DVDs. For this reason, it seems that DVDs are providing the most impactful source of foreign media within North Korea. Still, when watching a foreign DVD, defectors report that it is hard to settle into the experience and suspend reality because of the danger posed by the activity. The majority of people who watch DVDs are borrowing them from friends or purchasing them from a trusted connection. Ethnic Koreans in China (Chosunjok) and ethnic Chinese living in North Korea for work are the greatest source for DVD circulation. Within the black market, only those who have enough knowledge about the state's crackdown operations are confident enough to sell such illicit items.

The black market is a location where electricians have earned money modifying TVs and radios with dials fixed to domestic signals to facilitate picking up foreign content. If listened to at all, foreign radio broadcasts are usually tuned into very late at night, between 10 P.M. and 2 A.M. The content of media broadcasts such as Radio Free Asia, Voice of America, or Free North Korea Radio, run by defectors in South Korea, is more political than DVD content, which is typically movies and drama. Consumers of radio broadcasts are more likely to be men and of an older demographic. Unlike DVDs, radio broadcasts provide North Koreans with real-time information. Through foreign broadcasts, they can learn about international politics, joint military drills by South Korea and the United States, and black-market exchange rates. Such information impacts trade of illegal materials into North Korea, security checks, and exchange rates. Thus, for some, the foreign broadcasts help with their market activities. North Koreans are eager to consume various types of foreign media. In the past, North Koreans were keen to listen to anything that was non–North Korean; now they are more discerning as media consumers and search out information they find interesting and trustworthy.[7] There is a notable difference in what elites and non-elite, rural, less-educated (lower Songbun) individuals listen to in radio broadcasts. Generally, those of lower Songbun listen to more cultural and entertainment programs with music, letters home from defectors in South Korea, and dramatized radio programs.[8] This suggests the need for more "niche broadcasts" with information that will appeal to different audiences via AM-capable radios, which is what more people have access to. Shortwave broadcasts can be sent over longer distances and are harder to jam due to modulation. As such, these broadcasts should be continued as they reach the interior.[9]

Foreign Media and Domestic Perceptions of the Regime

Consumption of foreign media, both news and entertainment, has improved North Koreans' perceptions of South Korea and the United States, thus countering some of the state media rhetoric.[10] This is positive news. However, it has been observed that North Koreans' views of their own government and nation-state have not changed despite access to foreign media.[11] This finding parallels ominously with that of Holger Lutz Kern and Jens Hainmueller, who found that East Germans' access to foreign mass media didn't undermine authoritarian rule but rather led to greater life satisfaction for East Germans.[12]

Kretchun and Kim suggest that North Koreans' views of their government are not changing because the foreign media they consume generally cannot report on domestic events in North Korea due to the lack of access and transparency, and certainly cannot do so in real time. There is also a widespread domestic assumption that foreigners do not know about North Korea; thus, their information about the regime cannot be of significance. Although consumers trust the media they see, identifying it as reliable and accurate, they do not then take this information and begin to perceive their regime differently—as has been assumed by policy makers.[13]

Kretchun and Kim speculate that this may be because the reality of domestic issues faced by North Koreans is not represented in the media they are watching. Simply put, it is a content issue rather than a trust issue. DVDs and radio broadcasts do not, and cannot, cover domestic stories or local content.[14] The findings of Kretchun and Kim strongly suggest the need to link activist groups such as Asia Press's *Rimjin-gang*—which has been working with clandestine journalists inside North Korea to get information out of the country— with groups such as Radio Free Asia, Voice of America, and Free North Korea Radio, facilitating journalism and broadcasting from within North Korea material that is produced outside North Korea and then sent back in.[15] By doing this North Koreans would be able to get information about other parts of their country mediated through underground journalists and produced abroad in Japan, South Korea, and China. Since travel in North Korea is strictly controlled, media coverage from other parts of the country would enable fellow residents to get a fuller picture of the domestic situation, which would be particularly important for those elites in power.

North Koreans want entertainment and news media, but they also need to catch a glimpse of the banal and the ordinary via media platforms that are unmediated. Circulation of unedited, raw video and audio—such as is commonly seen on sites such as YouTube and other platforms—also has a role in the parched desert that is North Korea's media landscape. Kim Heung-Kwang, a former North Korean prisoner and currently the executive director of the North Korea Intellectuals Solidarity, an NGO that sends information into North Korea, explains his messaging as follows: "Films are films. I only knew parts of South Korea through films. I wanted to show North Koreans what the good life was. I want to send details of the basic conditions of life in South Korea through digital magazines and footage via USBs. For example, you turn the tap all the way to the left and there's a consistent source of hot water."[16]

Kim tries to take the audience with him, as if sitting on his shoulder, through his daily life in South Korea, so the viewer can have the experience, as much as possible, through him. He films his ordinary life, walking the aisles of the shopping market, capturing the rows of toothpaste, cookies, food, and other items. He films the aisles of pet food options, pet toys, and pet clothes. He tries to convey what ordinary life is like for regular people in Seoul.[17]

Clearly there is a critical need for non–state produced coverage of events inside North Korea. Imagine if a Pyongyang-based Kim Heung-Kwang could film his daily life, the privilege and access to resources he might have, and then have that information—in raw format, anonymized and free of attribution, circulated via underground groups such as Asia Press's *Rimjin-gang*—seen by North Koreans in the northernmost remote city of Chongjin.

While the North Korean state's media has eviscerated South Korea and other foreign countries, research with defectors suggests that inflow of foreign media ameliorated those representations somewhat. However, the same has not happened in terms of recasting how North Koreans perceive their own state. Inflow of foreign media seems to leave their perception of the regime unaltered. The domestic ideology that champions the personality cult of North Korea's leadership family is strong and likely a huge factor in the seeming stalwart perception of the government. However, if foreign media content could include audio and video captured from underground journalism within North Korea, such efforts could lead to considerable change.

Leaky Information

When foreigners, diplomatic or otherwise, travel to North Korea, activities are strictly controlled, and whole regions of the country and people are off limits. International humanitarian aid agencies working inside North Korea are carefully watched and regulated by the state. Aid agencies have been kicked out for failing to abide by controls or have left due to the frustration of having to deal with them.[18] North Korea's government directives instruct that understanding the DPRK from abroad and from the perspective of outsiders should be murky and unclear: "one of our strategies [is that] when the Americans look at our interior, we make it murky as if wrapped in a fog."[19] When speaking or writing internationally, North Korean representatives employ normative diplomatic language mixed with standard themes of the North's victimization by hostile states. They evoke arguments that mirror the radical far left or other authoritarian regimes. We may assume that state representatives are speaking the genuine demands of the state. However, high-ranking North Korean defectors have warned that the North Korean state cannot be trusted for diplomatic negotiation. If North Korea is negotiating with you, "it's a counter-intelligence operation. . . . North Korea uses dialogue as a tool of deception rather than of negotiation."[20] The state uses international "negotiation" to buy time, gain access to things it wants, and trap the enemy.[21]

High-ranking North Korean diplomats are carefully screened prior to international appointment, and while abroad they are under constant surveillance, often living in the diplomatic embassies. North Korea needs to ensure its internationally deployed citizens will not be seduced by foreign media or social influence. Of course, these individuals interact with the world, and as they do so questions are raised that reveal awkward incongruities between ideology and practice. Former North Korean diplomat Thae Yong Ho explains that "everyday activities and services were like leading a ceaseless double-life, which was psychologically difficult."[22] The most obvious questions such as how Kim Jong Un could kill his uncle, how the government could take humanitarian aid while building a nuclear arsenal, and how a communist country could have hereditary succession were, in Thae's words, questions that "made me increasingly realize the deep-rooted contradictions upon which the entire North Korean system is built."[23] So it seems that it is risky business for North Korea to have any kind of international interaction at all. To ensure that diplomats don't make the decision to defect as Thae did, the government has devised a system of family hostages, what defectors have called "love abuse."

As further insurance against defectors, the state requires all nationals dispatched abroad—whether as diplomats or export laborers—to ensure that at least one family member remains back in North Korea as an "anchor." Of course, it is typical that the individual will have almost her entire immediate and extended family in North Korea.[24] In this way the country anchors the ideology in the thoughts and actions of those abroad through the continued presence of loved ones within the state. If the person abroad strays, the anchor pays the price through reeducation, imprisonment, or execution, or the recent trend is to appear in video propaganda. The hostage program ensures that even if a person is tempted to engage with foreign media or receives some influence, overall loyalty to the DPRK is ensured. Even when a person is abroad, there are signs that diplomats avoid foreign media and foreign social contact as much as possible. When Thae Yong Ho and his family defected from the London-based embassy, he told his sons: "I'm going to cut the chain of slavery, you are free men." They asked him if they could freely browse the internet. He answered, "You can do Internet games whenever you like, you can read any books, watch any films."[25]

Just as North Korea is concerned with the kinds of information circulating domestically, so too is the state anxious about information about its activities that reaches the world. North Korea's international efforts to run damage control on its national image show the strong arm of the state and its brash, irreverent efforts to go to any lengths to ensure opacity. A former North Korean official, speaking with professor Kim Suk-Young, explained that almost all the employees at his government ministry, almost a thousand people, were asked to play the role of "shoppers, drivers, and pedestrians to parade around the city" to present an image of Pyongyang for visitors. In part, the objective in doing this is to obscure knowledge about human rights violations within the country. Internationally, North Korea tries to leave no trace of its abuses.

Spies who work internationally are trained to commit suicide if captured. Kim Hyun Hee, one of two North Korean spies responsible for the bombing of Korean Airlines flight 858, which killed 115 people in 1987, survived her attempted suicide and held out confessing for over a year of interrogation in South Korea, insisting she was not from the North.[26] Another example of going to any lengths to ensure state secrets is the recent attempted break-in at a Kuala Lumpur morgue where the body of assassinated Kim Jong Nam, half-brother of Kim Jong Un, was held. If Malaysian police had access to the body of Kim Jung Nam, they would have access to information about the nerve agent, a weapon of mass destruction, which killed Kim.[27] Tellingly, when the Korean Central News Agency finally did report the case domestically, Kim Jong Nam (who had lived in forced exile abroad from the Kim family and whom virtually no North Korean citizens knew existed), was not mentioned by name or relation at all; his identity and the cause of his death was wiped from the narrative. The newspaper reported that "a citizen with a DPRK diplomatic passport" died of stroke in Kuala Lumpur; the Malaysian state refuses to repatriate the body.[28]

The Voice That Defects

The work of activist and journalist Ishimaru Jiro reveals that there are people within North Korea who seek change and are doing so via nascent underground journalism. Ishimaru covered North Korea as a journalist for twenty years. However, he felt frustrated by the barriers to information set up by the state when he visited North Korea. Working along the Sino-Korea border, on the Chinese side, he established contacts with North Korean border crossers. His method of covering North Korean domestic affairs is through partnership with citizens inside the North. Over the last few years, Ishimaru and his team have produced several volumes of a magazine called *Rimjin-gang*, named after a river in North Korea that flows south.[29] The work is published in Korean, Japanese, and English. The team also records short clandestine videos in public spaces, such as in various city markets, in North Korea. The work of Ishimaru and his anonymous team inside the DPRK has revealed the presence of UN World Food Program food; aid from the Red Cross, the food from the UN Food and Agriculture Organization, and other sources; and medicine being sold on the black market. The videos, photos, and reportage confirm what we have heard for decades from the legions of testimony from defectors about orphaned children, starving elderly, emaciated soldiers, and profound, widespread destitution. The videos recorded by the clandestine team show that access to food is still highly precarious in North Korea. The work of Asia Press and *Rimjin-gang* has made considerable contributions to international awareness of domestic problems in North Korea. They have provided timely information that is harder to achieve from defector testimony.

Ishimaru's team has created what may be the first partial samizdat media in North Korea. I refer to it as a partial samizdat because, unlike samizdat of the Soviet Union, which circulated domestically, the information Ishimaru is collecting is not being circulated back into North Korea. It is instead flowing out of the country. Another proximate samizdat are the short-stories of Bandi, an author writing under a pseudonym that translates as "firefly." South Korea's monthly magazine *Monthly Chosun* identifies the several-hundred-handwritten-page manuscript titled "The Accusation" as written by an author who still resides in North Korea and is a member of the Chosun Writers' League Central Committee, North Korea's state-authorized writers' association. Bandi, born before the Korean War, witnessed North Koreans struggling through the March of Suffering (the 1990s famine). Those years moved him to write about the horrendous difficulties he witnessed in the lives of his friends and colleagues. His stories pinpoint the harsh contradictions of North Korean society. The pages were reportedly smuggled out of North Korea by a relative of Bandi's who defected and first published them in Korean by the Chogabje publishing house in 2014.

By flowing out of North Korea, this media is missing a trick in the social-change playbook. North Koreans need to consume media that is not state mediated. At the present moment, whether foreign or domestic, the media consumed by North Koreans is polished and professional—whether democratic or authoritarian. Activist resources need to be directed at facilitating circulation of North Korea's tiny nascent journalism and literature back into North Korea.

This would make it a samizdat, and perhaps as such it could be effective for circulating diverse information. North Koreans need the opportunity to witness the geographic, social, and political differences that exist in their country, which are absent at the level of their own media. The new frontier for the information wave into North Korea would benefit from including materials that are anonymized for safety and cover topics by and for North Koreans related to documentation of domestic affairs, class privilege, and inequality.

Another way that North Koreans exchange information and let their voices defect is via mobile phones. These phones are purchased in China using the Chinese telecom network and are smuggled back into North Korea via a friend or broker and then delivered to family and friends. These phones can then be contacted via telephones anywhere in the world. Thus, when North Koreans arrive in South Korea, even from the Hanawon Center, the facility where North Koreans are housed upon arrival in South Korea after they are debriefed by the National Intelligence Service, they use the local phone boxes or their own personal mobile phone to contact family in North Korea, speaking to them in real time and relaying information directly. There is no fear of North Korea being able to tap these phones as they are communicating through Chinese telecoms. The risk for North Korean residents comes if your conversation is overheard or if your phone rings when the wrong person is near. Defectors in China, South Korea, and Japan are able to maintain contact. If used near the border, these phones can receive signals from Chinese cell phone towers. Detection equipment is used by the North Korean government to determine who is using a Chinese cell phone, so clandestine, quick, and irregular use is essential to avoid getting caught with these illicit devices.[30]

Official cell phones in North Korea, known as Koryolink cell phones, and unofficial cell phones from China are transforming the unofficial economy in North Korea.[31] In contemporary Pyongyang about 60 percent of residents between the ages of twenty and fifty use official North Korean cell phones, with some residents such as adolescents and merchants identifying mobile phones as an essential item.[32] Mobile phones have existed in North Korea for more than two decades now, since the fiber cables were laid in the mid-1990s, but they are still a rare luxury item. A few years ago, the mobile phone made a person vulnerable to robbery and suspicion, but the increased presence of the objects has transformed their meaning into a status symbol of the new rich.[33] Koryolink phones cannot make international calls; they are understood to be under regular surveillance and subject to jamming by the DPRK government if the user tries to make calls in the border region using a Chinese cell tower, but there are creative and adaptive ways to use them to call internationally. Hyun-Jung Ryu, a scholar at the Seoul-based, DPRK-focused University of North Korean Studies, studied how, with the assistance of brokers based deep within North Korea, a person could call South Korea by linking up the microphone of the

Koryolink phone with the earpiece of a smuggled Chinese mobile phone that had dialed South Korea. The phones are aligned by microphone and earpiece, and two brokers are required.[34] With a smuggled Chinese cell phone and access to a cell tower network, calls can be made and received internationally.

When examining the impact of new information and communication technology, there is a tendency to focus on the internet. But research on poor, low-income countries and places where the internet is limited indicates that change in such places happens through the mobile phone, which is far more influential than the internet. It is an economical and efficient means of redistributing money among those who are poor and disadvantaged.[35] New social alternatives become possible through it.[36] The mobile phone speeds up and makes more reliable former low-tech ways of keeping in touch. When earlier defectors left North Korea, their contact with family was almost certainly severed; however, relations are maintained with the use of the mobile phone. Reuniting can be carried out more safely and with greater care through the use of the phone, but the mobile phone also provides the option to "reunify" via a short phone call.

The use of the mobile phone between defectors and their family assists in social behavior beyond the norm of acceptable, legal behavior in either North or South Korea due to the national security laws of both countries. The technology cannot be fully monitored or controlled by either country; thus, individual family relations are privileged through the modern, capital-driven loophole of mobile technological communication, which North Koreans appropriate for their own ends. Perhaps more than elsewhere, the use of mobile phones to communicate across the otherwise impassable geopolitical dividing line of North and South Korea demonstrates that public space and private dynamics can break free of controls. Maintaining contact with people who would otherwise be inaccessible across space and time is a key feature of modern global dynamics.[37]

Mobile phones are also used in ways particular to the cultural context of North Korea. For example, slang is used as a means to shorten expression and speed up talk time, to avoid getting caught.[38] If the State Security Department does catch someone communicating internationally via mobile phone, they can be punished to discourage others.[39] While there is, indeed, great risk, the ability of the state to achieve surveillance over all communication is shown to be impossible.[40]

Mobile phones can be used in the transfer of money and goods but also information. Clandestine radio signals have been sent into North Korea for decades, and since the early 2000s defectors in South Korea have used long- and short-wave radio to communicate with North Koreans. Their voice is a means of raising consciousness and democratic empowerment in North Korea. Kim Seong Min founded Free North Korea Radio in 2004. He had defected from North Korea in 1996 after being exposed to information in his job monitoring foreign broadcasts in the Korean People's Army, which helped him to learn that North Korea wasn't quite the country it has presented itself to be. He also recognized the power of the voice, carried in radio broadcasts, to influence the decisions that empower individuals.[41] Free North Korea Radio has been joined by Radio Free Asia, Open Radio for North Korea, Radio Free Chosun, and North Korea Reform Radio, all of which send radio broadcasts into North Korea that are accessible through radios that have not had their dials fixed by authorities. A survey conducted by the Korea Press Foundation asked three hundred newly arrived defectors about the impact of radio broadcasts in the North. Of the respondents, 4.27 percent had experience listening to the broadcasts while in the North.[42] As political scientist Danielle Chubb observes, "Activists argue that defector broadcasting directly into North Korea is a highly effective form of advocacy. Insofar as it allows North Koreans in Seoul to interface directly with their fellow nationals in North Korea, it is a unique and unprecedented form of activism in the history of the North Korean human rights campaign."[43] Once having left their home, defectors used to be voiceless to their loved ones left behind. They could not send letters, make calls, or stay in touch over the internet. They could not even get a spot on the broadcast schedule to send a direct message home.[44] The mobile phone has become a mini radio broadcaster, allowing voices to target those who matter.

Through the mobile phone, North Korean defectors are able to "voice" themselves and their current lived experience abroad back into North Korea. This is greater familial intimacy than the broadcasts of Free North Korea Radio can offer because it is no longer a monologue, no longer selected and acceptable messages broadcast to an audience of listeners but rather a dialogue, no matter how brief, between known subjects. The communications happen in real time, unlike prerecorded broadcasts, and the voice carries emotion and immediacy, as is so often the case when we speak with loved ones. It bypasses the obstacles of state censorship in both Koreas, albeit with great clandestine care, and passes beyond the physical distance that formerly made communication impossible. North Korean defectors and their North Korea–based interlocutors create mini broadcasting services between themselves, bypassing other media noise.[45] This enables the flow of individual, nonpublic narratives of personal experience that are outside the purview of states. It permits the transmission of defector voices into North Korea but also the transmission of ordinary North Korean voices out of their country without defection. The defector diaspora can be present in North Korea via their voices on the mobile phone, and North Koreans can be present in South Korea through their voices without defecting.[46]

Along with radio broadcasts, the mobile phone offers real-time connections between absent others. While mobile phones and money transfers are typically used to secure the safe passage of would-be defectors, remittances and quick exchange of information may keep people from making the decision to defect.

Would-be migrants to China benefit from remittances that are brought into North Korea, and they do not have to take the risky choice of heading into unknown territory in a new country. Sometimes the mobile phone is a site where the decision to defect is debated. Over dinner in a Seoul restaurant with a North Korean defector-friend, I witnessed this in real time. A call came to her mobile in the middle of our meal, and an angry, quick conversation took place in a matter of moments between North and South Korea. My friend's mother was unsure whether to defect even though the broker had been paid. Yes, she would live better, but she was afraid of being lonely, I was told. "She doesn't want to come, she doesn't want to be without her friends." The Database Center for North Korean Human Rights found that 78.1 percent of North Koreans intended to send remittances to North Korea to secure the safe passage of family out of North Korea.[47] But, as this phone call shows, this percentage doesn't necessarily reflect the intent of those back in North Korea.

Recently more North Korean defectors in South Korea and abroad are contributing new and different ideas to shape the content of material broadcasted into North Korea. For instance, Je Seong Ho, mentioned earlier in this book, set up an NGO called Now, Action, United and Human Right.[48] The NGO sends broadcasts with content aimed at developing critical thinking about market mechanisms. For instance, the broadcast features a few young defectors talking about which type of business would make more money, a chicken restaurant or a bakery? Would the location of the shop matter? How could the shop attract customers?[49] Defectors and activists who send information into North Korea do so with the hope that it may lead to on-the-ground changes that will eventually facilitate liberalization of the government. The effects of being exposed to media can be amplified through talking about it, so it is not just exposure to media at work here, but there are intermediate factors that amplify the effects.

Forbidding what is foreign has always been about creating and controlling what is properly North Korean. Improvements in access to non–state sanctioned information and communication technology is a huge advantage for ordinary North Koreans—setting aside the question of whether it will lead them to question the regime. North Korea's domestic information and communication technology suggests that Kim Jong Un is embracing digital advances just like the rest of the world. However, Kim Jong Un is using advances in information and communication technology to achieve greater digital censorship, surveillance, and control. Political scientist Sheena Chestnut Greitens argues that North Korea is switching from an approach emphasizing total control to one focused on surveillance and activism with "greater political benefits for regime survival."[50] This is a trend also observed in Russia, China, and the Middle East, as noted by Seva Gunitsky.[51] A former computer programmer from North Korea explained that Red Star OS 3.0, North Korea's version of Windows, has an invisible virus scanning application that runs in the background and cannot be removed called opprc, which keeps track of offline digital content and its distribution through users. Content-sharing history and the path that the content took are all available for the authorities to see with this software. This enables the authorities to track back in time to find the smugglers who brought the media. North Korea is working to create a "self-contained digital environment."[52]

Information trouble leads to a knock-on effect of other troubles in North Korea, particularly in spheres related to access to resources and the rule of law. These then further complicate issues faced by refugees, overseas laborers, and detained foreign nationals in North Korea. Media control constitutes North Korea's current dilemma because it creates a particular experience of the world by managing access to information and its interpretation. The way North Korea drips information and misinformation about human rights, in particular, to its people domestically and the way it stonewalls internationally explains how the human rights problem is held together in North Korea.

CHAPTER 6

CONTROL OF MOVEMENT

As the 24-year-old in the Korean demilitarized zone ran from his vehicle, his fellow soldiers came in pursuit, firing more than 40 rounds at him. He was hit at least five times—but clung to life as he kept crawling south.

He was found bleeding in a pile of leaves by South Korean soldiers and brought to doctors.

—Marwa Eltagouri, "What We've Learned About the North Korean Soldier Whose Daring Escape Was Caught on Video"

In November 2017 the world watched as a North Korean soldier was gunned down trying to drive over the demilitarized zone (DMZ) border into South Korea. A few days after this spectacular decision, Marc Knapper, the acting U.S. ambassador to South Korea, tweeted a picture of Korean People's Army soldiers digging a trench and planting trees in the spot where the young defector, Mr. Oh, had crossed. It is exceptionally rare for a person to cross the border between North and South Korea. Typically, such a journey is taken from North Korea across the Tumen River along the Sino-DPRK border into China. That route can take a few hours, for those with money, connections, and luck. Or it can take several years, for those who only have their wits. As with defection via the DMZ, few North Koreans defect by boat. In July of 2016 a young North Korean defector was found wandering the streets of the western Japanese city of Nagato, in Yamaguchi Prefecture. He told police he had jumped from a shipping vessel and swam ashore using a plastic flotation device.[1] He stated that he was born in 1990 but had no identification papers. In 2011 nine North Koreans spent five days at sea until the Japanese coast guard picked them up. They were resettled in South Korea.

The defection of Oh from North to South Korea caught the world's attention for a few reasons. He crossed into the South at one of the most dangerous, highly guarded, and politically spectacular points of connection between the two nations: the Joint Security Area (JSA). The second reason is that, for such an individual to be stationed at the JSA in the first place, he had to have been of good Songbun, and those of politically loyal class backgrounds are assumed to be unlikely to want to defect. Finally, CCTV cameras captured the defection and the response of the Korean People's Army soldiers at each stage.[2] This was the first time rights violations committed under order of the North Korean state were caught on camera through the actions of the Korean People's Army: as the young man ran from North Korea into South Korea, he was pursued and shot at dozens of times by fourteen comrades.[3] The Korean People's Army soldiers violated subsections 6, 7, 8, and 9 of Article 1 of the Armistice Agreement between North and South Korea by shooting across the DMZ, by physically crossing the DMZ (one of them crossed, seemingly to retrieve the wounded soldier who had fallen on the South Korean side), and for using AK-47 assault rifles within the JSA. Assault rifles are not permitted under the UN Command Military Armistice Commission, the body established to supervise the armistice agreement.[4] (Since March 25, 1991, North Korea has ceased to attend the UN Command Military Armistice Commission meetings. In 1994, North Korea declared the armistice itself to be meaningless.) Even granting the North's rejection of the armistice, basic rights were grossly violated.

North Korea has a de facto embargo on any of its citizens leaving the country without permission. This is a violation of the International Covenant on Civil and Political Rights, Article 12, sections 1 and 2, to which North Korea is a signatory. This covenant carries components related to the freedom of movement within your country and into and out of your country. When the Korean People's Army shot at the defecting soldier, they were also violating one of the most basic of rights: Article 3 of the Universal Declaration of Human Rights, the right to life, liberty, and personal security. Yet the soldiers were following the instructions of their commander, Kim Jong Un. Former officials from North Korea report that a person who defects from the North is deemed a treasonous individual who should be shot to death.

This policy dates back to the early 1990s.[5] If these soldiers had not chased Oh, the twenty-four-year-old defector, if they had not tried to kill him, they themselves would likely have been killed. The CCTV footage captures all of these men running for their lives, for very different reasons. In his book *On*

Strengthening Socialist Lawful Life, Kim Jong Il wrote, echoing the words of his father, "Our laws are important weapons for the realization of our national policies."[6] Under North Korea's revised 2012 penal code, Article 63, "Treason Against the Fatherland" encompasses "those who betray the Fatherland by fleeing and surrendering to another country" as acts punishable by capital punishment.[7]

The events of November 13 show that the DMZ sharpshooters are prepared to kill any of their comrades. How differently might the scenario have played out if Oh had been shot at the Sino-DPRK border, since the Chinese government cooperates with North Korea to repatriate defectors? It is less likely that soldiers on the Chinese side would have come to his aid, like the South Korean soldiers did. This naturally leads to the question of how many shots across that border have not been caught on camera. By way of comparison, if a South Korean soldier stationed at the JSA were to defect North (*wolbuk* is the Korean term), it is likely the sniper would not shoot to kill that enemy national. Why? Alive, he is of more use. He can be put to use in the service of propaganda. North Korean political power permits life and causes death according to ideological usefulness.[8]

Internal Migration

Since crossing the border is so dangerous, what about internal migration? In North Korea, there is a lack of labor mobility, which is a consequence of government control on migration throughout the country. This control is achieved through a household registration system called *hoju*, which allows the government to determine where people live. North Korea aims to maintain a stable population distribution within the provinces and regions that have habitable land. About 45 percent of North Korea's population is located in the central belt of the country (South Pyongyang, North Pyongyang, and South Hamgyong), and the least populated areas are those that border China. Overall, about 60 percent of North Korea's population lives in urban settings throughout the provinces. The most populous cities are Pyongyang and North Hamgyong. This level of urbanization is more like what occurs in developed economies rather than developing economies such as North Korea. Indeed, big gaps in development exist between the urban centers of North Korea and its rural areas. Ironically, this regional inequality—created by attempts to control movement—is a major factor in the kinds of illicit population movement that is seen within North Korea and across its borders.

North Korea is not the only country with a household registration system; both China and Vietnam also employ a similar system to control population movements. In each of these cases the household registration is also a means of determining entitlements to socioeconomic welfare such as allocation of food rations and provision of housing, medicine, and education.[9] However, where North Korea's *hoju* system differs is in terms of sectioning off the privilege of residing in Pyongyang from those in provincial cities and rural areas. Residents in Pyongyang have access to vital resources that are in dire need elsewhere in the country. Securing access to the capital city through the household registration system results in several benefits for the regime: it is possible to present a good image to the international world and even invite visitors to see things for themselves. It also ensures internal stability by containing populations who might be disgruntled at the inequalities and by eliminating the opportunity for people between these regions to become aware of regional inequalities.

Is it possible to get a privileged *hoju* and move to Pyongyang? It is not impossible but is highly restricted. If you are a university graduate with an exceptional academic and political background, if you are an entertainment or sports star who has made an outstanding contribution to society, or if you are a member of the military personnel with a record of excellent service, you may be able to get assigned to live in this coveted part of the country. One might assume that marriage could be a ticket to migration into Pyongyang, but it is required that both individuals be from the city to remain living there. However, even with these exceptionally high standards, there are other social barriers that curtail movement. First, individual social climbing would raise suspicion in North Korea. Second, many in provincial cities or rural areas are not necessarily aware of how much better their lives could be in Pyongyang. More often migration occurs in the other direction, as once-privileged residents in Pyongyang are exiled to less favorable regions of the country. During the 2000s migration within North Korea was reduced, even compared with its typical rate. However, demography scholars indicate that the situation has worsened as *hoju* control has "tightened in Pyongyang in its exclusion of one-half million of its former residents from privileged entitlement in 2011."[10]

According to the limited data available, the official rate of migration between provinces is very low. Annually, migration between counties is about 0.7 percent. More women (0.8 percent) than men (0.6 percent) migrate, while migration between provinces is only 0.2 percent. This rate places North Korea at an extremely low mobility ranking compared with countries like China with similar household registration systems. The higher number of women migrants could be due to such factors as marriage (typically the woman moving in with the man's family), male military conscription (which is of longer duration), and women being far more likely to be hired in the special economic zones and tourism sector.[11] Government directive, then, is the main way that official intra-country migration occurs in North Korea, and it appears that it is virtually impossible to move openly within the country without permission.

Despite the need for government-authorized permits for legal internal migration, unauthorized migration has occurred throughout the country. In contemporary times, the increased acceptability of bribery has facilitated movement both within North Korea and across the border, although neither action is officially sanctioned. North Korea's public distribution system once was the central means of political and economic control of people's movements within the country. One had to stay put to collect food, shoes, and wages, for example. But when this system failed repeatedly through the 1990s, there was hardly an incentive to remain in one place. In the late 1990s many children and young adults were distress migrants, and the government made efforts to contain this population through what were called "9/27" detention centers (after the date in 1997 when they were founded, September 27). In 2010 scholar Courtland Robinson found a migration rate within North Korea of 18.7 percent among the three thousand refugees he spoke with in China, a much higher rate than the government's official numbers.[12]

Danger at the Border

Given the challenges inherent in internal migration, migration out of North Korea remains the most viable way for individuals to try to achieve better circumstances. However, the main routes out of the country are rife with danger. North Korea shares a 1,420-kilometer border with China, and many of the negotiations around preventing migration from North Korea are with China. After the death of Kim Jong Il, Kim Jong Un reportedly dispatched "storm corps" military personnel throughout the country for population control, with emphasis on the Sino-Korean border.[13] Russia and North Korea have also negotiated a return agreement for illegal migrants.[14] The border between North Korea and Russia is only 17.5 kilometers in length, running along the Tumen River and Lake Khasan. The Korea Russia Friendship Bridge carries a train line from Rason to Vladivostok. Some North Koreans have defected across the Russian-DPRK border, but the number is very low. Nonetheless, the cooperation agreement between the two countries is an indication that migration occurs enough to draw government attention.

North Korea's penal code distinguishes between political and economic migration, but punishment is delivered to both. The penal code gives up to two years of "labor correction" to someone who crossed into China for economic reasons, but if the security agency finds they left for political reasons or had contact with activists while in China, the punishment could be long-term detention. The code also stipulates that those helping border crossers will be severely punished.[15] Individuals who help others to defect have been publicly executed, regardless of their rank and position in society. A border patrol guard who helped a family of five to defect to South Korea was publicly executed in 2013.[16] Pastor Han Choong-ryeol, an ethnic Korean man who had been helping North Korean refugees in the Changbai Korean Autonomous County of China since 1993, was killed in the area on April 26, 2016. The pastor was killed by someone who reportedly looked like a North Korean customs official and who took Pastor Han's personal items after the execution.[17]

Defecting, attempting to defect, or helping others to defect are all capital crimes under North Korean law. The criminal code states that defectors who return to the North will be sent to reform institutions for a minimum of five years. If the person has had contact with foreigners, Christian missionaries, or South Koreans, or if the person commits an act of grave concern, the code provides for imprisonment in a political prison camp or the death penalty.[18] Based on extensive interviews with North Koreans in China and elsewhere, Refugees International found "almost all North Koreans face severe punishment upon deportation back to North Korea, regardless of their original motivation for leaving their country."[19]

Border Crossings, Then and Now

How did we get here? Historically, migration has occurred both legally and illegally across the Sino-Korean border and from northern to southern parts of the Korean peninsula. In the past, patterns of migration within the ethnic territory of the Koreas was shaped by geography, where physical limits like mountain ranges made movement out of the country impossible. Cultural aspects such as strong loyalty to family and territory mixed with fear of foreign countries also provided inhibition to migration. But during the Korean War there were approximately 2.9 million internally displaced persons on the peninsula. Of these, about 900,000 were from the North moving south.[20] Not many years later, during China's Great Leap Forward Famine (1958–1961), ethnic Koreans in China, known as Chosunjok, and Chinese along the Sino-DPRK border area migrated into North Korea to find food. North Korea's 1990s famine saw a reverse of their direction of migration back to China. The famine and subsequent economic shocks in North Korea led to spikes in defection numbers throughout the 1990s up to 2012, when Kim Jong Un took power and cracked down on border crossings.

The China–North Korea border is often depicted as a location for refugee migration patterns that are recent, particularly since the famine of the 1990s, but this is not the case.[21] Indeed, an increased number of North Koreans have crossed since the 1990s, but there is a history of loose legal agreements between China and North Korea. What was new in the 1990s, international relations scholar Hazel Smith observes, is that ethnic Koreans in China would previously migrate into and out of North Korea. During the famine, the migration was outward to China.[22] The two governments communicated about border migration as early as 1957 through to the 1970s. Topics such as marriage between North Korean women and Chinese men, ethnic Koreans crossing into North Korea for reasons of ethnicity, crime across borders, and even the Chinese Great Leap Forward were discussed between the two states.[23] North Korea had work opportunities for ethnic Koreans who were living in enclaves in China's border area. At the time North Korea had labor shortages, and because most ethnic Koreans spoke the language, they were a natural fit to fill the gap. Migration was not ideologically motivated but driven by the need for work and food.[24]

In 1964 the two countries agreed to a protocol that distinguished types of border crossers and how they should be returned. Criminals were to be returned, but if people were driven across because of disaster, they "should be assisted."[25] The protocol also allowed for the exchange of information about infection and disease, the return of corpses discovered in the border region, and other concerns. The 1964 protocol, like the revised protocol that would come later in 1986, has a friendly tenor. A protocol between North Korea and China is still in place today, establishing when and who should be returned as well as how to deal with illegal border crossings.[26] Permission is given in clause 7 to "fire guns or release police dogs . . . [in] . . . special circumstances such as when the safety of their own lives is put in peril by an antirevolutionary element attempting destructive activities," which could be interpreted as permission to shoot to kill.[27] Prior to the 2000s, according to the agreement of the protocol, China returned North Koreans if they were criminals or individuals who had engaged in criminal activity in China. China's Jilin Province, where there are many ethnic Koreans, also has a local law that requires the return of North Koreans who enter illegally. This bilateral agreement and the Jilin law are in clear violation of the UN Refugee Convention. Collective deportation of non-nationals has been held to be prima facie discriminatory. States are obliged to ensure noncitizens are sufficiently guaranteed protection for personal circumstances if they are long-term residents or have family ties in the country. Furthermore, no country may refoul an individual if there is a well-founded fear of persecution upon return. The Convention Against Torture and Other Cruel, Inhuman or Degrading Treatment or Punishment, entered into force in 1987 and ratified by 146 countries, requires states to ensure that torture does not occur within their borders and prevents the forcible return of a person to a country where there are substantial grounds to believe an individual could be tortured. States may not discriminate against persons of any particular nationality. The International Covenant on Economic, Social and Cultural Rights establishes that states shall in general protect the rights of all people regardless of citizenship so that they can work in good working conditions and have an adequate standard of living. The covenant permits developing countries to determine to what extent they guarantee the economic rights of non-nationals.[28] China and North Korea's agreement on this issue is therefore in violation of these important covenants.

The precipitating factors that led North Koreans to migrate into China are highly complex, but trends can be identified over time. Severe socioeconomic stresses are push factors for migrants, even when borders are guarded by soldiers who shoot to kill.

During the 1990s the main cause for defection was linked to the famine. Later, during the 2000s, defections have been identified as "economic." However, both of these periods of defection are economic in nature; rather, it is the degree of hardship that is different. Digging deeper, as I did in my field research, we see the famine contributed factors that made living very difficult: illness, disease, domestic violence, alcoholism, abandoned children, and so on. While many North Koreans left for what we could identify as "economic" reasons, it is not common for North Koreans to identify these causes as having political underpinnings. A woman who is experiencing domestic violence at the hands of her husband, for example, has no legal avenue for redress in North Korea. Such individuals may opt to cross into China for a better life. Others cross into China with the assumption that crossing will be temporary, only to discover once there that they cannot return to North Korea without danger.

After the 1990s the reasons for North Korean migration have fallen generally into two categories. There are those North Koreans who are connected to the "straight shot" defection, which has come about as defectors who successfully arrived in South Korea are now bringing family members out. The brokered connection for this is fairly well established. Then there are those North Koreans who attribute "economic reasons" for their defection—here we see individuals who recognize that they can have a better life economically if they cross into China, and this is often divorced from politics. What has changed is that the migration is less directly attributed to food, but inadvertently it is connected to the same sociopolitical inequalities that brought the famine to the North. There are of course a small number of North Koreans who pass into China in hopes of reaching South Korea, and who do so for political reasons or reasons of political persecution. This group is very small, in my estimation and according to my research. So it seems there was the first wave that came as a result of the famine and its concomitant difficulties, and then there was a second wave that came after the failed economic reforms of 2002.

As large numbers of North Koreans began to cross into China in the 1990s, often to stay or move onward, China ended its general tolerance of Koreans in its territory and began returning large numbers. At the time, and now, China maintained that North Koreans in China are not refugees (nànmín) but rather economic migrants (jīngjì yímín), for whom the UN Refugee Convention does not apply. They are defined out of the convention. But there is no national procedure in China and no cooperation with the UN High Commissioner for Refugees (UNHCR) to produce an agreement that could help determine whether North Korean individuals are refugees. In an interview debate with Phoenix TV News, Dr. Huang Yun Song of Sichuan University explained that China lacks the mechanisms for screening refugees.[29] What complicates this matter further is the fact that North Koreans are legally dual nationals because of the wording of the South Korean constitution. This added dimension of complexity is something China is aware of, and it situates China in a tricky position between the two Koreas. Thus, the Chinese government feels it is safer to justify its denial of North Koreans as refugees because they have left their country for economic reasons, which is outside the terms of the UN Refugee Convention.[30]

There is no basis for China's claim that refugee status cannot apply to North Koreans. According to the UNHCR, any North Korean who has fled to China should have a prima facie claim to refugee status because they risk persecution *for having left* the North, a recognized fundamental right recognized in international human rights law.[31] Having economic motives for departure does not disqualify an individual from refugee protection if they face the likelihood of persecution upon their return. China violates the most fundamental obligation of international refugee law by taking no action to assess refugees on an individual basis; further, it contravenes the prohibition against forced return by refouling North Koreans. Adherence to Article 33 requires individual assessment. A "denial of protection in the absence of a review of individual circumstances would be inconsistent with the prohibition of refoulement."[32] Article 33 also prohibits forced return (refoulement). This prohibition is so fundamental that human rights advocates argue it reaches the level of customary international law and should be binding to states that are not even parties to the convention or protocol. Like the prohibition against slavery or genocide, it is a principle from which no state is permitted to deviate.

Embracing Loss and Illegality

Few things are more emblematic of North Korea's failure to provide for its citizens than the fact that its people will risk everything to defect, as demonstrated by the young Mr. Oh in the vignette that opens this chapter. The individual's act of moving from one sovereign territory to another, propelled by the nation's failure to uphold economic and civil rights, signals a crisis of human rights within the country. These individuals face further burdens whether as unrecognized refugees in China and third countries or in terms of basic mental and physical health once they settle in South Korea, Japan, or further afield. These knock-on effects are due to the constellation of human rights failures in North Korea. The disturbingly grotesque images of the long roundworms found in

Mr. Oh's intestines, typically contracted through eating food grown in human feces, testify to the poor agricultural conditions in North Korea that effect even the reasonably well-off Songbun classes. The agricultural and health conditions are an indictment of the North Korean state.

As mentioned, North Korea's de facto ban on citizens' right to travel out of the country means that individuals break national laws of several countries as they defect. This effectively means that the "state-citizen contract" between North Korea and its citizens is in conflict. The breakdown of domestic law leads to breakdowns between citizens and nations.[33] As a combination, these factors lead to a situation where North Koreans are not able to avail themselves of rights through official refugee status. As such, their physical journey through the region is much more circuitous than that of Oh's. Figure 6.1, a map modified by political science professor Jiyoung Song, demonstrates the great distances most North Koreans must travel to finally achieve legal status in South Korea.[34]

North Koreans are prevented from accessing rights because of geopolitical dynamics in the region and the inability to make the covenants of international human rights law binding. At the precise moment when North Koreans engage individual agency, when they throw off the net of their nation, which does not

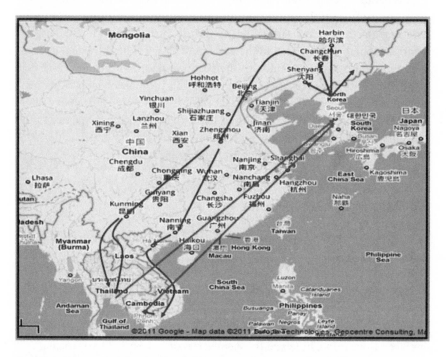

6.1 Migratory routes taken by North Koreans on their way to South Korea

Song Jiyoung, "The Complexity of North Korean Migration," *Asia Pacific Memo*, no. 229 (June 6, 2013), http://apm.iar.ubc.ca/the-complexity-of-north-korean-migration/

protect their rights, the international community confronts its inability to do anything. Precisely at the point when North Koreans lose everything—home, networks, statehood—is when they need human rights the most. And yet it is at this moment of being and having nothing but their humanity that they cannot gain access to human rights. They move from a place where their rights were not protected to a bigger space within the "family of nations" that excludes them from basic legality and basic humanity. This is the recurring contradiction at the heart of human rights. States are the primary abusers of rights, and yet they are also tasked with being the primary protectors of human rights. Political philosopher Hannah Arendt observed this flaw in 1951. Departing from the one nation to which they belonged, refugees are cast on the shores of the global network of nation-states. In that sphere, Arendt notes, they are compelled to engage in illegality to gain legality. There are few means of achieving legality in a world that has cast you out of legality altogether. The North Korean migrant is pushed into one of two situations. Either she transforms herself into a spectacle, hyperpoliticizing her actions in order to achieve recognition of her being, pressing states to recognize her. Or she lives in shadows, waiting, hoping she may one day safely access legality.

The person without the protection of their nation-state, the one who lives in a foreign land, has few alternatives. The options are thus: "either he violates the law of the country where he resides . . . or he violates the law of the country to which he is expelled."[35] What we have with the refugee is the ultimate embodiment of a subject for whom the very idea of human rights should find a perfect suitability. Yet refugees, instead of indicating the supreme success of the ideas of international human rights values, indicate their profound crisis.[36] At the point of leaving the North, many have nothing left in their possession but their humanity; their life is testament to the fact that human rights are not contained within one's being. Human rights are not born with us the way nationhood might be. We do not have or possess human rights but are only possibly able to access them upon certain conditions.

For the North Korean migrating into China, it is only through illegal acts that enable her to compel states to legally embrace her that her status as a refugee might possibly be achieved.

Breaking into the Law

The world's media attention was drawn to the plight of North Koreans in China in the early 2000s through embassy-storming activities organized by activists. On March 14, 2002, a group of twenty-five North Korean refugees jumped the walls of the Spanish embassy in Beijing, seeking political asylum and threatening suicide if they were sent back to North Korea. The twenty-five were made up of six families, including eight children. Around this same time, five North Koreans gained access to a U.S. mission in Beijing. Forty-four North Koreans pretending to be window-cleaning staff gained entry to the Canadian Embassy in Beijing on September 29, 2004. Prior to this two smaller groups of North Koreans gained entry to the Canadian Embassy in Beijing. Just a few weeks earlier eleven men, fifteen women, and three children from North Korea climbed cement walls and cut a metal fence to gain entry to a Japanese school in the same city.[37] They were transferred to the Japanese Embassy and sought asylum. North Koreans who successfully crossed through China to third countries jumped embassy walls elsewhere. In late September 2009 nine North Koreans entered the Danish Embassy in Hanoi, Vietnam, seeking political asylum and passage to Seoul.[38] Jumping embassy walls had a confusing effect on intelligence and diplomatic communications at the time. Thai intelligence thought the UNHCR was involved in trafficking North Koreans into Thailand. In fact, the UNHCR was facilitating refugees to South Korea via Thailand in order to reduce the likelihood of more cases of people jumping into embassy compounds.[39]

The embassy-storming activities led China to circulate memoranda to embassies in May 2002, contrary to the UNHCR mandate. China's diplomatic memorandum to all foreign embassies and missions in the country stated that safety and national security issues were being threatened by these intrusions. The memorandum asked foreign governments to "inform the Consular Department of the Chinese Ministry of Foreign Affairs in case the illegal intruders were found, and hand over the intruders to the Chinese public security organs."[40] In response to this, the UNHCR released a statement informing embassies that handing over North Koreans to Chinese authorities is an act tantamount to refoulement. The vast majority of embassies ignored China's demand.

In August 2002 a group of seven North Koreans approached the Chinese Ministry of Foreign Affairs and handed guards papers expressing their interest in applying for asylum. Chinese police arrested all seven. Known as "the MoFA 7," they have not been heard from since.[41] Since the mid-1990s the Chinese government and DPRK agents in China have reportedly captured refugees and those helping them.[42] When international media covered the refugee actions in 2002, China cracked down harder on North Korean illegal migration, searching safe houses and international airports for refugees who were intent on reaching South Korea. NGOs or religious groups with any connection to North Koreans continue to be targeted.[43]

Activists tried to provoke a "coercive engineered migration" on the Sino-Korea border in the early 2000s, mirroring a pattern of migration that occurred when Hungary opened its border with Austria, allowing East German tourists to escape communism; it was regime change by "refugee flow."[44] Behind the push for public attention to the refugees was the hope that China would be coerced by public pressure into building refugee camps along the Sino-Korean border, reducing the risks to life facing many North Koreans. China was having none of it and began a campaign to return North Koreans.

The mass refugee spectacle was also driven by the hope that, with enough people fleeing, North Korea would soon collapse. Further afield, in the United States, similar thinking prevailed that outward migration was an opportunity to hasten the fall of the regime. As political scientist Kelly M. Greenhill observes, a group of Bush administration officials made up of policy makers and legislators from both Democratic and Republican divides, along with Christian groups, pressured China against repatriating North Koreans with the hope that establishing camps might lead to a steady outward flow of people. There was talk of resettling North Korean refugees from China into the United States and other countries to "hasten the fall."[45]

The Chinese and North Koreans viewed this public display as the politicizing of human rights and the radicalizing of subjects. "We believe that politicizing human rights issues is not conducive towards improving a country's human rights," a spokesperson for the Chinese Foreign Ministry explained in early 2014.[46] He further elaborated by stating that taking such issues to the International Criminal Court is not helpful to improve human rights within a country like North Korea. Actions taken by activists in China, geared at saving North Koreans, led to wide-reaching crackdowns on the border and enforcement of formerly overlooked official agreements between the two states.[47] "Naming and shaming" campaigns aimed at China, which hoped to improve the lives of people suffering violations, and at North Korea, while said to be anecdotally helpful, have not been proven to be effective.[48] China "responded by severely implementing the provisions of the Protocol, rounding up and sending hundreds of North Koreans who had previously lived illegally but relatively securely in China, some for several years."[49]

Those who successfully scale embassy walls generate pressure in the form of a political crackdown from the state that descends on their brethren still in hiding throughout China. But they also force a face-to-face encounter between themselves and the state apparatus via the diplomatic channel, which compels norm-abiding states to permit their application for refugee status. Contrary to popular belief, diplomatic missions and embassies do not enjoy full extraterritorial rights; they are not the sovereign territory of those countries they represent but are rather bound to the laws of the host country. Their physical territory, however, is not to be trespassed by the host country unless given permission by the represented country. For this reason, refugees sometimes use embassies to escape the host country, with the arm of local laws being unable to reach within; diplomatic channels can thus be used to resolve the refugee problem. However, even this is not secure. Violations of embassy extraterritoriality have occurred.

North Koreans are compelled to break national and international laws repeatedly in an effort to access the legal instruments of human rights. In the course of any one individual defector's journey, the individual is compelled to act criminally to achieve legal human rights. She breaks North Korean national laws by crossing into China, becoming a traitor (traitorous, a terrorist) to her nation. Once in China, an assessment of her refugee status with the guidance of the UNHCR is not granted. By defining her as an economic migrant, China turns North Koreans into illegal migrants. Yet she is "inside" the jurisdiction of China's national laws; as such, the only route to full human rights, with reasonable safety but great risk, is through illegal channels such as jumping embassy walls.

She must seek out a broker or some other illicit system such as a false passport to gain entry to another country.[50] Perhaps she will purchase false papers, or she will trespass onto the premises of a foreign embassy, or she will travel and cross secretly to a third country. If she marries and has children, they are likely to inherit her precarious status, making legal access to education, health, and travel almost impossible. She has no right to rights; she is not within a community, and no law exists for her.[51] If she wants to activate her rights, she is compelled to wrest them from the sovereign by becoming criminal because she is, as Arendt observes, "outside the jurisdiction of these laws and without being protected by any other. The stateless person, without right to residence and without the right to work, had of course constantly to transgress the law."[52] By transgressing the law, the refugee enables it to include her, to provide for her act of criminality. "The criminal offense becomes the best opportunity to regain some kind of human equality, even if it be as a recognized exception to the norm. The one important fact is that this exception is provided for by the law."[53] Through state structures beyond their control, North Koreans are forced to become outlaws.

China and DPRK attempt to contain the migrants through state-level agreements defining what is excluded by law. North Koreans in China are "not, in fact, simply set outside the law and made indifferent to it but rather abandoned by it, that is, exposed and threatened on the threshold in which life and law, outside and inside, become indistinguishable."[54] This creates fault lines of power as access to human rights are practiced and interpreted, as abandoned by the law on the ground. The sovereign states withhold or grant human rights according to social conditions determined by a "web of hidden agendas."[55]

The Experience of Statelessness

There is safety in invisibility. Being stateless does not necessarily imply that an individual is automatically a victim. As rights scholar Bela Hovy observes, "millions of people continue to live and work outside their country of citizenship without discrimination."[56] So while all North Koreans in China are vulnerable to abuse, not all face abuse or the same type of abuse once in China. The pull factors offered by China such as access to food, medicine, and information can be had by North Korean refugees so long as they do not raise the attention of Chinese authorities. Not drawing attention to the self, being invisible and compliant, are aspects of life within North Korea. To continue life in that manner but in an environment that offers greater access to necessities may not be interpreted as radically illogical. And besides, when the state is so often troublesome to you, why bother with official methods of dealing with things? This goes some way to explaining why many North Koreans are willing to take the risk of going to China in the first place. That said, China offers different aspects of vulnerability to North Koreans, and different consequences for criminalized behavior than their home state, creating opportunities for new, unanticipated kinds of victimization.

Our embodiment impacts the types of rights violations we may be subjected to. For women and children, for example, the violations are often more severe. These groups are more likely to be trafficked for sexual exploitation. Women and children are biologically more likely to be at risk, with diminished or no access to basic health care and education. Within any category, children occupy the most vulnerable position in terms of rights, and yet there are human rights instruments aimed at children such as the Universal Declaration of Human Rights and the Convention on the Rights of the Child, and organizations such as the United Nations International Children's Emergency Fund (UNICEF) and Plan International, a development and humanitarian organization that advances equality for girls. But the rights of children remain particularly precarious. When children cross borders, they are open to a host of additional vulnerabilities. While North Korea claims that children are valued, their ability to access rights is nonetheless precarious. Children who cross into China may not represent those worst off in North Korea, but once in China, whether they remain in the territory or cross back and forth, they face a new set of rights violations within the international arena.

Statelessness is a problem facing children without a nationality, the de jure or legally stateless. However, it also applies to children who due to irregular migration are de facto stateless—"stateless in the sense that despite having a nationality, they cannot turn to the state in which they live for protection or assistance."[57] Another category of children are those who are effectively stateless, "children who have both a nationality and legal status but cannot prove either, typically because their birth is not registered."[58] Stateless children— whether because they cannot prove their citizenship or because they effectively have none—present the same human rights challenge.

Most defectors in South Korea and China originally migrate from the small northern towns and provinces of North Korea. This is also where a large proportion of homeless and begging children have been identified. Called Kotjebi (flowering swallows), homeless children live in packs, steal for their livelihoods, skip school, and suffer abuse. Access to health services, not to mention food and a fixed residence, is particularly precarious for these children.[59] Rates of tuberculosis among children in North Korea are not well known, but a World Health Organization report from 2014 claimed that 1.9 percent (2,090) of the 110,000 tuberculosis cases in 2013 were children.[60] Rates of tuberculosis among homeless children in the northern provinces are likely to be significant as this region was worst hit by the famine, is low-priority in state distribution of resources due to categories of Songbun, and has suffered a slow recovery.

Children are among the most vulnerable citizens in North Korea, and this vulnerability increases when they cross into China, casting off access to the North Korean state for the life of an illegal migrant in China. Brad Blitz highlights the dearth of analysis on what it means to be a child citizen. "Little political consideration has been given to what it means for a child to be a citizen. This is surprising given that many of the cardinal formal attributes of citizenship—including the right to vote, to serve on a jury, and to stand for public office—are denied children. No other group of citizens in the developed world today has such legally sanctioned partial access to the benefits of membership."[61] Christina Alfirev further identifies that children are often easily moved across borders as if without any sense that there may be an economic, social, and political price to the child.[62]

North Koreans who cross into China on foot, walking and wading through the Tumen River, which acts as a natural border between China and North Korea, often travel at night to avoid detection. Some people travel with children and infants or in groups. Drawing any attention to the act of crossing can be fatal. Travelers with children and babies reportedly dose them with sleeping pills, "a must-feed item for young children, despite the obvious dangers" to ensure clandestine passage for the whole team.[63] Not recognized as refugees by the People's Republic of China; they are compelled to migrate further; crossing still more borders into neighboring countries such as Mongolia or through Southeast Asia.[64]

If they are unable to access opportunities through official registration, North Korean children in China face daily, sustained deprivations that have consequences.[65] Technically, children born of North Korean women in China to a Chinese national father are entitled to Chinese citizenship under constitutional law.[66] A person born in China to at least one parent who is a Chinese national is a Chinese citizen. Significantly for the case of children born to a North Korean parent and a Chinese citizen in China, Article 6 of China's Nationality Law states that a person born in China to stateless parents or parents of uncertain nationality who have settled in China will have Chinese citizenship. This law provides much-needed relief from intergenerational statelessness, but it is worth noting that this law still does not provide protection for vulnerable migrants more generally.

The number of North Korean migrants in China is estimated to be between 30,000 and 300,000—a wide range.[67] The U.S. State Department, in a 2005 report, estimated the number at between 30,000 and 50,000.[68] In 2005 aid groups, popular presses, and governments estimated that about 150,000 to 300,000 North Korean migrants were in China.[69] The variation in numbers identifies the inability to accurately survey these vulnerable populations due to Chinese law. At present, 32,147 North Koreans have defected and settled in South Korea. Approximately about 200 have been granted special residence in Japan. The United States admitted 122 North Koreans—with 25 granted political asylum since the country adopted the North Korea Human Rights Act in 2004—and across Europe and Asia about 2,000 have been granted refuge.[70] Totaling these numbers and comparing with the number of North Koreans who remain at home reveals that defectors constitute a tiny portion of the overall population. However, the numbers indicate a migration pattern driven by socio-economic need: they are characterized as female (82 percent in 2014), between the ages of twenty and thirty-nine (58.2 percent in 2014), and unemployed or supported by someone else when in North Korea (48.4 percent in 2014).[71] Border-crossing migrants constitute a self-selecting minority that migrate for economic and social needs; only rarely do they overtly identify political persecution as a push factor, although political persecution is linked with the absence of socioeconomic rights.

It is impossible to assess the number of North Korean refugees in China. China does not recognize North Koreans as refugees, and there is no legal means to conduct a census among migrating populations from North Korea in the region. In 2013, 93,300 work visas were given to North Korean citizens in China, and 206,600 visits were made to China by North Koreans as tourists (some of these could have been repeat visitors).[72] Many North Koreans try to blend in with the community of Chosunjok living along the Sino-DPRK border, often learning to speak Chinese or marrying Chinese farmers. There is a possibility that they will blend in; sometimes defectors live out decades in such conditions. However, many North Korean refugees recall that their memories of life in China are far worse than memories of North Korea.[73] Based on extensive interviews with North Koreans in China and elsewhere, Refugees International notes that "almost all North Koreans face severe punishment upon deportation, regardless of their original motivation for leaving their country."[74]

China, despite being a signatory to international conventions on human rights, turns a blind eye to trafficking in women, forcefully repatriates North Koreans, and is generally inhospitable to North Korean refugees who, as a result of state failure to act, live in permanent fear of being captured and punished in China or North Korea.[75] The employment situation of North Koreans in China is extremely precarious, as is the condition of women and children. Abuse, trafficking, and other forms of exploitation are often facts of life that illegal migrants must endure; otherwise there is the risk of being repatriated to North Korea. North Koreans often have limited linguistic ability with Chinese. Longer periods of time in China may provide opportunities to improve their Chinese language ability, which has beneficial consequences for "passing" as Chinese. An environment of suspicion, encouraged by Chinese government payouts to those who catch North Korean "illegal migrants," pervades the Sino-Korean border area. This in turn generates difficulty in finding connections and establishing trustworthy alliances. Among the network of North Korean defectors in China—those who are in contact with one another—there is also great suspicion. The "true" identity of the person when they were back in North Korea is suspect—this response could be the result of mutual surveillance and distrust in North Korea combined with the legitimate concerns of capture and return. The North Korean government sends intelligence officials into China to capture defectors.[76]

Alternate Routes and New Dangers in Mongolia and Southeast Asia

Because of the complexity of achieving legitimacy in China, North Koreans are compelled to live a life of hiding or to migrate further into the continent on a circuitous route to South Korea. If traveling by land, most North Korean refugees must pass through China. At least two geopolitical factors have led NGO networks to facilitate the movement of North Koreans through China. First, the flow of North Korean refugees has been gradual but relatively sustained. Second, China's refusal to identify them as refugees has led NGOs to set up secret networks to facilitate the movement of North Koreans through China to bordering countries such as Thailand, Laos, Vietnam, and Cambodia, with the aim of achieving permanent settlement in South Korea, Japan, the United States, or elsewhere. The migration of North Koreans throughout the region, particularly when it catches media attention, generates political tension between the countries involved. Human security concerns are something many countries in the region would rather deal with silently and invisibly as domestic matters.

There are two primary routes out of China. The first is a northern route to Mongolia and, more exceptionally, Russia, which usually takes at least two days by train. The second route is over land and/or river to Southeast Asia.[77] Political scientist Jiyoung Song notes that most North Koreans make use of China and Southeast Asia via human smuggling networks with Thailand, the Philippines, Vietnam, Cambodia, and Myanmar as transit countries.[78] Some individuals may initially be sold as brides, Jiyoung Song notes, but then may turn into brokers as necessity or opportunity permits.

Yeonmi Park defected from North Korea with her mother at a young age. In her memoir *In Order to Live*, she tells of the easy slippage between being a trafficked girl and being a trafficker. "I had to pretend I was much older, because the women wouldn't listen to a thirteen-year-old girl. My job was to translate for them, buy tickets or hire taxis to bring them back to Hongwei [her "owner"], and persuade them to cooperate if they wanted to stay in China."[79] Many of the women suffer terrible consequences as a result of these experiences. It is not surprising that they might seek to keep migrating to find a better place. For Yeonmi and her mother, this was possible after years of working in illicit online sex chat rooms to make money and connections. Learning they could have a safe place to live and work in South Korea, she and her mother made the decision to try to reach the South via Mongolia. A group of religious activists helped Yeonmi and her mother.

Yeonmi writes, "Mongolia's state policy was to allow North Korean refugees from China safe passage to a third country, but events on the ground were much murkier."[80] Because Mongolia was a former satellite state of the Soviet Union, its relations with the DPRK and South Korea are complex. Since the 2000s North Korean refugees have fled the DPRK via China and sought asylum in Mongolia. The choice to migrate north to Mongolia was largely inspired by the belief that they would be better off there than in China. Russia and Eurasia analyst for the Sino-NK research group Anthony V. Rinna explains that Mongolia was operating for a time as an "underground railroad." These quiet rescue efforts were terminated after Chinese police intercepted the journey of twenty-nine North Korean refugees, repatriating them.[81] There were reports that Mongolia intended to build a refugee camp for North Koreans in the eastern province of Dornod.[82] Mongolia denies these claims on the grounds that it is not a signatory to the UN Refugee Convention.[83] Recall that even nonconvention countries are bound by the principle of nonrefoulement. The UN Refugee Convention is binding on all states as part of customary international law. Even if this were not the case, Mongolia's constitution asserts that "foreign citizens or stateless persons persecuted for their beliefs, or political or other activities and who are pursuing justice, may be granted asylum in Mongolia on the basis of their well-founded requests."[84] Through the Law on the Status of Foreign Citizens, "foreigners nationals shall have the right to seek political asylum."[85] In an unusual twist of logic, Bat-Erdeniin Batbayar, the Mongolian chairman of the Northeast Asian Association—an NGO involved in DPRK-Mongolian relations—expressed that it would be in Mongolia's interest to invite laborers from North Korea rather than to accept refugees.[86] Foreign laborers and refugees, while both migrants, are complex categories of non-nationals. The problem that causes North Koreans to out-migrate will not be resolved through inviting laborers who, as selected elites, are earning money in the service of the North Korean state. The proposal is totally incoherent.

As a policy of multiple tracks of engagement, people-to-people activities can be useful but can hardly resolve a migration crisis. After Kim Jong Un took power, the first head of state to reach out was Mongolian president Tsakhiagiin Elbegdorj, who visited Pyongyang in 2013. Since that time, Mongolia continues to pursue cultural engagement, in the form of academic exchanges, women's parliamentary exchanges, and mayoral forums.[87] These are likely doubling as efforts to keep channels of communication open between the two states. The most sensitive issue is the refugee problem.[88] Mongolian government agencies don't wish to publicize information about how many refugees arrive due to concern for the refugees and relations between the states.[89] Some estimates claim that at least six hundred North Koreans now settled in South Korea arrived there via Mongolia.[90] Foreign Minister Tsend Munh-Orgil clarified that Mongolia's police border guards are under instruction not to send the refugees, *no matter whom*, back into China.[91] South Korea's consistent open-door policy to North Korean refugees is an indictment against states like Mongolia that do not facilitate passage of North Koreans.

Cambodia, a party to the UN Refugee Convention and its protocol, has diplomatic relations with both Koreas. In July of 2016 local newspapers reported that North Korea sent operatives to terrorize defectors.[92] The action was in response to the defection of thirteen North Korean employees from a North Korean state-run restaurant in China. Of Southeast Asian countries, Cambodia and Laos have the closest ties with North Korea, and a North Korean citizen traveling there is not unusual. North Korea could have learned the details of the transfer of refugees via WikiLeaks diplomatic cables that—written with the assumption of security—carried names, gender, and ages of defectors. Although Cambodia has a track record of deporting other refugees—for instance, refouling twenty Uighurs to China in 2009—some evidence suggests Cambodia has provided North Korean defectors secret passage to South Korea via diplomatic channels.[93]

In 2012 a waitress from the Phnom Penh–based Restaurant Pyongyang defected to South Korea via Thailand.[94] Leaked diplomatic cables indicate that the U.S. Embassy in Thailand has tried to assist North Korean refugees in Cambodia but that Thailand has had a record of not helping defectors.[95] Thailand has not ratified the UN Refugee Convention or its protocol and does not recognize refugees. The Thai government claims to observe the convention in practice and applies a humanitarian approach to persons of concern.[96] They have diplomatic relations with both Koreas. Thai government officials block the work of the UN High Commissioner of Refugees. According to Human Rights Watch, UN workers were not allowed to conduct status determinations for individuals appealing for refugee status.[97] In 2006 Winai Phattiyakul, head of the Thai National Security Council, expressed concern about media coverage of North Korean refugee movement through Thailand.[98] Thai government policy, he stated, was to work with the United States on a discreet, case-by-case basis. Not wishing to raise the ire of North Korea, and with the possible aim of helping refugees from North Korea based in Laos, Phattiyakul stressed the importance of having no publicity. Revealing the complexity of managing geopolitical dynamics in the media glare, the same WikiLeaks cable identifies South Korean religious leader Rev. Chun Ki-Won as saying that the South Korean government leaked the story of North Korean refugees at the U.S. Embassy in Bangkok to the media. It reads: "Reverend Choi said the ROKG wanted to stop the movement of North Korean refugees to the United States and so was publicizing the presence of the North Koreans in Thailand who had approached the U.S. Embassy."[99]

Other Southeast Asian countries face similar complexities with respect to North Korean refugees within their borders. Laos is not a party to the UN Refugee Convention or its protocol. It has diplomatic relations with both Koreas. South Korea's *JoongAng Daily* newspaper reported that North Korea is sending operatives to Laos, as they had in Cambodia, to attack defectors and South Koreans.[100] As it does with anyone who defects from state-run enterprises overseas, North Korea accuses South Korea of abducting these individuals.[101]

Vietnam is a party to almost all core international human rights treaties, but it is not party to the UN Refugee Convention, its protocol, the 1954 Convention Relating to the Status of Stateless Persons, or the 1961 Convention on the Reduction of Statelessness. Vietnam has diplomatic relations with both Koreas. Leaked diplomatic cables from 2003 indicate that the Vietnamese government "generally does not take much note of North Korean refugees unless they cause a disturbance or generate 'political difficulty' by attempting to apply for refugee status or asylum while in Vietnam."[102] Once again, the necessity for North Koreans to not draw attention to themselves was identified as critical to ensure their safe passage to Cambodia. In July 2004 the Vietnamese government granted passage to 468 North Korean refugees. The South Korean government organized the mass airlift to take the group to Korea. The plan was a success but leaked to the media just prior to its operation.[103] Following this public incident in 2004, the underground railway via Vietnam all but disappeared. The incident "infuriated" Pyongyang, a fact that led Seoul to not take such public actions again.[104] Ten years on, Vietnam is accused of returning North Korean defectors to China.[105] Not having the proper documentation, many who try to access the UNHCR in Hanoi are returned to the point of entry, usually China.[106]

Myanmar is not party to the UN Refugee Convention or its protocol either. It has diplomatic relations with both Koreas but has senior-level exchanges with North Korea. Existing ethnic conflicts in Myanmar means that North Korean refugees there face particular vulnerabilities. In 2013 the South Korean newspaper *Dong-a Ilbo* reported that sixty-four North Korean refugees were being held by Myanmar militia groups.[107] An activist visited the site where they were held and identified twenty-five people who had died as a result of forced labor and illness. Concerned about the status of North Korean rights in the country in November 2008, Australian ambassador Michelle Chan brought up the issue with her North Korean counterpart in Yangon. Chan reported, "The DPRK Ambassador stressed (with a straight face) that except for Embassy officials, there is 'not one single North Korean' in Burma."[108] Concerning South Korean resettlement of North Korean refugees, the cable postulates the potential impact:

> The ROK DCM [Republic of Korea Deputy Chief of Mission] cited concerns that Burma's tilt toward North Korea could result in a decrease in GOB [Government of Burma] cooperation with his Embassy in facilitating the transfer of North Korean refugees from Burma to South Korea. The DCM reported that about 50 DPRK refugees a year show up at the ROK Embassy in Rangoon, having traveled over land from China. To date GOB immigration authorities have allowed the refugees to board flights for South Korea bearing provisional ROK passports. The cooperation has been on an ad hoc basis, which means it could quickly be reversed. The South Korean DCM noted that on two occasions North Korean refugees have been arrested and imprisoned on charges of illegally entering the country. In the first case the GOB eventually turned the refugee over to ROK officials for onward transit to South Korea. In the more recent case, however, the refugee remains in prison and GOB officials have so far refused to cooperate with the ROK Embassy, insisting that they first need approval from the North Koreans to release the individual.[109]

The Philippines, on the other hand, has worked with the United States to process North Korean refugees.[110] Some North Koreans have worked clandestinely in China and earned enough money to purchase illegal South Korean passports on the black market and have flown to the Philippines to request asylum in the United States and South Korea.[111]

The North Korean Refugee on the World Stage

An individual with more than one nationality must have a well-founded fear of persecution in each country of his or her nationality in order to be considered a refugee in need of international protection, according to the 1951 UN Refugee Convention. As noted in the UNHCR Handbook, this provision is "intended to exclude from refugee status all persons with dual or multiple nationalities that can avail themselves of the protection of at least one of the countries of which they are nationals." The Handbook further discusses the requirement that such nationality be "effective" and that, in general, the individual should request such protection and be refused before such protection can be deemed ineffective. While the implementation of this clause has been debated among refugee scholars, virtually all North Koreans could theoretically avail themselves of the protection of South Korea since the South Korean constitution claims the entire peninsula as the Republic and all the people there as its citizens. For this reason, UNHCR officially refers to North Koreans in China and elsewhere as "persons of concern" rather than refugees. This technicality, however, should not in any way diminish the fact that most if not all North Koreans outside their country clearly meet the substantive definition of a refugee.

The United States occasionally granted asylum to very small numbers of North Koreans. They were processed through the U.S. asylum system for persons who apply on U.S. territory rather than being admitted as refugees from overseas. But under international and U.S. law, dual nationality is a bar to refugee protection unless the individual fears persecution in both countries of nationality, or unless the nationality of the nonpersecuting country is found to be "ineffective." At a congressional meeting Secretary of State Colin Powell said that the United States could not legally admit North Korean refugees because all North Koreans are entitled to South Korean citizenship under South Korea's constitution. If Powell's interpretation were correct, this would be a barrier to asylum status as well. However, even prior to the North Korean Human Rights Act (2004), to remedy the problem of seeming dual citizenship, Sen. Sam Brownback of Kansas, a leading human rights proponent, sponsored legislation that eventually became part of the act.

On the global and virtual scale, we see greater exchanges of material items and people, and yet our contemporary world is marked by the ways that individuals become stuck between sovereignty and access to human rights. While a nation is a physical and ideological construct, it binds its citizens' access to rights by compelling citizens to access rights through sovereign territory. Departure from the territory, if illegal, means the loss of representation in the attempt to access rights. Hannah Arendt's 1951 observation still identifies the most compellingly contradictory aspect of human rights: that the rights of man alone do not exist unless they are bound up in citizenship to a nation-state that respects them.

International obligations for refugees began with the 1951 Convention on the Status of Refugees (Refugee Convention 1951) and its 1967 protocol. According to the first article of the convention, a refugee is any person who,

> owing to a well-founded fear of being persecuted for reasons of race, religion, nationality, membership of a particular social group or political opinion, is outside the country of his nationality and is unable or, owing to such fear, is unwilling to avail himself of the protection of that country; or who, not having a nationality and being outside the country of his last habitual residence

as a result of such events, is unable or, owing to such fear, is unwilling to return to it. (Art. I, A[2])

The convention sets out a system for promoting adherence to its provisions, such as requiring parties to cooperate with the UNHCR in the exercise of its operation and facilitating their duty of supervision in the application of the provision. States establish procedures to assess refugee claims in accordance with their own legal systems. The UNHCR "advocates that governments adopt a rapid, flexible and liberal process, recognizing how difficult it often is to document persecution."[112] The UNHCR is not binding on states but is a persuasive authority and is often cited by domestic courts as well as in conclusions adopted by the Executive Committee of the High Commissioner's Program during its annual sessions. For example, the Executive Committee has recommended that: "As in the case of all requests for the determination of refugee status or the grant of asylum, the applicant should be given a complete personal interview by a fully qualified official and, whenever possible, by an official of the authority competent to determine refugee status."[113] The requirement that a person be outside his country to be a refugee does not require departure from that country illegally, or even that departure is based on a well-founded fear. A person may ask for recognition of refugee status after being abroad for some time. A person who was not a refugee when he left his country, but who becomes a refugee at a later date, is a refugee *sur place*. A person becomes a refugee *sur place* due to circumstances arising in his country or origin during his absence. A person's own actions may lead him or her to become a refugee *sur place*. The act of applying for asylum could, in some cases, be regarded in this context.

Timely and where possible individual assessments are encouraged to determine if someone is a refugee. The Geneva Convention presumes that parties to the convention institute a recognition procedure to identify refugees.[114] If there are disputes between parties regarding the interpretation or application of the convention, such disputes are to be referred to the International Court of Justice. Yet, the court has never heard a case arising under the UN Refugee Convention. The convention itself is silent on the type of refugee identification procedures that will suffice. How refugee identification is decided has been unclear since the convention was adopted.

CHAPTER 7

PRISON CAMPS, TORTURE, AND EXECUTION

We finished our work and we were about to pick up this grass we knew was edible. Then the guard saw us. He came running and stepped on our hands. He brought us to this spot and told us to kneel. In the camp, you only do the work you've been instructed to do. We'd committed a crime because we'd reached out to pick the plant. . . . He told one of the heads of the work unit, "Pick up the plant. The roots included. The soil included." So the unit leader unearthed these two plants with soil and roots and they put it in front of us. Then they told us to eat . . . We were begging. We were asking for forgiveness. But they kept beating us. So, Young Hee and I had to eat this plant.

—Jee Heon A at the UN Commission of Inquiry on Human Rights in the
　Democratic People's Republic of Korea

Young Hee's family, before the Korean War, came from Jeju Island. She was in prison because her parents had tried to leave North Korea but were caught in China. Dragged back to North Korea, they were executed before her eyes. She was put in prison, where she met broadcast journalist Jee Heon A. The two young women became friends in the prison and decided that they would one day escape and meet on Jeju Island.

After being force-fed the plants and soil, both Young Hee and Jee Heon got sick with diarrhea.

> I always told Young Hee that she had to make it to Jeju Island and I promised that we would make it together. But suddenly she collapsed because of a serious case of diarrhea. She couldn't get up. She couldn't even eat. She began to lose a lot of weight to the point where she couldn't get up and eat with her own hands. She was lying down all the time. She couldn't even move her body. She was close to dying. That's when Young Hee said, "*Unni* [older sister], I don't want to die, but I think I'm going to make it first to Jeju Island. *Unni* you have to make it to Jeju Island. I will be meeting you in Jeju Island." That's what she told me. I said no, but there was nothing I could do. I couldn't give her any medicine. When she died, she couldn't even close her eyes. She died with her eyes open. I cried my heart out.
>
> In a penicillin bottle I wrote her date of birth, the day she died, and her name. I hung the bottle around her neck. I tied her hair. [The other prisoners and I] tied her legs. Her arms. We wrapped her body in a plastic bag. This is what happens in a prison camp in North Korea. That's how we wrapped the dead bodies. When the warehouse has twenty dead bodies, we take those bodies to a place called the *Kkot Dong San*, the flower hill. We dig a hole that can fit twenty bodies, we bury them there.[1]

How did a broadcast journalist, someone with good social ranking in North Korea, end up in a prison camp being forced to eat soil and having to bury her friend in a mass grave? Her story starts in January 1981. While visiting China, Jee Heon A's father overheard a radio broadcast from South Korea's Korean Broadcasting Station. When he returned to North Korea he told his family about what he heard: that the world and South Korea was not as they had been told. Her father shared with her and the family the difference between what they had been told and what was going on in the world. He urged the family to leave with him. Regarding that suggestion Jee Heon A said, "I thought that my father was becoming a capitalist so I told him we could not leave. Betray our dear general? My father was very serious about leaving. He persuaded me."

As with many journeys into China, crossing a border that takes only a moment to throw a stone across, so too for Jee Heon A, whose journey stretched into years of illicit passage, secreted lives, and being sold, traded, abused, and finally returned to North Korea. Returned to North Korea, she was imprisoned and tortured. Her punishment provides us with a jumping-off point to understand the most egregious human rights violations in North Korea—the use of torture, imprisonment, and public execution to retaliate against undesirable or disobedient North Koreans.

Individualized Punishment

According to North Korean criminal law, the principal punishments and supplementary punishments in North Korea are short-term labor, limited term of reform through labor, lifetime of reform through labor, or the death penalty. Individuals can also be divested of their right to vote (although this is arguably a performative act rather than a consequential one in the DPRK), have their property taken away, be stripped of qualifications, or have qualifications suspended.[2] As stated in U.S. State Department's Trafficking in Persons report for 2016, "Forced labor is part of an established system of political repression. The government subjects its nationals to forced labor through mass mobilizations and in North Korean prison camps."[3] Forced labor brigades (*dolgyeokdae*) may even involve teenagers and children.[4] These punishments are ostensibly meant to "reeducate" North Koreans as to the appropriate socialist behavior or to punish those whom the state deems beyond help.

The presentation of collective well-being is crucial to the myth of North Korea's socialist self-reliant state, but this image of North Korea is at odds with the individualized nature of punishment there. Defector Kim Hyuk lived as a street kid in North Korea, starving and scavenging for food. His experience revealed to him the contradiction of a society where people are meant to care for everyone, but the weakest and most vulnerable suffer profoundly. He said, "Structure-wise, it is a collective society. In North Korea we have the saying, 'the organization for one; one for the organization,' which means that paradoxically the people have to give up their benefits and rights for one single individual. But I think there is a double interpretation which means that a single individual must sacrifice oneself in order to sustain the collective group of people."[5]

Unless self-sacrificing for the collective, the individual cannot be absorbed in the collective and is expelled. Socioeconomic coping strategies that set the individual apart from the collective such as enfranchisement, entrepreneurial activities, or private selling run counter to expectations of the state. Anyone who slips out of the collective by siphoning an existence that runs afoul of the strict controls of the state runs the risk of being severely punished.

Reduction of crime is not the only purpose of punishment. Rather, as theorist Michel Foucault argues, the "concrete systems of punishment" are a social phenomenon that extends beyond the juridical structure of society. They act not only to suppress and eliminate but also to produce positive useful effects for the society in which they emerge.[6] As Foucault terms it, punishment and prison are a "political technology" operationalized on the body. Politics is invested in control of the body, and the twisted logic of justice pursues it.[7] North Korea relies on a politics of political purity existing in the very cells of its people and, by extension, ethnic qua racial purity.[8] The need to control this imagined purity is visible in how pregnant women are treated if refouled from China. Jee Heon A reported at the public hearing how she and her fellow prisoners witnessed the miraculous birth of a baby, which they were then instructed to drown.

> There was this pregnant woman who was about 9 months pregnant. She worked all day. The babies who were born were usually dead, but in this case the baby was born alive. The baby was crying as it was born; we were so curious, this was the first time we saw a baby being born. So we were watching this baby and we were so happy. But suddenly we heard the footsteps. The security agent came in and this agent of the Bowibu said that . . . usually when a baby is born we would wash it in a bowl of water, but this agent told us to put the baby in the water upside down.[9]

A pregnant woman who returns from China is prima facie assumed to be carrying a mixed child.[10] The testimony of a former commissioner of the Women's Group in North Korea stated that there is a policy that pregnant women refouled from China, without exception and irrespective of the father's assumed ethnicity, undergo forced abortions.[11] These abortions are not arranged through any sort of hospital or medical procedure but through beatings and horrific abuse by guards. Various methods are used to force abortions on these women. Force may be applied to the outside of the woman's body causing pelvic trauma. She may be forced to do heavy physical work and deprived of food. She may be forced to insert chemical or abortifacient herbs into her vagina. The fetus may be killed by being stabbed with a tong-like apparatus. If premature labor is induced, the baby—dead or alive—will be discarded.[12] Such treatment of pregnant women and the unborn can occur in holding centers, interrogation rooms, and detention centers.

North Korea's own People's Safety Enforcement Law (1992), Article 50, clause 3, states that a woman who is pregnant cannot be detained, and she cannot be detained if she is as many as seven months postpartum.[13] By forcing pregnant women to undergo these brutal forms of torture, North Korean officials discriminate against women on the basis of gender and the assumed ethnic identity of the unborn child. Forced abortion causes extreme mental and physical suffering and meets the threshold for torture as defined in Article 1 of the Convention Against Torture, which supplies the definition of torture for Article 7 of the International Covenant on Civil and Political Rights (ICCPR).[14]

Testimony from defectors indicates that punishment is personalized to the weakest vulnerability of an individual or to some aspect of their person that singles them out. This can be seen in the way that people with disabilities are treated in North Korea and in detention facilities. It is apparent that North Korea is disciplining bodies that "go wrong" just as it must discipline minds that go ideologically "wrong." The treatment of people who are physically disabled and pregnant women who are assumed to be carrying Chinese-Korean babies resonates with eugenics-based practices that influenced Korea from Japan, Germany, and the United States.[15] In the following example, Ji Seong Ho describes how he was treated by police, who singled him out for his disability after he had made an illegal journey to China.

When the police came to Ji's house, they questioned him about going to China, beating him as they questioned him. The police reduced him to his physical disabilities by calling him a cripple. Something that should not be seen abroad is a disabled North Korean. Ji reported that, while beating him, the police expressed concern over whether he had been seen in China and whether foreign media had captured an image of him, implying that his very existence brought shame on North Korea.[16] This example is particularly poignant because Ji had severely injured his left hand and leg at the age of thirteen, when he fell from a moving train while trying to steal coal—coal he could sell to buy food for him and his family to survive the famine, a full decade prior to seeking food in China. If the government had not criminalized coping strategies, he would not have had to take the dangerous risks he did. Ji lucidly explained in his public hearing, "I became a disabled person because of the North Korean government. I wasn't born with a disability. I got disabled and I got these disabilities because of North Korea and they were torturing me because of that."[17] Ji became disabled as a result of the state, he suffered hunger and the loss of family members through starvation, but his survival strategy of begging in China, North Korean police believed, must be severely punished because his *being seen* by foreign media would bring collective shame to North Korea. The national interests of North Korea are best served when the international community knows as little as possible about what's happening inside and how the state operates.[18] The state's obsession with a theoretical presentation of an idealized self is a practice that pervades daily life, particularly where a foreign audience may be present.[19]

The police officers who beat Ji Seong Ho were already aware that survival tactics such as border crossing reflected badly on North Korea, but they went further and personalized their abuse of him by targeting his physical disabilities. They knew that a starving young man, begging on homemade wooden crutches, with a left hand and leg mutilated by a train accident, could not reflect the state's promise that it upholds economic and social rights. Ji reported that as the police beat him, they drew particular focus to his disabilities: "You look like hell, and you are a cripple, and then you beg for food in China. You are defaming North Korea. You are putting shame on the North Korean regime."[20] Ji heard the police connect his appearance, disability, and begging in China with shaming the North Korean state. He caused the state to lose face.

Ji Seong Ho could be left by the state to die because he is not valued. By border crossing, he transformed into something powerful vis-à-vis the state. The calculus is flipped. He becomes important, noticeable, and *vital* to North Korea by border crossing because his act risks revealing the truth of his condition and the atrocious system that produced it. By potentially *being seen*, Ji embodies the equivalent of the state being seen for how it really is. In the language of law enforcement, everything is a "tell," and the body of Ji Seong Ho, in his act of begging in China, told too much. Control of what is said and what is seen is critical to North Korea. Control of how things are said and how things are seen is critical too. North Korea tries to operationalize an illusion that will resist the knowledge of facts.[21]

The police officers' singling out Ji Seong Ho's disabilities resembles the style of North Korean state media in singling out individual political figures or public defectors for individualized ridicule. The police locate the cause of North Korea's shame within the most vulnerable part of Ji Seong Ho's being: his disability makes North Korea look bad. The shame is not North Korea's but his. It is he who must be kept from the sight of foreigners who would misunderstand. It is not what Ji Seong Ho might say or get or do but simply his very being that causes shame.

The body is an area for coordinated discipline in North Korea. Even early in North Korea's history, it emphasized bodily hygiene, athletics, and purity. The well-functioning body manifested the functioning body politic.[22] Disability is the ultimate manifestation of bodily nonconformity. North Korea tries to manage a sanitized self-image by hiding those who do not conform.

Although North Korea passed a law in 2003 mandating equal access to public services for the disabled, there was no legislation passed to implement it. The UN Committee on the Rights of the Child noted de facto discrimination against children with disabilities because North Korea does not guarantee that these children have equal access to health care, nutrition, education, and other social services. As Ji Seong Ho explains, discrimination toward the disabled is common. "In North Korea, they use a derogative term to refer to the specific part of their body that is disabled. For example, if you don't have a hand, or missing a wrist like me, then they would refer to it as a gravel hand (*jagil son*). Instead of names, even to refer to my family, they refer to my family as the family of the gravel hand."[23] Degrading treatment of disabled people is widespread in North Korea. Ji recalls making fun of disabled adults when he was a child, prior to his injury. But discrimination takes a more pernicious aspect when supplies of food and medicine and access to other resources are denied on the basis of disabled people being less valued in society. Citizens' Alliance for North Korean Human Rights reports that the birth of a disabled child in North Korea is understood as a curse. The group also identifies "Hospital 8.3" as a location where abandoned and disabled children were used for chemical and biological tests.[24]

North Korea's discomfort with disability could lead to the observation that disability itself is seen to embody the failure of the state. In a similar way, the act of defection or border crossing announces the limitations and failures of the state. Without saying a word, border crossers articulate the varied failures of North Korea through their determination to take a risk for something that may be better. Each individual carries a nuanced narrative of how they just couldn't stay in North Korea anymore, whether because they couldn't make ends meet or because they were no longer welcome. Each carries an idea of what could be gained through the risk.

Walking five kilometers to China on crutches to get food for his family is a wordless articulation of Ji's mighty resolve and bravery. But because the individual act of defiant survival risked capturing the international media gaze, because it captured the essence of North Korea's cruel indifference and risked communicating that internationally, it must be punished. Tortured by the police to within an inch of his life, Ji Seong Ho would ordinarily be sent to prison, but the conditions of prison and the torture he suffered would have guaranteed his death. He begged the police to not send him. They granted him freedom from prison if he would sign a pledge stating he would not cross into China again.[25]

Early Lawfare

What are the juridical procedures and political devices that have stripped North Koreans of their rights? The legal code of North Korea was based on Soviet models.[26] By 1955 the penal system bore resemblance to those in China, the Soviet Union, and Eastern Europe. People held in internment camps were mostly political prisoners with no fixed sentence. Those in reform through labor camps had sentences up to one year and were given wages for their work performance.[27] Between 1954 and 1955, Eastern European dictatorships (except the Albanian regime) began to release political prisoners. Sometimes this involved rehabilitation of victims. This was the path of the Soviet Union's idea of rehabilitation, so many dictators followed, even if reluctant. Bulgaria released ten thousand prisoners from concentration camps in 1955. Romania pardoned political prisoners who had sentences of ten years or more. North Korea would not follow this trend until August of 1960.[28] In 1955 a Hungarian diplomat to North Korea reported that the North Koreans did not mention the large internment camps throughout the country—of which many of the interned were from South Korea.[29] North Korea's practice of crime inheritance or mutual responsibility can be seen in Soviet Stalinism. Historian Balazs Szalontai points out that a 1934 Soviet law instructed that any family member who knew of the intentions of a "traitor to the homeland" could get a prison sentence of up to five years. Those who did not know but who were related to a traitor could be exiled for up to five years. In 1935 the Politburo enabled the application of the death penalty to certain criminals aged twelve and older.[30]

North Korea is sometimes described as being like one big prison camp. Giorgio Agamben writes that the "camp" is a space of juridical order that is exceptional. It is exceptional in that all possibilities are included in this territorial space of exceptionality. The camp is a zone where outside and inside are without distinction, "the exception and the rule, the licit and the illicit, in which every juridical protection had disappeared."[31] Agamben stresses that the real question to ask is not *how* it could be possible for one human to commit such acts toward another. Rather, the more useful question is to ask what are the juridical procedures and political devices that have stripped humans of their rights and prerogatives "to the point that committing any act toward them would no longer appear as a crime."[32] We therefore have to acknowledge we are looking at a camp any time such a structure exists.

Above the Law

Governance of North Korea in its full spectrum—the constitution, civil law, regulations, the Korean Worker's Party Charter, and so on—falls within the control of Kim Jong Un. His decree is shielded, reinforced by a monolith of principles dictating day-to-day moral practice for all. Kim Jong Un sits at the top of the hierarchy of authority, ruling the grand and the granular. Within this framework it is thoroughly incomprehensible that the leader could be brought to trial at the International Criminal Court or accused of responsibility for crimes against humanity identified in the United Nation's Commission of Inquiry report of 2014. No laws in North Korea bind the leader; he is above and outside of them. And yet there are different views on how things should run within the North Korean government organs, as shown by the research of political scientist Patrick McEachern. The government organs are not a total monolith of strategy, but there are fissions between them over how to approach problems in the country.[33] This ensures robustness to the overall structure. It is normal that there would be disagreements in how the country could resolve problems. Contrary to how it may look, McEachern finds that North Korea is not a "one-man rule" state. Eliminating the leader, as we have seen with the deaths of Kim Il Sung and Kim Jong Il, has not spelled the elimination of North Korean governance as we know it. There is an order of governance and control that works as follows:

1. Kim Jong Un's words and directives.
2. Ten Principles for the Establishment of a Monolithic Ideological System.[34]

3. Korean Workers' Party directives (most notably the policy guidance of the Korean Workers' Party Secretariat's Organization and Guidance Department).[35]
4. Korean Workers' Party Charter and domestic civil laws.
5. Democratic People's Republic of Korea Constitution.[36]

The strength of democratic process can be measured through criminal justice and due-process guarantees. The degree to which North Korea strays from its self-proclaimed description as democratic can be measured in the ordering of power, which is so total as to eclipse any legal apparatus entirely at the highest levels. The constitution and criminal code appear normative, mimicking performative codes common to all states. Identifying and sidestepping the "fog" that North Korea tries to wrap itself in with these normative documents, sociologist Christopher Green points to the Ten Principles as evidentiary of how power operates and dominates in practice.[37] Green cites one of the highest ranking defectors, Hwang Jang Yop, who emphasized the centrality of the Ten Principles in all human affairs since their announcement by Kim Jong Il in 1974. The principles and their sixty-five subclauses should be memorized by all Koreans, young and old, regardless of Songbun, and whether resident in North Korea or abroad. They are:

1. We must give our all in the struggle to unify the entire society with the revolutionary ideology of Great Leader Kim Il Sung.
2. We must honor Great Leader comrade Kim Il Sung with all our loyalty.
3. We must make absolute the authority of Great Leader comrade Kim Il Sung.
4. We must make Great Leader comrade Kim Il Sung's revolutionary ideology our faith and make his instructions our creed.
5. We must adhere strictly to the principle of unconditional obedience in carrying out the Great Leader comrade Kim Il Sung's instructions.
6. We must strengthen the entire Party's ideology and willpower and revolutionary unity, centering on Great Leader comrade Kim Il Sung.
7. We must learn from Great Leader comrade Kim Il Sung and adopt the communist look, revolutionary work methods and people-oriented work style.
8. We must value the political life we were given by Great Leader comrade Kim Il Sung, and loyally repay his great political trust and thoughtfulness with heightened political awareness and skill.
9. We must establish strong organizational regulations so that the entire Party, nation and military move as one under the one and only leadership of Great Leader comrade Kim Il Sung.
10. We must pass down the great achievement of the revolution by Great Leader comrade Kim Il Sung from generation to generation, inheriting and completing it to the end.[38]

Because these principles are intended as the guiding moral vector in North Korea, it is worth pausing for a moment to examine them. The first thing apparent is a numbing repetition in the language of the text echoing the collective "we" and the founding leader Kim Il Sung. Every principle gives the directive "must," which carries out a dutiful action or belief in honor of the leader. Reading the Ten Principles as aspirational rather than as achieved social outcomes suggests that society struggles to unify with the ideology of the leadership. Struggle is expected, and it is reasonable that it will be dealt with. A separation between society and ideology is indicated. Only the leader is ideologically pure. The principles remedy the separation of society and identity by honoring the authority of Kim Il Sung. Principles 4 and 5 internalize the ideology as "our faith" and "our creed" through obedience; 6 and 7 turn outward to revolutionary unity and work methods; 8 identifies political life as something *granted* by the leader, not inalienable or natural; 9 calls for total unity of the institutional national body; and 10 evokes every person's duty to indoctrinate the next generation in the achievements of the leader, a veiled reference to sustain Songbun purity. Defectors acknowledge that the Ten Principles are above constitutional law in North Korea. Jang Hae Sung, a former reporter for the Korean Central News Agency, clarified that "the constitution can be violated, but if you do violate . . . if you go against the Ten Principles that is not going to be forgiven."[39]

Law as Weapon

Law can be a shield, protecting an individual from harm. In such cases, the law itself is upheld, and the individual in question, offense committed or not, is entitled to protection from abuse within the law. When law is used as a shield, all are entitled to a fair trial. In such a case, the court is not under the state but rather separate from it. Alternatively, law can be a weapon used to criminalize, detain, and end life. It can also be used as a mode of educational reform for public and criminal alike.[40] In such cases, guilt is extrajudicial, and there are no legal avenues for recourse. Law is not a tool the individual can turn to as a shield to defend herself against charges. Instead, law resolutely finds her culpable. The task of law in such cases is to determine the degree of punishment—how deeply the sword will cut. The constitution, legal documents like the criminal code, and laws in general in North Korea are not ultimately the most powerful binding documents; rather, the words and dictates of Kim Jong Un and the Ten Principles are the strongest governing principles. In the DPRK, law is a weapon. This is the way Kim Il Sung phrased it: "The law of our country is an important weapon for implementing the policies of our state. The policies of our state are the policies of our Party. It is impossible to enforce the law without knowledge of the political line and policies of our Party."[41]

The criminal code of North Korea should *not* be read as law-in-practice. Rather, like other North Korean state documents, it reveals details of what the state values and how it legitimates abuse of power. Article 1 explains that the objective of criminal law in North Korea is to defend the sovereignty of the state and the socialist system. In countries where rights are upheld, criminal law serves to protect society and the accused, not the state. In North Korea's criminal code, the rights of the accused, an essential requirement for just law, are not mentioned. Instead of having access to legal rights, the accused can repent of wrongdoing and surrender to the state, at which point the state may show leniency. When the criminal code is read alongside the Ten Principles and Songbun, several features stand out. First, and most obviously, Articles 59 through 72 explicitly address crimes directed at the state and nation (there are 303 articles in total). According to the classification of Songbun, the hostile class is prima facie guilty of these thirteen criminal articles. The code also contends with merely thinking about crime toward the state. Articles 21 and 22 explain that a person who thinks up an offense shall be punished more severely. Planning a crime carries criminal liability with Article 19.

The code indicates that the law is not the same for all people. For instance, Article 40 states that when an offender has "previously contributed greatly to the country," their penalty shall be mitigated. Article 53 states that a criminal may have their penalty canceled through special pardon from the chairman of the National Defense Commission of the DPRK, Kim Jong Un. General pardons can be granted by the presidium of the Supreme People's Assembly; at current writing, the presidium is Kim Yŏng-nam.

According to Articles 193, 194, and 195 of the code, it is a crime to impair socialist culture. These articles criminalize the import, keeping, making, and distribution of "decadent" culture; the "conduct of decadent acts" such as dancing that reflects carnal content; and listening to "hostile broadcasts" (broadcasts from abroad). People caught violating these articles are subject to reform through labor for up to five years. However, adopted by degree No. 2483 of the Standing Committee of the Supreme People's Assembly on December 19, 2007, are the additional clauses of criminal law that classify an act as "grave." Most notable is Article 23, "Exceptional Application of Crimes which Fall Under Life-Term Reform Through Labor and the Death Penalty," which states: "In cases where multiple acts of crime committed by one perpetrator are particularly grave, or where there is no possibility of rehabilitation, the punishment shall be life-term reform through labor or the death penalty." The Retroactivity and Non-Retroactivity Principle, Article 9 of the criminal code, imposes punishment on offenders according to the penal law in force at the time the offense was committed, regardless of later revisions to the criminal code.

Article 1 of North Korea's criminal code states that the objective of the law is to "defend the state, and the socialist system," revealing a spectacular inversion of the rule of law that guarantees due process as detailed in Article 14 of the UN ICCPR, which states that "all persons shall be equal before the courts and tribunals" and "presumed innocent until proven guilty." Further, Article 27 of the ICCPR explains, "All persons are equal before the law and are entitled without any discrimination to the equal protection of the law. In this respect, the law shall prohibit any discrimination and guarantee to all persons equal and effective protection."[42] Application of the law in North Korea is inherently biased and yet also arbitrary.

Detained for Punishment

Setting aside for a moment whether detention itself is right or wrong, ideally detention is punishment in and of itself, not a place one goes *to be punished*.[43] However, people are incarcerated in North Korea *as* punishment and *for* punishment. The same logic can be seen in how law operates in North Korea. Law is upheld not so much to protect people but to convict transgressors toward the state. Punishment in North Korea is dehumanizing, cruel, and humiliating. In political prisons and ordinary prison camps, the North Korean government physically uses up the prison population by extracting as much labor as possible. The physical structure of penal facilities seems designed for degradation through treatment of the prisoner: the social and physical environment of the prison is physically and psychologically dangerous, opening the prisoner to more violence. The prisoner is doubly or triply punished, first through detention and then additionally through overwork, poor nutrition, inhumane treatment, physical abuse, and exposure to unhygienic conditions with little access to health care. Such problems are not merely a concern for a human-rights-based approach to criminal justice. They are also a concern for North Korea and the region as contagious diseases and other pathologies flourish in such conditions. Population groups sometimes cycle through the system; this is particularly the case with reeducation facilities. Through this, contagion is spread to other population groups. In this way a biovulnerability of prison life opens people within and beyond the prison to greater risk. Deprivation of the right to food is widespread in North Korean political and ordinary prison camps, regardless of fluctuations in external food availability.[44] The natural hunger of prisoners is used to punish them in detention facilities where ration portions are slashed. Guards are trained to use food and hunger as a means of punishment.[45] Prison deaths are typically due to starvation, overwork, or illness.

The Commission of Inquiry found North Korea in violation of several basic human rights through arbitrary detention, torture, executions, enforced disappearances, and political prison camps. North Korea has certain obligations to uphold the rights of all citizens, including detainees, according to several articles in the ICCPR.[46] North Korea's practice of "crime by association" or "crime by inheritance" (*yongchwajae*) leads to the imprisonment of children—this is why there is the seemingly incongruous mention of classrooms and school lessons in camps in the accounts of former prisoners—the state is in violation of the rights of children under the Convention on the Rights of the Child.[47] North Korea's legal system and detention facilities—whether political prison camps, reeducation centers, or holding facilities—function as parts of a networked apparatus instilling a culture of enforcement for North Korea's socialist system.

Any effort to show respect for the dead was responded to with cruelty from guards. Family members who asked to see their deceased loved ones were scolded: "Have you come to honor and cry over a dead prisoner? Go home!"[48] At Camp 13 three children were mauled to death by military dogs. According to a former guard at the prison, these children were descendants of political prisoners and were attending the prison-run school at the time of the attack. The dogs were not put down, and the dog trainer was praised by the battalion leader. Former prison guard Ahn Myong Chul reported, "He actually praised him because the dogs had mauled and killed political prisoners."[49]

Treatment in so-called reeducation camps is indistinguishable from prisons. Defector Lee Jun Ha describes torture in the reeducation center at the hands of the Security Department secretary. He was asked to select a wooden bat from among a pile of bats and put it behind his knees. Then kneel. A single piece of paper was placed between his buttocks and calves. He was instructed not to move and hold the position. When the paper fell he was beaten. After four hours of this he was instructed to stand up but could not.[50] His hands were beaten black by the official. He was then put in solitary confinement for twenty days. Lee witnessed the torture and the public execution of a prisoner who tried to escape. The entire reeducation camp was gathered to witness four gunmen shoot the man dead. The security department head, Nam Byung Shik, instructed the other prisoners to watch carefully to learn what happens to an escapee. The prisoners were then subjected to a lengthy lecture about the benefits of reeducation through labor, a gift from the leadership that should not be refused.[51]

In a memoir about his reeducation camp experience, Lee Jun Ha reports that a male prisoner named Ma Il had a sexual relationship with another male prisoner. For this he was given an extra nine years in the reeducation camp. Ma Il had a defiant character, according to Lee Jun Ha. He challenged and defied the guards. He was eventually assigned to another section of the prison where he was beaten to death by a mob on the guards' request. Lee mused that if Ma Il had been born during the Japanese colonial era, he would have been a hero for the people and nation due to his resistance toward authority, but instead he was born in North Korea and died in a reeducation camp in a small town.[52]

After release from reeducation, Lee Jun Ha's punishment didn't end. Being sent to reeducation taints former detainees with greater vulnerability postrelease because of the social stigma connected with detention. Lee Jun Ha described being bullied by safety and security police even after his release. He was also repeatedly pressured for money and other bribes by employees of the People's Safety Agency.[53] As is permitted by the criminal code of North Korea, Article 30, under section 2 on punishments, a citizen's rights are "partially suspended" during the period of detention.[54] Citizen identification numbers are erased or recreated via the prison system in North Korea. Jeong Kwang Il explained that Yodok was a little different from other prison facilities. "[In] other prisons they give you a permit, that's the end of it. . . . *in order to ensure secrecy*, they gave me a new identification card [upon release] that I used to work as a laborer in the military. Except for the people who are very close to me, except for my close family, [no one knows about my imprisonment]."[55]

The North Korean government goes to great lengths to keep prisoners from talking about these camps. "When I was released from Yodok, I had to sign a letter to not disclose that I had been in Yodok. I was not to disclose that I was in Yodok or that I knew anything about it. If I were found out to be talking about Yodok, I would be penalized for it," Jeong Kwang Il explained.[56] When defector Kim Eun Cheol was released from the camp, people who knew him were surprised to find him alive, thinking he had died. "I did not tell [them] that I was in the prisoner camp, but instead I used the name, the number of the army and said that I worked there. . . . People thought that I had worked in the army, not [that I] did my sentence in the prison camp."[57] Could he have known on meeting someone in the streets that that person had been in the camps? This question was put to Jeong by Marzuki Darusman during the UN public hearing in 2015. "No we could not," he explained. "It's difficult to recognize people. It doesn't really show that you have been in the camps. But there are rumors. So there would be rumors or stories of people having received interrogation or questioning from Bowibu [the secret police] or the pre-trial board."[58]

As mentioned, North Koreans are sent to prison *for* punishment, not *as* punishment. Reports from former guards, prisoners, and construction workers who witnessed the conditions of political prison camps reveal the cruel and degrading treatment toward people held there—not only in their nourishment, which is paltry; their clothing, which is threadbare; and the psychological treatment but also the built space of the prison, which is designed to devalue the prisoner. The structure of prisons was set up so that people would have to kneel down to enter them and then crawl throughout the interior. Mr. K—the name given to an anonymous witness at the United Nations—worked in a special shock troop unit. He and his team were dismantling Political Prison Camp 11 to build a villa for the leadership. The former population of the camp was sent to Political Prison Camp 16, and the other half went to Hoeryong prison camp.

Mr. K described his surprise seeing the prisoners' quarters which he was ordered to dismantle. Expecting to see an ordinary sized building, he found something half underground and built like an animal hutch. The walls rose from the ground for about eighty centimeters (about thirty-one inches), and there was a straw roof. The "house" structure sat over a dugout in the ground, about eighty centimeters deep. The huts were interspersed with dugout areas where pigs were held. During his testimony, Mr. K drew a depiction of the huts on the white-board. Prisoners were living in dirt dugouts with small three-foot-high shelters erected above them. The effect of this architecture on the prisoner is that their eye level would be just a foot or so above ground level, at the feet of the guards.[59] The testimony of Jee Heon A and Young Hee that opens this chapter highlights that the behavior of guards is opportunistic and cruel. However, the architectural details provided by the testimony of Mr. K indicate a widespread and systematized dehumanization of detainees that is not arbitrary but thought through.

The obfuscation of prison camps is also thought through. Former political prisoner Jeong Kwang Il explained to the UN commissioners that the location of Yodok camp was changed after the international community released information about the location of the camp to media following the testimonies of former prisoners. The same principle applies when naming camps. While many people in North Korea know of prisons, they may not know precisely about them. Ahn Myong Chul, the former guard, was from a privileged class family. After he graduated from the agriculture university in 1987, he went on to a position as a defense guard for a detention center. He admitted to having no knowledge of detention centers prior to his post. Subsequently, he worked in several detention facilities throughout the country. His work colleagues mostly came from privileged families. He eventually worked in other facilities where his rank was among the lowest; his comrades belonged to families of descendants of those who fought Japanese colonial rule. Ahn recalled the curious way the camps were named. The camps are not called "Prison (*suyongso*) such and such," for instance. They are named through a set of words lifted from the army unit number tasked with defending the prison and whatever item might be farmed in the camp. Ahn explains: "We sometimes would add specific vegetables or fruits that came from that region to the end of the number . . . so we have to furnish the expressions to refer to these political camps."[60] This failure to officially name prison facilities suggests the state's efforts to mask information while also systematizing it.

In the case of foreign invasion or domestic revolt, prisons are supposed to be eliminated. Ahn Myong Chul, speaking about his role in the prison camps, said,

> In case of a revolt, we are supposed to suppress it and shoot them. In case a
> war breaks out, in order to eliminate any evidence, we were supposed to wipe

[the prisons] out so that there is no evidence of inmates. In each political camp there are tunnels. Those tunnels were dug so that we can eliminate inmates in case we had to erase any evidence of their existence and in case of possible revolt or runaways or should a war break out. The guards are supposed to arrive in the area they are in charge of and shoot everybody who is under their supervision.[61]

Ahn explained that outside the walls of the prison camp, guards lied about their occupation to keep the camp a secret.[62] He recalled that North Korean authorities became concerned about maintaining secrecy of prison camps in 1993, around the time that Sungho-ri (Sŭnghori), a camp for political criminals, was disclosed by an international human rights organization.[63]

Guards selected to carry out public executions in North Korea must have been in the military for three years, have good aim with a gun, and have a strong ideology. Ahn explained, "Training of the guards is done in a new camp called Number 26. The new guards are trained there for a minimum of three months. Then you are allocated to your own post where you receive an additional three months training. What we are taught and trained the most in is how to suppress riots, and we also receive mind training to make us understand that these inmates are enemies."[64]

There were cases of male guards sexually abusing women prisoners. If a woman prisoner became pregnant, her pregnancy would be forcefully terminated because criminal classes are not typically permitted to reproduce.

> The leader of my team battalion was Han Dae Chul. He raped one of a inmates, and the woman actually got pregnant and gave birth to a baby in the field. The baby and the woman were taken to detention houses. The guards were trying to find out who the father was, so they asked her and the inmate said she was raped by one of the soldiers. The baby was put in a pot [to die] where meals are made for the military dogs. I think the woman was sent away. This was a big issue. The soldier who raped her had his rank taken away.[65]

Again there is an inversion of logic here in the camp. The rape and pregnancy of this woman was a "big deal" not because of the guard's blatant abuse of power but because, as Ahn explained, "If a woman gives birth then that's a really big problem in the camp because the camp was established at the instructed order of Kim Il Sung since 1958."[66] By definition, the camps are aimed at eliminating antistate elements. Prisoner reproduction is totally antithetical to this.

According to Kim Il Sung's instructions, three generations of the inmates should be annihilated. In his UN testimony, Ahn explained how this principle played into his work. "Kim Jung Il said that all escaping political prisoners should be caught. So the camp is there in order to make sure that there are no future generations of political prisoners."[67] He further elaborates on the sexual abuse of women prisoners and the consequences for perpetrators and victims. "If the father is an inmate, the guy would be shot to death and the woman sent to the harshest coal mines to work. However, if the father is from the Secret Police, the Bowibu, he has to retire from his job."[68] However, he reported that some guards take matters into their own hands. "I think it was prison [Gwan-risa] Number 13 or 19—he [the guard] committed suicide."[69] The child of such a union could not hope to survive the political environment governing the prison camp.

> If the guard rapes or has sexual intercourse with an inmate, the political pris-oner will be sent to a really harsh place. If she gives birth, then she will be secretly executed.[70] If she was just ["only"] raped, she would be sent to the harshest workplace like the mines. The guy who rapes her would be sent out back to the society because he would be deemed as having not sufficient alle-giance or loyalty, and he would be stigmatized. He will not be able to get a good job in the military.[71]

It is proximity to prisoners and the social relations that such closeness could engender, rather than abuse of prisoners, that raises the concern of the state and, thus, the punishment of guards within the prison system. Those who min-gle with prisoners are instructed on their indiscretion through demotion, which naturally raises ire in the North Korean Songbun system. As Ahn elaborates, the battalion had an emergency gathering to strip Yang Sung Chul, a superior to Ahn in Camp 22 and a guard, of his rank because of his sexual assault on a prisoner. The rape was reported to authorities through the system of mutual surveillance among the prisoners. His victim, Han Jin Duk, was tortured by fire and sent to work in a mine. For Yang, an emergency meeting was gathered; "his rank was taken away because he had a relationship with the enemy. He was forcefully and dishonorably discharged from the army."[72] The message that is reinforced is that connections between the social groups must be maintained through the purity of right action and punishment of indiscretion.

According to the testimony of guards, sexual indiscretion was treated dif-ferently than other types of abuse. Harming or killing prisoners often solicited praise. While working at Camp 22, Ahn saw his superior hit a prisoner over the head—a man of forty years of age who was working in a brick factory. The prisoner's eventual death was reported to the Bowibu. The superior reported that the man was hit because he wasn't working very well. In the end, the fore-man of the factory where the inmates worked was scolded. The superior who hit and killed the man was rewarded by being sent to the university.[73]

Lee Jun Ha's memoir about his reeducation experience details how guards treated inmates at his location. Because food in the detention facility was so poor, family members would sometimes gather what little they could and bring it to their loved ones. Guards would gather these items together, dump them into a collective bowl and feed it to the inmates "like animal feed." If the guards were in a bad mood, they would splash boiling soup in the faces of inmates. The guards drove nails through oak clubs used to hit inmates, causing severe injury.[74]

The penal system in North Korea consists of an array of detention facilities. These can roughly be classified as political prisons, ordinary criminal prisons, and reeducation prison facilities. There are other types of detention that have been reported, such as the euphemistically termed "guest houses" run by the State Security Department and holding stations operated by the network of police and interrogation detention centers.[75] The difference between who gets detained where is typically determined by the type of crime a person is said to have committed.

While the causes that lead to detention in these facilities may be different, in some cases the treatment of people in them is almost indistinguishable. However, the testimony of former penal system detainees establishes political prison camps as among the most difficult to survive and reeducation facilities as being places one is reasonably expected to survive or be released. The Ministry of People's Security in charge of the network of police stations deals with less severe economic crimes while political crimes are deemed more severe, and punishment for these is given by the State Security Department of the Korean People's Army Military Security Command. As stated in a 2016 U.S. State Department report on North Korea, there are about 80,000 to 120,000 prisoners held in political prison camps in the country's remote areas at any one time.[76]

All prisoners, including children, are subject to forced labor for long hours under harsh conditions. Typical tasks include farming, logging, or mining.[77] Prison authorities abuse prisoners or those in interrogation to get money and other resources through bribes. According to reports from defectors, the penal system circulates large numbers of people through for short periods of time.[78] In the process, they are subjected to physical, psychological, and emotional abuse. They may also be in danger of contracting illnesses and spreading the contagion upon release. Research by Stephan Haggard and Marcus Noland shows that refugees who have cycled through penal system are less likely to trust the regime.[79]

Defector Lee Jun Ha describes two types of people that are created through the reeducation camps. The first are people whom the bad atmosphere (the dog-eat-dog survival methods) of the prisons does not influence; they follow the values of life outside the facility, trying to understand the pain of those who suffer more. Then there are those who pick up the poor values and coping skills of the prison and have trouble overcoming the criticism and mocking they receive from society outside of the camp once they get out. They have difficulty

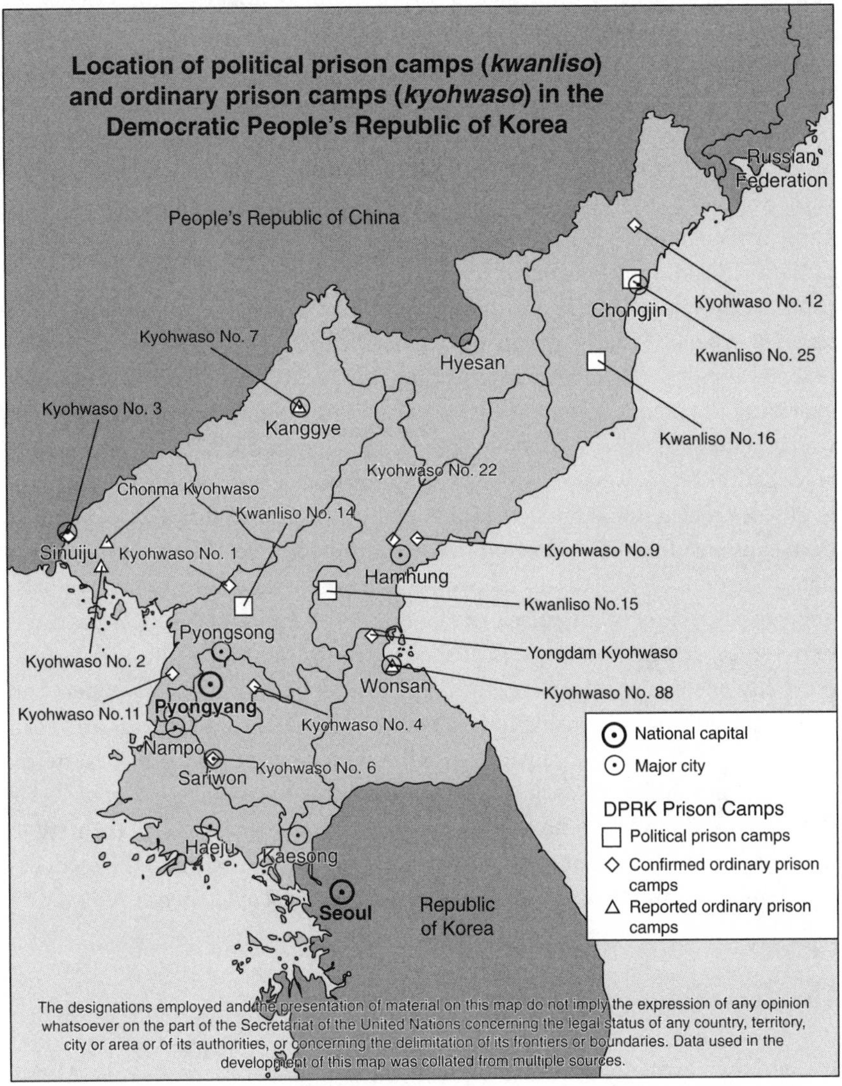

Location of political prison camps (*kwanliso*) and ordinary prison camps (*kyohwaso*) in the Democratic People's Republic of Korea
People's Republic of China
Russian Federation
Kyohwaso No. 12
Chongjin
Kwanliso No. 25
Kyohwaso No. 7
Hyesan
Kwanliso No.16
Kyohwaso No. 3
Kanggye
Kyohwaso No. 22
Chonma Kyohwaso
Kwanliso No. 14
Sinuiju
Kyohwaso No. 1
Kyohwaso No.9
Hamhung
Kwanliso No.15
Pyongsong
Yongdam Kyohwaso
Kyohwaso No. 2
Kyohwaso No. 88
Wonsan
Kyohwaso No.11
Pyongyang
Kyohwaso No. 4
Nampo
Kyohwaso No. 6
Sariwon
Haeju
Kaesong
Seoul
Republic of Korea
National capital
Major city
DPRK Prison Camps
Political prison camps
Confirmed ordinary prison camps
Reported ordinary prison camps
The designations employed and the presentation of material on this map do not imply the expression of any opinion whatsoever on the part of the Secretariat of the United Nations concerning the legal status of any country, territory, city or area or of its authorities, or concerning the delimitation of its frontiers or boundaries. Data used in the development of this map was collated from multiple sources.

7.1 Location of political prison camps (*kwanliso*) and ordinary prison camps (*kyohwaso*) in the Democratic People's Republic of Korea

United Nations Human Rights Council, "Report of the Commission of Inquiry on Human Rights in the Democratic People's Republic of Korea," A/HRC/25/63, February 7, 2014 http://undocs.org/A/HRC/25/63

reestablishing themselves in society and sometimes turn to drink or commit another crime, ending up back in the reeducation facility.[80]

Lee Jun Ha was held in Jeongeo-ri Reeducation Camp, also known as No. 12 Reeducation Camp, about twelve kilometers from Hoeryong in the direction of the coastal town of Chongjin. He estimated that about two thousand people were held in that camp, guarded by about three hundred security forces. The camp was founded in 1970 as No. 22 Juvenile Reformatory, but in the 1980s the name was changed to No. 12 Reeducation Camp.[81] The description Lee provides of the reeducation center in his book makes it difficult to distinguish it from political prison camps. From the moment he arrived, guards beat him and shouted orders. He saw a group of prisoners loading logs onto a truck, and he realized the logs were corpses. At several points in his memoir he mentions that surviving the reeducation camp is not a certainty. Almost 80 percent of those who enter do not survive due to overwork and starvation.[82] The facilities in the reeducation center were primitive, with living quarters infested with lice, bedbugs, cockroaches, and fleas. The toilet and washroom facilities were dysfunctional and insufficient for the number of detained people. He reports there was one washroom for one thousand prisoners. Despite the huge numbers of prisoners, each section of the prison was only given one new blanket per year, and between seven and twelve pairs of shoes, padded clothes, and underwear to meet any needs that might arise in the entire section that year. Prisoners had to eat "everything" according to Lee, just to survive, including grass and corn found in cow feces. During work mobilizations, prisoners ate weeds, newly sprouted cabbage leaves, corn seedlings, "anything that wasn't poisonous."[83] He states that there was a time around the year 2000 when as many as thirty to forty people died per month from malnutrition and overwork in the reeducation center and were cremated. The bodies were not sent to their loved ones.[84]

The Human in the Prisoner

Despite the horrendous and widespread abuse of prisoners by guards, Ahn, a former prison guard who defected, reported some human sentiment in the guards toward the prisoners. He explained that this came about for two reasons. First, the guards in the political prisons are not as strict as the Bowibu in terms of ideology. Second, the camps are, for strategic reasons, located in the wilderness, surrounded by high mountain ranges. Cut off from the rest of North Korean society, their community *is* the political prison camp.

> It's quite difficult to see other people. The only things that we see are birds and the inmates. At first, we are disgusted with them, but as we've been living with them for a long time, we become sort of relaxed, so some of my comrades felt

bad about some inmates. I also felt bad about some inmates, but I couldn't express it because if I do express my sympathy, I would be punished. However, when we have conversations I was able to get the hints that some comrades were feeling bad or were feeling sad for some of the inmates.[85]

During Ahn's public hearing, Justice Michael Kirby asked him if he ever felt ashamed of his behavior as a guard. Ahn's answer illustrates his initial impression of the prisoners. His awareness that most prisoners had "no idea" why they were in prison eventually dovetailed with his own family's trouble with the law. He explained, "At the time, I thought the inmates were truly bad. When I became a driver, I met political prisoners and sometimes I met people who were really good workers. When I had free time, when I got bored, sometimes I would strike up a conversation. I would ask where their hometowns were and why they were there. 90% of the people had no idea why they were in the camps."[86] Naturally, at first he was suspicious of this nearly unanimous claim from the prisoners. Later, when he was permitted a trip home to visit family, he learned that his family was going through something very similar to the stories he heard about in the camps:

> My father was in the top position of the distribution center, so he often had occasion to meet people in high positions at dinner meetings. He made a mistake of saying to these higher ranking officials that the reason for the food shortage was because people at the top were not doing their job right. That is considered a betrayal of the party. My father was drunk at the time, and next day he regretted saying that. He knew he made a mistake. So he committed suicide. Committing suicide is also a crime in North Korea. That's why my mother was arrested and she was being investigated in the political prison camp.[87]

Ahn's siblings were rounded up from their respective schools, military academies, and occupations for questioning at the political prison camp.[88] He saw how easily someone can slip into the prison maze of the state. Drunken expressions of discontent—something highly plausible—are not interpreted lightly by the North's criminal code. Perhaps such comments would happen too often if they were permitted. The code states: "Criminal liability shall not be imposed on an offender who commits socially dangerous acts while he or she is unable to judge his or her conduct or control himself or herself because of chronic mental disease or temporary mental disorder; medical measures may be adopted in such cases. The foregoing paragraph does not apply to a person who commits an offense under the influence of alcohol."[89]

When he learned of this story from home, Ahn knew that the Bowibu would be trailing him and that his time in North Korea was limited. He returned to work at the political prison camp having already made the decision to defect. He invited two political prisoners whom he had befriended to join him—two brothers aged twenty-four and twenty-six who had been imprisoned since the ages of two and four. Ahn met the brothers when he was a driver, transferring coal. He put them in the truck and told them they may have to engage in fire if the group was caught trying to flee. Ahn gave each of them a pistol and instructed them to shoot when he ordered. But the brothers were scared and ran away in the middle of the escape attempt. They never got away from the camp, Ahn reported. "I was the only one who did. I drove the truck out of the political prison. Because I was the driver, I had freedom to drive around the area. I drove all the way to the Tumen River, left the car there, and went to China."[90]

Redress and Complaint

Oversight of the detention process is by the office of the prosecutor, not the courts or any other judicial office. The law facilitates the ability of the security agency to search, seize, and arrest during investigation and pretrial examination phases.[91] North Korea's Code of Criminal Procedure states that the prosecutor must issue an arrest warrant and that this warrant must be presented to the suspect upon arrest. If the suspect is to be detained for a continued period, confirmation of this must be requested from the prosecutor within forty-eight hours of arrest.[92] Family members of detained suspects must be notified and informed of the whereabouts of the individual within forty-eight hours of arrest according to Article 183 of the code. When the South Korean Bar Association surveyed North Korean defectors in South Korea on these procedures, they found that only 49.4 percent of respondents had been notified.[93] According to the findings of the UN Commission of Inquiry, these arrests amount to disappearances according to the definition in the UN Declaration on the Protection of All Persons from Enforced Disappearance (A/RES/47/133), adopted by the General Assembly in December 1992, although North Korea has not yet signed this Convention.[94] North Korea does not consistently follow the letter of the law, domestically or internationally, where the safety and security of individual rights are concerned. The Korean Bar Association reports in a white paper from 2012 that only 18.1 percent of respondents were presented with an arrest warrant or some type of document to justify their detention at the time of arrest.[95] Sometimes an individual wasn't even told the reason for arrest.[96] The most compelling concern with this procedural matter is that, with or without a warrant, there are no assuredly safe means of questioning arrest and detention.

In 2005 North Korea reformed its Code of Criminal Procedure and put a time limit of two months on interrogation and detentions prior to trial. However, it is difficult to know if this merely speeds up the process of getting to detention and thus to less care when there are trial procedures. Lee Jun Ha, the young man who was in reeducation, mentioned earlier, was assigned a lawyer who only argued for one thing—a reduced sentence—and only because Lee was young. His guilt or innocence was not examined under evidence in court. The judge eventually gave him seven years, which even Lee thought was a good result, despite his innocence.[97]

To complain or raise a question about state procedure, regardless of how it is followed, is a political gesture. The more political a crime is deemed to be, the more likely it is that criminal proceedings will lack due process even within the limited due process offered through the constitution and criminal code.[98] During the UN Commission of Inquiry investigation, Justice Kirby asked former detainees if appeal was possible. When he asked defector Kim Young Soon about her time in Yodok prison, she replied, "There was no way I could complain. In North Korea, you don't complain because we [would] die. But they saved us at least from death because the dear leader took pity on us. We were just laborers, just workers. We could not complain a single word. And every day we were instructed about the ideology. . . . Anyone who contravened this ideology was chained and was never seen."[99]

Another defector, Kim Hyuk, was held in a reeducation center with little to eat apart from the rodents he caught. Justice Kirby asked him if he ever complained about the lack of food given to him at the detention center. Kim explained, "If you complain, then that would be a cause for another crime. I mean, that is you are resisting government or party policies. So I was given three years. But if I complained, I would have been sent to a political prisoner camp or there would have been a longer sentence given to me." Kim connects complaints with increased sentencing or increased severity of punishment. But how did you *know* that that would happen?, Kirby asked. Kim's answer is intriguing because he simply ties it back to not saying what one wants to say—the desire that is felt cannot be articulated. He also links this seamlessly with Kim Il Sung, which suggests that, for Kim, his felt desires were antithetical to the leadership. Any speech that is negative about North Korea is "taken away." Kim Hyuk explains:

At that time in North Korea, we couldn't say all the things we wanted to say because everyone knew we couldn't talk about Kim Il Sung. And if somebody said you know a neighbor said something in China about North Korea and somebody heard that and that he came back to North Korea, and then that was known, then he would be taken away. So whenever you say the name of Kim Il Sung or Kim Jong Il you would have to say it in a very honorific way. So you just couldn't complain. You just could not, you know, resist.[100]

The information that detainees receive about complaint procedures is that they should not even think of complaining, and if they do complain, more punishment will be given. Complaint or questioning the law is by definition a contravention of state ideology. What comes across in the accounts of former prisoners is that complaint and appeal, if they do occur, do so not through official bureaucratic channels but through personal appeals of mercy from the direct abuser. In the earlier account, Kim Young Soon explains that their lives were spared because the leader "took pity" on them. Young Hee and Jee Heon A begged for forgiveness from the guard in the story at the start of this chapter.

Ahn Myong Chul recalled only one incident when guard conduct was questioned at the camps. His direct manager was a comrade who didn't like working in the military, Kang Young Chul. To vent his frustrations while supervising a group of indentured workers farming a field, Kang would summon an inmate and shoot him. The killing would be explained by Kang as preventing the inmate's attempted escape. Kang killed five inmates in the time he worked at the camp. There was an investigation—not into the conduct of Kang but rather into the factors that would be leading five inmates to attempt to escape. Escape was virtually impossible from the camps, so it was highly unusual that five inmates would attempt an escape in the first place. The Bowibu was brought in to do an investigation, and they found that the inmates had no intention to run away. However, to maintain high spirits within the camps Kang Young Chul was not punished severely. If knowledge of the attempted escapes had been reported, it would have been a scandal, he stated, so results of the investigation were not publicized.[101]

No such mercy was afforded the prisoners in the camps, of course. Justice Kirby asked Ahn if there was any form of appeal or review in the political prison camps where he worked, prior to prisoners being sentenced for additional indiscretions during their time there. Ahn answered:

> In the restricted area, the inmates are no longer registered citizens, so you don't need a law to decide the sentences. The bowibu agent is the person who decides whether you are saved or you are executed. There are no other criteria other than his words. The prisoners are already eliminated from society. [As for] those who are in the revolutionizing area, I haven't heard of any due process. I think we don't have any judge's trials. It's the word of the bowibu agent that decides everything. Before execution is done, the bowibu agent reads what type of crime has been committed and orders the execution.[102]

Although they are imprisoned as political prisoners, such individuals are completely outside of political life as lawfully entitled subjects.[103]

Despite this, prisoners did find ways to resist and survive despite the earnest efforts of prison camp officials to remove them from society. In a country that operationalizes collectivity, it is through recourse to individual and mutual bonds of proximity that survival is negotiated. Kim Eun Cheol, who was held in Yodok prison camp, gave testimony to the UN Commission of Inquiry about constant hunger. Justice Kirby asked him if the guards did anything to help his hunger. It was not the guards, but the fellow prisoners who helped. "I was hungry, so we traded things." Kim explained, "I traded clothes, between inmates, we exchanged things like clothes, or we traded food so that we can keep ourselves just a little bit more full but it was not enough. It was never enough. We just had to comfort ourselves with what we had."[104] In seeking to ameliorate suffering, individualized paths of least resistance are chosen. Of course, for each of these choices, there is the risk of others bearing the consequences. After he escaped Yodok and defected to South Korea, Kim Eun Cheol explained, his brother was executed through the system of crime by inheritance (*yongchwajae*), and his sister then committed suicide.

Executing the Public

Public execution in North Korea is another manifestation of the state's intolerance for indiscretion and the pursuit to eliminate it. It is not enough to kill the person who has violated the law; the person must be killed in a particular way, and the method and moment of killing is used for meaning. The individual who transgresses is used by the state to reincorporate the collective. Young, old, male, female—anyone can be killed.[105] An audience is gathered to attend the criminal's moment of "correction." Anyone may attend. Those gathered to watch the killing will hear the gun blast, smell the sulfur, see the head explode, see heat rise from the blood, but they also witness a gathering of people who do not intervene against this moment of death. The audience is the other part of the apparatus of this style of killing. Public execution is a profoundly performative gesture in North Korea's exercise of state power. This type of killing operationalizes anticipation, risk, and the moment of action/inaction for both the individual and the collective. It is a performance, the climax of which is the moment the state acts—which is precise, grotesque, and entire—while the audience and the victim absorb the action of the state. The audience and the victim are so thoroughly acted upon by the state as to be rendered inactive, inert non-things. The audience sees the killing and sees a collective that does not intervene. What is killed along with the executed individual is any lingering belief among the citizenry that the collective *can* act against the overwhelming power of the state. It is the public, the populace, that is executed.

There is no special provision for public executions in the penal code. Until the 1970s North Korea carried out public executions in large stadiums in Pyongyang that could accommodate huge audiences. Nowadays public executions occur in the provinces.[106] The audience is an essential component of the public execution, although it should be noted that private executions can be powerful disciplining sources too, capturing audiences here and there through rumors about execution. In North Korea's 1999 Criminal Procedure law, Article 297 states that a death sentence can be carried out only with the approval of the Supreme People's Assembly Standing Committee. Firing squads and other methods are mentioned in Article 32 of the Decisions and Sentencing Law as methods of killing.

The history of killings in North Korea tracks the socioeconomic stress of the times.[107] Public executions have increased since the 1950s, peaking during the 1990s and declining after 2010. However, given the closed nature of North Korea, it is impossible to assess the actual numbers of executed individuals who are deprived of their right to life through legal execution, summary execution, or related methods.[108] The Database Center for North Korean Human Rights indicates that the vast majority of violations reported occurred in the North Eastern provinces of North Hamgyong, South Hamgyong, and Yangang. The concern here is rather the impact of public executions on the living rather than a precise calculation of how many were killed. North Korea carries out executions to remove criminal elements. It carries out public executions to achieve this *and* to psychologically execute rogue elements within the audience gathered to observe, as a way of setting an example. Psychological studies conducted in 2001 and in 2004 with North Korean defectors found that witnessing a public execution was the second-most-traumatic event reported by North Koreans. (The first was witnessing someone die of starvation.)[109]

North Korea is one of few countries in the world that conducts public executions and is one of twenty-one countries that carry out executions.[110] By retaining the death penalty and the arbitrary use of it, North Korea is in violation of the right to life. Through the arbitrary use of execution, North Korea is also violating the prohibition against the arbitrary deprivation of life.[111] Conducting executions publicly is not compatible with respect for human dignity.[112] In 1982 the United Nations mandated a special rapporteur on summary or arbitrary executions. This was renewed and widened to include extrajudicial killings in a 1992 mandate that covers all countries, regardless of ratification of international conventions. According to this report, North Korea is not enacting the legal application of the death penalty and thus is carrying out unlawful killings.[113] Further, the report states that fair trials should be guaranteed, but if a state is unable to conduct trials, then executions should be halted until they are able to ensure respect for fair trials. A report on executions by the International Federation for Human Rights found that North Korea does not respect any of the international obligations outlined by the UN Special Rapporteur on executions or the Human Rights Committee and is in breach of a peremptory norm of public international law.[114] Special rapporteur reports on human rights in the DPRK explicitly condemn the use of the death penalty as punishment in crimes for misconduct of the political or religious variety.[115]

The spectacular manner of public execution still occurs in North Korea, and some of this has reached international media attention. When Kim Jong Un took power, the public killing of exceptional criminals became highly stylized. Ordinary public executions typically follow set norms: an audience is brought to attend, the criminal target is tied to a spot, the crimes are read out, and three executioners shoot simultaneously three times. After the execution, the criminals' remains are put in a sack. Prior to execution a V-shaped spring is inserted in the mouth so that if victim tries to speak, his words are unintelligible. Former state poet Jang Jin-Sung explained the purpose of the device in his memoir *Dear Leader*. "The device had been officially sanctioned for use at public executions so that a prisoner could not utter rebellious sentiments in the final moments of his life before it was taken from him."[116] The public execution is "not so much to re-establish a balance as to bring into play, as its extreme point, the dissymmetry between the subject who has dared to violate the law and the all-powerful sovereign who displays his strength."[117] But what of that situation where the public execution is highly spectacular? The closer someone is to the top of the DPRK hierarchy, observed state poet Jang Jin-Sung, the "more violent his end when it comes."[118]

Burned by the Sun

At the Kanggon (Gang Gun) Military Training Area, twenty-two kilometers north of Pyongyang, satellite imagery indicates that a spectacular exhibition of public execution took place. At the academy's firing range on or around October 7, 2014, six ZPU quadbarreled antiaircraft guns were placed in line.[119] The ZPU each have four 14.5 mm heavy machine guns mounted on a towable wheeled carriage. The total weight of fire produced by such guns is equal to twenty-four heavy machine guns. Experts indicate that the use of ZPUs in a small-arms range, such as they were, was not only dangerous but unusual. Behind the ZPUs, facing the direction of fire, satellite images captured what appear to be troops or equipment, and behind this, five trucks of different sizes, a large trailer, and a bus. The presence of these automobiles suggests that an audience, possibly of VIPs, may have been brought to observe the shooting of a target, thirty meters downrange.[120] Greg Scarlatoiu, executive director of the Committee for Human Rights in North Korea, and Joseph S. Bermudez Jr., expert on defense and intelligence affairs, observe that the rounds fired had a range of eight thousand meters and could reach an altitude of five thousand meters. Positioning the guns to "fire horizontally at targets situated only 30 m downrange could have no conceivable utility from a military viewpoint."[121] Scarlatoiu and Bermudez write that the most plausible explanation for the event captured by satellite imagery is a public execution. If true, the physical damage to the two men allegedly executed would be total destruction.[122]

Since taking office Kim Jong Un has conducted sweeping purges and public executions of high-ranking officials and family. For each known execution, there are likely dozens of people sent to political prison camps. Convicted of treason in late 2013, Jang Song-thaek, uncle of Kim Jong Un, was executed at Kanggon Military Academy. Jang was considered the second-most-powerful man in North Korea, and he wanted to reform the country. State media publicly announced the execution of Jang by stating he had developed a faction of antiparty counterrevolutionary elements. An unusually long article published by the Korean Central News Agency detailed his journey to "self-destruction" and his "special military tribunal." He was described as a "despicable human scum" and "worse than a dog" who betrayed the "profound trust and warmest paternal love shown by the party and the leader."[123] Jang was summarily charged with violating Article 60 of the DPRK Criminal Law: terrorism against the state. In cases of "grave offense," this is punished by life-term reform through labor or the death penalty as well as confiscation of property. According to the former deputy director of South Korea's National Intelligence Service, Ra Jong-yil, author of a biography on Jang Song-thaek, there is no indication that Jang was appointed a lawyer or even permitted to speak during his trial.[124]

North Korea's central television agency reported on the story. The broadcaster explained Jang's crimes and his military trial while the camera cut to a photograph of Jang Song-thaek being arrested at an enlarged meeting of the Workers' Party of Korea Central Committee Politburo on December 8, 2013. In the big seating hall Jang was removed from his post, deprived of titles, and expelled from the Workers' Party. This was a public arrest staged to occur before all of the senior party officials in the Politburo meeting.[125] In fact, Jang and his deputies had been arrested and put under house arrest weeks earlier. The broadcast cut to two men and two women on a windy, snowy Pyongyang street reading a single broadsheet of the *Rodong Shinmun*. Next the camera was looking over their shoulders. The readers' shadows were cast on the article about the specially appointed military tribunal investigating Jang Song-thaek. The men were interviewed for their thoughts on the matter. They expressed no sympathy. One of the men said execution was too light a punishment.[126]

The offense Jang and his deputies committed is so exceptional that, to the state, it requires something more than mere killing. It is not enough for the state to deprive the criminals of physical life for indiscretion toward the state. It is not enough to shoot them dead. As the man-on-the-street in the interview said, execution is too light. Something more must be done. The criminal must be killed in an exceptional way. But the limitless cruelty of the state encounters a stubborn impasse with death itself. Though the state may wish to kill him again and again, each life yields only one death. So the method of killing, the performance of it, must manifest the desired excess. The state rolls out the ZPUs. Nothing could remain of the prisoners after such an execution. They would be pulverized. They would be extinguished as though they never were. Nothing for family burial. No grave for mourning. It is wrong to mourn a political criminal's death anyway. To match this erasure, all records of Jang's experience with the Worker's Party of Korea were also wiped.

Several elite North Koreans have reportedly been killed in this manner.[127] Killing in this way takes up where death leaves off, gives life to death again and again. It is so spectacularly horrific that the phrase "killed by antiaircraft missile" occurs in the mind of those who hear of it. While his singular death is an experience that refuses to be multiplied, and although he cannot take his suffering with him, the state finds satisfaction for its excess nevertheless in the lives of others such as those related and proximate to the accused. Spreading out around Jang and his deputies were shockwaves of purges through their families as dozens were sent to political prison camps.[128] When high-ranking North Korean party cadres have been executed in the past, other people connected to them (yongchwajae) were executed or sent to prison camps. Numbers of those killed via association are released through official Workers' Party lectures.[129] North Korean defector groups in South Korea lodged an official complaint with the Office of the Prosecutor at the International Criminal Court regarding the execution of Jang Song-thaek.[130]

Around the time of these extraordinary killings in November 2014, the Ministry of State Security and Ministry of People's Security rolled out implementation of the 9.8 Measures, the name evocative of the date of North Korea's founding (September 8), which are instructions for the weeding out of "impure and hostile elements."[131] The 9.8 Measures achieve greater regulation and order throughout the State Security and Peoples' Security organs and increase their power "to the greatest degree" so that they can uphold the state system. In short, the measures call for a total militarization of people and State Security in North Korea in defense of the state. Soldiers commanded by the Ministry of State Security and Ministry of People's Security were negatively impacted by these measures. For instance, in the past they may have been able to manipulate their position of privilege vis-à-vis their role in surveillance to bypass the control of the Workers' Party of Korea.

In line with the military thrust of the 9.8 Measures, public executions for political indiscretion are seen as acceptable under Kim Jong Un—far more than they were under Kim Jong Il.[132] Through the 9.8 Measures public executions are the preferred method of destroying impure and hostile elements of society. The order reads, in part: "The sound of gunshots must accompany the destruction of impure and hostile elements, and when necessary, public executions are to be used so that the masses come to their senses."[133] The measure also permits State Security to extrajudicially decree if an antiregime act has occurred and, if so, to carry out execution by gunfire. After the crime is determined and the death sentence delivered, soldiers are instructed: "afterwards file a report on the person and crime to Pyongyang."[134] The order also calls for the relatives of antiregime criminals to be punished. To reduce discussion of trafficking and other rights violations in the international community, defections were to be limited through orders to shoot to kill. This measure violates Article 7 of the ICCPR, which states that no one should be arbitrarily deprived of life.

The 9.8 Measures are likely to further entrench the importance of Songbun in weeding out hostile elements throughout all classes of society. Jang and his deputies were among the closest to the leadership; thus, their punishment as antirevolutionary forces needed to be severe. This indicates that punishment in North Korea is measured by a calculus of crime plus Songbun. Defectors with experience of political prison camps reported differences in punishment periods for prisoners based on Songbun. Further, decisions about whether to release or confine a prisoner longer were also devised from Songbun status.[135] In a cruel twist, the higher social position that prevents someone from discrimination in North Korea can lead that person to receive a harsher sentence—even death—for daring to transgress.

CHAPTER 8

EXPORTING RIGHTS VIOLATIONS

Deaths from accidents at work can be horrific. Chŏn Kyŏngsu worked as a welder, mostly on ships from Norway and Denmark. Over the nearly two-year period he was at Crist Shipyards in Gdynia, Poland, he worked on ten projects before an accident occurred on site. In 2014, he was working his usual 12-hour day. He was welding pipelines inside a tank when a flame suddenly ignited, engulfing him in fire. He was brought to the hospital with burns to 95% of his body. His injuries were so severe, he died the next day.

—from an article in Onet.Biznes (Poland), June 15, 2016

For many, the idea of North Koreans being posted overseas for work or forced labor may seem unusual. Given that North Korea is typically represented as a prison "unto itself," the chance to work overseas might be interpreted as singularly positive—and possibly also a risk the North Korean state would be foolish to take by exposing its citizenry to the world. North Korea sends workers overseas primarily to gain foreign currency. The calculus of who to send is simple: who can generate the most money to send back to the government while also being the least likely to defect while abroad or to bring illegal information back. In the earliest days of this state enterprise, the latter part of the equation was less of an issue than it is today.

Immediate family back in North Korea serve as "anchors" against major infractions, such as abandoning the homeland, or minor ones, such as raising concern about dissatisfaction with work conditions.

South Korea's National Intelligence Service estimated in 2015 that the North Korean government was "earning $230 million a year on average from 58,000 workers in 50 different countries overseas."[1] According to some sources, the history of North Korea's export of human labor dates back to the 1950s.[2] Other reports identify the earliest records dating to 1967.[3] The goal of labor export is to achieve foreign currency for the state, which is particularly critical during economic sanctions. In the earliest years of exported labor, the practice had a double benefit for North Korea: the state gained foreign currency earnings *and* the state exported politically undesirable citizens. In the 1970s North Korea sent laborers with politically unsavory backgrounds, those with bad Songbun, abroad to places like Russia for logging. As one worker explained, "I had bad family background [Songbun], so I was sent to the most difficult logging site in Russia."[4] Jobs that were dangerous and a risk to life were matched with individuals who were seen to be a political risk to the DPRK. As one interviewee put it, "I left North Korea in August 1970 because a list of names came down. The list included only those whose life the regime did not care about. Interestingly, nowadays, the majority of these overseas workers come from Pyongyang, the most privileged of cities in North Korea."[5] In the past, many of these agreements were between states. Today they are typically between the North Korean state and private companies.

North Korea not only commits rights violations within its borders; increasingly, North Korea exports them. The state lends individuals it deems ideologically "safe" to work in unsafe jobs abroad. Workers are sent out of the country to work in restaurants or other businesses as a privilege but must give most of their pay back to the state and submit to heavy surveillance while away. In addition, investments in for-profit ventures that harm foreign nationals, like shoddy medical clinics or lethal arms sales, are undertaken without hesitation. North Korea even takes its most egregious human rights violations on the road, killing or kidnapping dissidents or representatives of hostile states. This chapter unpacks all of the diverse ways that North Korea violates human rights in other countries.

Workers of the World

North Korea's practice of export labor has a history of exploitation. Since the UN Commission of Inquiry report of 2014, several studies have directly itemized the widespread exploitation of this practice as it operates today. North Korea is using the global neoliberal market to dispatch earners who are contracted workers in temporary, insecure, and precarious jobs. The state claims up to 90 percent of their earned wages and charges the workers for their upkeep in terms of food and lodging.[6]

As increased public scrutiny cast a harsh light on these activities, North Korea sought to hide its workers on the high seas as sailors and fishermen.[7] Two factors indicate increased concern for the state of workers' rights in such conditions. The Tokyo MOU (an intergovernmental cooperative organization on port state control in the Asia-Pacific region) rated North Korea's ships as among some of the most unsafe at sea.[8] A search of their site shows hundreds of North Korean ships designated as unfit for service due to fire safety, water tightness, and other safety features.[9] Protecting the rights of workers at sea is difficult due to several factors germane to the workers themselves. They may be irregular workers without access to information in their own language, for example. Such things could be remedied, but matters are complicated because they are working in the quasi-territorial space of the high seas, where human rights laws are even murkier.

Scholars Shin Chang-Hoon and Go Myung-Hyun, of the Asan Institute for Policy Studies based in South Korea, produced a report in November of 2014 raising awareness of the issue, noting that the UN Commission of Inquiry report didn't examine this area of rights abuses.[10] The United Nations report of the special rapporteur on the situation of human rights in North Korea produced a report in 2015 stating that over fifty thousand North Korean citizens were working overseas at that time.[11] More recently, a group of scholars based in Europe at the Leiden Asia Centre published a detailed report on their findings into North Korean forced labor in the European Union.[12] More scholarship is needed in this area. Particularly useful would be research into North Korean export workers in the Middle East and Africa as well as into dispatched sailors and fishermen in Montevideo, Uruguay, and possibly elsewhere, such as Peru.[13] North Korea is not a member of the International Labor Organization, but states that host North Korean exported laborers are members.

Russia is the country with the longest relationship with North Korea's export labor, and it currently has the largest number of North Korean laborers of any cooperating country. Data from the Russian Federal State Statistics Service indicate there were 8,700 North Korean laborers in Russia in 2000. By 2005, this rose to 20,100, and 36,500 by 2010. By 2015 there were 50,000.[14] Workers are primarily employed in the logging industry in the eastern part of Russia. China follows with approximately 19,000 workers. North Korea's export laborers are typically men. When they are posted abroad, women are typically sent to restaurants and *onsen* in China, although as many as 150 women from North Korea worked in the Czech Republic in the early 2000s manufacturing shoes and clothes.[15] There are several branches of a Pyongyang-run restaurant franchise, called Pyongyang Restaurant in Cambodia, which also permitted North Korea to build a $10 million museum in Siem Reap.[16] China deported several North Korean workers when it was found that they were engaged in prostitution. The women were asked to work in the sex industry by their over-seer while officially working at a Chinese food factory in Donggang. The exec-utive of the company, a Chinese and the North Korean minder, in addition to the women, were said to split the profits from the sex work.[17] In May of 2016 thirteen North Koreans defected to South Korea while working in an official capacity at a North Korean–run restaurant in China.[18]

North Korea and Russia worked on an agreement for overseas workers and illegal migrants in 2014.[19] Around November 2014, the draft agreement drew criticism from numerous Russian NGOs working for the protection of human rights. The groups state that the agreement contravenes existing laws on migrants and refugees in Russia and should not be applied.[20] After the dissent from the NGOs, there is no word, official or unofficial, on the agreement. In June 2015 Russia's biggest nongovernmental news agency, Interfax, published an article quoting Sergey Naryshkin, the chairman of the State Duma (the Rus-sian lower house of the Federal Assembly). The chairman announced that the Russian government was planning to sign the Treaty on Mutual Legal Assis-tance in Criminal Matters with the DPRK.[21] The document focuses on the con-ditions under which a person can be handed back to his state of origin. Infor-mation on the new treaty is still unavailable as of this writing. There could be

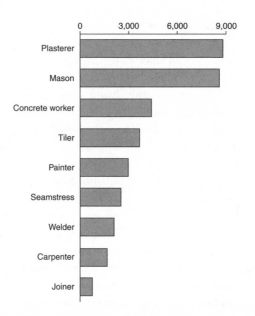

8.1 North Korean Workers in Russia on 2017 work permits

Ian Talley and Anatoly Kurmanaev, "Thousands of North Korean Workers Enter Russia Despite U.N. Ban," *Wall Street Journal*, August 2, 2018, https://www.wsj.com/articles/russia-is-issuing-north -korean-work-permits-despite-u-n-ban-1533216752

several reasons for this. The Russian government might be facing some difficulties ratifying the agreement. The agreement may have been signed, but they have not published it. There may be reasons to keep the document private. Russia's policy on North Korean workers is more transparent than its policy on illegal migrants. The website for the Federal Agency for the Development of the State Border Facilities of the Russian Federation provides the text of the agreement between the governments of the Russian Federation and DPRK regulating the conditions under which North Korean citizens can enter and stay in Russia.

Countries Hosting North Korean Overseas Workers

Country	Number of Workers
Russia	20,000–50,000
China	19,000
Kuwait	5,000
United Arab Emirates	2,000
Mongolia	1,3000–2,000
Qatar	1,800
Angola	1,000
Poland	400–500
Malaysia	300
Oman	300
Libya	300
Myanmar	200
Nigeria	200
Algeria	200
Equatorial Guinea	200
Ethiopia	100
Total	52,300–83,100

Additional Countries Hosting North Korean Workers as of 2017 (exact numbers unknown)

Bangladesh	Mali	Tanzania
Belarus	Mozambique	Taiwan
Cambodia	Namibia	Thailand
DR Congo	Nepal	Uganda
Ghana	Peru	Uruguay
Guinea	Republic of the Congo	Vietnam
Indonesia	Rwanda	Zambia
Kyrgyzstan	Senegal	Zimbabwe
Laos	Singapore	

In January 2007 the Czech Republic ended the employment of North Koreans after the UN Security Council unanimously passed Resolution 1718, a resolution that imposed a series of economic and commercial sanctions after the DPRK's October 9, 2006, nuclear test.[22] At the time 408 laborers, almost all women, were employed as seamstresses in textile and leather factories, as bakers, and as manual laborers throughout the country. The workers were typically employed through one of two types of work contract: group contracts between a Czech labor broker agency and a Czech firm or direct contracts between individual North Koreans and their employers—the latter being less common.[23] Various inspections had been conducted by Czech authorities, and they found the working conditions to be satisfactory according to the law; however, the government of the Czech Republic found the case troubling.[24] According to the deputy minister of labor, Petr Simerka, the labor conditions of the women were not the area of concern but rather their "personal freedom outside" the work environment.[25] He noted that procedures were in place that, if workers wished to seek asylum, they would be permitted to remain in the Czech Republic. In 2002 Kim T'aesan, then serving as president of a North Korean–Czech trade association since July 2000, sought and received asylum. Simerka expressed the importance, however limited, of "exposure to the West," and that Czechs appreciated the plight of North Koreans, having survived authoritarianism themselves.[26] Of considerable concern, however, was where the money was going. Investigators found that wages were deposited directly into one bank account, but under Czech law they did not have the authority to investigate the bank account further unless there was evidence of the law being broken. In 2007, under the concept of forced labor, North Korean laborers were returned home.

Men are sent to work in logging, shipbuilding, mining, and construction. Export labor of this kind started in Africa in the 1970s. Nigeria, Algeria, and Equatorial Guinea have hosted about two hundred workers each, while Ethiopia has hosted one hundred and Libya, three hundred. Angola hosted as many as one thousand.[27] In the 1990s North Korea began sending workers to the Middle East. Kuwait hosted approximately four thousand workers, while United Arab Emirates hosted two thousand. Qatar had eighteen hundred, and Oman, about three hundred. Over the years forty-five different countries have hosted North Korean foreign workers at some time, including countries such as Syria and Iraq. Globally, the total has been estimated between fifty thousand and sixty thousand people.[28] Due to pressure and embarrassment, some countries such as Poland and Qatar have made efforts to terminate employment of North Korean workers where their fundamental rights are violated.[29]

The U.S. State Department's *Trafficking in Persons Report 2016* states that North Korean laborers in Mongolia do not have freedom of movement or choice of employment. They are only permitted to keep a small portion of earned wages, and they endure difficult work and living conditions.[30] Although the

Mongolian government had an intergovernmental agreement with North Korea to regulate the number of imported workers and their salaries, the Mongolian government made no effort, the report states, to investigate labor conditions of foreign contract laborers.[31] The same report identifies that North Korea has sent over four thousand laborers to Kuwait to forced labor on construction sites through a North Korean company operated by the Worker's Party of Korea and the DPRK military.[32] Up to 80–90 percent of workers' wages are taken by the company, and workers are expected to work fourteen to sixteen hours a day in bad conditions and with poor nutrition and little health care. Workers are monitored and confined.[33] There are strong indications that North Koreans are forced to work in hazardous conditions for long hours and with their salary controlled for a period of three years.[34]

The Experience of Being Exported

The physical health of candidates is checked prior to permission and passports being granted. A 2015 report by North Korea Database Center found that workers with hepatitis and tuberculosis had passed the selection process through bribery in the provinces, so further health checks were conducted in Pyongyang.[35] This indicates the attractiveness of overseas jobs for North Koreans. Work conditions abroad are very dangerous and wages are "unimaginably low," yet North Koreans have payed bribes to be able to work overseas.[36] The Leiden Asia Centre report also indicates preexisting health concerns, with one interviewee identifying that 30 percent of applicants fail the threshold for health demands because of tuberculosis; a sick individual can "pass" the health test at the cost of fifty dollars.[37]

Prior to being sent abroad, an individual's background is checked to ensure ideological loyalty. If an individual is known to have had a grandfather or a great-grandfather with connections to the United States or the southern part of Korea during the Korean War, that individual is unlikely to be selected. Additionally, the call for applicants to go abroad for these posts is not made public in the DPRK but rather is exclusively aimed at those of special classes. The recruitment process is informal, and there are many stages of assessment and potential elimination.[38] The president of the neighborhood association (*inminban*) and three colleagues must vouch for an individual's good ideological standing.[39] Laborers are often men married with children back in the DPRK, and marriages have to be official and in good standing. According to Kim T'aesan, former manager of a textile factory in the Czech Republic, for eligibility you have to be "formally married and your children have to remain back home in North Korea—they are hostages to prevent you from escaping."[40] As the Leiden report shows, "there is an implicit threat to North Korean workers that their families are being held hostage to ensure against flight risk and to guarantee adherence to rules."[41] Having an immediate nuclear family is crucial for eligibility for going abroad, yet workers are severely restricted in correspondence with family and friends, often only getting letters via other deployed workers.[42] This use of family members who remain back in North Korea has been referred to as a system of love abuse.[43] The state abuses the love that exists between family members, keeping the majority of family back in North Korea—who will be punished if the citizen abroad defects. This ensures they maintain loyalty to the nation.

Individuals are always sent abroad in groups. Passports are kept by managers and only used by the individual at the point of customs immigration control.[44] This might not seem odd to North Koreans, as most of them do not own passports. Workers typically have no idea what to expect, only knowing their placement will last three years. Workers report not seeing employment contracts. They understand that the agreement is made between the state and the institution through which they are hired. According to the Slaves to the System Project, proper explanations of contract terms and work conditions were lacking for every host country and position, regardless of occupation. The social pressure to conform also discourages North Koreans from complaining or suggesting alternative opinions to managers. As one former overseas laborer explained, "If you complain or go against their opinion, you become an outcast. No one can act that way. Workers think [of] it as a natural thing and just go along with it. Of course we complain among ourselves. There is a possibility that the manager's informant can hear us but I believe he is on the same side. It is all right unless you make a statement against the system."[45]

Workers are frequently unaware of pay and remuneration. Sometimes they only find out how much they are paid once they take up the position, if at all. According to one interviewee, workers never knew how much they were earning, and never knew the cost of room and board. For this reason, the extent of abuse is also beyond awareness.[46] The small amount of wages they were permitted to keep also had to be self-managed in terms of getting that money back to North Korea, as there were no institutional management processes in place for international transmission.[47]

One of the incentives for going abroad is the promise that, upon successful completion of the contract abroad, workers will be given household appliances such as televisions when they return to North Korea. "Because an average North Korean could not purchase even a black and white television with a lifetime's worth of savings, most people considered these compensation arrangements to be generous. Therefore, overseas opportunities were in high demand."[48] The other reason for these types of nonmonetary rewards is that the movement of money into North Korea has become considerably more difficult in the wake of the UN Security Council resolutions that aim at cracking down on financial transfers into and out of North Korea.[49] Workers are kept in the dark about how much they are being paid by the company as their salaries are deposited into accounts controlled by the North Korean government and signed for or forged by managers. They are unaware what percentage of their income goes to the government. They also face punishment from North Korean managers if they fail to meet production targets. Since wages are given to workers via managers, these wages can be withheld to push workers into working harder as they face increased precarity without access to their wages.[50]

Rent and other charges are deducted from wages, but workers are not allowed to know details or itemized information. They are unable to trace what money is coming in and what is going out. Workers are obligated to return part of their salary back to the government of North Korea since working abroad is a privilege of the state. The state takes this payment automatically from workers, and they never learn what their real salary is prior to these government deductions.[51] Reports indicate that the amount of money the North Korea government clawed back from workers was considerable. "If one receives a hundred dollars, they took away ninety. Even the remaining ten dollars are not entirely given to me," a logger based in Russia stated. As a way to make extra money, laborers turn to working illegally outside of the company.[52] If workers did not finish their tasks, they were deducted pay for that part of the job left unfinished.[53] If companies provided the cost of food to North Korean workers, North Korean managerial staff intercepted this opportunity to extort by providing lower-quality food.[54] It is almost unimaginable to raise concerns with managers over wages, work conditions, or the desire to change or stop work. "The workers wouldn't dare to raise an issue against the system, for instance, regarding their wages. If they do, they know they will be sent back home (to the DPRK), where they will face punishment."[55]

Exporting Thought Control

The Leiden Asia Centre report shows that, along with its laborers, North Korea exports its entire ideological structures and practices, such as surveillance.[56] This means the expectation of regular self-criticism sessions and ideological training, customary back home, is also commonplace abroad. North Korea reproduces the hermetic, controlled, and isolated ideological vacuum of home. These "micro-versions" of North Korean ideological thought-life are a pervasive feature of the lives of workers abroad.[57] When a suitcase containing several handwritten notebooks was left in Montevideo, Uruguay, media captured a rare glimpse into the private life of a North Korean sailor. The notebooks contained dozens of pages of carefully written notes. There were poems and songs about Kim Il Sung, Kim Jong Il, and Kim Jong Un as well as notes about Juche and the Charter of the Korean Workers' Party. Not a single personal, or personal-izing, note was reportedly found apart from the fact that the notes were hand-written.[58] The notebooks appear to be study guides. An overseas laborer explained, "If you don't [participate in all study sessions], they count it as a vio-lation. It is a political obligation for North Koreans. Meeting and studying are a must."[59] And yet it is possible that some of North Korea's ideological control might slacken while abroad. There are indications of this happening, accord-ing to one worker: "Indeed, there once was the time we did not hold the meet-ing for a month and procrastinated writing notes until the end of the month."[60]

Yet, even if there is some slack in ideological practice, the education it pro-vides can often be broadly influencing of behavior. Prior to going overseas, primary "training" concerns ideological preparation. As one interviewee reported,

> There is the working abroad training. This teaches manners, customs and eti-quette we should follow abroad. The last one is [a] higher-class course, and this is interesting, they teach us how to stay secure. It deals with the many South Korean national security agents abroad and how we have to be careful since they will otherwise kidnap us. . . . They show us videos about people who were blinded by the lure of money and went to South Korea, people who got kid-napped and all kinds of miserable lives of people who went to South Korea and were tortured to death, while their deaths were camouflaged as traffic accidents.[61]

The state uses videos of return defectors to encourage a state-led ideological framing of life elsewhere. To date, detailed research into North Korean work-ers' rights abroad has mostly focused on the European Union, predominantly Poland.[62] As noted earlier, few North Korean workers are sent to Poland com-pared with other countries such as China and Russia. However, the fact that even among this small number of workers there are serious human rights con-cerns indicates that in scaling up, engaging in more arduous labor such as log-ging, and moving to countries with worse labor rights records, things are unlikely to be better. North Korean overseas laborers' rights are violated in six key areas: the right to work or change jobs, the right to free movement and to choose where to live, the right to privacy and correspondence with family, the freedom of opinion and religion, the freedom of expression without interfer-ence, and an adequate standard of living and wages.[63]

Workers report that their personal identity documents such as passports were only in their possession at the moment of passing through immigration; at all other times their identity papers were kept by managers. The only time workers might otherwise get access to their documents would be if they had to go to the hospital.[64] Interviews with former exported laborers reveal that they lived in near total isolation from non–North Korean workers, blocked from accessing the host country by barbed wire and other barriers in the compound. If workers asked why the barbed wire was there, they were told it was standard for all workplaces with foreigners. In addition to physical barriers, there are also linguistic barriers and rules against contact with the host community.[65]

Some workers did suspect the wire was there to manage their free movement. The workers indicated awareness that their living and working conditions were far from ideal. Kim, former manager of women laborers in the Czech Republic, described work conditions as "slave like." "They don't have access to [the] outside world, no access to TV, radio and such, and they are not allowed to talk to foreigners."[66] The Leiden research team found closed-circuit TV cameras outside the homes of North Korean exported laborers. Workers were controlled and surveilled in other ways too. An interviewee explained that according to the "general principles of DPRK's overseas labour," they were not permitted to go out. If supplies of food or other necessary items were running out, then a trip to the shops could be permitted. And yet, "individually it was not possible to go out"; one had to go in a group, and only with permission of a supervisor.[67] Little time for rest and physical recovery is permitted, with only one day off per month—some workers only had one day off per year—and no other holidays. If national holidays were in place in the host country, North Koreans were sent to work by their supervisors anyway. North Korean national holidays were similarly ignored.[68]

Czech Republic Labor Inspector General Hahn noted that in an investigation of the workplaces, it was clear the workers were under a "microscope." He said "it was frustrating that the individual workers refused to talk with inspectors one-on-one without other coworkers present, usually the designated North Korean translator. Even in one-on-one situations where a Czech-provided Korean translator was present, the workers would not talk with inspectors."[69] A western journalist, a resident of Prague, visited a textile factory in Nachod where North Korean women worked. She observed "North Koreans laughing amongst themselves and with their Ukrainian coworkers as they sewed"; upon asking questions directly, however, she found that the North Koreans gave no response. The Ukrainian coworkers told the journalist that the North Koreans understood Czech and seemed happy to be living and working in the country. Working conditions in this factory, at least, appeared to meet or exceeded Czech standards.[70]

Not all overseas work is dangerous, but there are reports that men's work, in particular, has a higher degree of risk and danger. Deaths from accidents at work can be horrific. Chŏn Kyŏngsu, the man whose story opens this chapter, worked as a welder, mostly on ships from Norway and Denmark. Over the nearly two-year period he was at Crist Shipyards in Gdynia, Poland, he worked on ten projects before an accident occurred on site. In 2014 he was working his usual twelve-hour day. He was welding pipelines inside a tank when a flame suddenly ignited, engulfing him in fire. He was brought to the hospital with burns to 95 percent of his body. His injuries were so severe that he died the next day.[71] The Polish National Labor Inspectorate investigated and found illegal practices by the employers.[72] Polish labor officials were not able to prosecute because North Korean workers' documentation identifies them as self-employed and beyond Polish jurisdiction.[73] Prior to the accident that killed Chŏn, the Polish inspectorate found twenty-nine North Koreans working illegally at the shipyard.[74]

Testimony from logging workers in Russia indicates that the work is very dangerous and extremely physically demanding, particularly because workers lack the adequate equipment needed to perform tasks, work takes place in long shifts, the weather is harsh, and the workers are inadequately prepared in terms of clothing and tools.[75] Workers were not given proper clothing for work tasks and had to borrow from other workers or lay out money from their meager wages to buy sturdy clothes.[76] Conditions of work pose great risks to safety. If an injury on the job required medical attention, the worker or the hiring enterprise in the host country paid the cost. An injury that prevents a worker from producing is egregious because the injured worker would be freeloading on the system, an expensive prospect while abroad. Such workers are shipped back to North Korea.[77] Compensation or support for death on the job is not offered.

When the negative aspects of life for overseas North Korean workers have come to light, many human rights groups have marshalled to campaign against the violations. However, raising awareness of human rights violations does not necessarily generate improved conditions for those under concern. Sometimes rights campaigns can have unexpected and compounding negative effects.[78] When rights campaigners raised awareness about working conditions for North Koreans in Kuwait, for example, workers were given safety gear to wear, and they would be fined if they failed to wear it properly.[79] They may have been physically safer, but were financially worse off as the payment of these fines came out of personal savings. In the case of exported rights violations, the solutions really need to address the real problem—the North Korean state—instead of the symptoms of misconduct abroad.

Exporting Prisoners

The rumor of an overseas North Korean prison in Equatorial Guinea has yet to be confirmed. The Congolese newspaper *Le Potential* published a story about the prison, said to be in Santiago de Baney. After the article went to press, the local DPRK ambassador arrived at the newspaper office to complain about how North Korea was represented. The government official requested the names of the source for the information, but was denied. *Le Potential* was not the first to publish the story, explaining that Equatorial Guinea is "one of the few countries to have acceded to the request of the North Korean regime to accommodate prisoners to work in inhumane conditions at the boundary of slavery."[80] The Spanish paper *Diario rombe* first researched and published the story in 2014, claiming North Korea is expanding its overseas prisons in Africa, with special emphasis on Equatorial Guinea.[81] Prisoners are sentenced to forced labor in the small town of Santiago de Baney. According to witnesses interviewed by *Diario rombe*, the prison is located between the towns of Rebola and Baney and is filled with convicts who are politicians, criminals, and murders sentenced to hard labor with inadequate food, beatings, poor health, and poor living conditions. The prison is within a farm area, guarded by armed military. The paper states the prisoners are unable to leave, and their sentences are for life. The reporter explained that it was not possible to speak to any of the prisoners. It is difficult to know if these prisoners are laboring on behalf of the North Korean or the government of Equatorial Guinea.[82] The paper reports that Equatorial Guinea feigned ignorance of the prison, claiming they merely rented the land to North Korea and didn't know its true purpose. For those who drive by on the roadway from the airport to Sipopo, the prison can't be seen through the forest. The article claims that the situation of indentured North Korean laborers in Equatorial Guinea is similar to that of the overseas laborers in Siberia. *Radio Free Asia* reported on the case in 2016, indicating that the prison was in fact in operation.[83] Early in 2018 Equatorial Guinea called upon its domestic businesses to halt dealings with North Korea.[84]

Exporting Medical Malpractice

Part of North Korea's overseas money earning involves medical practice and pharmaceutical sales. North Korea operated two medical clinics in Tanzania as part of its foreign currency earning efforts. The clinics "used fake medicine, unqualified doctors and ineffective treatments that could actually harm patients."[85] Medicine being sold by the North Korean doctors in Tanzania contained levels of mercury not permissible by international standards.[86] Analysis found traces of lead, arsenic, and other poisonous heavy metals in medicine from these clinics.[87] According to *Radio Free Asia*, "Before the shuttering of the two clinics, 13 such facilities in Tanzania, including four in Dares Salaam, were remitting about $1 million a year to Pyongyang."[88] Illegal medical service, in the form of producing defective medicine and medical instruments, is criminalized in North Korea's own criminal code. Yet, when done overseas and to turn a profit for the state, the crime apparently passes the bar of acceptability.

Countries with North Korean Medical Clinics (as of 2017)

Angola	Nepal
Cambodia	Nigeria
China	Republic of Congo
Mongolia	Tanzania
Mozambique	Uganda

Clinics lacked business licenses yet accepted patients. Most of the doctors at the clinics had no work permits. The list of concerns about the clinics was considerable, including unverified treatments, unverified therapeutic apparatuses, unlabeled drugs, and fake or improperly labeled medicine. North Korean doctors based in Kenya, for example, could not speak Swahili and were also not proficient in English.

North Korea has sent doctors to other countries in Africa. A "technical exchange" exists with local hospitals in Nigeria. Three male North Korean doctors who had been working since 2005 in Potiskum selling polio vaccines were allegedly killed by Boko Haram.[89] A Cambodia-based diplomat not authorized to speak to the media told the *Diplomat* that North Korean doctors were dispatched overseas in eight other countries: Ukraine, Bangladesh, Kurdistan, Tanzania, Russia, Uganda, Ethiopia, and Nepal.[90] There are indications that doctors are dispatched to Libya and Mozambique as well.[91] A 2015 report by *Radio Free Asia* claims that there have been as many as twelve North Korean medical clinics in Dar es Salaam, Tanzania, since 1991. Staff has numbered as few as twenty in the early years to a hundred in recent times.[92]

Local media indicate that patients who visited the clinics did not receive proper medical care. Conditions that precipitated a visit to the doctor worsened. Local stories strongly suggest abuse and manipulation of patients in order to increase financial takings in exchange for "treatment."[93] A local source spoke to *Radio Free Asia*, saying clinics were earning between US$1 million and US$1.3 million a year. Of those takings, about 90 percent was sent back to the regime.[94]

Ties between Tanzania's local health officials and the North Korean government make it difficult to resolve issues. There are suggestions the clinics may be evading taxes in Tanzania and may be partially owned by the ruling Chama Cha Mapinduzi (Party of the Revolution) party.[95] When investigated, the North Korean personnel claimed that their business was a joint operation with Chama Cha Mapinduzi—the Tanzanian governing party. Deputy Minister of Health Hamisi Kigwangalla found the claim to be false after checking with the ruling party. After this finding the clinics were shut down. Despite these scandals, deceptions, and abuses, North Korean medical personnel remain employed abroad. In Cambodia two North Korean doctors are employed at a hospital called Lipo Long Hua International. They live at the hospital and are on call twenty-four hours a day.[96]

Exporting Militarism

North Korea provided training and equipment to anticolonial and communist fighters in the 1960s and 1970s. When the Soviet Bloc collapsed, the international connection changed with the times, morphing into providing help—building tunnels in the early 2000s—for Hezbollah and Hamas and putting weapons into the hands of Tamil Tigers. Hard currency and weapons trading were Kim Jong Il's developments to his father's international engagement, switching up from revolutionary zeal to "brutal pragmatism."[97] Today these efforts continue in the form of laundering hard currency, trading weapons, and selling illicit and counterfeit drugs through front companies.[98]

Recent investigations by the UN Panel of Experts reveal that North Korea continues to carry out prohibited military cooperation throughout Asia and Africa. There is ongoing ballistic missile cooperation between North Korea, the Syrian Arab Republic, and Myanmar. Evidence also shows that North Korea is conducting conventional arms deals and using cyber operations to steal military secrets.

Security is also threatened through cyber operations outside of the realm of the military. The UN's Panel of Experts on human rights found that their email accounts were compromised. Their passwords were accessed by an adversary in May 2017 and were later targeted with spear phishing attacks. Microsoft contacted the UN Panel of Experts and gave the assessment that it was a "persistent and sophisticated attack by a professional adversary."[99]

North Korean diplomats play a pivotal role in these prohibited activities by providing logistics support for arms transfer, providing technical and intelligence operations, and acting as fronts for commercial activities—these acts violate UN Resolution 1874 and the Vienna Convention on Diplomatic Relations.[100] North Korea uses "sealed diplomatic shipments" to undertake prohibited activities that involve UN-sanctioned entities. In a similar fashion to avoid detection, the North uses front companies to obfuscate the timing, route, and content of prohibited shipments.

Until January 2017 an eighty-member North Korean military advisory mission was in Angola training the Angolan presidential guard and other units. Angola has yet to provide the United Nations with a list of names and ranking of the members. In August 2016 a shipment of thirty thousand rocket-propelled grenades and components on route to Al-Sakr Factory for Developed Industries, in Cairo, was seized by the Egyptian authorities. These entities are violating the arms embargo provisions and have failed to provide the UN Panel of Experts with information on the identity of the exporters from the DPRK or any financial information related to this. Eritrea also has established arms-related cooperation with DPRK via the company named Eritech. The Panel of Experts found military cooperation projects between the DPRK and the Sudan. A group of ballistic missile technicians affiliated with North Korea's Academy of National Defense Science, an organization sanctioned by the United Nations, visited the Syrian Arab Republic in November 2016. Prior to this trip a technical delegation from North Korea visited Syria and transferred materials known for use in chemical weapons programs such as special resistance valves and thermometers. Syria acquired several tons of conventional armaments (30 mm grenade launchers, six-barreled 7.62 mm machine guns, and six-barreled 30 mm autocannons) through a North Korean front entity called Chonryong Technology Corporation in September 2016.

✳ ✳ ✳

As their involvement with selling chemical weapons and running fraudulent medical clinics shows, North Korea's attempts to bolster or protect its regime's power through human rights violations are not limited to surveilling and controlling citizens who are permitted to travel beyond its borders. On top of the other human rights violations they have exported, North Korea has also allegedly carried out abductions and political executions abroad. The state's international abductions of citizens from so-called hostile nations in their own countries are well documented—they are discussed more in the next chapter. In February 2107 Kim Jong Nam, the exiled brother of Supreme Leader Kim Jong Un, was killed using VX nerve agent in the Kuala Lumpur airport. While the investigation and trial are still ongoing at the time of this writing, many experts believe the murder was an assassination carried out on Kim Jong Un's orders. By taking their most egregious human rights violations on the road in this manner, North Korea shows that national boundaries cannot contain their disrespect for human rights and the international laws meant to protect them.

PART II

THE DENIALS

CHAPTER 9

FROM THE MOUTHS OF FOREIGN NATIONALS

Speaking to a large gathering of reporters at the People's Palace of Culture in Pyongyang, twenty-nine-year-old U.S. citizen Arturo Pierre Martinez delivered a breathless speech about American imperialism. For a while it was precisely the sort of message that might have come from the Korean Central News Agency (KCNA). But it took a turn. "About halfway in," writes political economist Stephan Haggard, "the unraveling becomes apparent as Martinez takes up the issues of an American-run UFO (not drone) program, 'weaponized satillital Octocopters' used for official drug-running and 'infrasonic generators' . . . that have been used to implant thoughts and voices in US citizens and give cancer to five South American heads of state."[1]

It seemed North Korea got a little more than they bargained for with this American.[2] No matter. He served a function to debunk allegations of rights abuses. During the question-and-answer period, a North Korean reporter—unfazed by ravings about 'Octocopters'—sought Martinez's thoughts on the "U.S. smear campaign" concerning North Korea's human rights. Martinez answered lucidly, "I do believe that the arguments or accusations the U.S. has been making against the DPRK are completely unfounded. During my stay here I witnessed how happily [sic] the nation is. There have been many accusations against the DPRK. People here are very happy. People are taken as a priority. Even they were treating me well."[3]

* * *

The inherent weakness embedded in human rights is that persons are only able to avail themselves of rights when they can access the protection of a receptive nation-state. This paradox can be examined from another angle: the links between citizen and state, particularly where foreign nationals—willing or detained—are concerned. The cases here highlight how North Korea operationalizes individuals from foreign nations as part of soft power political agenda to present an image of a nation that respects rights.

It is hard to imagine nowadays why anyone would want to defect *to* North Korea. Nevertheless, *wolbuk*, as it is called in Korean, has occurred. It is more common, though, for North Korea to detain unwitting wayward foreigners to use for similar ends. These acts do not sit outside of the geopolitical sphere. Instead, such movement of people readily reveals the human security dimension of international relations and the power play between nations. These cases are often highly mediatized, both in North Korean and international news. They may involve high-level government officials from the United States. Officials from the United States are involved not because the vast majority of foreigners illegally crossing into North Korea have been Americans but because the Americans are more likely to be operationalized. Kenneth Bae, an American evangelical Christian missionary arrested in North Korea, was told, "Contact your government and tell them to make the most ardent efforts for the following: the United States needs to validate the DPRK legal system; they must acknowledge your guilt; they must apologize for your crimes; and they must promise that these types of illegal acts by Americans will not happen again."[4] It becomes North Korea's opportunity to flip the "shame game" campaign by literally naming and shaming someone for breaking their national security laws. This individuated shaming is a metonym for the North's desire to throttle but then, on their own terms, forgive the United States.

With each foreign national who is caught and cast in this role, the same message is reiterated again and again. It goes a little like this: U.S. citizens are breaking North Korea's national laws; they are infringing on national sovereignty to change the North Korean state. On the mediatized scene, these acts create an opportunity for North Korea to make personal and intimate an otherwise cold, distant, and impersonal geopolitical quandary that exists in the U.S. imaginary somewhere "over there." These individuals are antagonists in a North Korean historic narrative that can finally gain global attention as David (North Korea) wrestles and wins against Goliath (the United States). The antagonist is an individual manifestation of the United States, whose transgressions are a stand-in for U.S. grand geopolitical ambitions. In the glare of the press conference spotlight, the adversary is revealed for what he really is: pathetic, defeated, and convinced his former thinking was in error, his behavior hostile and wrong. The North Korean state treats the wayward antagonists (sometimes) mercifully yet firmly. Sometimes they are housed in a prison but more often in a hotel—with a bill to follow. American citizen Merrill Newman was held in a hotel for forty-two days. Upon his release and return to the United States, he was billed $3,241 for his "hotel room, meals, a $23 phone call to his wife and $3 for a lost plate."[5] Brought down to the minutia scale of dinner plates and phone calls, these cases may seem comical, but the message conveyed is steadfast: this state takes itself deadly seriously, and woe to those who don't. There must be acknowledgement of errors, sincere impassioned apology, and international media attention.

The Willing

Before Newman and other operationalized sojourners, there were the soldiers. The willing.

Technically these soldiers were deserters of the U.S. military. Six U.S. soldiers went to North Korea after the Korean War. James Joseph Dresnok, the key figure of the documentary *Crossing the Line*, went to North Korea in 1962, the same year that Larry Allen Abshier crossed. Jerry Parrish claims that he crossed into North Korea on December 6, 1963, because he feared his father-in-law would kill him upon return to the United States from South Korea. Parrish worked as a teacher for two decades at North Korea's Reconnaissance Bureau Foreign Language College. Charles Robert Jenkins crossed on January 4, 1965. The factors that led them to cross were by and large personal and immature—remarkably irreconcilable mistakes.[6] Speaking to author Jim Frederick, Jenkins explained,

> I decided that I was going to walk north across the DMZ and into North Korea. Once there, I would ask to be handed over to the Russians and request a diplomatic exchange for passage back to the United States, where I would face charges for desertion. I had heard of this happening before. . . . I still feel my biggest mistake was the way I went AWOL. I was so ignorant. I did not understand that the country I was seeking temporary refuge in was literally a giant, demented prison.[7]

Life in North Korea was undoubtedly different from what these men were used to. Within a few years of arriving, in 1966, several sought asylum at the embassy of the Soviet Union in Pyongyang. The Soviet Union rejected their plea and notified DPRK officials. Parrish tried to seek asylum at the Chinese Embassy but got the same result.[8] In the foreword to Jenkins's memoir, Jim Frederick describes Jenkins's life—and likely the other foreigners in North Korea: "a life of quiet desperation, of suffering an almost unbearably understated evil. He and his fellow Americans were considered special by the Organization [Jenkins called the government "the Organization"]—about that, there can be no doubt."[9] But the North Korean government also didn't know what to do with these deserters. A little over a decade later Roy Chung, a South Korean citizen who grew up in the United States, went AWOL while serving in West Germany in 1979. Shortly after, he was heard on Voice of Korea, then known as Radio Pyong-yang. In 1982 U.S. Army infantry soldier Joseph T. White also crossed the demilitarized zone.[10] Over time, all were used by the North Korean government through its state media. They appeared in North Korean movies and on maga-zine covers as villainous American imperialists. Their voices were broadcast over the demilitarized zone using loudspeakers in an effort to persuade U.S. soldiers stationed in the South to defect northward.

Following their defections to North Korea many of these individuals mar-ried. Typically matches were made by the state between defectors and abduct-ees.[11] Dresnok married Doina Bumbea, from Romania, who, according to Jen-kins, had been abducted by the North Korean state. Jenkins was married to an abductee from Japan, Hitomi Soga.[12] Children of these unions are carefully positioned within the media. In recent years, James and Ted Dresnok spoke to Korean American journalist Roh Kil-nam. Roh is the face of the Los Angeles–based news publication *Minjok Tongshin*. Sympathetic to North Korea, Roh has been called a "cultural spy" for North Korea.[13] In their interview with Roh, the white Dresnok brothers—one dressed in Korean People's Army attire and both

9.1 James (left), Ted Dresnok, and Roh Kil-nam from *Minjok Tongshin* (screenshot 20.50)

"Dialogue with Two Children of an American Who Crossed the 38 Parallel 54 Years Ago," *Minjok Tongshin*, YouTube, May 21, 2016, https://www.youtube.com/watch?time_continue=36&v=xoxIp NKqhus)

speaking fluent, Pyongyang-accented Korean—explain, "The American Imperialists caused the division of the Korean Peninsula." The scene reads like a geopolitical mashup: two young white men born in North Korea to an American military deserter father and Romanian abductee mother praise North Korea to a South Korean–born, naturalized U.S. citizen. The brothers were gracious to clarify that Roh wasn't representative of the American Imperialists—they didn't hate *him*—but rather the top U.S. government officials.[14]

High-profile deserter announcements were not the only way that North Korea tried to change the global narrative about itself in the postwar era. North Korea tried to gain support in the international community through connecting with radical leftists or Juche international study groups abroad. They continue to do this today. In the 1960s North Korea invited international supporters to its homeland to help tailor their material to different audiences. To contemporary minds, the notion that North Korea would try to promote itself internationally might seem like an impossible task. The 1960s through the 1980s was a phase of political and economic success for North Korea, which was particularly contrasted by political strife in South Korea. In 1965 socialist economist Joan Robinson determined that the country had accomplished an economic miracle. Revolutionary Che Guevara told media that Cuba aspired to model itself after North Korea.[15]

The personal papers of Eldridge Cleaver reveal connections between the Black Panther Party and the North Korean state in the 1960s and 1970s. Cleaver saw Pyongyang as an "earthly paradise" where U.S. imperialism was admirably resisted.[16] Historian Benjamin Young's examination of Cleaver's personal papers exposes favorable commentary on the DPRK, Kim Il Sung, and Juche ideology. Visiting the country in 1969, Cleaver described basic needs being met in terms of food, education, medicine, and so on; although he wasn't unaware of the "brainwashing and unsubtle racism," he still found the country impressive.[17]

Aligning with African American movements was an attempt to join in collective international anti-imperialist struggle against the United States, but for North Korea the aim was about reunifying the Korean peninsula.[18] Young reveals that North Korea believed connecting with the Black Panther Party could help to shift public opinion in the United States toward sympathy for the case of North Korea. North Korea justified its connection with African Americans by creating a sense of shared subjugation at the hands of imperialists, thus giving the sense of a mutual struggle against a common enemy.

The Black Panther Party sought to align with postcolonial states in collective revolution against the fascism and imperialism of the United States. North Korea's anti-imperialist campaign wasn't solely targeted on the United States but extended into the third world. North Korea connected with the independence movement in Puerto Rico, Castro's Cuba, neo-Nazis, and Grenada as well as African states. The goals were many: to spread propaganda about Kim Il Sung, to access money, to stir unrest in the United States and among its allies. The international outreach, what Young calls "guerilla internationalism," was aimed at improving North Korea's international reputation particularly as it compared with South Korea's status at the United Nations.[19] In the late 1960s and 1970s North Korean propaganda tried to establish Kim Il Sung globally as the new leading Asian communist and ideologue; the work was successful.[20] In some circles Kim Il Sung was viewed as on par with Friedrich Engels, Karl Marx, and Joseph Stalin for leading a global revolution.[21] Social scientist Adrian Buzo identifies that North Korea placed large advertisements with extracts of Kim Il Sung's speeches in popular Western newspapers such as the London *Times* and the *Washington Post*. When the advertisements weren't always interpreted as the North would have liked, efforts were abandoned.[22]

Despite North Korea's international engagement, foreigners who go willingly to North Korea—then and now—sometimes find themselves unwillingly detained. Originally from Venezuela, poet Ali Lameda moved to North Korea in 1966 after receiving an invitation to work with the government's Department of Foreign Publications. His duty was to undertake translation of the works of Kim Il Sung into Spanish. He was also charged with the promotion of these texts throughout the Spanish-speaking world. While at the DFP, Lameda met other foreigners tasked with similar assignments, in other languages. One of these individuals was Jacques Sedillot, of France, a man who would also face imprisonment and torture.

Although Lameda was interested and sympathetic to "the great work of national construction of the Korean people," he always felt a pervading feeling of stifled isolation in Pyongyang.[23] When he was arrested, it came as a complete surprise.[24] In September of 1967 nine people showed up at his apartment to arrest him. Two were in police uniform, and the remainder were Public Security agents. He was arrested for being an enemy of the DPRK and ordered to confess. Lameda describes this period of imprisonment as torture by hunger and continual cruelty. He reports a year of starvation rations, filth, beatings, cramped and damp cells, sleep deprivation, chronic fever, and the endless tortured cries of other inmates. This first arrest and imprisonment with the Ministry of the Interior lasted a year. Upon release, he returned home in such a condition that no explanation was required for what he endured. In his account to Amnesty International, Lameda explains he was returned to his home in Pyongyang, "covered in sores and suffering haemorrhages" and weighting 22 kilograms (48.5 pounds) less.[25] It was obvious to his companion, even without explaining it, that his year of imprisonment was one of extreme suffering. He was led to believe that after two months of house arrest, he would be released without condition.[26] Naturally, Lameda shared details of his year of imprisonment with his companion, a foreign woman who lived with him in Pyongyang.

Lameda speculated in his report to Amnesty International that the security services must have bugged his home because upon his second arrest they accused him of denouncing North Korea, spreading propaganda against North Korea, and acting as an imperialist spy. Authorities referred to Lameda's literary work as "bourgeois filth," confiscated it, and ordered it burned. "The authorities wanted me to tell my companion that on my own orders it was to be burnt. It was unbelievable that I should tell her any such thing about my work, my life's work."[27]

After his second arrest Lameda was given a trial that lasted one day. He was provided a defense attorney but was not permitted to defend himself. "It was demanded that I confess my guilt. The tribunal did not make any specific accusations—there were no formal charges—but the accused has to accuse himself before the tribunal. Thus there was no necessity for the tribunal to produce any evidence. I had no right to defend myself, I could only admit guilt."[28] Lameda asked for a lawyer of his choosing. He asked for the tribunal to be made public. His requests were "dismissed as bourgeois." The prosecutor averred that Lameda was in Korea to "sabotage, spy and introduce infiltrators," that he was "under the control of the CIA."[29] They requested the maximum penalty according to the Penal Code. His defense counsel, whom he met for thirty minutes, delivered a speech of praise to Kim Il Sung and asked that Lameda receive twenty years in prison. The tribunal retired for five minutes to determine a sentence of twenty years forced labor.

Lameda was to be reeducated through labor; thus, he was to be taught a trade. However, he was never taught one. Lameda speculates that it was because they did not wish for a foreigner to mingle with Koreans in the camp. In the Amnesty International report, Lameda states he was held in Suriwon prison, which took three hours of driving on winding dirt roads out of Pyongyang. There are no records for a camp called Suriwon, but he could have been held in Sariwon, which is to the south of Pyongyang. It is also possible that he was held to the north of Pyongyang at Kwanliso No. 14, the nearest political prison camp to Pyongyang. Lameda had no pen or paper in prison but wrote verses and memorized them. He later published a poem, "Dawn," composed in camp. One stanza states: "Human suffering pierces the uprightness / of your orthodoxy. You see banners / of gold in your labyrinths. But one Tuesday it all comes crashing down unexpectedly."[30] Lameda was held in solitary confinement for six years.

North Korea released him in September 1974. The release resulted from multiple geopolitical pressures between North Korea and Venezuela. His release was a quid pro quo between the two countries. Venezuela wanted to get Lameda released. The government pressured two visiting North Korean "correspondents," saying that they would only be received if they could get North Korea to release Lameda. Releasing Lameda would make it possible for North

Korea to angle for diplomatic relations with Venezuela.[31] They did establish diplomatic relations. The foreign ministry's director of international policy, Diaz Gonzalez, stated that relations between the two countries would be "nominal" with no residence for either nation in the other's territory "for some time to come."[32] To this day, relations remain nominal, and Venezuela has no diplomatic compound in Pyongyang.[33]

Sedillot met North Koreans in Algiers. He was over sixty years old when he accepted an invitation from North Korea to work as head of the French section in the Department of Foreign Publications. The department, the same that Lameda worked at, was "virtually a foreign ministry of information and propaganda."[34] As part of a North Korean plan to improve the reception of North Korean propaganda in the French-speaking world, Sedillot was sent to France to determine its effectiveness there. He was also tasked with recruiting more French translators for the team. Sedillot faithfully reported what he found:

> When such people [the French] encounter propaganda which says that, at 14, Kim Il Sung was the leader of the Communist Party, had launched a revolution and directed an army—a child leading a communist party revolution in a country without a communist party, beating the Japanese army, and so on, it seems very hard to believe. Commenting ironically, the French said they had heard about [Augusto] Sandino, but not a word about Kim Il Sung in the 1920s. Otherwise they would have sent him some assistance.

According to Lameda, who relayed the deceased Sedillot's story to Amnesty International, these disagreeable responses were "what everybody says when they read those publications."[35] Lameda advised Sedillot to remove this portion of the report. Sedillot insisted the insights were valuable to the North Koreans because they were true and based on public opinion polls with hundreds of people. Sedillot had the misguided thought that North Koreans should reflect on how their propaganda was received in France, making it more palatable.

The message and its timing were disastrous. Even as Sedillot was collecting his data in France, arguments were occurring at the top of the party and government. "Reflected in the exaggerated exaltation of the personality of Kim Il Sung," he explained, were problems in DPRK politics.[36] The Cultural Revolution's elevation of the Chinese leader was mirrored for Kim Il Sung in Pyongyang. The Seven-Year Economic Plan had failed. Another three years were tacked on. This was "a great blow to Korean pride," Lameda states, because they had been proclaiming it a success, and that would have to be retracted.[37] Indeed, these were years of crucial economic and political change for both Koreas. South Korea would soon change from an authoritarian dictatorship and poverty to a democracy with a leading global economy, while North Korea would sink deeper into economic and political entropy. Thus, Sedillot's perceived challenge to the regime hit a nerve. As with Lameda, Sedillot was accused of being an infiltrator and given no chance to defend himself. He was stalwart throughout his "trial," refusing to make a false confession. He was imprisoned and released in 1975. He wished to return to France but died in Pyongyang in 1976.

The Detained

The earliest and most famous case of North Korea's use and abuse of foreign nationals—outside of prisoners of war—is that of the eighty-three Americans captured from the USS *Pueblo* seized at noon on January 23, 1968. The U.S. ship was in East Sea international waters when a North Korean SO-1 class subchaser approached.[38] The men on board the North Korean ship were at general quarters, which means they had followed an announcement signaling all hands must attend battle stations. Deck guns were trained on the USS *Pueblo*. On board the *Pueblo*, the ensign raised the flag indicating that hydrographic research, not combat, preparations were under way. As they did this, several North Korean P-4 motor torpedo boats approached. The subchaser hoisted the signal flag "Heave to or I will open fire on you." *Pueblo* hoisted a response: "I am in international waters." The signal came again, "Heave to or I will open fire." The U.S. ship: "Thank you for your consideration: I am departing the area." They began to depart at one-third speed. Torpedo boats crisscrossed the ship's bow and the subchaser again hoisted the message: "Heave to or I will fire." Seconds later, North Korea was firing at the American ship. The *Pueblo* did not fire back. Despite the *Pueblo* raising the international signal for "Protest," two thousand rounds hit the *Pueblo* and wounded one crew member. Then two North Korean officials and around eight to ten enlisted men with AK-47s boarded the ship. The eighty-two men and the wounded Duane Hodges—who would later die from his injuries—were taken hostage.[39]

The men were taken ashore, put into two groups, blindfolded, and put on a train to Pyongyang. At the station they were shouted at and spit on by a gathered crowd. One of the captured crewmen later reported that the most distressing thing was the "total and complete hatred" the North Koreans had for them. "You could just feel it," he said.[40] There was no intention to kill the men, but they would not be treated well. They were tortured physically and mentally. The crewmen were photographed for evidence, and the United States was contacted to begin negotiations for their return. Determined to communicate with the homeland, three of the crewmen posed with their middle fingers out as a means of signaling coercion. They were later beaten for this. Their living conditions and treatment were very poor until the United States agreed to apologize.

Then there was a turnaround. Eleven months later the men were finally transferred across the DMZ's Bridge of No Return. To get them back, the United States had to formally acknowledge the government of the DPRK and apologize. Representing the United States as a negotiator was Maj. Gen. Gilbert H. Woodward, who signed an English- and Korean-language document explaining that the crewmen of the USS *Pueblo* had crossed illegally into DPRK territorial waters "on many occasions" and conducted spy activities into military and state secrets. The United States, the document further elaborated, "shoulders full responsibility and solemnly apologizes for the grave acts of espionage committed by the US ship against the DPRK after having intruded into the territorial waters of the DPRK."[41] Before signing the document General Woodward made a formal statement repudiating the claims.[42]

Prior to their eventual release in December, the crew of the USS *Pueblo* sat through two press conferences on August 13 and September 12, 1969, in Pyongyang.[43] North Korea produced a dossier of falsified evidence about the USS *Pueblo* intrusion, which was later examined by the U.S. Office of Naval Intelligence. At the press conferences the men were forced to repeatedly rewrite statements that the United States needed to admit, apologize, and affirm that they had intruded into DPRK waters. Cdr. Pete Bucher also made a final confession about the "heinous crimes" of the crew.[44]

9.2 North Korean photograph of USS *Pueblo* (AGER-2) crew at a press conference in North Korea

U.S. Naval History and Heritage Command Photograph / Public Domain

A French journalist in attendance reported that the crew members' faces were insincere, and their body language was odd. Of course, North Korean propaganda was trying to present the men as contrite. A declassified cable indicates that the men subtly communicated their unwillingness to participate. "They sat unusually still, with few of the physical movements that would be natural during a long conference. They did not react to the audience," a journalist reported.[45] Although North Korea tried to operationalize these foreigners for its own benefit, recently released Romanian documents reveal that the Soviets were deeply concerned with the "warmongering."[46]

Since the formation of the country, North Korea has made use of foreign detainees and defectors of all stripes in different ways for its political agenda. In claiming the bodies of foreign nationals by force, coercion, or persuasion, North Korea claims an opportunity to speak *and be heard* by the international community through the bodies of foreign citizen-hostages. The message remains the same: North Korea is merciful but no joke and not to be mistreated by imperialists. When "ideological enemies" cross into North Korea and are detained according to national law, the state maximizes use of these opportunities. The world may have forgotten the Korean War, but the North Korean government has not. Merrill Newman was a U.S. infantry officer in the Korean War.

In October of 2013 Newman traveled to North Korea as a tourist with Juche Travel Services. According to Stephan Haggard, "Newman fell afoul of North Korean authorities not simply for his Korean War service in 1953 with a unit running partisans from the island of Chodo into the Mt. Kuwol area. The crime was to have spoken about an interest in re-connecting with partisans and their descendants and sharing an email exchange Newman had with a South Korean veteran."[47] The North Koreans knew of this, according to Mike Chinoy in *The Last POW*, because two North Korean guides reported it to authorities. Chinoy's book carries the following eyebrow-raising quote from Newman: "It was clearly my error to indicate I'd like to make contact with any North Korean survivors" whom he had trained in the anti-Communist guerrilla brigade.[48] With Merrill Newman, North Korea put words into the mouth of a former U.S. war veteran, turning him into a living puppet. He read from a script that was obviously prepared for him. Grammar mistakes and all, his speech concluded with:

> I realize that I cannot be forgiven for my offensives but I beg for pardon on my knees by apologizing for my offensives sincerely toward the DPRK government and the Korean people and I want not punish me. Please forgive me. I will never commit the offensive act against the DPRK Government and the Korean People again. On this trip I can understand that in US and western countries there is misleading information and propaganda about DPRK. If I go back to USA, I will tell the true features of the DPRK and the life the Korean people are leading.[49]

North Korean media reported the story of Newman—detained for forty-two days—with the headline, "Apology of U.S. Citizen for His Hostile Acts in DPRK," revealing it didn't matter *who* Newman was but rather *what* he was: an apologetic American.[50] Newman read a lengthy handwritten letter of apology to a gathered press and endorsed each page with red thumbprints to the clattering sound of cameras. It was obvious from the grammar errors the letter had been written for him, and Newman later confirmed this. Additionally, it bears all the characteristics of North Korean state rhetoric. These media spectacles that involve foreign nationals, especially Americans, secure far more views online than other videos from North Korea that take the typical approach to propagate dissemination. At present writing, the KCNA-released view of Newman's "apology" has been viewed 49,688 times.[51]

Newsman's assumption that the Korea War is over and long since forgotten is not isolated to him. It is clear that North Korea's response to such errors in thought and deed, by citizen or foreigner alike, is used to animate the present with the past.

One does not even need to be born anytime near the Korean War for the war to affect them. No matter. The past will rise up to meet you as it did with a young American named Otto Warmbier. The twenty-one-year-old was detained in North Korea on January 2, 2016, for attempting to steal a Kim Jong Un banner from the wall of a North Korean hotel. Warmbier claimed he was promised

9.3 Merrill Newman, "American Vet Held in N. Korea, Reads 'Apology Letter'" (screenshot 01.22)

jonnydopplr, "Merrill Newman, American Vet Held in N. Korea, Reads 'Apology Letter,'" YouTube, November 29, 2013, https://www.youtube.com/watch?v=ShpW9qCuwGE

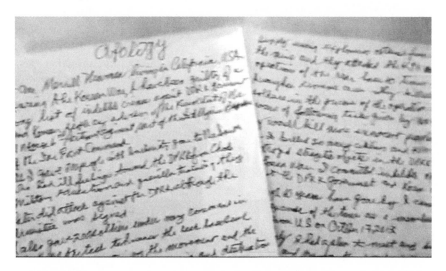

9.4 Merrill Newman, "American Vet Held in N. Korea, Reads 'Apology Letter'" (screenshot 01.24)

jonnydopplr, "Merrill Newman."

compensation if he brought back some artifact from North Korea (as if he were going to the moon). Political economist Stephan Haggard expressed it best. The banner was not worth much, but "the value of humiliating foreigners with earnest confessions, replete with positive references to the fairness of the DPRK legal system? Priceless."[52] Haggard identifies a critical truth: North Korea makes use of these human resources for its own aim. The detention, press conferences, and trials of these foreigners take a very public and theatrical stage. Will Ripley of CNN has relatively good access to many of the detained. Such a platform gives viewers a seemingly "Americanized" take on the cases while relaying North Korea's state message through the conduit. Each case reveals a deadly seriousness to protect sovereign territory, reiterating that the Korean War is unfinished.

Otto Warmbier was sentenced to fifteen years of hard labor after a one-hour trial on March 16, 2016. Former U.S. ambassador and New Mexico governor Bill Richardson, who previously served as special envoy to North Korea, was in place trying to negotiate for Warmbier's release. Warmbier was returned to the United States a year later, on June 13, 2017, and was found to be suffering from a severe brain injury. North Korea claimed he had contracted botulism and had taken a sleeping pill, which caused the condition.[53] He was alive but not responsive. He died on June 19, after his parents requested that his feeding tube be removed. No autopsy was conducted on the body.[54] The coroner listed the manner of death as undetermined. His cause of death was listed as complications of blood and oxygen shortage to the brain, due to an "unknown insult" one year prior.[55] The parents of Otto Warmbier maintain he was tortured while in a North Korea prison. U.S. representatives are a little more muted in their accusations. Richardson said that North Korea needs to "explain the cause" of the coma.[56] During his State of the Union address in 2018, Donald Trump brought up the story of Otto Warmbier to, curiously, indicate the mercilessness of North Korea's nuclear development program. Otto's parents and surviving siblings were asked to stand as acknowledgment of their sacrifice for this revelation. They did, although they were clearly still rocked by devastation over their loss.

Warmbier's manner of death remains inconclusive. It is clear that North Korea did detain and sentence the young man to fifteen years' hard labor. It is not clear whether they tortured him, causing his brain damage and eventual death. Given that the cause of death was identified as due to complications emerging from lack of oxygen to the brain, the only clear indication is that somehow his brain was deprived of oxygenated blood; this could have happened in any number of ways. The coroner's report indicates a round tracheostomy scar at the sternal notch, indicating he was given medical therapy while in North Korea.[57] The North Koreans may not have known what to do with the young man in a brain-dead state and, not wishing to have him die on Korean soil, shipped him home after keeping him on life support for nearly a year. We may never know what happened to Warmbier, but it is clear that he was used as a political tool by North Korea until he became a risk to them. Similarly, the United States evokes his death as a soft power political tool, swaying public opinion just as North Korea tried to do with him.

Detaining Americans enables North Korea to trigger the involvement of international diplomatic parties. Because the United States does not have diplomatic relations with North Korea and, thus, no embassy in the country, the rescue of an American typically involves the Swedish Embassy. The Swedish, having relations with both the DPRK and the United States, act as a liaison between the countries. Further to this, when Americans are rescued from North Korea, former presidents or high-ranking government men are preferred intermediaries. In 2009 U.S. journalists Euna Lee and Laura Ling were working on a documentary about defectors in China; it is unclear which side of the border they were on, but North Korean border guards ultimately arrested them. Lee and Ling were detained for 140 days until former president Bill Clinton negotiated their release. An earnest apology from Bill Clinton, delivered to the DPRK government, was published in North Korean news.[58] The KCNA article touts the gracious benevolence of Kim Jong Il, who "issued an order of the Chairman of the DPRK National Defence Commission on granting a special pardon" to the two journalists. The article commends their release as the "manifestation of the DPRK's humanitarian and peaceloving [sic] policy" and states that Clinton's visit to the DPRK "will contribute to deepening the understanding between the DPRK and the U.S. and building the bilateral confidence."[59]

In 2014 the U.S. director of national intelligence was tasked with freeing two Americans imprisoned in North Korea. The case of one of them, Matthew Miller, is informative because he was an American who traveled to North Korea *wanting* asylum. Against his wishes, his nation was contacted, and diplomatic channels opened to remove him. Bizarrely, he told South Korea–based *NK News*, "My main fear was that they would not arrest me when I arrived."[60] Miller tore up his visa and passport when he arrived in North Korea. He did not want the United States to be involved in his case. However, several months later, while Miller was in prison, Director of National Intelligence James Clapper was tasked with removing him and freeing Korean American prisoner Kenneth Bae. Bae had been arrested in the special economic zone of Rason in North Korea and was charged with trying to overthrow the regime. When he was eventually released, North Korea tried to slap him with a bill of almost $300,000 for his hospital stay—he was sick during his detention—but he refused to pay.[61]

Recently three Korean Americans—Kim Hak Song, Tony Kim, and Kim Dong Chul—were released after being detained in a North Korean prison for more than a year. Kim Hak Song and Tony Kim worked at the Pyongyang University of Science and Technology. The North Korean state accused them of "hostile acts," but the men have not elaborated on why they were arrested. Kim Dong Chol was arrested on October 2, 2015, and accused of committing espionage. A press conference was held in Pyongyang on March 25, 2016, during which Kim Dong Chol read from a prepared script and confessed he had planned to overthrow the regime. He was given ten years for his crime.[62] He had reportedly been caught with USB drives containing classified documents related to nuclear, military, and other activities inside North Korea. With the help of Secretary of State Mike Pompeo, who visited Pyongyang in the lead-up to the 2018 Singapore Summit between Kim and Trump, all three were released.

The news reports and press conferences that North Korea generates with foreign illegals operate in a similar way to the spectacle of the refugee who jumps embassy walls. As mentioned previously in this book, North Korean refugees break the law by jumping embassy walls in order to access diplomatic legal channels. With news reports and press conferences, North Korea makes use of foreign nationals who break domestic laws, or who are accused of breaking domestic laws, to force diplomatic engagement. North Korea is showing the international and the North Korean domestic community that it operates "within the law." In a kind of reality TV gone wildly authoritarian, North Korea casts genuine Americans and need only supply the script.

North Korea presents itself domestically and internationally as rule abiding but also flexible, and their language is humanitarian and peace loving.[63] They imprison errant foreigners and absolve them of crime, when sufficiently appeased. Recall how this resembles the obsequious, humiliating, and dehumanizing acts required of prisoners as they beg for mercy but do not get it (see chapter 7). Foreigners willingly identify their mistakes, and earnestly request forgiveness while identifying North Korea as a good country and unlike what they had expected. This enables North Korea to import into a foreign voice the message it has long been sending: See for yourselves, we are not the problem.

The Abducted

In the late 1970s and 1980s people began disappearing from Japanese shores without explanation. In the wake of a failed assassination attempt on South Korean president Park Chung-hee in 1974, North Korea devised plans to abduct foreign citizens to improve its international intelligence gathering. The assassination was attempted by Mun Se-hwang, an ethnic Korean sympathetic to the North Korean government and living in Japan. After the attempt, South Korea tightened its security against would-be North Korean spies. To circumvent this, North Korean authorities turned their attention to Japan as a site to gather resources for human intelligence, abducting and recruiting citizens in an effort to teach North Koreans the ways of Japanese language, culture, and customs.[64] From 1977 until 1983 seventeen Japanese citizens vanished. Other missing persons are suspected to be part of the abduction campaign, but North Korea has not confirmed these suspicions.[65]

Kume Yutaka was the first to disappear, a fifty-two-year-old security guard. She was last seen on the coast of Ishikawa Prefecture in the fall of 1977. Next was a thirteen-year-old girl taken as she walked home from badminton practice. A former North Korean spy later confirmed that the girl, Megumi Yokota, had been abducted to North Korea.[66] Following her abduction, the North Korean government targeted individuals and couples in Japan as well as Japanese traveling in Europe.[67] In July of 1978 two couples disappeared. One couple left their car behind; the other, their bicycles.[68]

The abduction issue was first picked up in the public media in an article in the January 7, 1980, issue of the *Sankei Shimbun*, a conservative Japanese newspaper. Initially the police thought the story pure imagination, but in time this would become one of the most central diplomatic concerns between Japan and North Korea.[69] Speculation over abductions gave way to certainty when surviving North Korean bomber Kim Hyon-hee, of KAL flight 858, was interrogated by South Korean intelligence and revealed that she had learned to speak Japanese from Japanese-abducted nationals living in Pyongyang.[70]

It was only in 2002 at the first Japan–North Korea Summit meeting in September of 2002 that North Korea acknowledged it had abducted Japanese citizens. An early draft of North Korea's Pyongyang Declaration did not make direct reference to the abductions or to North Korea's culpability in the disappearance of Japanese citizens.[71] It was under the urging of Abe that Prime Minister Junichiro Koizumi adopted a more pressing position against North Korea to formally admit their role in the abductions. Five individuals were reported alive, but eight had passed away in North Korea. Two others had no record of entering North Korea. In 2004 North Korea returned cremated remains that it claimed were those of Megumi Yokota, but DNA analysis of the material in Japan indicated that the remains were not hers.[72] Japan has repeatedly made demands for North Korea to return the abductees. At the start of 2006 a government-wide team was established to deal with the issue, the Special Abductions Issue Team (Rachi Mondai Tokumei Chīmu), which encompassed all ministries and agencies. In the fall of 2006 the government of Japan set up the Headquarters for the Abduction Issue.[73]

The abduction issue in Japan has received far more public and government attention than similar abduction cases from South Korea.[74] Scholars have identified political agency, ideology, media-activism, and media environments in the public sphere as factors that result in these differences.[75] North Korea has abducted far more South Koreans than they have citizens of other countries. The two most famous South Koreans abducted to North Korea are Shin Sang-ok and Choi Eun-hee. Abducted separately, the couple—already famous for filmmaking and acting in South Korea and divorced at the time of kidnapping— were reunited in North Korea. Kim Jong Il arranged for their abduction in order to improve the country's filmmaking.[76] British filmmakers Rob Cannan and Ross Adam produced a documentary about the bizarre story in 2016, *The Lovers and the Despot*. In 1986, after many years of plotting to escape, the two were able to win enough confidence to be left alone in Vienna where they escaped to the U.S. Embassy.

In South Korea, the abduction of citizens by North Korea was known about for decades, unlike in the case of Japan. The issue of abductions has been raised between the two Koreas since the 1970s. At the time South Korea's authoritarian leadership was busy committing violations against its own citizens and was far from concerned over how other countries might do the same to its people. In 1972–1973 and again in 1985, the South Korean National Red Cross led efforts to reunify families, which included abducted individuals. In 1994 Amnesty International released a report indicating that forty-nine South Korean citizens had been abducted by North Korea. As political scientist Celeste Arrington identified, prior to the 1990s, South Korea's authoritarian leaders operated a *yeonjwaje* principle (guilt by association—yes, the same practice as in the

North), which cast any individuals with association to North Korea, however obliquely, as a communist sympathizer.[77] As a result, family members of abductees faced the double misfortune of having loved ones taken and then having official civilian and military service opportunities in South Korea stripped from them.

Amid the softening of views toward the DPRK, and the Kim Dae-jung and Kim Jong Il "Sunshine Summit" of June 2000, groups in South Korea became concerned with the abduction issue. The group Families of Abducted and Detained in North Korea was founded in February 2000 by seven abductee families. Eventually other groups gathered to form the Korean War Abductee Family Union, which, among other work, has compiled a list of approximately ninety-five thousand abductions by North Korea.[78] In 2009 a group was founded by returned abductees. Seven South Koreans who were kidnapped to North Korea and held for decades escaped to South Korea and founded the Returned Abductees' Committee.[79] The South Korean abductee groups have a variety of goals that roughly define them. Some aim to gather information and establish fact-finding missions inside the DPRK to justify their claims. Other groups wish to maximize the compensation offered to returned abductees through the April 2, 2007, legislation titled the Law for the Victims of Abduction to the North in the Postwar Years.

In 2011 the South Korean government established a committee called the Rules on the Installation and Operation of the Abductees Committee. One of the many tasks of the committee is to maintain and raise public awareness about war abductions and their determination to resolve the issue. On the anniversary of the beginning of the Korean War (June 25), the committee worked with broadcasting stations to raise awareness. They aired a program called the "Feature Program for the Korean War" on the Korean Broadcasting Station's TV music show *Gayo Mudae* on June 24, 2013, and aired a documentary on KBS titled *People Who Have Not Returned* on July 27, 2013. Families of war-time abductees were invited to attend field-site visits to Panmunjom and Cheorwon, in the demilitarized zone. Photo exhibits were displayed in six of South Korea's largest cities. However, press coverage of the abduction issue in South Korea has been sporadic, and conservative newspapers like the *Chosun Ilbo* attend to the abduction issue more than progressive newspapers.[80]

North Korean Defectors Return Home

Return defection, also known as "double defection," refers to North Koreans who have left the North, resettled legally in another country—usually South Korea—but then return to North Korea. It is inconclusive whether these cases are genuine or forced. Yet, as scholars Adam Cathcart, Christopher Green, and

Steven Denny observe, "the goal and outcome of re-defection is the same," no matter whether the individuals came by choice; they can all be used in media to support domestic public opinion for North Korean dominant consensus.[81] As with the foreign nationals mentioned earlier, the movement of defectors back into North Korea can be a boon for North Korean media. These cases highlight how individual choice or state coercion become a power play between nations.[82] Return defectors who appear in North Korean media play the powerful role of denouncing life in South Korea, demonstrating the merciful forgiveness of Kim Jong Un for their errant mercantile choices.

As mentioned earlier, North Koreans who are refouled from China face extreme punishment. So how it is that these double defectors escape the same fate? In recent years, it has been estimated that as many as one hundred North Koreans have returned to the North from the South, although many suggest this number is too high and impossible to accurately calculate.[83] The South Korean Ministry of Unification puts the number at thirteen.[84] South Korea keeps track of North Korean defectors, and eight hundred are reportedly unaccounted for.[85] There are reports that North Korean defectors in South Korea have gone missing. Prior to their absence, they were contacted by brokers in China and lured to the Sino-Korean border area under the assumption that they would be reconnecting with family from North Korea. Thus, it is not known if the "return defections" are being orchestrated by North Korea to alter perceptions of both North and South Korea.[86] Family ties are used to lure defectors back to North Korea under threat of punishment of children if defected parents do not obey.[87]

Some defectors, however, might wish to return willingly to North Korea. Doing so could give them a high-profile opportunity to protest their treatment as defectors in South Korea and possibly win the favor of North Korea.[88] With return defectors, North Korea has the chance to counter the dominant narrative about its failings. In state media and international media that are granted access, North Korea presents the living, breathing, sobbing returnees—young and old, male and female, and an array of voices. The returnees apologize for letting their bourgeois egotistic ambitions lead them astray from the motherland. They singularly embody the propaganda North Korea produces. These individuals are a rare resource that North Korean cannot fail to use. The returnees "name and shame" themselves and South Korea, detailing how they were led astray until, realizing their error, they return to the homeland, tail between their legs. The returnee is presented as a credible witness because she has lived in both North and South. She speaks bravely, though humbly, of errors in judgment that would otherwise be fatal to reveal. Perhaps these are thoughts her listeners may have had. In a method mirrored in Korean Central News articles that played through the scenario of Jang Song-thaek, so too these dramatizations play through the plan of would-be defectors. She takes the fateful decision and returns alive to tell the horrific tale. It is a story of awakening. Does her narrative dissuade them? At least it tries to support her description of defectors' lives in South Korea; she cites statistics gathered from the South Korean Ministry of Unification on defector unemployment and suicide rates in South Korea.[89] North Korea cleverly endeavors to inoculate those who may wish to leave: South Koreans may do well, but *you* will not do well in South Korea.[90] And that is a reasonably compelling argument for poor migrants. Absent are the stories of defectors who have fared spectacularly well, of course.[91]

In addition to discouraging defection, the returnees' narratives present an opportunity to shame South Korea for its treatment of North Koreans, and this stands in for South Korea's treatment of North Korea. South Korea, "under" the United States, has become the quasi-occupier—mistreating Koreans, focusing on greed. Through the returnee, North Korea shows the prodigal citizen returned to seek pardon from the motherland for the error of her ways. The narrative devices used by the state deviate little from those found in the apology letters of foreign detainees. North Korea treats the wayward antagonist firmly but with benevolence; after an emotional performance where the antagonist begs for mercy and forgiveness, Kim Jong Un grants amnesty. At least that's how we are meant to interpret the end of the story. The true fate of these return defectors can't be confirmed.

Individuals with the extremely rare experience of what could be called revolving-door defection (defection to South Korea, return to North Korea, and defection to South Korea again) report severe abuse, imprisonment, and torture post press conference. Kim Nam-Soo is said to be the first known case. He left North Korea in January of 1997 and settled in South Korea. However, after struggling with business failure in the South, he went to a DPRK embassy in China in July of 2000 with 70 million South Korean *won*—approximately US$60,000—requesting permission to return to North Korea. North Korean media stated, "Our Comrade is coming in with party membership fees." He was reportedly permitted to run a bathhouse and barbershop after his return. In 2003 he redefected again, claiming the regime was too oppressive.[92]

Another individual named Yoo Tae-Joon returned to North Korea in 2000 in order to reconnect with his family. Crossing back over the Sino-Korean border, he learned that his family had been killed as punishment for his defection. He was subsequently arrested by the police. At a press conference in the DPRK, he said the government treated him well and gave him food. Later they tortured him.[93] He managed to leave North Korea once again in 2001.

Jun Yong-Chol gave his press conference in the People's Palace of Culture on July 19, 2012.[94] Images of this press conference appeared later in North Korean posters, intermixed with North Korean Socialist Realist art, to press the message of destroying the imperialist agenda.[95] Choi Seung-Chan returned to North Korea with the equivalent of $50,000 he had saved working at the

9.5 Return defector Jun Yong-Chol gives his press conference in the People's Palace of Culture, July 19, 2012.

Adam Cathcart and Brian Gleason, "North Korean Claims of Terrorism from Inside Chinese Territory: An Annotated Analysis," *SinoNK*, August 14, 2012, http://sinonk.com/2012/08/14/north -korean-claims-of-terrorism-from-inside-chinese-territory-an-annotated-analysis/

South Korean Nonghyup Bank from May 1997 to January 2004. He gave $30,000 to the North Korean government and several thousand to friends. He was reportedly treated well; Kim Jong Il ordered officials to not send him to prison. These cases have been publicized in the *Rodong Shinmun* as well as on televised programs showing interviews with the returnees.[96] In the KCNA video recording of returnee Pak Jung Sok's press conference (she went by the name Park In Sook in South Korea), she is highly emotional, particularly when she reflects on returning to the motherland. Between tears, as she dries her eyes, she reads from a prepared script. At the end of her speech, flanked by two North Koreans, she briefly sings a song of praise for Kim Jong Un. KCNA later reported she was living in a beautiful Pyongyang apartment and her leg—wounded in South Korea—was being treated.[97]

Some returnees' stores are more suspicious. North Korean media has, from time to time, painted refouled refugees as having left the country against their will and then later returned. North Korea released a video of nine teenagers being interviewed by KCNA. Known as the "Laos 9," these youths were making their way to South Korea with the help of activist-missionaries through Laos when they were caught by police, detained, refouled to China, and then repatriated to North Korea.[98] North Korea reported that the teenagers "returned" to the homeland after being "kidnapped" (*napchi*) by South Korea. State media

showed the youths at school. When CNN interviewed them, they stated grati-
tude for the help of the motherland.[99] International media attention followed
the story of the nine youths after they were detained in Laos and refouled to
China. KCNA reported a "round-table" press conference with the youths, where
they explained the kidnapping.[100] The recent defection of thirteen overseas restaurant workers has also been described by North Korea as an act of abduction. The male supervisor and twelve female employees were working in China
when they defected to South Korea. They are the children of elites in government and administration in North Korea.[101] North Korea appealed to South
Korea to permit the thirteen to meet family members still in North Korea. The
North has also threatened the South over these so-called abductions.[102]

South Korea–based defector Kim Ryen Hi applied for political asylum at the
Vietnamese Embassy in Seoul on February 29, 2016. She stated that she wanted
to return to North Korea to be reunited with her aging parents, her husband,
and her daughter. She is the first known North Korean defector to have entered
a foreign embassy in Seoul in an attempt to return to North Korea. Her arrival
in South Korea was the result of meeting smugglers in China, she reports, who
lured her to South Korea under promises of making money and returning to
North Korea. She claims she arrived in Seoul by mistake.[103] Such a narrative—
publicly aired, fabricated or real—falls in line with a story North Korea might
be willing to accept for a price of cash currency or the currency of propaganda.

Recently a return defector tore her South Korean–published memoir while
she was filmed by North Korea's KCNA.[104] She had lived for years in South
Korea, eventually writing her memoir about life in North Korea and her con-
version to Christianity in the South. Son Ok-Sun tells state media that the memoir was written at the behest of enemies.

North Korea is showing us what we might otherwise only hear about via
word of mouth. Such stories are a boon for North Korea's position on human
rights accusations. It is difficult to know how many North Koreans may have
returned to North Korea after defecting to South Korea, but North Korea has
put a few of them on film and broadcasted their stories domestically and in the
public domain.[105]

Some return defections appear linked to North Korean espionage in South
Korea. Han Chang-gwon, president of the North Korean Defectors Groups'
Coalition, stated that one person, while at South Korea's education center for
North Korean refugees, known as Hanawon, videotaped the inside of the build-
ings and compound. He then disappeared from South Korea in 2009 with the
video. He has reportedly been spotted back in North Korea; his father, man-
ager of the Hoeryong police substation, "did not suffer any punishment after
his son defected," leading to speculation that the son had been working for
North Korea as a spy.[106] Other secret agents have infiltrated South Korea–based
North Korean groups such as *Daesung kongsa*, a newspaper run by defectors.

9.6 Son Ok-Sun on DPRK TV. The subtitles read: "But because she has finally realised and understood."

James Rothwell, "North Korean Defector Returns Home after 16 Years and Rips up Her Memoirs on Camera." *Daily Telegraph*, January 21, 2016, https://www.telegraph.co.uk/news/worldnews/asia /northkorea/12112246/North-Korean-defector-returns-home-after-16-years-and-rips-up-her -memoirs-on-camera.html

9.7 Son Ok-Sun tears her memoir apart on DPRK TV.

James Rothwell, "North Korean Defector Returns Home after 16 Years and Rips up Her Memoirs on Camera." *Daily Telegraph*, January 21, 2016, https://www.telegraph.co.uk/news/worldnews/asia /northkorea/12112246/North-Korean-defector-returns-home-after-16-years-and-rips-up-her -memoirs-on-camera.html

South Korean intelligence captured other spies before they had the opportunity to return to North Korea with information. Jung Hwa Won was arrested in August of 2008. Kim Myung Ho and Dong Myung Kwan, two agents sent to South Korea to assassinate former secretary of the North Korean Workers Party defector Hwang Jang Yop (one of the highest-ranking North Korean defectors), were also arrested.[107]

* * *

What message can be taken from these cases of defection, return defection, triple defection, and North Korean abduction of former defectors? These highlight the agonizing complexity of geopolitics on the Korean peninsula as it meets the soft, ambiguous, and changing struggles of individual relationships. These cases identify the very personal journeys through choice that each defector makes—the gamble and negotiation with states not because one wants to but because one has few choices—and the states themselves cannot and will not permit the powerful banality of ordinary human need.

In repenting, in the act of forced confession, the individual is twice disgraced: first because one is caught "in the act," which must be repented and confessed, and second, for having repented, for having falsely confessed.[108] Of course, there is an inherent problem in this: how to prove authenticity? The interior state of the actor is unknowable. But this doesn't undo the potential power of those who bear witness. Consider this: Elaine Scarry writes that within societies, when there is a crisis of belief, "the sheer material factualness of the human body will be borrowed to lend that cultural construct the aura of 'realness' and 'certainty.'"[109] And the voice bridges that body to the world as it narrates experiences of South Korea. The body and the voice are our closest travel companions in this world. Scarry observes that they are the "most elemental and least metaphorical categories"; as such, the two—particularly when transmitted via audio and video—can give a sense of veracity to those who witness.[110] The redefector is brought back from the hell of South Korea, body and voice. Resurrected, she tells of horrors.

With return defectors and foreign nationals, their voices, written or recorded, can be "broken off from their speaker so that they can then be taken off and made the property of the regime."[111] Their uses are legion.

CHAPTER 10

THE STATE NEWS STRIKES BACK

Under the present grave situation where the human rights issue is at the crossroads of sincere cooperation or war, the DPRK Association for Human Rights Studies releases a detailed report to lay bare the secret behind such political fraud as the anti-DPRK "human rights resolution" which has no relevance with the protection and promotion of genuine human rights and clarify the responsibility for the ensuing consequences.

. . .

The recent farce orchestrated at the UN is a shameless political chicanery to put down justice with injustice and conceal truth with lies and the height of brazenfaced burlesque to deceive the world people with intrigues and fabrications.

—"Detailed Report on Secret Behind Anti-DPRK 'Human Rights Resolution' Released," *Korean Central News Agency*, November 28, 2014

North Korea primarily responds to allegations of rights abuses by denying that rights are being violated. But they cannot just simply deny. North Korea, by denying accusations, is at least in a process of international socialization. They are implicitly aware that there is a problem with their rights situation as interpreted by international norms— which they interpret as "Western Imperialist norms."

First, North Korea responds with discourse that positions state sovereignty as the bulwark of true human rights. This is not unusual and is arguably typical for a nation that identifies as postcolonial in the nonaligned movement and of the Global South. Appeals to national sovereignty and outright denial of rights violations are typical initial reactions of norm-violating states.[1] Second, North Korean discourse combines emphasis on state sovereignty with a tireless reliance on tu quoque argument style. Tu quoque is a Latin term that refers to the accused turning the accusation back on the accuser, also known as an appeal to hypocrisy. Words like "hypocrisy" and "double standard" appear many times in North Korean discourse and representatives' speeches. One representative at the United Nations even went so far as to say that the United States should "mind your own business."[2] For North Korea, human rights are impossible without state sovereignty, and tu quoque irresistibly offers historic wrongs and contemporary U.S. atrocities that name and shame accusers who point the finger at North Korea. These first two techniques embody North Korea's critique par excellence.

Employing tu quoque easily leads to a voluble discussion of the rights violations of those states that North Korea believes are levying the critique—the United Nations makes the critique, but North Korea sees the United States and South Korea as its true accusers. In fact, North Korean media at no time addresses the rights violations it is accused of committing. Instead they cut straight to critiquing South Korea and the United States, using words such as "rape," "racism," "prison," and "torture" as key points of accusation.

To assess North Korea's interpretation of the UN Commission of Inquiry report, this portion of the book draws on a snapshot of materials produced by the North Korean state available in the public domain. The first source is the Korean Central News Agency's *Rodong Shinmun* online articles published between January 1, 2014, and May 27, 2015. This large corpus is taken as a representative sample of North Korean news. The *Rodong Shinmun* published a total of 17,603 articles during the time under investigation, of which 1,038 mentioned human rights and 116 mentioned the 2014 Commission of Inquiry report (*inkwon kyului*). I performed a corpus analysis on the *Rodong Shinmun* articles looking for key words "human rights" and "Commission of Inquiry report" as well as words collocated (appearing before or after the words "human rights" [*inkwon*] and "human rights report" [*inkwon kyului*]).[3] Of the 17,603 articles, only 1,038 (6 percent) cover the topic of human rights, and only 116 articles discuss the UN Commission of Inquiry report directly (0.6 percent). The small fraction of articles covering human rights do so in a manner presented in the paragraphs that open this chapter—the denial dance that distracts and elaborates on the violations of the United States and South Korea.

Drawing on this data, my analysis shows that the North Korean state presents the following critiques—in no particular order—against the UN Commission of Inquiry report:

a. Citizens of North Korea were not interviewed.
b. UN Commissioners did not visit North Korea.
c. Interviews were conducted in states that don't respect rights (elaborate atrocities).
d. Interviews were conducted with North Korean "human scum" paid by the United States.
e. The United States is using the United Nations Commission to destroy North Korea.

The timing of the UN Commission of Inquiry report is also interpreted as conspiratorial. Critique of North Korea's human rights comes, they claim, at a time when the United States has tried all other methods to bring down the regime and having failed is striking out about human rights. The argument lobbied against the United States and the international community is as follows:

a. Sanctions didn't work.
b. Isolation didn't work.
c. Therefore, the United States will try the "human rights racket" to destroy the social system of North Korea.

The United States and South Korea, nations and leaders alike, are variously described in hyperbolically negative ways that highlight the senseless cruelty and selfish ignorance toward their own people and the international community. The "rights racket" is a ploy to destroy North Korea. Past cases where the United States evoked human rights as justification for international invasion, such as the invasion of Iraq, are put forward.[4]

Not surprisingly, North Korea does not directly address the allegations of atrocity raised in the Commission of Inquiry report. North Korea does acknowledge the activities of the international community regarding an "anti-DPRK human rights racket" built on the "lies of human garbage" that are the "puppets of the US" and its followers. None of the articles goes into detail about the accusations of forced imprisonment, torture, famine, discrimination, and so on. At no point does the *Rodong Shinmun* parse the accusations individually to discredit them. Rather, the UN Commission of Inquiry report as a totality is discounted with the repeated phrase "a report based on lies."

Affect and North Korean News

Reading North Korea's news once in a while doesn't leave too great an impact. The *initial* impression—reading it here and there, without a deep dive—is that the media in North Korea is unsophisticated and sophomoric. Close reading reveals it is actually deeply sophisticated, exacting, and skilled at manipulation.

If you read North Korean news every day for months as I did while writing this book—by all means, give this a go—it has a narcotic, vertigo effect. With regular reading, the ribald edges sluff off—they are so commonplace, so standard that they drop out of view—and what is left behind are the droning messages that pulse like heartbeats in each sentence. Topics may vary, but the message is virtually unchanging: North Korea is the best, forever-challenged underdog who will struggle against its greatest abuser, the United States. To be fair, the cumulative effect of reading seventeen thousand North Korean news articles may not be representative of what it is like to live with that media—and pretty much *only* that media—for a lifetime. This chapter began with an amuse-bouche. Here is another taste, from an article critiquing the United Nations' report on North Korea in 2014:

> The "report" misrepresents the true picture of the DPRK people enjoying genuine rights and is peppered with sheer lies and fabrications, deliberately cooked up by such riff-raffs as those who defected from the DPRK and criminals who escaped from it after committing crimes in the country. [Commissioner Michael Kirby] has neither been to Pyongyang nor met with government officials of the DPRK. The US is a kingpin of human rights violations, which slaughters innocent people bringing untold disasters through aggression and intervention worldwide. It has killed civilians in Iraq, Libya, Afghanistan, Pakistan and other countries, openly supplied weapons to rebel forces in independent countries including Syria, flagrantly violating their sovereignty. It operates prisons in different parts of the world, including Guantanamo, mal-treating the inmates. The US, tundra of human rights and veritable hell, is infamous for systematic worldwide tapping and surveillance. Therefore, it is preposterous for the US to talk about other's "human rights violations."[5]

At no point does North Korea acknowledge the accusations leveled against it or take the crimes one by one to refute or discount them. Rather, they simply dismiss the UN report in total and evoke tu quoque, the appeal to hypocrisy. They dismiss the report and change topics. But at this point I need to clarify something because perhaps you, like millions of North Koreans, have not seen or read the Commission of Inquiry report, which is nearly four hundred highly detailed and painstakingly researched pages long. The commissioners interviewed over two hundred people and worked with nine experts in the research and writing of the report. If you only read North Korean news, you would never know this. You would think the report was maybe a page or two long. You would believe that just a handful of defectors spoke and were paid for the speaking, but no one was actually paid for giving testimony to the UN commissioners. You would think that the defectors who spoke were the worst of the worst by any moral standard: murders, rapists, and child molesters. Never is it mentioned in North Korean news that they were instead victims of torture and rape. If you only read North Korea's news, you wouldn't know that experts gave testimony or that those who testified had visited North Korea on several occasions.

Changing the Subject to the Wrongs of Others: Whataboutism

The seventeen months of news articles examined here did refer to rape, torture, and prison camps, but such words were entirely associated with the United States and South Korea. Turning the accusation back on the accuser, North Korea's news deflects and obfuscates through detailing rights violations committed by other nations. As such, the news articles reframe the UN Commission of Inquiry report as hypocritical and agenda driven. A Korean Central News Agency article from March 15, 2017, reported on a "white paper" on the human rights situation in the United States. Starting with the shockingly high cost of the 2016 presidential election, the article covers the great swath of supposed violations in the United States. As always with North Korea, some of the statistics are correct, but the context is removed. For instance, a few years prior the North Korean news reported, "The number of impoverished people increased to 46.5 millions [sic] last year, and one sixth of the citizens and 20-odd percent of the children are in the grip of famine in New York City."[6] Fact-checking North Korea's rights report, Matt Ford noted in the *Atlantic*—with some relief—that there wasn't a famine in New York. Indeed, although many children in New York City are food insecure, a famine is quite another matter.[7] Other KCNA articles go into tireless detail on costs of medical procedures in the United States. "It costs USD 500 to have a tooth pulled out, tens of thousands of dollars for appendectomy, USD 1 000 for a day in hospital for first aid, and USD 100,000~200,000 for an operation on the emergency case in the first-aid room."[8]

Violence and discrimination in the United States or committed by its citizens abroad also warrants mention. One account reads: "There occurred ceaseless GI [serviceman] crimes last year alone. To cite just a few examples, GIs gang-raped a woman in her twenties on a subway electric car, GIs made shooting spree against passers-by in the center of Seoul, driving their car over a local policeman before taking flight and a drunken GI drove his car at breakneck speed, causing a traffic accident, and beat the victim who chased him."[9] These accounts are not erroneous, but, again, they lack context and detail. The stories are incomplete and omit from the narratives the resulting accountability and justice. The GIs were arrested and charged for their crimes.[10] In the Korean Central News Agency's articles, these cases serve to highlight the licentious character of American soldiers and their treatment of South Korean women. It all serves to distract from the human rights report; it is whataboutism at its finest.

Making Multitudes from the Singular

To avoid the sense of unreliability and doubt that naturally arises from a singular narrative voice, North Korean media creates a sense of multiplicity and credibility by employing the perspective of international sources. Allied countries' spokespersons often appear, as do representatives from Juche organizations abroad. The International Socialists make an appearance here and there. Through these other voices North Korean human rights are framed favorably and review United States' rights badly.[11] If an American citizen shares something positive about North Korea, this gets picked up. For instance, the Korean Central News Agency reported on the thoughtful reflections of a few unnamed U.S. Army officers who shared their preconceived notions about North Korea prior to visiting. "A U.S. army officer who had once visited the DPRK as a member of the group for finding remains of GIs told a group of U.S. lawyers who was on a visit to the DPRK in the same period that he had been told when leaving Hawaii for the DPRK that it is a veritable hell on earth but while staying there, he could realize that it is good to live in and what he heard from Western media and his seniors were all sheer lies."[12]

The army officer's account is paraphrased. Even still, the language of his paraphrase is identical to the language North Korea uses—notably, "sheer lies" and "veritable hell on earth." These are textual examples of the North Korean state throwing its voice into the body of others to give credence to the state's view, and we saw this method in chapter 9. Sometimes, of course, the state doesn't have to throw its voice but merely relay what is printed in radical leftist news outlets internationally. Case in point: *New Eastern Outlook* published a piece by a Canadian criminal lawyer who—along with a group of other lawyers as part of the National Lawyers Guild—visited Pyongyang in 2003 and reported that there were no rights violations.[13] The National Lawyers Guild is a pro–North Korean organization for lawyers and law students that has a history of support for Stalin, Mao, and like-minded dictators globally. Nevertheless, the North reflected the views of a Canadian criminal lawyer, Christopher Black, on the United Nations report:

> The report itself is an amazing document, not only because it is entirely contrived, but also because the "crimes" which the Commissioners allege take place in the DPRK are exactly the conditions that exist inside the United States itself. The hypocrisy is stunning but no one can be surprised when we learn in paragraph 31 of the report that the "public hearings" held by the Commission were conducted with the help of the governments of the United States, Britain, Japan and South Korea, all enemies of the DPRK, who arranged, according to the Commission itself, all the logistics, venues, interpreters, technology, security,

press services and, importantly, the "witnesses." Nor can we be surprised when we look at the three members of the Commission.[14]

Christopher Black, a member of the Canadian Communist Party, traveled to Pyongyang with the National Lawyers Guild. The Guild is not viewed credibly among the human rights activist community or within the legal field; it would seem that they deem North Korea's legal system to be without flaw.[15] Nonetheless, this is a method North Korea uses to validate its perception of rights.

As part of the framework of tu quoque, the *Rodong Shinmun* brings the reader news of the United States' violence in Iraq, Afghanistan, the former Yugoslavia, and the Korean War; of South Korea from military occupation until the present; of the United States' surveillance and wiretapping of allies in Europe; and of the United States' torture of illegally detained foreigners in offshore prisons such as Guantanamo Bay, Cuba. To drive home the hubris of the United States accusing North Korea of human rights abuses, abuses on U.S. soil are itemized in detail. The killings of unarmed black men by white police officers throughout the country are frequently mentioned. The high suicide rate and unemployment rate of youths in South Korea are also elaborated. There is summary dismissal of these countries as capable of honoring human rights because, by definition, their joint military exercises endanger life. The exercises pose a threat to international security, and the United States, North Korea believes, should be recommended to the UN Security Council. The provocative and dangerous exercises, North Korea argues, are a clear indication that South Korea has no sovereign rights and cannot uphold citizen rights. The exercises also indicate that the United States wishes to violate the sovereign rights of North Korea, which would simultaneously mean the violation of citizen rights.

This is the basic approach of North Korea's argument: deny and change the subject. Use of tu quoque is powerful because the cases leveled against the United States are true. However, that approach only goes so far. To engage a rebuttal against accusations on that basis is incoherent. But in a politically immature public, such an argument style is distracting and seemingly powerfully persuasive. The human rights report is not about the United States or any other country; it is about North Korea. Looping in a discussion of U.S. rights abuses is a poor argument trick to displace attention; it is a powerful distraction that seems to resolve the argument by bringing up something thematically related. Whataboutism, a technique popularized by the Soviet Union, is, in my assessment, the only type of argument style used in North Korean state media.

Whataboutism creates a race to the bottom. Some might argue that whataboutism is ineffective for intellectual debate but functions well in the "real world." To challenge this idea, I evoke John Oliver, who, although a comedian, seems to have a better grasp of law than Christopher Black, quoted earlier. During the 2017 season finale of *Last Week Tonight*, Oliver identified the callous deviance inherent in whataboutism: "A defense attorney could not stand up in court and say, 'Maybe my client did murder those people, but I ask you this: What about Jeffery Daumier? What about Al Capone? What about the guy from Silence of the Lambs?' I rest my case here people. I rest my case. The problem with whataboutism is it doesn't actually solve a problem or win an argument. The point is to muddy the waters."[16] It is hard to imagine what might be more real world than human rights violations.

Distracting Emotion

In addition to deflection, changing the topic gets an emotional jumpstart. The emotional language turns on fear and anger in shaping a seeming personalized relationship to the topic. Not unlike other nations, North Korea's state rhetoric is highly emotional.[17] Emotional language is significant in mediating different worlds of experience as the text performs the correct emotions for readers.[18] Where North Korea's media differs is in its use of highly polarizing extremes that mimic extreme emotional reactions. Along with this, nation-states are personalized and debased or exalted accordingly. There is no simple, objective telling of events. Adjectives are always negatively modifying nouns to firmly capture the emotion required to understand enemy states: bastard Americans; puppet South Korea. Nouns are overworked to relay the awful behavior of enemy states: the human rights *racket*. The newspaper narrates emotion according to metaphor, metonym, or expression.

North Korean news is not all glum. There is also love, pride, and relief for life inside North Korea. For example, Kim Jong Un inspected the conditions of a dental hygiene supplies factory on June 24, 2017, observing that "the Party and the government are taking full responsibility for people's lives and health and that such socialized health care is one and only in the world."[19] The *Rodong Shinmun* distorts the foreign world by decontextualizing facts and events. Even when accurate in relaying facts, the discourse chosen for impact is highly emotional, "securing truths" through an emotional form of knowing.[20]

Close reading of the news shows that, in the *Rodong Shinmun*, the strongest word linkages with UN Commission of Inquiry are the names of nation-states (see figure 10.1). The phrase most associated with the report is "the United States," followed by "the United Nations," and "South Korea." Considering that North Korea considers South Korea a colony of the United States, and the United Nations as equivalent to the United States, the following graph is stark in revealing which nation North Korea identifies with the United Nations Commission of Inquiry report.[21]

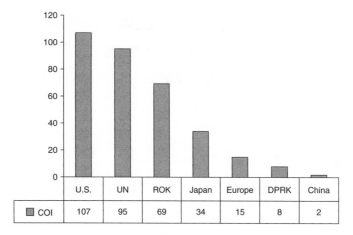

	U.S.	UN	ROK	Japan	Europe	DPRK	China
■ COI	107	95	69	34	15	8	2

10.1 Words most often associated with "UN Commission of Inquiry report" in North Korea's *Rodong Shinmun*, January 1, 2014–May 27, 2015

Words most frequently associated with the UN Commission of Inquiry were "invasion" and "threat to peace" (figure 10.2). Other key words of association are highly emotional, connected with suspicion and fear. Recalling that human rights are framed in North Korea as respect for the rights of the sovereign state so that the rights of individuals may be respected, it is clear that the UN report is viewed as grounds for invasion, a threat to peace (*p'yŏnghwarŭl wihyŏp'ada*), as a document based on lies, and driven by the pretext for war. This generates fear that the report is a threat to North Korea, to the collective, and, thus, to individual North Koreans. North Korea's central news explicitly calls the UN Commission of Inquiry report a "new slogan for war."[22]

Combining the two trends of emphasis on nation-states and emotional language, it is possible to see what emotional words were most collocated with the United States and South Korea. Emotions, their expression, and their cultural manifestations are all learned, pliable, and have behavioral aspects. It is not without reason to grant that jingoistic aggression and ethnocentric beliefs are useful for mobilizing populations at times of war or in the lead-up to war.[23] Emotion-laden words associated with the United States and South Korea describe both behavior and character in highly vituperative language. Most notably, the United States is associated with dangerous scheming behavior. South Korea has these features too, but with fewer occurrences. Both counties are deemed a threat to North Korea.

Further description of the United States and South Korea as diabolical, stupid, and nonsensical raises the sense of alarm for their unpredictable behavior (figure 10.3). The words "United States" and "dangerous" were collocated nearly

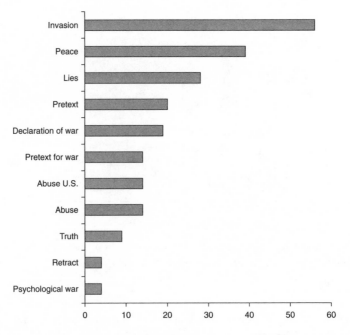

10.2 Emotional words associated with "UN Commission of Inquiry report" in North Korea's *Rodong Shinmun*, January 1, 2014–May 27, 2015

eight hundred times in the newspaper, followed closely by "South Korea" and "dangerous" at over seven hundred. Related words like "scheming," "diabolical," "unfortunate," "fascism," and "destructive" appeared more than two hundred times each, all collocated with the United States and South Korea: correlations of danger and scheming with diabolic behavior and stupidity frame the United States and South Korea as operating under illegible, unreliable logic. In official North Korean letters to the United Nations, the word "arbitrary" appears frequently alongside expressions such as "indiscriminate" and without seeming awareness of a contradiction, "double standard."

Throughout North Korean state media, South Korea and the United States are identified as sovereigns that are dangerous to their own people *and* North Korea. Those states fail to protect their people through the most primary of elements in North Korea's human rights project: national sovereignty. Two other elements are needed and fall within the sovereign, namely: the duty of the collective and the duty of the individual. In the following analysis of North Korean news, we can see how North Korea identifies the role of the collective and the individual in terms of their destruction of human rights in the United States and South Korea. The graph in figure 10.4 shows that both the collective and

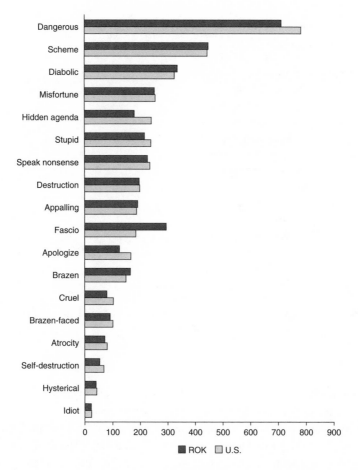

10.3 Descriptive words associated with the United States and South Korea in North Korea's *Rodong Shinmun*, January 1, 2014–May 27, 2015

the individual in the ROK and the United States become victimized and victimizer, living in what North Korea calls the "tundra" of human rights violations. Through quality-of-life words, North Korea highlights the unequal social and economic rights of the United States and South Korea. The analysis shows overwhelming reference to crime in the United States, over eight hundred articles, and in South Korea, about six hundred articles. The United States is responsible for crimes within its country in terms of rape, sexual violence, famine, and racial discrimination, but it is also culpable for international crimes in the form of massacres, fascism, torture, and slavery. Quality of life within these countries cannot be guaranteed either, and the impact of these nations on other countries ensures the proliferation of rights abuses elsewhere.

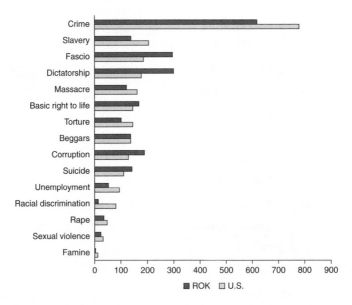

10.4 Socioeconomic words associated with the United States and South Korea in North Korea's *Rodong Shinmun*, January 1, 2014–May 27, 2015

With the rights of citizens so thoroughly disrespected, says the *Rodong Shinmun*, it is a wonder that the United States wants to raise the issue of human rights in a place like North Korea, where life is ideal. There is no logic to it other than that the United States has its agenda to destroy North Korea. The tu quoque distracts from North Korean rights while also revealing the agenda of the United States as insidious. This message is relayed further in person, and writing, at the United Nations.

A range of emotions appears in the language of the newspaper, but they can be classified as affectively generative of anger and fear. Anger variously manifests as annoyance, indignation, shock, incredulity, and rage that the United Nations, under duress from the United States and South Korea, would make false accusations against North Korea using the lies of state enemies (defectors). Fear variously manifests as terror, fright, agitation, alarm, and panic that the United States will use the UN report as pretense for invasion. This would thereby violate the rights of North Korean citizens by bringing them into a state of active war and a potential return to colonization, this time under the United States, which North Korea perceives to be the current state of South Korea. The function of anger and fear in the *Rodong Shinmun* is critical, particularly when it is operationalized as political public opinion and linked with historic wrongs. Contemporary scholarship in a range of disciplines has identified the crucial role of emotion in politics in stimulating and sustaining conflict.[24] Recent studies in the field of psychology have shown that anger leads to optimism while fear leads to increased risk estimates and preparedness.[25] While Lerner and Keltner, among others, identify the need to differentiate types of emotion when studying human behavior, their findings on fear and anger raises an interesting point of reflection. First, anger and fear mutually sustain one another. A reader of the *Rodong Shinmun* may be angry that false accusations are made against North Korea by the United Nations but then feel fearful of being trampled under the agenda of the United States. Second, we can see that anger and fear function together to legitimate political opinion on how to understand and protect human rights within North Korea. Affect is about convergence.

The affective impact comes from what runs through the state media: a blending of objective truths decontextualized with subjective ones, facts with inaccuracies, emotional reasoning, and hyperbole with deflection and obfuscation. The material is profoundly negative at points, reaching new lows of racism, sexism, and misandry. At other points it reaches new heights of thin-aired clarity in its piercingly accurate critique of the United States' crimes and South Korea's political and social failings. There is such a thorough mixing of accuracy and inaccuracy, "truth and lies" that the effect is like a maze. Let's try to imagine what effect this would have on a reader who has no regular sources of news beyond rumor and black-market chatter. I imagine the effect would be bewilderment or, perversely, certitude that North Korea is on the right track. In these confusing, labyrinthine passages, one thing remains clear: North Korea's news is *always* good news, and the rest of the world suffers terribly.

The emotional words that link negative metaphors associated with the United States and South Korea are strengthened, and their affective impact made more immediate through use of metonyms that stand in place for the United States and South Korea (see figure 10.4). Metonymy is when we use one thing to stand in place of another. While it was curious to find metaphors for the United States and the South Korea as a "stupid wife" (*p'unsuŏmnŭn a'nangne*) and vampire, metonymically the two countries are most often identified as "sin" and "beast" in more than 250 articles each. Synecdoche, where part is meant to stand for the whole, operates within metonymy. Figure 10.4 identifies the metonyms for the United States and South Korea. Perhaps the greatest metonym that appears in the *Rodong Shinmun* is how the UN Commission of Inquiry is interpreted as entirely spearheaded by the United States.

Defectors who gave testimony about rights violations publicly are totally subsumed under the term "human scum" in North Korean state rhetoric. Very rarely do their actual names appear. My computational analysis shows that, of 17,603 articles between January 1, 2014, and May 27, 2015, the *Rodong Shinmun* made few references to individual defectors. Instead, defectors were grouped collectively under the term "human scum" (*inkan suraegi*, or human trash/

garbage). Indeed, the term "human scum" appears in 242 articles, while the number of references to prominent defectors all together totals only five mentions (see figure 10.5).

As figure 10.5 shows, metonymy is also used for defectors. This primarily functions as referential—one thing stands for another—but it is not only referential. It provides an immediate message within the word or phrase that goes beyond either of the two things represented; it becomes a crucial means of interpreting and understanding a thing. Metonymy achieves something different from metaphor because it creates greater focus on some particular aspect of what is being identified; the conceptual framework is narrowed. Thus, we can arrive at the observation that there is a difference between understanding the *meaning of words* and understanding how people *understand experience*. When reflecting on the emotional language North Korea's central newspaper uses, it is clear that the *Rodong Shinmun* operationalizes language to shape an affective experience of things.

The language of North Korea's state news provides data that leads to a general framework for understanding the North Korean affective experience of the international community, the United Nations, the human rights report, and the commission's findings. The truth of domestic human rights violations is of no concern for North Korea's news. What is of concern is how the human rights

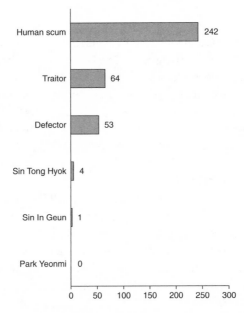

10.5 Frequency of references to defectors by derogatory terms or name in North Korea's *Rodong Shinmun*, January 1, 2014–May 27, 2015

violations of other states should be perceived and interpreted, and what kinds of actions should follow from this.

The affective impact of North Korea's print media is palpable. Prolix material of this sort is disorienting. The language is tirelessly bombastic. Hyperbole is the norm. It is as if an irate scribe gained control of a printing press and, in profound seriousness, took to circulating vitriol on a daily basis to a captive audience. I identify a singular scribe because, forensically, the discursive style of the articles is wiped clean of individuation. The message is singular, heady, distressing, and anodyne. It is reminiscent of what Elisabeth Anker calls a melodramatic discourse.[26] Its power comes not only from how the story is told but also from the particular mix of the contents of its telling: the abundance of what is written about—the rights violations of enemy states—and that other larger bit that remains untold: the rights violations of North Korea.

CHAPTER 11

NORTH KOREA'S RHETORIC OF DENIAL AT THE UNITED NATIONS

What matters is that the noisy "human rights" racket of the United States against the Democratic People's Republic of Korea is nothing but hysteria kicked up by the human scum who fled to south Korea after having been forsaken even by their kith and kin for all their evil doings and vices perpetrated in their hometowns. In other words, it is a charade staged on the basis of the misinformation provided by them.

The great irony is that a country as big as the United States uses those human scum, who are more dead than alive, for its campaign to hurt the dignity of the Democratic People's Republic of Korea. This must be a tragicomedy of the twenty-first century orchestrated by Washington.

National sovereignty is more important than human rights.

This is probably the reason why the United States keeps more prisoners than any other country in the world, mercilessly brandishing sharp swords against any forces opposed to the state and endangering its existence.

The Democratic People's Republic of Korea also does not show any mercy or leniency towards a tiny handful of hostile elements doing harm to the ideology and social system chosen by all its people, who are the masters of the sovereignty.

This is because they are riff-raff and dregs of society and good-for-nothings, as useless as slag in molten iron in the furnace.

—Letter from DPRK ambassador Ja Song Nam to the UN Security Council,
  March 15, 2014

Thanks paragraphs are taken from a four-and-a-half-page letter written by Ambassador Ja Song Nam, permanent representative of the Democratic People's Republic of Korea, to the president of the United Nations Security Council.[1] Less than a month earlier, the UN Commission of Inquiry report was published, confirming allegations of extreme, systematic, and widespread human rights abuses by the North Korean state. North Korea was under a new level of attention regarding the conditions of its citizens. North Korea had engaged with the United Nations on the topic of human rights before, but this was the first time for the North to receive such a pointed level of critique.

It would be inaccurate to imagine that North Korea is unfamiliar with human rights theory or norms. Indeed, North Korean state representatives are clearly schooled in international human rights norms; this is demonstrated in the masterful way they leverage the delicate claims within rights language toward state ends. North Korea wrote and submitted an assessment of their own human rights situation to the United Nations. Their rights report highlights the existence of free speech and free press for citizens according to their Law on Protecting Intellectual Property Rights. The text also justifies limitations on these rights under the "special duties and responsibilities" they command from the bearer, referring to Articles 19 and 20 of the UN International Covenant on Civil and Political Rights, or ICCPR. North Korea is operationalizing part of the ICCPR, which states that rights may "be subjected to certain restrictions." The statement from North Korea conveniently ignores the rest of the sentence in the covenant, which states: "these [restrictions] shall only be such as are provided by law and are necessary." North Korea picks and chooses what applies and what does not come into force with the second clause in Article 19: "[necessary] for the protection of national security or of public order." Article 20 resonates with many authoritarian states: "Any propaganda for war shall be prohibited by law."[2] It is the boundless scope of what is considered propaganda for war that is left undefined by North Korea.

The Origins of North Korea's Stance on Human Rights

There are early references to human rights in the speeches of Kim Il Sung and Kim Jong Il. State-controlled journals such as *Workers* (*Kulloja*) and *One Thousand Mile Leaping Horse* (*Chollima*) also carry articles about human rights.[3] North Korean awareness of the concept of human rights is not new but has existed since the founding of the country in 1948. Most references to human rights have emerged since the early 1990s due to increased attention from international countries, primarily the West, about North Korea's human rights conditions in the wake of the Soviet Bloc collapse.[4] Many of the reflections on human rights that appear in North Korea's main newspaper have appeared elsewhere in North Korean state propaganda. Political scientists Jiyoung Song and Robert Weatherly identified three main themes in North Korean human rights discourse: rights are conditional (they must be earned, but only if you are the right type of person), collective rights are above individual rights, and welfare and subsistence rights have special importance.[5]

Loyalty to the nation takes precedence over class as the factor that determines entitlement to rights in North Korea. The classification of individuals according to class was a system set up in 1958 primarily as a means to protect North Korean democracy and human rights from "the enemy of the working classes." People were classified as "hostile," "wavering," or "core" according to their class background of origin. Song and Weatherly describe this as a way to classify people according to their state of mind.[6] With Kim Jong Il, the state of mind became loyalty to the nation. Kim Jong Il wrote, "Anyone who loves our country and our people is eligible to serve the people and ultimately to be a member of our society."[7] By emphasizing loyalty to the nation as the basis for membership and entitlement to rights, this shifts responsibility to the individual and her demonstrated love for the country in determining her entitlement to rights. Entitlement to rights is thus contingent on the right kind of character. The character of a person is linked with the greater community to which the individual lives, principally via the family.

North Korea prioritizes collective rights, and the interests of the family are the basic unit of society enabling the collective to function. Each of the three North Korean constitutions written after 1948 indicates the importance of collective principles over individualistic ones.[8] The individual depends on the collective for her rights, and it is only when the collective has rights that the individual can have them.[9] Within this frame it doesn't make sense for an individual to seek or demand rights for herself by herself. Making demands alone could be seen as greedy and selfish. It would also jeopardize the collective interest. The notion of collective rights emphasizes national sovereignty. One of the fundamental arguments put forward by North Korea is that it is not possible for people to have human rights in a country that is not sovereign. Thus, no South Korean enjoys human rights because the country, as North Korea understands it, is a colony of the United States. As colonized subjects, they are as slaves. Kim Jong Il states, "People who are under foreign rule can never enjoy true human rights."[10]

North Korea emphasizes welfare and subsistence rights. The state's principal obligation to the people is the provision of welfare rights, although it clarifies that this can only be achieved if the country remains secure in sovereignty. The human right to subsistence is contingent on the national right of survival within the international community, which leads to the need for self-defense against hostile forces seeking to destroy the country from within or without.

This is used to justify all types of derogation from basic rights and justify the need for nuclear defense. However, it is not justified by the standards of international human rights norms.

In examining North Korean responses to the UN Commission of Inquiry report both at the United Nations and in its state media, the message is consistent and clear: North Korea has no human rights problems (best look at the United States) and is impervious to international efforts to force change through criticism. Close analysis of how North Korea constructs its response shows that it claims to be impervious, and yet it clearly has taken actions as a result of criticism—although such actions may not be to the betterment of rights. The international community might assume North Korea categorically dismisses the UN Commission of Inquiry. Indeed, North Korea has *said* as much. However, it has said and done much more than this too. Just prior to and in the wake of the UN Commission of Inquiry, both domestically and internationally, North Korea was uncharacteristically outspoken on the topic of human rights. The state, via representatives, made dramatic gestures to contest UN findings. This chapter examines this discourse and other performative gestures.

The major outcome of transnational advocacy for human rights in North Korea has been the UN Commission of Inquiry, its 2014 report, and the permanent addition of North Korea's human rights abuses to the UN Security Council agenda. North Korea has responded to these allegations internationally and domestically, not as activists may have wished, but the consequences still hold potential for improvement. The regime's response clearly shows denial and minor tactical concessions. According to patterns observed by other norm-violating states, these characteristics place North Korea within a process of international human rights normalization.[11] If states are denying that they commit rights violations, this indicates the state is at least interested in international socialization with rights norms—otherwise, why be part of the United Nations at all? Real change of human rights conditions and implementation of recommendations is of course the goal.

Examining the regime side of the rights equation, this portion of the book demonstrates that North Korea has a hyper concern with image control. While this typically takes a rhetorical form, image control is sometimes coupled with performative gestures embodied by state representatives and ordinary citizens aimed—like the rhetoric—at roundly refuting allegations of rights abuses.

Prior to the publication of the UN Commission of Inquiry report in 2014, an interactive dialogue was held with the Commission of Inquiry members on September 17, 2013. At this meeting Justice Michael Kirby stated that North Korea had been invited but declined to participate with the commission.[12] In the audience, Kim Yong-Ho, representative of the DPRK, spoke from a prepared script. He stated that North Korea "totally rejects" the oral update from the commission because it is fabricated from "defectors and rivals" as part of a political plan to "sabotage our socialist system by defaming the dignified image of the DPRK . . . under the pretext of human rights violations."[13] Kim stated that the violations mentioned in the update "do not exist" in North Korea. He clarified that the special rapporteur and the UN commission are motivated by hostility. He concluded by saying that the UN commission would not result in any changes in the DPRK but that the country honors dialogue and cooperation on human rights.

Several months later, at the Interactive Dialogue with the Commission of Inquiry on March 17, 2014, North Korean representative So Se Pyong stated that his delegation "categorically rejects" the commission because it is fabricated by the United States for "ill-minded political objectives."[14] Based on the "fabricated stories" of "criminals," the report is "defective and unable to condemn" North Korea. So detailed the U.S.-led war in the Middle East and the Balkans as well as the false documents used to support those interventions. Finally, he addressed the issue of the recommendation of North Korea's referral to the International Criminal Court as a "desperate attempt to eliminate" their society. He stated that the North Korean social system "protects human rights and fundamental freedoms both legally and in practice" and that the DPRK will "faithfully fulfil its obligation in the international area of human rights." So's response echoes the argument style in state media: the lies used to justify the United States' war in Iraq and the "fabricated" testimony of defectors are framed as discrediting the UN commission's findings.

In October 2014 a side event was held at the UN headquarters in New York, organized by the missions of Australia, Botswana, and Panama. The event included participation from defectors. Kim Song, the DPRK deputy head of mission, attended the event and challenged the UN Commission of Inquiry's report. Speaking without looking at his notes, Kim denied the allegations and denounced the "antagonist style" of the panel-led approach. He was given an opportunity to ask questions: "The testimony of defectors was conducted in a leading fashion. What does the panel think of this? What policy, at high level, is the source of crimes against humanity? Have you read the DPRK constitution? Have you read North Korea's human rights report?"[15] He accused the UN commissioners of being unfair because the investigation was conducted without seeing things directly. It is evident from these two public speaking events that the North Korean state is keeping pace with accusations leveled by the United Nations. The evocation of the phrase "high level" is an attempt to address the findings of the UN commission, which found the state responsible "at the highest level" for crimes against humanity.

Later North Korean representatives held a press conference at the United Nations on January 13, 2015, to give their side of the story to journalists accredited to the United Nations and to share their own report on the North Korean human rights situation, which they sent to the United Nations (examined momentarily in this book). At the event, An Myong Hun, deputy permanent representative of North Korea, asked that the United States temporarily halt the annual joint military exercises, identified as a threat to human rights. If this request was granted, the logic went, North Korea would not hold a nuclear test.[16] In March 2015, for the first time, North Korea's foreign minister attended the UN Human Rights Council at Geneva to defend the country's record.

North Korea also engaged in two rounds of the Universal Periodic Review process in 2008–2011 and 2012–2015. The Universal Periodic Review is a process where all United Nations member states undergo a review of their human rights record, indicating what actions they have taken to improve the situation in their country. All states are reviewed every four and a half years. The fact that North Korea participated in the Universal Period Review can be identified as a small change in their response to international rights norms, but this should not readily be interpreted as positive. Former North Korea United Front Department propaganda writer Jang Jin-Sung explained: "Despite Pyongyang's deceptive ways, many people in the outside world continue to believe in the theoretical North Korea in which dialogue with the regime is seen as the way to effect change. But I know from my years inside the government that talking will not get Pyongyang to turn any corners, not even with the North's current leader, Kim Jong Un."[17] In the first round of Universal Periodic Reviews—"astonishingly," Michael Kirby remarks—North Korea "rejected all the criticisms and recommendations proposed in the Human Rights Council" although North Korea has been part of the United Nations since 1993.[18] North Korea received 167 recommendations in December 2009. Immediately North Korea rejected 50 recommendations on the basis that they "seriously distorted the reality of and slandered the country." North Korea typically delays or fails to submit reports related to obligations (its state party report to the ICCPR was two years late). Their submission to the Committee on Economic, Social and Cultural Rights was submitted ten years behind deadline! Reporting obligations for other UN mechanisms are similarly delayed. The next—and, for North Korea, the third—cycle of Universal Period Review will take place in 2019.

One of the most dramatic performances of the state's rhetoric on human rights occurred at yet another side event at the United Nations in New York. At the event called "Victims' Voices: A Conversation on North Korean Human Rights" at the United Nations, a North Korean representative interrupted the event partway through.[19] Three North Korean defectors were providing details about their lives. Joseph Kim, speaking in English, shared his story and thanked the audience for attending.[20] The next speaker, Jin-hye Jo (Jay Jo), was about to speak when the DPRK representative, sitting with two colleagues, interrupted the proceedings. Because he was initially speaking without a microphone, it was hard to hear him. The audience at the New York UN headquarters looked bemused and uncertain. One of the North Korean panelists shouted at him, but the defector continued to read from his script without flinching. His mic was turned on. At this point in his speech he was explaining that the United States committed some of the world's worst human rights violations. U.S. ambassador to the United Nations Samantha Power asked for the control room to turn off the mic but then decided the man's speech was informative: "It's better to allow the DPRK to speak as it's a self-discrediting exercise," she stated.[21] Jin-hye Jo addressed the diplomat with poise and confidence, stating that he shouldn't bother speaking up just to tell lies. The panel speakers discussed whether the UN security staff should be called or whether they should let the North Korean representative speak. He continued to read. Defectors in the audience collectively shouted "out with you." Jin-hye Jo spoke up and began her story. She stated that she was now a U.S. naturalized citizen and held up her U.S. passport. The audience clapped loudly, and the North Koreans left the room.

North Korean representatives were cool, calm, and collected at these events. They read their speech, during which the defectors sitting in the audience were provoked and came off looking rowdy and boisterous, and then they left. Perhaps this was the intention. The speech that the DPRK representative read echoed the state rhetoric precisely. Close listening of other speeches at other events reveals further eerie uniformity. At a regular session of the Human Rights Council, the North Korean representative addressed the panel, describing the report as a political agenda. He said there is a Korean proverb that the panel should heed: "mind your own business."[22] The representative spoke for five minutes, his allotted time, and categorically rejected the allegations. He stated that the panel actually has nothing to do with human rights but rather is part of a political campaign with the agenda of eliminating North Korea. The speaker claimed "even Western media" outlets have identified that the human rights report is not genuine but is aimed at regime change. He further stated that the sponsors of the panel are "unqualified" to speak on issues related to its topic because panel members are from countries that committed human rights violations. Here he was referring to Japan sitting on the Security Council. Japan is not a permanent member to the Security Council (like China, the United States, France, the United Kingdom, and the Russian Federation) but was elected to the position.[23] North Korea interprets the presence of Japan on the Security Council as a contradiction due to the rights violations and crimes against humanity committed by the country during its occupation of China and Korea.

A second North Korean press conference was held on November 15, 2016, at the United Nations in New York after the adjournment of the General Assembly's Third Committee meeting. The room was mostly empty; sitting at a table in front were representative Kim In Ryong, North Korean ambassador and deputy permanent representative to the United Nations; Kim Yong-Ho, representative of North Korea and self-identified human rights expert; and Ri Song Chol, councilor to North Korea's permanent mission. The representatives issued the same state response: categorical denial, the case is "fraudulent," this is like Iraq. However, they furnished more detail. The United Nations commission "reminds us of the time, 13 years ago, when the United States was telling the lie in the United States that there were weapons of mass destruction in Iraq," said Kim In Ryong. "The resolution even touched on the nonexistent issue of exploita-tion of our workers sent abroad and nuclear weapon and ballistic missiles that have no relevance to human rights."[24] The representatives' responses show that North Korea is keeping up with research by rights groups and NGOs. North Korea's use of tu quoque turned to the contemporary. The representative stated: "The EU should rather pay attention to cleaning up their houses first by reflect-ing upon and bringing to justice those responsible for the crime against humanity including xenophobia, Islamophobia, defamation of religion and Neo-Nazism that are rampant in their own territories and the worst ever refu-gee crisis caused by the United States and Western countries themselves."[25] Japan's past crimes against humanity are itemized and identified as an area requiring compensation.

In the final portion of his speech, Kim In Ryong addressed the natural disas-ters in North Korea and the resulting hardships for people. He explained that the government of North Korea was making efforts to ensure people were being taken care of. "The people in the DPRK take immense pride in the socialist system of the country which was chosen and consolidated and further devel-oped by their own will as well as the genuine system of ensuring human rights which capitalism can neither achieve nor imitate at all."[26] The UN Commis-sion of Inquiry report is once again identified as "illegal and unlawful," part of the plot to undermine the social system of North Korea.

After the twelve-minute speech, the group took questions from the press. Kim Yong-Ho, who was tasked with answering questions, spoke without the assistance of notes and began by stating that he would answer questions related to human rights issues. This focus and emphasis on rights is something new for North Korea's UN representatives. He began by stating that the abduction issue was resolved. (While he didn't elaborate on what he means by this, it is presumed he was referring to a deal between Kim Jong Un and Shinzo Abe to allow investigation into the abductions from Japan.) On whether the current special rapporteur on human rights in North Korea, Tomás Ojea Quintana, would be permitted entry to the country, Kim stated that he would always be welcome in Pyongyang—as an individual, not as the special rapporteur.[27] This echoes the argument put forward by political scientist Jonathan Chow in his analysis of North Korea's participation in the Universal Periodic Review. North Korea wants to be in control of the narrative, and that is why the review, with North Korea submitting its own data, is acceptable while a visit from the spe-cial rapporteur is not.[28] Ambassador Kim In Ryong offered concluding remarks, which he read from a prepared document: the U.S.-led forces are pressing the DPRK with nonexistent and politicized human rights issues. The United Nations Commission of Inquiry, he said, intends to "defame and eliminate the DPRK," which is "far from a constructive dialogue."[29]

A third press conference was held by North Korea on December 13, 2016, to give the standpoint of the North on the human rights issue to the UN Security Council. Ambassador Kim In Ryong spoke from a prepared statement.[30] Putting the North Korean human rights issue on the agenda at the UN Security Council was described as beyond the mandate of the Security Council and a result of pressure from the United States. The ambassador mentioned that other developing countries and the Non-Aligned Movement group of states rejected the placement of human rights on the Security Council agenda as beyond the remit of the council. He called for nothing less than the reform of the council.[31] His statement is similar to an article in Korean state news on an earlier date, December 11, 2016.[32] Several members of the press audience asked about the North's domestic news rhetoric, identifying it as threatening—indeed, it does make several veiled threats to the United States. Kim did not answer the question of rhetoric.

On November 23, 2016, North Korea's own state-run Association for Human Rights Studies forwarded an open questionnaire to the United Nations in response to the Third Committee of the 71st UN General Assembly resolution on human rights in North Korea.[33] The Korean-language version is worth mentioning here as it is significantly longer and answers each of the questions itself by highlighting the failings of the United States and South Korea.[34] The article highlights the mistreatment of overseas workers, an issue studied by the South Korean-based Asan Institute for Policy Studies in late 2014 and later by the Leiden Asia Centre–European Alliance for Human Rights in North Korea and the Database Center for North Korean Human Rights.[35] North Korea explains that overseas workers are proud to be dispatched to help the motherland prosper. The article details the North's strong medical health system, which is sharply contrasted with that of the United States and South Korea, including granular detail on the cost of medical exams, laboratory tests, and biopsies.

North Korea's Self-Discrediting Discourse

North Korea's state discourse is self-discrediting, as Samantha Power put it. By rebutting the findings with such extreme denials and defamatory accusations, the state reveals its own guilt. North Korea tends to criticize the interlocutor at a personal level and evoke misogynist, racist, ablest, mentalist, and homophobic language to defame the subject. Former president Park Geun-hye of South Korea was referred to as an "old prostitute coquetting with outside forces," and former U.S. president Barack Obama was her "American master reminiscent of a wicked black monkey."[36] Generally, the United States and South Korea are referred to as "mentally ill." Justice Kirby, investigator for the UN Commission of Inquiry, was also verbally abused as a "political swindler" and a "disgusting old lecher with a 40-odd-year-long career of homosexuality . . . still anxious to get married to his homosexual partner."[37]

The writing personalizes politics by identifying private aspects of Justice Kirby's life phrased to create an image of him as a frustrated, sexually deviant suspect with an alternative agenda. This language discredits North Korea because it supports inequality directly from the representatives of a state that purports to support equal social opportunity. Hate speech, defamation, and violation of a person's honor and dignity occur not only with reference to Justice Kirby but also whenever former presidents Obama or Park are mentioned. The same is true when defectors are mentioned; they are rarely named but are instead referred to via the metonym of "garbage" or "scum."

Defamation also occurs at the United Nations. In his statement read at one of North Korea's press conferences, Ambassador Kim refers to Obama as a lackey who is defeated in office as opposed to having fulfilled his maximum term of service. A state news article and Ambassador Kim In Ryong's speech carry exactly the same words and grammatical errors: "A lackey of Obama who will soon be compelled to leave the Oval Office after sustaining his bitter defeat went so reckless as to dare hurt the dignity of the supreme leadership of the DPRK at the United Nations Security Council in a sinister bid to tarnish its image and stir up the atmosphere of pressurizing it. But the lackey is sadly mistaken if he calculates that such ill-minded act can work on the DPRK and other countries."[38] However, Ambassador Kim adds further insights that are not elaborated on in the state newsprint article. In a "gangster like act of the US to insult the UN and its actor states, the US brought a small number of unknown NGOs and defectors, human scam [sic], at UN headquarters to fan [inaudible] the DPRK human rights racket even though most of the UN member states oppose such a politicized event. This shows clearly that the US is out all reasons [sic] and became the mental disabled who is not able to distinguish even the elementary things." He further states that the United Nations cannot function due to U.S. pressure to push its "ill-minded racket of slandering one of the sovereign member UN states."[39] Unlike the earlier press conference, the December 2016 press conference evokes the affect-laden language of the North Korean state media, which is highly insult driven.

There were seventeen official letters written by the DPRK permanent mission to the United Nations during this period; three specifically address the Commission of Inquiry report. The North's letters to the United Nations focus overwhelmingly on the protection of national sovereignty as the primary right of North Korea under threat of violation through the commission and "hostile forces." In other words, the state is turning the rights claims into a political claim against its national sovereignty. To ensure protection of their national sovereignty, they request that the United Nations prevent the United States and South Korea from carrying out joint military exercises. Again, this is diversionary. And the claim that it is about human rights rings hollow when they threaten to retaliate with nuclear tests if their demands are not met. North Korea identifies the United States, evidenced in the joint military exercises and historical legacies of violence, as the primary reason for testing missiles, which are a means to safeguard security.

In January 2014 North Korea's permanent representative to the United Nations, Sin Son-ho, called a public press conference in New York at the United Nations.[40] The subject: South Korean activists' practice of dropping antigovernment leaflets into North Korea, which the North identifies as an act of psychological warfare.[41] The argument about the North's claim on human rights was unchanged by the Commission of Inquiry report.

North Korea's Own Rights Report

Ri Su Yong, foreign minister of North Korea, addressed the UN General Assembly on September 27, 2014. He stated that abusing the human rights issue for political purpose is in itself the biggest human rights violation.[42] On September 15, a few weeks before Ri's address to the General Assembly, the North sent a letter to the United Nations with a large attachment. It was the North's own human rights report. This 119-page document, authored by the DPRK Association for Human Rights Studies, covers the earliest history of North Korea— from the foundation and ideology of the social system, through the Korean War, right up to the present. The preface to the document sets the tone throughout:

> Recently, distorted views are floated by anti-DPRK hostile forces about the realities of the DPRK, especially its human rights situation, causing serious misunderstanding thereof.
>
> The United States and its followers are pursuing persistent anti-DPRK human rights campaigns aimed at interfering in its internal affairs and eventually overthrowing the social system by fabricating [the] "human rights issue" of the DPRK to mislead international opinions and raise it to the United Nations.
>
> However, truth will always prevail and cannot be covered by whatever means.[43]

There are two main areas of concern in this statement, the first regarding a considerable contradiction within the text itself. The North sees itself as in a state of war (the armistice) as well as in a state of constantly preparing for war. The joint military exercises between South Korea and the United States are identified as provocations that necessitate the North's practice. Therefore, it is curious to read the following:

> The Korean War (June 25, 1950–July 27, 1953) provoked by the US brought the Korean people untold sufferings and calamities.
>
>   . . .
>
>   . . . However, the *people's livelihood was relatively stable* during the 3-year war period, and there *was not a single case of death due to starvation or cold* other than those killed by the US indiscriminate and brutal air bombing and artillery shelling.
>
>   . . .
>
>   . . . The DPRK Government has taken people-oriented legal measures such as the enactment and enforcement of legislation to *ensure the rights of people in the circumstances of war, which other countries couldn't imagine even in peacetime.*[44]

Reading these passages in light of the North's views on sanctions—which it identifies as a stranglehold on the country that prohibits the government's efforts to provide for its people—it is remarkable that the state was able to provide during times of war but sanctions now tip the balance. Further, in the Association of Human Rights Studies report, the above claim seems incoherent if during three years of catastrophic war *there was not a single case of death due to starvation or cold* unless brought about from the United States.[45] The document states that the North cannot uphold certain rights because of the pressure of the international community, principally the United States. This is odd because the situation, though far from ideal, is hardly as violent and turbulent as during the Korean War.

As we transition from the historical part of the report, above, to the section on contemporary conditions, there is a shift in sympathy for how "economic difficulties" threaten the right to life. "*Many countries undergo economic difficulties and people's rights to existence are threatened.* This is entirely attributable to the economic blockade and sanctions imposed by the US and other Western countries. The issue of ensuring human rights at [the] international level becomes ever more complicated with each passing day due to the high-handed and arbitrary practices and double standards of the US and other Western countries."[46]

Another section speaks about the need for sovereign development and prosperity "first" so that the human rights matter can be properly addressed. The economic connection with human rights is of course linked with the socialist and third-world emphasis on economic and social rights, which the United

States and others still struggle with, but we can see a contradiction in the logic between the earlier passage and the claims below:

> In order to properly address the human rights issue, independent development and prosperity of each country and nation *should be secured in the first place.*[47]
>
> . . .
>
> *Economic sanctions* and blockades are *one of the manoeuvers of interference* that the arrogant US is employing against other countries to interfere in their internal affairs and [is a] method of strangling.
>
> For decades, economic sanctions and blockades by [the] US and its satellite forces against [the] DPRK are extremely persistent and wicked.
>
> In a word, [the] US-sponsored economic sanctions and blockades against DPRK are intended to economically stifle the DPRK and destabilize the country to topple the government.[48]
>
> . . .
>
> The US economic sanctions and blockades towards [the] DPRK by stirring up its followers, *obstruct the right of development of sovereign state[s] and impose negative influence to enjoyment of human rights.* They are anti-human rights and anti-popular in character and [a] crime of genocide far surpassing the wartime mass slaughter.[49]

Other portions of the human rights report acknowledge the necessary curtailment of rights for the safety of the nation in a manner that mirrors the "state of emergency" justification now seen in neoliberal capitalist societies. So, while North Korea finds no end to its rancor for the censorship and surveillance practices of South Korea and the United States, the end justifies the means when it comes to their own practices of curtailing human rights. Again with the tu quoque. Of South Korea, the Korean Central News Agency states:

> South Koreans have no place where they may complain even though they are deprived of everything by the U.S. and their rights violated by it. . . .
>
> In the eight months of the present regime [in ROK,] more than 23,790 articles were deleted from [the] internet site for being "articles following the north" and hundreds of internet sites were forced to shut down. People demanding the right to existence were harshly suppressed.[50]

Of U.S. invasion of privacy, it says,

> The U.S. engaged in a tapping program, code-named PRISM, exercising long-term and vast surveillance both at home and abroad. The program is a blatant violation of international law and seriously infringes on human rights.[51]

The U.S. National Security Agency illegally monitored and snooped e-mails and internet information of inhabitants. This numbers a total of 56 000 cases in 4 years until 2011.[52]

Yet the DPRK clearly identifies the need to curtail rights in order to protect national sovereignty.

All kinds of advocacy of war of aggression, discrimination and violence, acts of instilling national, racial and religious antagonism and propaganda to threaten or harm the security of the state and social order are absolutely prohibited. Such acts are also prohibited by articles 19 and 20 of the international treaty on citizens and their political rights.[53]

. . .

Prohibition of anti-government associations is a matter of vital importance related to the destiny of the Republic and the prospect of the protection and promotion of peoples human rights under the situation where the US and Western countries are attempting to undermine the socialist system of the DPRK by creating and instigating such associations.[54]

. . .

Freedom of religion is allowed and provided by the State law within the limit necessary for securing social order, health, social security, morality and other human rights. Especially the Government prevents religion from being used to draw in foreign forces or harm the state and social order.[55]

North Korea invests considerable text in argument styles that rely on ad hominem attacks, particularly toward the United States and South Korea, as well as logical fallacy and generalization: "According to a nation-wide opinion poll conducted by the U.S. opinion poll institution GALLUP on March 26 last year [2013], 43 percent of its respondents regarded the issues of starvation and housing as serious social problems."[56]

The United States is also depicted as a twisted country that seeks to bring the DPRK down to its level. "It has persistently pulled up the DPRK over its strict control on such impure publications as pornography, in an intention to instigate alien elements. It went the lengths of claiming that the DPRK's strict step of removing the modern-type factionalists who seriously violated popular masses' human rights, construction of sports facilities and sport enthusiasm are contrary to the 'human rights standard.'"[57]

In sum, this official report to the United Nations uses its signature rhetorical attacks to deflect attention from the issue of its own human rights violations. It is not a real report of any kind but instead is a repetitive evasion of the matter at hand—one that continues to make the North look more, not less, guilty.

A Public Conversation

On October 20, 2014, the Council on Foreign Relations held a conversation with North Korean ambassador Jang Il Hun.[58] This was the first time that a representative from the DPRK spoke at length and took questions from an audience on the topic of North Korean human rights. Not surprisingly, Ambassador Jang stuck to the official North Korea stance on human rights. He began by identifying North Korea's own human rights report that was submitted to the United Stations. He clarified that there is a system for promoting and protecting human rights in the North. He echoed the first part of the report with, "The main obstacle to the enjoyment of human rights and fundamental freedoms by our people . . . is the United States' hostile policy against the DPRK. And through its political, military pressure and economic sanctions, it tries to isolate and stifle our system. . . . The prospect for human rights enjoyment by our people as a society evolves when the economic conditions of our people improve."[59]

It is not surprising that any government employee would repeat precisely the government's stance on an issue. What is impressive is the cavalier manner of Jang's delivery. During the question-and-answer session at the end of his talk, members of the public pressed Ambassador Jang on a few points of contention. When he was asked directly, "Why are you here today?" Ambassador Jang explained he was there to speak about the human rights situation in his country and "correct the wrong understanding of some people, given by the so-called defectors." Mr. Jang was trying to contain information about the DPRK that circulates freely in the international arena. This effort at containment takes the form of providing the explanation for the situation of the DPRK. But he does this without addressing rights directly. When questioned about the existence of political prison camps, he explained: "We totally reject the existence of the— whatever form it takes, the camps. *The terminology—I don't like it. . . . We call it* reformatory, right? And my colleague, I heard at the time that we mentioned about education through labor, detentions, but the Western media says that he admitted to the existence of labor camp[s]. *That's not true. I was there. I listened to him. So any camp of any kind does not exist* in my country."[60]

Jang is trying to walk back something his colleague let slip on October 8, 2014. Choe Myong-nam, a North Korean foreign ministry official in charge of United Nations affairs and human rights, "misspoke" in claiming that there were "reform through labor" camps aimed at improving people's political mentality.[61] Jang clarifies that there are detention facilities, not camps, turning attention toward his claim that the international community would rather not use terms that are amenable to North Korea.

There is a layer of metacommunication happening at this point in the public discussion, between the speech of Jang's colleague in the past, the reportage of it in Western media, and what Jang is saying here: through these three layers, he identifies what is true. Truth is established through being *there*. Not *there* in the camps, but *there* at the moment his colleague spoke. He "listened to him," and it is through this that he established "any camp of any kind does not exist." The words that Jang used were chosen operationally. This portion of the conversation reminded me instantly of the many hours I spent listening to North Koreans speak about the experience of the famine.[62] Speaking directly about hunger or starvation in North Korea was sometimes more dangerous than being hungry itself. To speak about hunger *created* hunger. To speak about starvation death *created* starvation death. Conversely, by speaking indirectly about hunger and starvation—someone died from food poisoning, not starvation; or high blood pressure, not hunger—make a new world.[63] Speaking, but also hearing, is a careful exercise in power. Ambassador Jang is at the Council on Foreign Relations in order to correct the words of his colleagues—and, of course, defectors—so that the internationally community can hear "more accurately." He said, "We *never have had* such kind of system in my country. That's for sure."[64] He hopes by saying it to the rest of the world, he makes it so.

Silencing the Voice

On April 30, 2015, the United Nations held a panel discussion to continue the dialogue about human rights conditions within the DPRK.[65] At the event, a small voice speaks up in the large room: "As for the DPRK. . . ." The speaker was drowned out by Barbara Demick, author of the best-selling book on North Korea *Nothing to Envy*. She told the speaker he would have a chance to speak later. But the speaker raised his voice. The representative began to speak loudly because his mic had been turned off. Only parts of his speech are audible. This effort is emblematic of what the North hopes to achieve: the silencing of North Korean defectors and those who give them a platform to speak.

What we witness in this instance of international relations at their most intimate is how truth and language operate inside North Korea on a regular basis. This moment appeared again and again in the oral testimonies I collected from North Koreans who survived the famine of the 1990s. Repeatedly they told me that, when in the North, they could not speak directly about their experiences because doing so would mean the end of life altogether.[66] The voice of the defector has become paramount in recent years, particularly in the wake of the Commission of Inquiry's report. As Samantha Power explained, "We must see that their voices, and those of other defectors, are amplified—here at the UN, at the Security Council, and beyond. And we must not be satisfied with telling the stories, but with asking what we can do to stop a system built to strip people of their most basic rights and dignity, and bring the perpetrators to account."[67]

After the event, a press release from North Korea's mission to the United Nations appeared online.[68] In the statement Ri Song Chol expressed the North's stance: The three-page document identifies the United States as "No. 1 in murder and crimes," identifying the murder of people of color, sexual abuse, and the "number of prisons and prisoners."[69] The text identifies physical violence by white police officers against black Americans in Ferguson, Missouri, and Baltimore, Maryland. It also mentions the CIA's use of torture and imprisonment without trial. It asks the United States to prepare a report on its human rights violations and permit international investigation into those crimes and punishment for offenders. Then South Korea is addressed. The *Sewol Ferry* disaster is identified as a violation of many children's rights; North Korea also claims that the State Security laws of South Korea violate the rights of those citizens who wish to praise the DPRK. The North identifies sexual tourism near American military bases since 1945 as another instance of South Korea's violation of rights. The statement turns to the assistant secretary-general to the United Nations for his participation in the "one-sided political drama." Finally, it addresses the North Korean defectors. They are "human scum" and "parasites." Shin Dong Hyuk, a defector who born and raised in a political prison camp, is accused in the North's statement of raping a thirteen-year-old girl.[70] Because portions of Shin's account were later recanted and amended, the North deems his entire testimony and (conveniently) all defector accounts as fabrications. In summary, it dismisses the entire commission report as based on lies, and the UN Security Council and UN General Assembly as biased as well.

Silencing takes the form of intimidation at the United Nations, but it can also take a very definitive form as well. Early in February 2015 the foreign minister of North Korea sent a letter to the United Nations asking for information on the identities of the North Korean defectors who participated in the Commission of Inquiry report. North Korea explained, "We are ready to reveal to the whole world the true identities of each and every one of them and the crimes committed and the lies told by them one by one."[71] Many who gave public testimony are under twenty-four-hour guard in South Korea and the United States due to threats from North Korean or pro–North Korean agents. North Korea is seeking more information on individual defectors so that it can unleash a campaign of harassment. As early as 1991 North Korea was killing defectors in South Korea. The most famous case is that of Yi Han-yong (Ri Il-nam)—a relation of the Kim family who defected in 1982.[72] After making his story known in a book titled *Kim Jong Il's Royal Family*—he was hunted down and shot by North Korean agents. He was silenced forever.

CHAPTER 12

BROADCASTING DENIAL

We are parents of the 12 girls separated overnight by the tremendous atroc-ities of the South Korean authorities who lured and kidnapped them through the gangsters of their national intelligence service.

—from a letter reportedly sent from North Korea to the United Nations
   in 2017

In a documentary produced by North Korea, a mournful letter appears, one reportedly sent to the UN secretary-general and High Commissioner for Refugees, Antonio Guterres, and to the president of the UN Human Rights Council, Ambassador Joaquín Alexander Maza Mar-telli.[1] In the video, violins sustain a wrenching, tearful note. A woman's voice is humming a sorrowful tune. The names of twelve women are read aloud. Photos of them fill the screen. The camera scans over three pages of the letter fanned across the desk. This is cut with an image of a woman writing a letter—that letter; she is squinting into the sentences and crying. The camera scans back and the scene shows several middle-aged men and women in a room behind a large conference table, standing over the epistolary. Everyone is crying. Some-one reads the letter aloud again, over shaky video montage.[2]

It is not new for North Korea to claim that defectors are instead victims of abduction. North Korea made similar claims when students sought, and were granted, asylum in Moscow between 1958 and 1961.[3] In an effort to repatriate these so-called abductees, North Korea hunted them. The aforementioned documentary from 2017 shows how North Korea operationalizes its citizens, the language of international human rights, and the institutions of human rights practice to present an image of the nation and people as vulnerable, bullied, and abused by other nation-states. Pity is the dominant emotion. In another video, a voiceover explains,

> Just as something called the North Korean Human Rights office opened in Seoul, a bastard going by the name of Jeong Kwang Il put his head in the door. The bastard said he got tortured and suffered in all kinds of ways in a North Korean political prison, and then escaped. He delivered to the office a list of people he says were in the political prison camp with him, living in these inhumane conditions. Evil defectors are all shameless liars, but he is even more advanced than the others.[4]

This vignette is from a video denouncing Jeong Kwang Il, a man who survived torture in a North Korean political prison, as mentioned in the introduction to this book. North Korea's state-run website *Uriminzokkiri* (Our People Together, a news source that is hosted out of Japan but tied to North Korea) has a subsection of videos titled "Human Rights—Lies and Truth."[5] As this book goes to press, there are 115 videos documenting, uncovering, and denouncing allegations of rights abuses. They appear in Korean, and some have Russian, Japanese, and English subtitles. The title of the documentary doesn't have a particularly nice ring to it. Located on the state-run website, in a section with over a hundred other documentaries like it, this documentary denounces a man who survived a political prison camp. His crime—now—is that he speaks about it. Titled *A Terrible Human Wreck Who Steals a Person's Name and Career*, the story doesn't have a logical narrative arc and at points seems to be edited in a fashion that is almost deliberately bad. This video, like the others, roundly discounts allegations against the North Korean state and defiles the defector who is making the allegations.

North Korea's state broadcasting service produces documentaries and news reports covering the topic of defectors.[6] Documentaries on the topic of rights, defectors, and return defectors increased after the publication of the UN Commission of Inquiry (COI) report in early 2014. North Korea also uploaded documentaries and man-on-the-street-interviews created by its own Korean Central News Agency to YouTube, though these are often taken down by YouTube, and the *Uriminzokkiri* site.

These video responses target what North Korea identifies as the weakest link in the United Nations' claims of rights violations: that the allegations are based on the "falsified" testimony of defectors. These videos are artifacts of the state, and as such they are objects worthy of analysis. Rather than trying to determine whether these videos should be believed or the manner of their reception domestically or internationally, this chapter forensically examines the videos to see what the state achieves in these creations. The artifacts distinctly show the coercive function of the state in presenting *the* correct response to defectors and their claims. My examination pays particular attention to features of the footage, such as the presence of family photographs, the use of images of defectors at the United Nations, images of scarification on the bodies of defectors, descriptions of the personalities of defectors, types of editing such as jump cuts and montage, facial reactions and body gestures of persons in the videos, voice tone, indications of prompting, the use of teleprompters, and overall narrative message.

It would be easy to dismiss these videos out of hand as the vehement ravings of a nation-state responding to a perceived threat. But under close analysis, the videos confirm and further reveal rights violations in North Korea in ways the state may not have realized. The videos employ typical methods of so-called authentic documentary making such as taking a seeming investigative-journalist approach and interviewing the man on the street. Yet the videos boldly eschew norms associated with reliability, trust, and rigor all the while professing accuracy and truth.

While North Korea has made documentaries in the past, and Kim Jong Il was a self-proclaimed cinema expert, contemporary productions in North Korea have a new and growing subject of critique in defectors. The primary target in these videos are those who have spoken publicly at the United Nations and other public platforms. These individuals, living or dead, are the objects of horrendous slander through character-assassinating narratives populated with friends, family, and neighbors—all clearly stage-managed. The insults are so abusive that, even if the claims were true, it is almost impossible not to have sympathy for the accused. It just isn't possible that every defector who has ever spoken out accusing North Korea of rights violations is a rapist, pedophile, sex trafficker, or murderer. And not only them but their kin as well, should they also have defected. Rather, these videos add insult to injury. The state is committing defamation against rights activists and foreigners too (see figure 12.1).

Unlike print media, the videos offer a chance to study how North Korea constructs its response to rights abuse allegations. The addition of English subtitles in these materials indicates that the videos are intended to communicate with an audience beyond North or South Korea. It is difficult to determine if the documentaries were aired within North Korea; possibly they may have been—and, certainly, the testimony from overseas workers indicates that some form of inoculator ideology is provided to those sent overseas. As more people defect, the state may use videos as preventative discouragement. The news broadcasts of interviews with the man on the street were aired inside North Korea as part

12.1 The title sequence, repeated in both parts, shows pictures of high-profile male defectors (above, left to right) Kang Chol-Hwan, Shin Dong Hyuk, Jang Jin-Sung, and others not pictured. These photos scroll past a still shot of Robert R. King, special envoy for North Korean human rights at the U.S. State Department. This title sequence reappears several times throughout both parts of the video (screenshot 0:10/17:12).

"Who Is Sin Tong Hyok?" Tv.uriminzokkiri.com, part 2, March 5, 2017, http://www.uriminzokkiri .com/itv/index.php?ppt=lie_human&no=33227

of a larger news sequence available to those who have television. Even if the videos are not believed by the domestic North Korean audience, they still operate as a discouragement. This is a form of what the philosopher Hannah Arendt calls "organized lying," which forms an "*adequate* weapon against truth."[7] These videos don't peddle truth; instead, they work with opinion, and that is a powerful tool of the state. They could provoke anxiety in the North Korean viewer that the state could do the same to them: make public opinion of them and their family— for right or wrong—a desecration. From the perspective of human rights violations, these videos are useful for tracing the intent of the state. In this respect, the insights of Arendt are useful further still. She continues: "As every historian knows, one can spot a lie by noticing incongruities, holes, or the junctures of patched-up places. As long as the texture as a whole is kept intact, the lie will eventually show up as if of its own accord."[8] In this case, the incongruities in the film's narratives and presentation reveal the truth of the state's efforts to silence defectors and manipulate public opinion at home and abroad.

At least one purpose of these videos is to undermine the credibility of North Korean defectors wholescale, within North Korea and beyond. But how do the videos achieve their purpose? What is the evidence of their false construction?

The videos typically start by identifying the testimony of defectors, on which the human rights report is based, as the greatest weakness. They then launch into a defamation campaign to name, shame, and discredit defectors. The obvious question raised by these documentaries is: Why do they exist and why now? The content of the documentaries and the context of their emergence reveal that the state is trying to satisfy a wholly legitimate request from the United Nations: for access to the country and its citizens. Through the documentaries, North Korea provides a quasi-access. The content of the documentaries and their construction reveals this.

Capturing Character: Photographs in Defector-Denouncing Documentaries

Shin Dong Hyuk is a North Korean who was born and raised in a political prison camp. His story shocked the world when, with the help of his coauthor, he published his memoir first in Korean and then in English. *Escape from Camp 14: One Man's Remarkable Odyssey from North Korea to Freedom in the West* tells the story of growing up in a prison camp in South Pyongan Province, North Korea. A few years after his story went public, Shin clarified parts of his story. He wasn't in the prison his entire life but rather in two different prisons (Camp 14 and Camp 18) and had tried to escape several times. He had a part to play in the execution of his mother and brother (he had told the prison guard about their escape plan in order to get an extra serving of rice and a better position in school). He wasn't tortured at the age of thirteen but at age twenty. North Korea had already been defaming defectors for years, but they saw Shin's public act of clarification as a "confession" that he had lied about everything. It was an opportunity to drive home the point that defectors are lying—even they admit it!

Shin's primary testimony concerned the political prison camps in North Korea.[9] In January 2015, a year after he gave his UN testimony, Shin explained that some of the dates and places of his narrative were inaccurate. Prior to Shin sharing his testimony at the United Nations, between the Korean-language publication of his book in 2007 and the English-language collaborative book with Blaine Harden, a U.S. journalist, a key portion of Shin's narrative had already been clarified. In the Korean version, he states that the guards learned of his mother and brother's plan to escape. The two were subsequently hanged. The English-language book reveals that Shin "exchanged" his mother and brother's escape plan with a prison guard with the hope of getting a portion of rice to eat and being elected classroom leader. Factually, the English version of Shin's story remains the same. The basic aspects of his story remain. He was born and raised in a prison camp, not Camp 14 but Camp 18, he was tortured, and he witnessed his mother's and brother's executions. When Shin publicly identified that he had got some details of his story wrong, the *Rodong Shinmun* seized it as an opportunity to identify the inherent deviant nature of former North Koreans.

In the two-part documentary *Lie and Truth* produced by the North Korean state about Shin Dong Hyuk, his father and a few other individuals are shown a childhood photograph.[10] The photo, truthfully or falsely attributed, links Shin to the narrative account in the documentary. As a photograph, his presence in the documentary is totally at the edict of the state: emptied of the ability to move, speak and act as an agent in the narrative. He is entirely acted upon, and this is the only reliable way for Shin Dong Hyuk to appear in the documentary.

Family photos are typically used to maintain relationships, particularly between people who are geographically separated, but in these documentaries the photograph confirms and reestablishes a relationship between the speaker and the defectors. The photographs disconnect the defector and testimony, rendering both deceptive. The photograph is not about aesthetic but rather functions toward a particular representational task. As photographer, writer, and filmmaker Allan Sekula observes, the photograph is "harnessed" for a particular representational task.[11]

Photographs are also mistakenly assumed to have a "primitive core of meaning" that purely relays their message, and this assumption "elevates the photograph to the legal status of document and testimonial. It generates a mythic aura of neutrality around the image."[12] So it is not unusual that photographs appear in the documentaries tasked with exonerating the state and denouncing the defector. The photographs in the documentaries are objects within the object of the video. Their representational task is to make the narrated reality authentic. The photograph becomes an active witness and an object of evidence; its seeming objectivity is conflated with actual objectivity.[13]

Photographs taken at moments when defectors gave testimony at the United Nations or other high-profile speaking engagements are used as an investigative reporting technique to achieve a sense of authenticity (figure 12.2). A connection is made between the individual's former life in North Korea and their present international life. This is achieved through a singular, consistent narrative about the defector's character pre- and postdefection. In each case, no matter the defector, stories about their former lives thoroughly characterize them as inherently devious. The photographs are used as a foil to link past, when the seed of deviance was only beginning, and present, when deviance is in full bloom. In the screenshot in figure 12.2, Shin's father and stepmother are shown a photograph of Shin Dong Hyuk. It is a photograph taken at an international speaking engagement. Unexpectedly, for a fraction of a second, both seem to be smiling at the photo.

The documentary shows Shin Dong Hyuk's father and stepmother sitting on the living room floor discussing the early years of Shin's life. They dismiss the claim that they lived in a political prison camp (figure 12.3). This portion of

12.2 Shin's father and stepmother view a photograph of Shin at the United Nations (screenshot 01:23/16:44).

"Who Is Sin Tong Hyok?" Tv.uriminzokkiri.com, part 1, March 4, 2017, http://www.uriminzokkiri.com/itv/index.php?ppt=lie_human&no=33226

video footage is edited to include footage from the United Nations showing Shin and members of the COI. The audio plays a continuous testimony-debunking narrative over these images.

In figure 12.4, Song Kyong Ran is given a recent photo of Shin. In this image, she uses her index finger to trace the lines of his face, confirming he is indeed Shin Dong Hyuk—or, as he was known in North Korea, Shin In Gun—and that there is resemblance to his father, Shin Kyong Sop (in figures 12.2 and 12.3). Song Kyong Ran elaborates on Shin and his mother's devious character. Other individuals appear in the narrative. A hairdresser is duped by Shin's mother. Shin's mother and brother (Shin Hi Gun) plot to murder the hairdresser to steal her money. The mother, we have been told, was money obsessed. While the hairdresser is in front of the mirror—a detail in the story that baffles—Hi Gun strikes her on the head from behind with an axe. The hairdresser's body was bundled into the storeroom only to be discovered later by Shin In Gun (Shin Dong Hyuk) and his father. The authorities were contacted, and Shin's mother admitted her crime. This allegedly occurred in 1996. According to the speaker, finding the body, knowing his mother was a murderess, she speculates with a reasoning that doesn't quite follow, that this caused Shin's "antipathy against the country, leading him to treason."[14]

Photographs are used throughout the filming of documentaries as prompts to the narrative. Another documentary denouncing Jeong Kwang Il uses the same technique. In addition to photographs, the documentaries place

12.3 "We've never lived in a so-called political prison camp" (screenshot 01:56/16:44)

"Who Is Sin Tong Hyok?" part 1

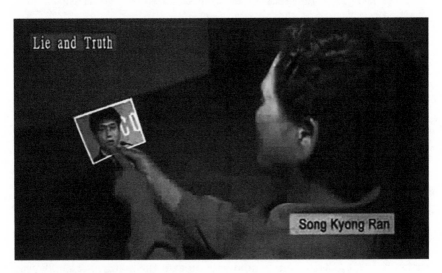

12.4 A neighbor with Shin Dong Hyuk's photo (screenshot 05:56/16:44)

"Who Is Sin Tong Hyok?" part 1

handwritten letters, certificates, and identity papers as "evidence" (figures 12.4, 12.5, 12.6, 12.7). Jeong Kwang Il gave testimony at the UN COI about his experience being tortured in a North Korean political prison camp—he was sent there because of illegal market trading. While there, under torture, he falsely confessed to spying for the South Koreans.

12.5 The documentary denouncing Chong Kwang Il (aka Jeong Kwang Il/Jong Kwang Il) (screenshot 09:58)

Meng Kyung Nam's interview, in "Terrible Human Wreck Who Steals a Person's Name and Career," tv.uriminzokkiri, September 11, 2015, http://www.uriminzokkiri.com/itv/index.php?ppt=lie_human &no=25376

12.6 A man holds a photograph of Jeong Kwang Il

"Terrible Human Wreck"

12.7 Closeup of the national identification card of Chong Kwang Il's daughter (aka Jeong Kwang Il/Jong Kwang Il)

"Terrible Human Wreck"

Yeonmi Park is a young North Korean defector who gained the world's attention through YouTube and public talks. Parts of her life story were also jumbled and confused, according to Maryanne Vollers, Yeonmi's coauthor on her memoir for Penguin.[15] Parts of Yeonmi's narrative were inconsistent. These were chalked up to a language barrier when she was not so fluent in English and sharing her story during the early days of her international activist career. However, for other reasons, certain parts of the story were not revealed. For instance, she omitted the parts related to the sexual abuse she suffered, the sexual abuse her mother suffered, and the fact that Yeonmi got caught up in human trafficking herself as a way to earn enough money to survive in China. I attribute many of these omissions to the social stigma of patriarchal society where a woman's value is attributed to her sexual "purity." Further, it is difficult to explain the process whereby someone can be a victim of human rights violations and yet complicit in the suffering of others at the same time. An additional aspect of trauma, according to Judith Herman (as Vollers also notes in her article), concerns how "traumatized people don't give you a perfect, complete narrative on the first go-round. You see this all the time with refugees seeking asylum. That doesn't mean their story isn't credible, because the gist of their story is consistent."[16] What we must hear when we listen to North Koreans' stories is that the events they relay are part of a broader personal narrative, a chronology, that identify the mechanical ways their rights were violated (torture, deprivation of food). Their narratives also reveal the conceptual ways their rights were violated. The conceptual understanding of how their rights were violated recognizes that the injury is to the whole person and to their life.[17]

Park's and Shin's stories confirm that even when there are visible signs of suffering, as in the case of Shin's scars, and even when speech is all that is accessible as "evidence" of a life lived, the telling of a story always means the risk of its erasure. In fact, as North Korean defectors tell their stories, the North Korean state responds domestically, through its central news agency in print, radio, and television, but also internationally through multilingual news and videos.[18] This act of the state speaking back to defectors, their families, the domestic audience, the international community, and activists highlights a steep imbalance of power. It is a monologue that masquerades as dialectic, reportedly clarifying the truth as it creates greater antagonism, suspicion, and hate.

In her book, Yeonmi Park didn't hold back from describing her family's struggle with food, medicine, and safety in North Korea. Nor did she hold back about the difficulties she faced in China. Some of the details of her narrative, such as facilitating the trafficking of women from North Korea into China when she was thirteen, were omitted from her public talks, which predated the book. North Korea produced several documentaries denouncing Yeonmi and her family. She now lives safely abroad with her mother and sister—her father died in China. All of them, including her deceased father, are targeted in the videos.

The documentary accuses her of faking the photographs of her father in China in an effort to authenticate her narrative. To add authenticity, the video shows a screenshot of an article by John Power that appeared in the *Diplomat*. Power interviewed Felix Abt, a Swiss-born entrepreneur sympathetic to the North and resident for seven years in the 2000s, about defector testimonies. The title of the article, "North Korean Defectors and Their Skeptics," is shown in the video as overlaid text accuses Yeonmi of "playing with the world" (figure 12.8).[19] During the documentary, Yeonmi is shown with other denounced defectors such as Jang Jin-Sung, author of *Dear Leader*, and details of Yeonmi's and her family members' education, work, and family history are detailed.

Penguin Books published her book *In Order to Live*, and so the press and its editorial staff are identified and threatened in the documentary for their involvement with the "book of lies" (figure 12.9). During this threat, the video shows blurry images of an anti-repatriation protest: Suzanne Scholte, an American human rights activist and president of the Defense Forum Foundation, is with Jin-hye Jo (Jay Jo), a defector who spoke at the United Nations (figure 12.10).[20]

The documentary accuses Yeonmi Park of fabricating her story and makes generous use of an article published in the *Diplomat*, from December 10, 2014, as support. That article, written by Mary Ann Jolley, is a sensitive treatment of the issues related to trauma and memory. However, the title is ideal for North Korea: "The Strange Tale of Yeonmi Park: A High-Profile North Korean

12.8 Overlaid text in the documentary reads: The little girl who is playing with the world (screenshot 06:03).

"Uriminjokkkiri vs t'albukcha pakyŏnmi ch'uaksangŭl tashigŭm p'ahech'yŏ ponda" [Our people vs. defector Yeonmi Park, digging up the beast again], YouTube video, 45:18, *Cihiribey Japene*, March 23, 2016, https://www.youtube.com/watch?v=__sIBm8eH3A)

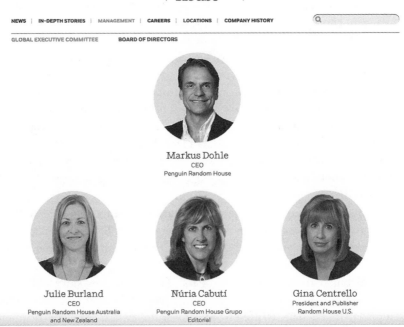

12.9 Penguin Books (screenshot 23:16)

"Our people vs. defector Yeonmi Park."

12.10 Suzanne Scholte and Jin-hye Jo, anti-repatriation protest (screenshot 23:54)

"Our people vs. defector Yeonmi Park"

Defector Has Harrowing Stories to Tell. But Are They True?"[21] The subtitle is useful for the documentary, particularly since no one in North Korea will be safely able to access it to find the answer.

Damaged Bodies

More than many other defectors in the public eye, Shin Dong Hyuk's body bears witness to the suffering he endured. His scars were presented at the United Nations—as was the case with other defectors—as part of their testimony about torture or injuries they suffered in North Korea. In this way, the scarification presents as an objective accounting of the experience. As with the words and images of defectors, scarification is reinscribed (figure 12.11). In the documentaries about Shin, his scars are attributed to childhood and work-related injuries through the stories told by his father, neighbors, and former coworkers.

Like testimony given at the United Nations, the body's scars and injuries are subjected to reinterpretation. North Korea's documentaries explain that, with investigative reporting, they revealed the lies of defectors who use both body and word to denounce the state. The body is injured or scarred in North Korea—through torture or accident during coping strategies—and this account is laid forward at the United Nations. But the meaning of the body's injury is undone and retold by the state—the scar is unmade as a sign of torture and remade as a sign of the defector's deceit. In the second part of the documentary about Shin,

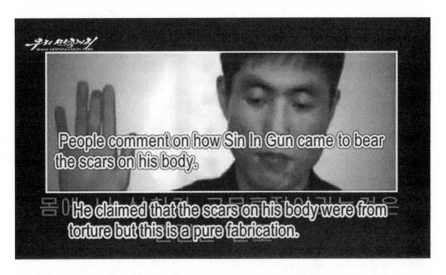

12.11 Shin showing his physical injury at the UN (screenshot 16:52)

Chang Hao Jin, "We Reveal, Once Again, the True Identity of the Human Trash Sin Tong Hyok." tv.uriminzokkiri, March 11, 2015, https://www.youtube.com/watch?v=xbd4TqipHYk

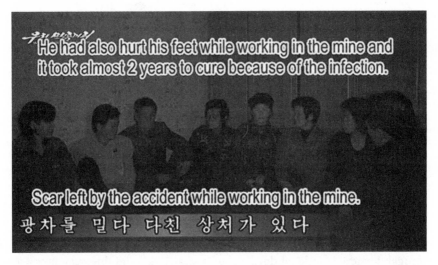

12.12 Neighbors in North Korea comment on allegations of torture (screenshot 17:51).

Chang, "We Reveal, Once Again"

Lie and Truth

The story was like this:
There was an ore-dressing plant near our pit. There was a settling pond and a pile of waste ore products next to it. He stumbled over while walking along the stony field without a torch, and he fell down and hurt his finger by rolling stones.

12.13 Shin's former work leader testifies about his injury (screenshot 03:13).

"Who Is Sin Tong Hyok?" part 2

the narrator investigates what caused Shin to lose his fingertip. A voiceover relays Shin's UN testimony in a jaunty, flippant tone. Shin is saying his fingertip was cut off by a prison guard as punishment for dropping a sewing machine. The footage cuts to the investigative journalist interviewing Shin's former work leader at the mine where he allegedly lost his finger.

The body and its genetics are also linked to a person's character. In figure 12.4, lifted from the *Lie and Truth* documentary, Shin's deceptive character is identified as genetically rooted. Another documentary about Shin, "We Reveal, Once Again, the True Identity of the Human Trash Sin Tong Hyuk," explains that he "inherited genetically" the habit of deceiving through lies and fraud (figure 12.14).[22]

Perhaps in the cruelest twist possible, just as both body and voice were subjected to political manipulation in North Korea, both continue to be manipulated after defection. The voice of the defector, delivered to a listening international audience, opens up the possibility for North Korea to reach them again, biopolitically, and to continue abuse. It is not only the state that wants to abuse again; other North Koreans in the documentaries articulate the desire to beat and kill defectors (figure 12.15). This demonstrates the almost inevitable revictimization that a survivor faces when he dares to speak, and the abuse is made perversely public as the state reaches them again in this strange public form of defector denouncement via video.

For North Korea, the body of the defector—like his oral testimony—is subjected to reinscription. Figure 12.16 is from a South Korean broadcast where

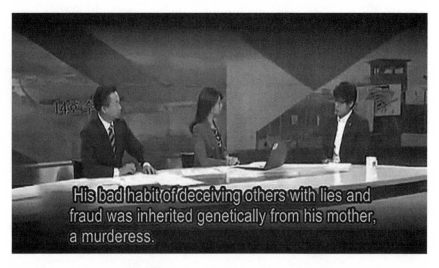

His bad habit of deceiving others with lies and fraud was inherited genetically from his mother, a murderess.

12.14 "Deceiving others is inherited genetically" (screenshot 30:38)

Chang, "We Reveal, Once Again"

Shin was interviewed by news anchors, with a voiceover that identifies his body, mind, and thoughts as lies. North Korea's investigative reporting reveals that defectors use their bodies to manipulate and lie as easily as they do their words. The scarred body displayed as evidence at the United Nations is separated from the individual's testimony and is covered over with narrative attributed to friends and neighbors. The citizen—within North Korea's borders or without, living or dead—is an empty signifier, a container waiting to carry the state's message. If the cipher becomes filled up with erroneous signifiers, such as allegations of crimes against humanity, it is evacuated of these virtually through denouncing documentaries or actual assassinations.[23]

North Korea repeatedly appeals to the international community to depoliticize the subject of human rights. Yet within state media there is no reticence to politicize the body and voice of the defector who testifies about rights violations—these individuals are not cast out from politics; rather, they are the very material to ignite political ferment. They are not beyond the scope of politics but are the object of its operation.

In my previous book, *Marching Through Suffering*, I showed how both body and voice are subject to political manipulation inside North Korea.[24] With these videos, another cruel twist related to body and voice is apparent. Just as torture unmakes and remakes the world of the tortured—objects used for torture take on new meaning, are split from their former meaning—so too the state continues the act of unmaking and remaking violence that becomes *metaphysical*.[25] As long as the survivor surfaces in the public realm to accuse North

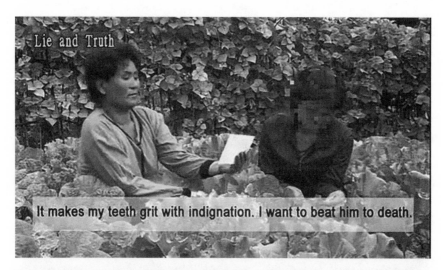

12.15 "I want to beat him to death" (screenshot 07:27)

"Who Is Sin Tong Hyok?" part 2

Korea, North Korea will attempt to claw back the account and furnish it with their own narrative. And yet when Shin points out the scars on his body, the violations to his physical integrity, he signals points of abusive contact between himself and the state. The testimony returns the origin narrative of abuse back to the state: the abuse *belongs* to the abuser, as the scars belong to Shin. It is that relationship that is made perversely public, which is agonizing to the survivor and yet in a different way is also agonizing to the state. They are brought into a biopolitical, humiliatingly public struggle for recognition of human over sovereign rights.

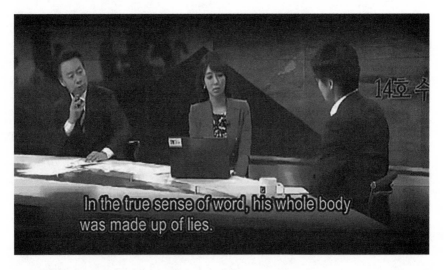

In the true sense of word, his whole body was made up of lies.

12.16 "His body was made up of lies" (screenshot 30:44).

Chang, "We Reveal, Once Again"

Feeling in Public

Critical theorist Lauren Berlant identifies the political sphere "as a scene for the orchestration of *public feelings*—of the public's feelings, of feelings in public, of politics as a scene of emotional contestation."[26] In the documentaries, North Korean public feeling toward the defectors is orchestrated through a singular, seemingly omniscient narrative voice embodied variously in family, friends, neighbors, and coworkers. The voices contest. The documentaries contest. How dare these people—defectors—who are inherently evil claim that the homeland abused them? Such hubris is emotionally voiced by each speaker. They create a shift from a rational to an emotional political public with an opinion. Berlant explains that the "political sphere is not void of rational thought, its dominant rhetorical style is to recruit the public to see political attachments as an amalgam of reflexive opinion and visceral or 'gut' feeling."[27]

This is not out of step with what Kim Jong Il would have wanted, particularly as film enables a subtle medium for the melding of emotion and politics. In Kim Jong Il's *The Cinema and Directing*, the word "emotion" appears 153 times.[28] In addition, there is an entire chapter titled "Emotions Should Be Well Defined in Directing." In that chapter, Kim states, "Providing a prerequisite based on true life is a necessary condition, for preparing the escalation of emotion. . . . When the emotional flow formed through change and development in life is consistently maintained, an emotion can develop and the accumulated emotion can move gradually toward the climax."[29] Later, he elaborates, connecting

It was on the 4th of April 1996 when the murder took place. In Gun's mother was not a decent human being.

An Ryon Hui
(Eye witness of the murder committed by Jang Hye Gyong)

12.17 A neighbor recounts the murder committed by Shin Dong Hyuk's mother (screen-shot 19:03).

Chang, "We Reveal, Once Again"

the role of character to emotion, "if the emotions are to be defined in depth it is necessary to control them by following the character's destiny."[30]

Emotional reactions to shocking events smooth over inconsistencies in narrative logic in the defector-denouncing documentaries. In *Lie and Truth*, a woman named An Ryon Hui tells the story of a murder committed by Shin Dong Hyuk's mother. Although An is identified in the documentary as an "eye-witness," she admits that she didn't see the event herself (figures 12.17, 12.18). Yet she relays the emotional features of the event as though she were there. She also provides details on the lazy housekeeping skills of Shin's mom (figure 12.19).

Acting as a guiding thread through the documentaries, a phenomenon that matches North Korean news, is an eerily singular narrative voice. Whether voiceover, interviewer, or interviewee (of whom there are dozens), all speak about the defector's character without nuance and with absolute certitude of the defector's devious nature. The destiny of the defector was written from the start; the end is seen in the beginning. There is no gray zone here. The defectors are *exclusively* and *entirely* bad.

A Singular Narrative

What does it tell us that the documentaries are about clarifying the character of defectors and thereby undermining the stories they have told, rather than directly addressing the claims of defectors? The message of the documentaries

12.18 A neighbor provides details of the murder she did not witness (screenshot 26:53).

Chang, "We Reveal, Once Again"

12.19 A neighbor describes the character of Shin Dong Hyuk's mother (screenshot 28:38).

Chang, "We Reveal, Once Again"

is singular, but their method of generating this message is not. Dozens of friends, colleagues, and family members are interviewed. This gives the illusion of a collective, diverse, objectively speaking public, yet the narrative is entirely singular. This method of making pluralities from singularities can be observed in North Korean state media, as discussed earlier.

It is a common feature of contemporary documentary to make use of multiple voices to tell a story.[31] The North Korean documentaries seemingly do this, but throughout all of the documentaries, despite who speaks and which defector they speak about, their messages are entirely the same. Documentary is supposed to show different points of view, yet these don't. Canadian film artist Aleesa Cohene states, "When you situate a singular as a multiple it becomes the world. It doesn't prompt you to question it because it creates a world upon itself."[32] Using multiple individuals to tell a singular story, the documentaries appear multifaceted but they are not. Pulling in the viewer occurs entirely through affect and the repeated onslaught of affect, not reasons of logic. We associate multiple voices with multiple perspectives: such is the way of the world unless coerced into uniformity. So this is the imaginary relationship that is created through the documentaries: an imagined relationship to a multiplicity that speaks uniformly on the defects of defectors.[33]

The documentaries tell more by what is absent—but would customarily appear—than what is present. The documentaries use seemingly ordinary North Koreans or relatives of defectors. The interviewees speak with flowing repartee. There are none of the typical hesitations, speech disfluency (when someone pauses, inserting an "um" to recall a thought) or fillers common to spoken communication. Interlocutors relay a message that is unvaried from the state's message: the defectors are lying, the report is based on lies, none of the investigators bothered to enter North Korea to see things for themselves, the United States has tremendous violations and should not point the finger, and the DPRK has a wonderful quality of life.

The Edit

From virtually any professional standard, these videos appear low quality, low budget, and amateurish. However, when I set that aside and look at the film footage forensically, the object is constructed very deliberately and almost shamelessly, obviously. All films undergo editing. However, close viewing of the North Korean documentaries and news broadcasts show that the narrative is deliberately constructed through the edit. In other words, the narrative is completely remade at the point of editing. How is it possible to identify this? In the videos there are dozens upon dozens of "jump cuts," points where the cutting and pasting of footage patches scenes together as if they occurred sequentially when they have not. The cuts in film footage are apparent in the obvious changes between footage marked by different tones of voice from the same speaker (midsentence) and different light changes in the room due to the passage of time (when, according to video, no time has passed). Attention to linguistic speech patterns shows that jump cuts happen midsentence at points where the speakers says "however" and "but," and this is clear when the tone of voice doesn't match with what came before or after. This means that the editors are telling the story in postproduction, in addition to the story that was told at the point of the interview.[34]

In addition to unusual edits, the body language of interviewees is worthy of note. I do not wish to *interpret* the body language here but rather to identify that this is something that would typically be edited out or avoided in standard documentaries, unless such mannerisms were within remit to capture. In the documentary denouncing Jeong Kwang Il (aka Jong Kwang Il), former colleague Meng Kyung Nam's interview (pictured in figure 12.5) is given a significant amount of coverage.

Throughout Nam's narrative, the type of body language he displays is not typically associated with confidence but with anxiety. Such anxious, repetitive handwringing is distracting to viewers, creating a sense of distrust toward the speaker. He fiddles with a pen and keeps his fists clasped together for the entire portion of his interview. Only four minutes of it are used in the documentary (out of a total twenty-eight minutes). This clip, like others, has jump cuts mid-sentence, where two halves of a sentence are pasted together in the editing process. Additionally, his eye movements—moving from left to right and unblinking, which occurs close to the end of the clip—indicate he is reading from text held off camera.

Considering these somewhat sloppy features, it is hard to imagine they could be overlooked for their oddity. However, it is also possible that the very things that appear low budget and unprofessional might be the very same things that engender a different meaning for some viewers. It could engender a sense of being "looked after" by the editors. Perhaps this should be interpreted as, sure, the editing is rough and sloppy, but this is because the detritus of the video has been scrapped for what is most necessary. Through this sense, the message has not been manipulated but rather clarified and streamlined through deliberate construction.

Objectively, the videos undermine their own credibility through the obvious and heavy-handed editing. This could seem like disregard. And yet this unskillful cutting and splicing brutally exalts the message, the rhetoric, the core meaning, which is the ultimate seat of value—disregarding the bourgeois careful edit. The power of this deliberate manipulation is in its ability to communicate *care* for the message being communicated itself, rather than for the truth of moments in which the message was being created. What is strikingly totalitarian about these videos is that they take a set of impossibilities and force their possibility: to wit, sloppily put together footage, witnesses who all say the same thing, defectors who are 100 percent evil, a nation-state that is always good: yes, this is possible. In standard documentary making, value is determined by making the thing well; here, however, the poor quality and deliberate editing is a powerfully blatant disregard for craft in favor of message.

Broadcasting Citizens

Another bold move since the publication of the UN COI report is the mediatized distribution of North Korea's imitation of a civil society. It is best called an "ersatz civil society" because, rather than speaking up for the undoubtedly plural interests of the citizenry, it speaks the uniform, singular rhetoric of the state. Around November of 2014—the same year the UN report was published—the ersatz civil society appeared and communicated via North Korean state media echoing state discourse. The ersatz civil society held a massive demonstration against the UN report in Pyongyang's Kim Il Sung Square.

At the protest, the Korean Central News Agency interviewed three representative groups about the UN report: men (and one woman) on the street, family members of defectors, and returned defectors. The content of their responses suggests ignorance of the inquiry's findings. Analysis of the ersatz civil society rhetoric reveals a precise echo of state discourse in its entire nuance. North Korea has adopted one of the most vital techniques in the rights advocacy playbook: the existential contingency of civil society for human rights advocacy. The ersatz civil society appears in North Korean news both as a mass and as individuals, impersonating a domestic advocacy network. The state is a ventriloquist, throwing its voice: the mass and the individual flawlessly speak its message.

North Korea's primary comfort zone vis-à-vis human rights is in the control of discourse: both what is said and how it is said. Yet the UN COI and the international human rights norms process has ushered North Korea into a discursive trap that turns the argument North Korea wields at the United Nations back on North Korea like a boomerang. The trap for North Korea is also their greatest justification for innocence where human rights violations are concerned: that violations have not been observed by the United Nations inside North Korea, so the United Nations cannot say they exist. This is ludicrous because they ignored any requests by the United Nations or any other neutral proxy body to access the country to validate or invalidate claims.

By denying on-the-ground investigations, North Korea maintains control of its citizens' knowledge of international human rights norms. The state also attempts to maintain control over the international community getting more information. By injecting the question of on-the-ground verifiability, North Korea attempts to suspend the human rights allegations in the realm of debate. This is a weak approach and will likely undermine North Korea. By suspending claims to veracity in this realm, North Korea loops itself into a tricky and obvious contradiction. North Korea tries to get past this snag by manufacturing a civil society presence.

North Korea sets up a catch-22 for itself through overreliance on discourse that excoriates other states for denying social and economic rights while touting its own respect for human rights. The discourse is bound to clash with the day-to-day reality on the ground. Furthermore, as North Korea produces its ersatz civil society, it engages a portion of its population directly in voicing the state's version of human rights, however normatively flawed. North Korea views the UN report as a fabricated nuisance, and yet it responds to the report, which is thus far the most powerful outcome of transnational advocacy. North Korea *is* concerned about claims of rights violations because they see these claims as a threat to sovereignty. They are adapting, albeit through technological media savvy, to the international community's pressure over human rights. North Korea is not responding by improving rights, but their way of responding might inadvertently hold potential for positive change toward respect for rights within international norms.

The main weakness North Korea identifies in the UN COI is that it is based on the words of alleged liars. Inversely, the same method is used to give their position: North Korea's statements are allegedly true. A discursive loop, or noose, if you will, is created because it catches North Korea in a contradiction that it cannot escape without revealing more.

By creating an ersatz civil society, North Korea tries to address the contradiction inherent in suspending the human rights debate in discourse: it "gives access" to civil society groups who claim to support human rights. North Korea is giving the international community what it has been demanding, on its own terms: access to the people with the voice of the state. However, the seeming civil society manufactured in the video footage introduces another complexity to human rights advocacy. Where international human rights are concerned, the voice of the citizen speaking up for herself is possibly the penultimate emblem of democracy and the foundation of rights lobbying. In North Korea's videos the ersatz civil society is raising its voice and making demands, but it advocates not for individual rights but the rights of the state.[35]

Thousands of protesters marched in Kim Il Sung Square carrying printed banners in classic North Korean font, praising the leadership and ideology of North Korea (figure 12.20).[36] The audience appears to be almost entirely male and of a similar age group.[37] This domestic response is not unusual among autocratic polities. In fact, it could have been predicted. Governments that deny rights abuses have successfully mobilized national movements against such claims, strengthening domestic support for the state. Heightened perceptions of threat and fear—as the UN COI is framed in North Korea—can "dramatically extend" these stages of domestic support for the state.[38]

The news broadcasts reference international views on North Korea that are favorable. In one case, a video begins by referring to a Russian news article that says North Korea has the best human rights situation in the world.[39] The broadcaster quotes from a Russian newspaper: "Everyone over the age of 17 has the right to vote and be voted into political participation. Everyone can participate

12.20 North Korea protests the UN Commission of Inquiry report, screenshot of a 2014 "protest" in Pyongyang. Placards read: "Let's smash the human rights report." "Complete rejection of the human rights resolution." "Unite."

Sandra Fahy, "DPRK Protest Against United Nations Human Rights Report Pyongyang November 25, 2014," YouTube, April 4, 2018, https://www.youtube.com/watch?v=Or6XiIftMDo

freely in political life, the right to publish, gather in social groups or enjoy the media and religion is legally guaranteed." This text is verbatim from the report by the DPRK Association for Human Rights Studies.[40] The news broadcast aired November 25, 2014, and the report appeared in KCNA print media at the end of October 2014.[41] The article explains:

> Everyone naturally participates in political life and has access to quality media and publications. The country provides everyone more than enough food to eat, clothes to wear, and things to use so that people can live a secure life. There is no poor get poorer and the rich get richer in North Korea. The students all receive scholarships to study at school for twelve years, the students don't even know what the word "tuition" means. If people who have no one to care for them, the country cares for them. Everyone gets free medical care. The old and the disabled are all cared for by the country. Juche, which identifies that people are the strength of the nation, is what enables North Korea to guarantee human rights. Juche thinks that the human is the most powerful thing, so everything in the universe exists to serve humans.[42]

The visuals that accompany this broadcast show North Koreans in traditional dress, people roller-skating around a square of pavement, soldiers walking

engaged in friendly banter, a man getting his teeth drilled by a dentist, generations of a family gathered around a table to eat. Everyone is smiling except the
man in the dentist's chair getting his teeth drilled.

Dated around July of 2014 (presumably July 8, given the content), a video by
Uriminzokkiri identifies the UN human rights inquiry amid reference to the
anniversary of the death of Kim Il Sung. The video switches to show the Arduous March (the March of Suffering): images of a bridge slightly flooded, people
on their haunches, young and old, building something unidentifiable with gray
bricks. "An experience," the video explains, "that helped turn the country into
a strong and prosperous nation with nuclear power. And," it concludes, "today
the people of North Korea are living the dream of socialism." Here we see images
of children playing in a pool park. The broadcast ends with a recommendation
that people of the world reexamine their interpretation of North Korean human
rights.[43] "Those countries that support the U.S. in its critique of North Korea's
human rights, has any one from those countries ever visited the DPRK? If they
did it must have been in 1994 when we were all weeping for the loss of Kim Il
Sung." A broadcast that aired around the end of November 2014 states that various media outlets from Russia, India, Brazil, and Uruguay reported the words
of a DPRK spokesperson at the United Nations who said that the testimony
from defectors was fabricated and false. The broadcast further elaborates that
because of these false and politically orchestrated allegations from the United
States, North Korea had to hold another nuclear test. "To defend ourselves
from U.S. invasion in the future, DPRK must limitlessly prepare for war."[44]

On November 18 the UN General Assembly voted on the resolution to rec-
ommend DPRK's human rights violations to the UN Security Council for
review. On November 19, North Korean television covered a November 11
article from their state news, the *Rodong Shinmun*, stating that the United
States and South Korea should stop the "human rights racket."[45] And the news
covered the new Yugoslavian party in Serbia, explaining that Serbia stands
together with the DPRK in their fight against the United States.[46] They interviewed two professors of law from Kim Il Sung University who explained that
the people of North Korea are "furious" over the UN COI.[47] Professor Park Hee
Chul said,

> The U.S. submitted a report on human rights in North Korea using the name
> of the UN. This shows the invasive instinct of these political fraudsters. This
> was fabricated, ignoring the most basic international procedure and law. We
> can never permit this. They didn't use proper procedure. They base it on the
> lies of a few human scum who left their country and family and use that for
> the basis of their report. As a scholar who studies international law I cannot
> understand it at all. Ordinarily to make this kind of report about a country
> there must be some previous documents submitted by the country under

investigation. The COI should have done fair and objective field research in North Korea before making such report. This report was not a matter of justice but a product of U.S. bribing and lobbying.[48]

Professor Park Hee Chul's comments are not accurate. The United Nations is not the United States. For over a decade the formal standard was applied in reporting to the United Nations about human rights violations in the DPRK. International law was followed in investigating allegations of violations and crimes against humanity. And, finally, the United Nations sought access but was ignored. A second professor also offered his views. Professor Kang Won Woo, also in the field of law, changes the subject:

> Really, a COI report should already have happened for the tundra of human rights violators like the United States, Japan, and South Korea. Everyone knows that the U.S. is the world's biggest human rights violator. Everywhere U.S. military boots go there are atrocities that even animals would be ashamed to commit. Even now we can still hear the screams of many souls who suffered the crimes of Japan. And one doesn't even have to mention South Korea's human rights situation where even the most basic right to life is violated. Even now, if you look you can see the *Sewol* ferry disaster, the antiblack racial violence. The human rights violations are endless. It is nonsensical that such countries would criticize other country's human rights situation. This is violating international law. Human rights are a nation's rights, and a nation's right is sovereignty.[49]

The video loops back to Professor Park, who clarifies that "everyone in North Korea will try to protect our territory and defeat this fabricated human rights racket." The insights of Professors Park and Kang are nothing new, and this facilitates observing their physical manner in the videos as opposed to their discourse. Close attention to the interviewees' mannerisms shows their eyes trail along as if reading text held behind the camera, suggesting they needed help remembering all the points they wished to express.

Around the time of the mass Pyongyang demonstration against the UN COI report, North Korean television conducted man-on-the-street interviews (one woman was interviewed) to capture their view on the report.[50] The broadcast is presented as part of the 8 o'Clock Evening News for November 25, 2014. Each interview occurs in a different location. The message of each interview works collectively to echo the message carried in the *Rodong Shinmun*, the UN letters, and the DPRK Association for Human Rights Studies report in the framework of their argument: (a) the COI is a fabrication; (b) it is an act of war that actually violates rights by threatening nations; (c) the DPRK has great human rights, and the United States has terrible rights; (d) South Korea has terrible rights; (e) human rights are a nation's rights; and (f) the United States and others should stop "or else."

The interviewer's microphone is in their faces. They speak. The voice is individual, personal, but the message is a synchronized echo of the state media; each person interviewed echoes a piece of the message. Each person is a character type lifted from the state media. These are types, types of sentences that the state writes in its media. The state is sovereign. The UN COI report is a war effort. America commits horrendous violations. Defectors are criminals. South Korea has horrible Park Geun-hye. The eyes move the voice along a line of words off camera, left to right, reading from a teleprompter.

The first citizen states that he is "furious from hearing what is reported in the news broadcasts. This fabricated report is a big political plot. It is political fraud and clownish play." A second man says, "The UN COI report is an invasive attempt to eliminate everything we have; it is a declaration of war. Our sovereignty is severely violated. They have declared war on us, and our military and citizens will never put up with this." A third man states, "For me, living in a people's country, I enjoy genuine rights. I heard that the U.S. fabricated a report about our human rights. Do they know anything about human rights to talk about it? Aren't we given free education, free medical treatment? Everything is guaranteed for the people. That is our system. The U.S. tries to dominate the world with the logic that 'I can live only by killing you.'"[51]

Finally, a very articulate woman is interviewed:

> They don't have any rights to speak of to criticize our rights. Truly, the South Korean puppet government should feel ashamed about human rights; they should hide their head in a mouse hole. Everyone knows that they drowned the innocent young students in the sea [a reference to the sinking of *Sewol* in April 2014]. The Park government even cruelly suppresses the families of these victimized students, and then they talk about our human rights. This makes me angry.

The fifth interviewee states, "Human rights are a nation's rights, and a nation's right is sovereignty. The human scum who betrayed our country and abandoned their family and ran away fabricated the human rights report. This is an intolerable challenge to our country. We are filled with a burning determination to protect our system and pursue the U.S. and their followers to the end of the earth to punish them."

The sixth interviewee: "We have been putting up with this for a long time. We should stop talking and start taking action. We have been building an extremely strong military and nuclear power for decades and these are not for decoration they are for today. The U.S. is acting crazy, not knowing that it will die. We are going to let them taste the gun of the 'military-first' North Korea. The U.S. and its followers have responsibility for this result."[52]

Uriminzokkiri cites a report by the American-based Society for the Study of Juche. The announcer, Kim Hyun Hee, identifies the linkages between a sovereign nation's rights and human rights. She says that human rights are inseparable from national sovereignty. She quickly adds, "We have the experience deep in our bones; Japan took our sovereignty and we were forced to live like slaves." Her story then begins to cover familiar ground: "Still the U.S. is colonizing South Korea and robbing from them under the name of democracy and human rights protection. The human rights imperialists are talking about the special privilege to do anything if you have money. The imperialists who don't even protect basic human rights of workers cannot speak about human rights."[53]

The broadcast shows riots and protests in the United States, particularly those following white police officers beating and killing black Americans with impunity. The broadcast then switches to North Korea as an ideal protector of human rights. "We have no taxes, no unemployed people, we raise orphan children with care; the new generation grows up without having to envy anyone for anything." The image of the man in the dentist's chair (he appears in other videos) is shown. Subsequent images show women in traditional dress; orphan children holding flowers; women in a living room, marveling with mystifying expressions of ecstasy; children at a water park; and boys playing a martial arts computer game. The report says that North Korea operates on love and trust. The United States and South Korea should not provoke North Korea. North Korea is like one life (one body) ready to defend sovereignty as if it was their own life. "They are blaming us for the Sony picture hacking, and the U.S. is helping the human scum to send leaflets into our country," the video explains.[54]

The Voice of the State

North Korea has begun to invite U.S.-based CNN, who formerly would have been denied, to interview its people about human rights. North Korea's relationship with CNN's Will Ripley began in 2014. Since that time Ripley has received impressive access to the country—albeit with the typical restrictions of seeing, hearing, and recording only what North Korea wants. In June 2015 Ripley was invited to meet with eight individuals in Pyongyang so they could speak on camera about human rights.[55] These invitations have followed in the wake of high-profile public defections and overseas labor rights reports. Ripley reports that each individual "asked to be there." The first man to speak challenged allegations about prison camps: "How could they have survived?" he asks. This interview is insightful for taking the current evidence that North

Korea exports forced labor overseas—something that wasn't covered in the otherwise extensive UN COI report. The interviewed men claim that they are happy to work overseas to earn money for their government. In 2016 Ripley was invited to return to Pyongyang to meet the family of a woman who defected to South Korea. Again, the family volunteered to be interviewed. They were pleading for their daughter's return, saying she was "abducted" and South Korea should return her.[56] Family members read letters to her, demonstrating the agony of family left behind and the benevolence of the state, should the wayward member return.

Using CNN as a pipeline, North Korea achieves two aims. First, they emotionally target family members in South Korea—love abuse—and they get to frame the defection as abduction, injecting the element of doubt.

North Korea's decision to use the ordinary citizen's voice is almost ingenious. First, and most obviously, it connects with the notion of democracy. The individual's ability to use her voice, and for it to be captured in media for dissemination, is one of the hallmarks of democracy. In this case it remains a scripted pantomime. But the voice is powerful for another reason. It ties the "subject and the other together"; it brings what is invisible and interior to the exterior.[57] The voice is a strange thing; it is magically synesthetic. Through sound, a visual image is created. Through sound, a thing becomes known. Critically for our case here, the voice is positioned as that which can bring something out of the depths, that which can disclose, that which can lay bare.

North Korea is that inaccessible interior par excellence. They make the interior of North Korea, which cannot be seen because there has been no access, exterior by giving the citizen a voice. But it is an act of ventriloquism. The voice is thrown into the wooden doll. And, indeed, there is a hollow emotional stoicism to the delivery. We get the voice of the state within the citizen.

In 2015 and 2016, following an internationally released human rights report about overseas labor exploitation, North Korea invited CNN's Will Ripley to interview citizens in Pyongyang who had worked overseas. The state's obsession with a theoretical presentation of an idealized self is a practice that pervades daily life, particularly where a foreign audience may be present. CNN was given the chance to speak to men who had once been laborers in Kuwait. They wanted to set the record straight. Speaking through a translator, they explained it was preposterous that their rights were violated; the United States should focus on its own problems. In a similar video, CNN's Will Ripley was invited to speak with family members of women who had been allegedly abducted to South Korea. The video operates much like the others wherein selected citizens are put before the camera where they deliver expected messaging on life in North Korea, and human rights violations abroad.[58]

The state media has taken a shift in propaganda style from word to voice as dozens of documentaries and broadcasts animate the state's discourse on human rights through the ordinary citizen's voice. Here we have the illusion of access, but things are still suspended in the realm of discourse, without genuine communication. There is the illusion of access but no real access. There is the illusion of a civil society via the demonstrations, the family members denouncing, the return defectors spouting the state's rhetoric, but it is solidly without civil society. There is the individual's voice, the individual's actions, but it is the state's meaning that sits inside the voice, the state's actions that sit within the body of the citizen. The United Nations has continued to seek access and has continued to be ignored.[59]

Capturing Evidence

Photography and film have long been associated with capturing evidence, linking perpetrators with crimes, generating empathy, and ensuring justice for rights violations. Think of Claude Lanzmann's heartbreaking nine-hour documentary film *Shoah*, Joey Boink's *Burden of Peace*, or Joshua Oppenheimer's *The Act of Killing* and *The Look of Silence*. Each opens a window onto landscapes of widespread suffering that compel the viewer to contemplate inhumanity. In the United States, video footage of Los Angeles police beating Rodney King catalyzed a movement to arm citizens with the ability to "capture" brutality and move toward justice, most notably resulting in the Witness Media Lab, a global project aimed at empowering ordinary citizens with the ability to record rights violations on camera and work toward their elimination and reconciliation.[60] Video documentation empowers. It offers the survivor a record of the experience that they may "cry out to the 200 million" as Solzhenitsyn once hoped to do, and did.[61]

The North Korean human rights campaign has swiftly gathered momentum in the last ten years through efforts of international nongovernmental organizations as well as through films, documentaries, and memoirs. The greatest push of late has come from the force of the United Nations through its Commission of Inquiry into alleged atrocities in North Korea. The result was a mammoth report confirming the existence of widespread and systematic crimes against humanity. The testimonies are in the public domain, and the video and audio testimony are available to anyone with internet access.[62] In the last few years, the testimonies are crying out to millions; even North Korea is listening.

A great democratic evening-up has taken place due to highly portable recording equipment and the instant upload of footage to social media platforms. We are in a new era where the visual, human rights, and survivors are concerned. Where justice seekers sought to record atrocity to avenge wrongs, a reversal is taking shape that challenges our neat association between documentation and justice. From ISIS to Boko Haram to the DPRK, perpetrators are recording their abuses and using it to galvanize support, celebrate ideology, and demonstrate power. As the scholar Sam Gregory puts it, "participants, witnesses, and perpetrators, are all filming."[63]

One of the most critical tools for improved human rights is the presence of a civil society that interacts with the international community, and vice versa. This interaction is referred to as a boomerang or spiral because the interaction moves back and forth between the civil society and the international community, with the aim of improving things, despite the presence of a coercive state that would wish otherwise. The absence of civil society in North Korea makes the human rights problem that much more entrenched. The "ersatz civil society" speaks the state's message, North Korea is giving the international community what it has been demanding, but on its own terms: access to the people with the voice of the state. The domestic society, who is given a voice, can only use it in defense of the state.

CONCLUSION

Ascent

The truthteller, whether he knows it or not, has begun to act; he, too, has engaged himself in political business, for in the unlikely event that he survives, he has made a start toward changing the world.

—Hannah Arendt, *Between Past and Future*

It is no easy task to ponder these things, to delve into them for pages and pages and to imagine. If the accounts alone induce anguish, rage, indignation, how much more to live it? As my North Korean friend reminded me: "That was our life—we *lived* that." And there are those who did not live through it. This book is a grave marker to those, and a record for the rest. I began this record by reflecting that the experiences here are so *endlessly winter* that only in wintering through them can the heart survive. To be tougher than what is tough. Yet, to read and close the pages of this book marks an ascendance from the rights violations described herein. To lift the eyes and continue to other things. To forget, ignore, and move on with the day. Reading is a trick of the mind that brings the lives of others into us—lives that would otherwise mean the end of us.

* * *

This book explores rights violations committed by the North Korean state, domestically and globally, to citizen and noncitizen, throughout the country's existence. North Korea's bold response to allegations is carefully crafted, and its pursuit of those who speak too loudly, relentless. Political rights were never possible in North Korea, since its founding. Although the state claimed, and claims, to provide socioeconomic rights, these have gone unfulfilled for generations. These earliest of violations were the seeds for what came later. The 1990s opened the eyes of the world wider to conditions inside the country as stories were carried out in the words of defectors. Bit by bit the global pressure to protect human rights grew strong as the evidence has mounted.

On the ground, the underlying causes of violations to social, economic, and political rights are difficult to parse. This is all the more so for individuals with little access to information about international human rights norms. When violations to physical integrity rights occur, the perpetrator is right there. In North Korea, the state justifies these as necessary measures for the protection of the state. Many turn a blind eye until they are implicated. Respect for rights, and their violation, occurs *as a plurality*. Rights bear relation to each other: the failure to uphold one means others will also fail. The violation of socioeconomic and political rights in North Korea leads to violations of physical integrity rights.

The state adds insult to injury. The evidence shows that North Korea doesn't give up pursuit of those who defy it. Its memory is long and open to edit according to political whim. When defectors speak about violations internationally, to those with power, the hand of the state reaches out again for abuse. Where possible, North Korea is listening, watching, recording, to target those who speak too loudly to too large an audience. Through threats and shame, the state tries to silence. Silence is not possible *because* abuses continue.

The argument presented by the evidence in this book is that rights violations committed by the North Korean state are ineluctable. They are intrinsic to the state and ongoing. Ensnarement in these violations occurs as a matter of course in the day-to-day life, domestically and abroad, of its citizens. But it doesn't end with that. North Korea violates the rights of its citizens abroad, those who defect and those who raise a loud voice of critique. North Korea uses foreign nationals as sympathizers, operationalizing them to discount human rights allegations. North Korea makes use of foreign nationals as pawns, using their nation's respect for international human rights norms to angle for state interests. North Korea produces media for domestic and international consumption aimed at denouncing standard, globally accepted legal defense for human rights. It denounces foreign citizens who try to protect and fight for the rights of their fellows. The state co-opts foreign media to legitimize and distribute its message globally. Finally, North Korea's international engagement on the subject of rights indicates that it is taking few practical steps at improving conditions while making elaborate efforts to seem as though it is accepting responsibility (but dodging it).

Recognizing human rights violations is a challenge to the domestic propaganda image, and it is the main interest of North Korea to keep propaganda intact and deny abuses. In 2018, with the Kim–Moon Panmunjom Agreement, North Korea won a small war against soft power activism. Activist groups struggle for funding and support of the ROK government because their activities are interpreted as hostile toward the North and a threat to peace on the peninsula. Those who circulate information into the North through activist networks have generated the greatest social change in North Korea. The circulation of information into North Korea, and out, holds the potential to inspire citizen-led changes that are independent of the state. For North Korea, the real enemies don't live in the United States, Japan, or South Korea. Let us remember, "contemporary history is full of instances in which tellers of factual truth were felt to be more dangerous, and even more hostile, than the real opponents."[1] Far more dangerous for North Korea is the accurate telling of life on the ground by those who are least acceptable to the state.

On January 11, 2019, Tomás Ojea Quintana, the UN special rapporteur for human rights in North Korea, said that "human rights on the ground remain unchanged."[2] In the most basic areas of life, access to the most essential of human rights, such as clean water, adequate food, health care, and sanitation, is going unfulfilled. Due to lack of access to North Korea, it is difficult to know to what extent sanctions are negatively impacting ordinary people on the ground. Quintana has requested that North Korea permit the UN Security Council to access the country to determine that sanctions are not negatively impacting the people, but to no avail. The challenge is to set a balance between exploring and opening new diplomacy tracks and applying sanctions, and the success of this balance is difficult to assess without access.

Since 2014 the UN Security Council has held yearly meetings on human rights under the agenda item known as "the situation in North Korea." To hold these meetings required a procedural vote each year, which passed, but at the end of 2018 it didn't. Signatures of nine members are required, but proponents couldn't gather nine signatures.[3] Tensions between Russia and the United States over sanctions seem to have impacted the annual meeting on the agenda item of North Korea's human rights. Russia is said to be violating sanctions (with illicit petroleum sales) while Russia accuses the United States of negatively impacting the humanitarian situation through sanctions. Russia and China are pushing for sanctions relief on North Korea in return for seeing positive signs of action by the DPRK. What kind of positive actions could North Korea make? Even before going so far as to talk about peace on the peninsula, or denuclearization—things that are tangentially connected to rights—what other signs might North Korea take to signal its sincerity in taking actions to improve rights? Improving human rights in North Korea could happen as effortlessly as the state not taking action to inflict the most egregious harms. The do-no-harm approach would mean not carrying out public or private executions, not carrying out forced abortions, not practicing the system of crime inheritance, not imprisoning border crossers. But would they do it? The state rhetoric, highlighted in part II of this book, indicates otherwise.

Access to the condition of people on the ground is the biggest barrier. It was the most frequent critique North Korea wielded at the UN Commission of Inquiry report. This is why state media was mobilized to create a mediatized civil society on video. If there are allegations that sanctions are worsening the lives of ordinary people, then access must be granted to verify. If there are promises that nuclear proliferation has ceased, then access must be granted to verify. The most critical unmet need right now in terms of sanctions and nuclear proliferation is verification through access. Without access, it is difficult to assess the humanitarian situation and the proliferation of nuclear materials. And naturally this also connects to assessing whether the rights situation is improving. North Korea needs to provide access for neutral observers. Until then, other methods of access must be tried.

* * *

The case is dismal, but it is not hopeless. There is evidence for hope despite the exceptionally complex nature of North Korea's human rights situation. Even in destruction, the greatest possible manifestation of life must be tried. This book ends, then, where it began.

We were in a traditional Korean coffee shop in a small town outside of Seoul. It was early 2018. Snow sat on the mountains, and ice floated on the Yellow Sea in heavy chunks. The coffee shop was empty except for Jeong Kwang Il, his bodyguard, and a fellow activist friend. Mentally, Jeong struggles to leave the prison camp. But he is pulling the bricks down around him in his own way.

In the chilly February weather, South Korean rap music blaring, we set out in the car before sunrise to reach the watery border between North and South Korea.[4] This is not the DMZ you see on the news. It is an inconspicuous tail end of it—a border nonetheless, but remote. And at such an early hour, we are not expected. Here is the place where activists and former North Koreans gather with bottles heavy with rice, money, and information, throwing them into the sea, into the current that carries them north. The question naturally arises: Does anyone get them? The North Korean activists in the group confirm that fishers catch the bottles in nets, and people near to shore in the North seek out the bottles and make full use of them. This hopeful launching of bottles is a way for us to duck beneath the power of the two nation-states on this peninsula, to hand something off to those we don't know, but care about, with the sea as our ally.

Con.1 Messages in bottles near the border between North and South Korea, February 2018. The photograph shows USBs—loaded with movies, music, and other information—U.S. dollar bills, white rice, and anthelmintic. The empty space in the bottles helps them float.

Author's photograph

Con.2 Messages in bottles near the border between North and South Korea, February 2018

Author's photograph

Other cars, other activists, will meet us there. A pickup truck filled with bottles of rice is also making its way. The typical delays and confusions associated with coordinated activism ensued. Someone needed coffee, another needed the bathroom. Were we on the right road? Would the water be too frozen to carry the bottles? At one point it seemed everyone in the car, driver included, was on a mobile phone shouting directions and queries down the line. As planned, a foreign journalist and her translator—hyped about the event they were about to witness—got picked up en route. Defiance, like all acts born of passion that run deepest in the heart, is exhilarating.

Like protagonists nearing the end of a long and difficult journey, our fortitude was tested by one final snag. A kind of border-before-the-border, in the form of an angry farmer, momentarily waylaid us. Unfortunately for him, his land was too ideally positioned for defector guerrilla activists to resist. Common courtesy meant we had to get in and out quickly so as not to raise his attention. Evidently his attention had already been raised by previous visits because the narrow dirt road to the water's edge, which sat upon his land, was blocked. A towering midweight excavator, its crane arm positioned like a fist pounding the earth, meant we couldn't drive the rice truck to the edge but had to unload and walk a kilometer with the supplies on our backs. This back and forth between the truck and the water took time, some rice was lost on the path, and several people, as if to mourn the loss, stopped and stared. No matter. Such a block—compared with the DMZ, compared with the regime of North Korea, compared with years of illicit border crossing or prison-torture—was child's play.

Near the edge of South Korea, along the coast of the water, we cluster in batches around piles of used one-liter PET bottles, each half-filled with white rice. We undid the tops and fed each three more items: a USB with movies, books, and information; a U.S. dollar bill; and a single pink pill in a plastic-foil bubble, an anthelmintic, inspired by the roundworms found in the young defector who had dashed across at the DMZ. Those gifted with strong forearms were tasked with tightening the caps on the bottles in preparation for their long voyage into North Korean waters, into the nets of fishers, into the hands of black-market sellers, into the homes of a lucky few. The rice could be sold, the U.S. money used on the black market, the pill sold or taken, the USB a portal into another world. Would those who capture the bottles be civilians or soldiers? Would they be deserving? It is not the people who are the enemy; the state makes the gray zone.

Before the final sending off—as if we were commissioning a ship—an activist-leader among us spoke: "A North Korean can live for a month or two on what is in this bottle," he said, holding one aloft. We stood around the mountain of bottles. Pictures were taken. Some said prayers. Finally, he shouted: "Throw them as far into the water as you can!" And, knowing they had to make it all the way to North Korea, we did.

NOTES

Introduction: Descent

1. Rainer Maria Rilke, "Sonnets to Orpheus," Part Two, XIII, in *Duino Elegies and the Sonnets to Orpheus*, ed. and trans. Stephen Mitchell. Vintage International Series (New York: Knopf Doubleday, 2009).

2. In various publications Jeong Kwang Il's name is romanized as Chung/Jung Gwang Il. Readers should note this is the same person.

3. Uri Friedman, "Coming of Age in North Korea: A Man Who Served the Regime Recounts His Efforts to Bring It Down," *Atlantic*, August 26 2016, https://www.theatlantic.com/international/archive/2016/08/north-korea-defector-jung/496082/.

4. Penguin Random House, the publisher of a defector's critical memoir, was threatened by North Korea—this is addressed later in this book. See also Reuters, "North Korea Sentences South Korean Reporters to Death over Review of Book About Country," September 1, 2017, https://www.reuters.com/article/us-northkorea-southkorea-media-threat/north-korea-sentences-south-korean-reporters-to-death-over-review-of-book-about-country-idUSKCN1BB2J0.

5. Ji-Young Lee, *China's Hegemony: Four Hundred Years of East Asian Domination* (New York: Columbia University Press, 2016).

6. For more on this, see William Stueck, *The Korean War: An International History* (Princeton, N.J.: Princeton University Press, 1997); and Andrei Lankov, *The Real North Korea: Life and Politics in the Failed Stalinist Utopia* (Oxford: Oxford University Press, 2014).

7. Sun Young Pak, Daniel Schwekendiek, and Hee Kyoung Kim, "Height and Living Standards in North Korea, 1930s–1980s," *Economic History Review* 64 (2011): 142–58.

8. The full UN definition of crimes against humanity, adopted from the Rome Statute, applies to rights violations that are "committed as part of a widespread or systematic attack directed against any civilian population, with knowledge of the attack." See the Rome Statute of the International Criminal Court, Article 7, https://www.icc-cpi

.int/NR/rdonlyres/EA9AEFF7-5752-4F84-BE94-0A655EB30E16/0/Rome_Statute
_English.pdf.

9. For a full list of Commissions of Inquiry, see the United Nations Library "Research Guides," http://libraryresources.unog.ch/factfinding/chronolist.

10. United Nations Human Rights Council (UNHRC), *Commission of Inquiry on Human Rights in the Democratic People's Republic of Korea*, February 2014, http://www.ohchr .org/EN/HRBodies/HRC/CoIDPRK/Pages/CommissionInquiryonHRinDPRK.aspx.

11. Jed Lea-Henry, "The Korea Now Podcast #21—Michael Kirby—'Human Rights in North Korea—Looking Back on the Commission of Inquiry,'" August 30, 2018, http: //korea-now-podcast.libsyn.com/the-korea-now-podcast-21-michael-kirby-human -rights-in-north-korea-looking-back-on-the-commission-of-inquiry.

12. UNHRC, *Commission of Inquiry on Human Rights*.

13. The hearings in Bangkok may have been held privately as there is no publicly available record of these on the OHCHR website. See the UNHRC "Public Hearings" page: http://www.ohchr.org/EN/HRBodies/HRC/CoIDPRK/Pages/PublicHearings.aspx.

14. Human Rights Council, "Detailed Findings of the United Nations Commission of Inquiry into Human Rights in the Democratic People's Republic of Korea," A/HRC/25 /CRP.1, February 7, 2014, p. 365, http://daccess-ods.un.org/access.nsf/Get?Open&DS=A /HRC/25/CRP.1&Lang=E.

15. Human Rights Council, "Detailed Findings," 212, 338, 355.

16. However, North Korea has always had some rhetoric related to rights—albeit not necessarily in line with international human rights law. For an excellent analysis of this, see Jiyoung Song, *Human Rights Discourse in North Korea: Post-Colonial, Marxist and Confucian Perspectives* (New York: Routledge, 2014).

17. Will Ripley, "North Korea Defends Human Rights Record," *CNN*, June 30, 2015, https: //edition.cnn.com/videos/world/2015/06/30/north-korea-denies-abuses-pkg-ripley.cnn.

18. Jennifer Williams, "Read the Full Transcript of Trump's North Korea Summit Press Conference," *Vox*, June 12, 2018, https://www.vox.com/world/2018/6/12/17452624/trump -kim-summit-transcript-press-conference-full-text.

19. Williams, "Read the Full Transcript."

20. Reuters, "Trump and Kim's Joint Statement," https://www.reuters.com/article/us -northkorea-usa-agreement-text/trump-and-kims-joint-statement-idUSKBN1J80IU.

21. Christy Lee, "UN Official: 'Time' to Talk Human Rights with North Korea," *Voice of America*, June 17, 2018, https://www.voanews.com/a/un-official-now-is-the-time-for -north-korea-human-rights/4441668.html.

22. A computer-simulated model measuring the impact on human well-being and multi-decadal climate disaster for the globe with the exchange of one nuclear bomb between India and Pakistan can be found in Michael J. Mills, Owen B. Toon, Julia-Lee Taylor, and Alan Robock, "Multidecadal Global Cooling and Unprecedented Ozone Loss Following a Regional Nuclear Conflict," *Earth's Future* 2, no. 4: 161–76. https://agu pubs.onlinelibrary.wiley.com/doi/abs/10.1002/2013EF000205.

23. Lea-Henry, "The Korea Now Podcast #21."

24. Jiyoung Song, "Why Do North Korean Defector Testimonies so Often Fall Apart?" *Guardian*, October 13, 2015.

25. Some interviewees requested that the commission hear their testimony off the public record.

26. UN General Assembly, "Report of the DPRK Association for Human Rights Studies," September 15, 2014, A/69/383-S/2014/668, https://digitallibrary.un.org/record/781479 /files/A_69_383_S_2014_668-EN.pdf.

27. United Nations Human Rights Office of the High Commissioner (OHCHR), "End of Mission Statement by the United Nations Special Rapporteur on the Rights of Persons with Disabilities, Ms. Catalina Devandas-Aguilar, on Her Visit to the DPRK, Delivered at the Taedonggang Diplomatic Club, Pyongyang," May 8, 2017, https://www.ohchr.org/EN/NewsEvents/Pages/DisplayNews.aspx?NewsID=21610&LangID=E.

28. OHCHR, "End of Mission Statement."

29. Song, "Why Do North Korean Defector Testimonies so Often Fall Apart?"

30. The two-part documentary is examined in the final portion of this book. North Korea refers to Shin by his North Korean name in the following romanization: Shin In Gun.

31. Research into testimony delivered at South Africa's Truth and Reconciliation Commission found that when women testified publicly, they edited out portions of their stories related to gender-based violence. Shelia Meintjes, "South Africa's Truth and Reconciliation Commission and Gender Justice," Gunda Werner Institute: Feminism and Gender Democracy, March 12, 2012, https://www.gwi-boell.de/en/2012/03/12/south-africa%E2%80%99s-truth-and-reconciliation-commission-and-gender-justice.

32. Meintjes, "South Africa's Truth"; and Anne Cubilié, *Women Witnessing Terror: Testimony and the Cultural Politics of Human Rights* (New York: Fordham University Press, 2005).

33. Jacob D. Lindy and Robert Jay Lifton, eds. *Beyond Invisible Walls: The Psychological Legacy of Soviet Trauma* (London: Taylor and Francis, 2001), 215.

1. The History of Human Rights Violations in North Korea

1. Kim Il Sung, "On the Establishment of the Workers' Party of North Korea and the Question of Founding the Workers' Party of South Korea," September 1946, in *Kim Il Sung: Selected Works*, 1:102–20, Marxists Internet Archive, https://www.marxists.org/archive/kim-il-sung/1946/09/26.htm. For an excellent historical analysis, see Jiyoung Song, *Human Rights Discourse in North Korea: Post-Colonial Marxist and Confucian Perspectives* (New York: Routledge, 2010).

2. Andrei Lankov, *From Stalin to Kim Il-sung: The Formation of North Korea, 1945–1960* (New Brunswick, N.J.: Rutgers University Press, 2002).

3. Andrei Lankov, *Crisis in North Korea: The Failure of De-Stalinization* (Honolulu: University of Hawai`i Press, 2005), 213.

4. Lankov, *Crisis in North Korea*, 212.

5. Lankov, *Crisis in North Korea*, 12.

6. Balazs Szalontai, *Kim Il Sung in the Khrushchev Era: Soviet-DPRK Relations and the Roots of North Korean Despotism, 1953–1964* (Stanford, Calif.: Stanford University Press, 2005).

7. Lankov, *From Stalin to Kim Il-Sung.*

8. Lankov, *From Stalin to Kim Il-Sung.*

9. Lankov, *Crisis in North Korea*, 10.

10. Lankov, *Crisis in North Korea*, 15.

11. Lankov, *From Stalin to Kim Il-Sung.*

12. Lankov, *Crisis in North Korea*, 16.

13. Yoon Yeo-sang, Chung Jai-ho, and An Hyunmin, *2016 White Paper on Religious Freedom in North Korea* (Seoul: NKDB, January 4, 2017), Database Center for North Korean Human Rights, http://www.nkdb.org/en/library/Books_list.php., 26.

14. Yoon, Chung, and An, *2016 White Paper on Religious Freedom in North Korea*, 26.
15. Szalontai, *Kim Il Sung in the Khrushchev Era*.
16. Yoon, Chung, and An, *2016 White Paper on Religious Freedom in North Korea*, 32.
17. Szalontai, *Kim Il Sung in the Khrushchev Era*, 213.
18. Szalontai, *Kim Il Sung in the Khrushchev Era*, 42.
19. Lankov, *Crisis in North Korea*, 196.
20. Lankov, *Crisis in North Korea*, 195
21. Quoted in Lankov, *Crisis in North Korea*, 152.
22. Lankov, *Crisis in North Korea*, 214.
23. Lankov, *Crisis in North Korea*, 42.
24. Lankov, *Crisis in North Korea*, 42.
25. Quoted in Lankov, *Crisis in North Korea*, 81.
26. Lankov, *Crisis in North Korea*, 180.
27. Lankov, *Crisis in North Korea*, 208, 200.
28. Szalontai, *Kim Il Sung in the Khrushchev Era*, 20.
29. Szalontai, *Kim Il Sung in the Khrushchev Era*, 20.
30. Andrei Nikolaevich Lankov, In-ok Kwak, and Choong-Bin Cho, "The Organizational Life: Daily Surveillance and Daily Resistance in North Korea," *Journal of East Asian Studies* 12, no. 2 (2012): 193–214.
31. Szalontai, *Kim Il Sung in the Khrushchev Era*, 11
32. Lankov, *Crisis in North Korea*, 57–59.
33. Lankov, *Crisis in North Korea*, 148–49.
34. Lankov, *Crisis in North Korea*, 152.
35. Lankov, *Crisis in North Korea*, 150.
36. Lankov, *Crisis in North Korea*, 195.
37. Ministry of Unification, Institute for Unification Education. *Understanding North Korea: 2014* (Seoul: Ministry of Unification, 2014), 336–40.
38. Szalontai, *Kim Il Sung in the Khrushchev Era*, 22.
39. Szalontai, *Kim Il Sung in the Khrushchev Era*, 212.
40. Szalontai, *Kim Il Sung in the Khrushchev Era*, 212.
41. Lankov, *From Stalin to Kim Il-Sung*, 5.
42. Lankov, *From Stalin to Kim Il-Sung*, 9.
43. Lankov, *Crisis in North Korea*, 181–82. The forced relocation was called the Resolution 149 of the Cabinet of Ministers.
44. Lankov, *Crisis in North Korea*, 181–82.
45. Lankov, *Crisis in North Korea*, 181.
46. Lankov, *Crisis in North Korea*, 181.
47. Szalontai, *Kim Il Sung in the Khrushchev Era*, 64.
48. Szalontai, *Kim Il Sung in the Khrushchev Era*, 65.
49. Szalontai, *Kim Il Sung in the Khrushchev Era*, 65.
50. Szalontai, *Kim Il Sung in the Khrushchev Era*, 71.
51. Szalontai, *Kim Il Sung in the Khrushchev Era*, 71.
52. Szalontai, *Kim Il Sung in the Khrushchev Era*, 231.
53. Szalontai, *Kim Il Sung in the Khrushchev Era*, 248.
54. Lankov, *Crisis in North Korea*, 99.
55. Lankov, *Crisis in North Korea*, 98.
56. Human Rights Council, "Report of the Detailed Findings of the Commission of Inquiry on Human Rights in the Democratic People's Republic of Korea," A/HRC/25/CRP.1, February 7, 2014, http://daccess-ods.un.org/access.nsf/Get?Open&DS=A/HRC/25/CRP.1&Lang=E., p. 207.

57. World Food Summit, "Part 1: Issues and Concepts for Protecting and Promoting Good Nutrition in Crisis Situations," Food and Agriculture Organization of the United Nations, n.d., http://www.fao.org/docrep/008/y5815e/y5815e05.htm.

58. Donald Clark, *Living Dangerously in Korea: The Western Experience, 1900–1950* (Norwalk, Conn.: EastBridge, 2003).

59. Hazel Smith, *North Korea: Markets and Military Rule* (Cambridge: Cambridge University Press, 2015), 63.

60. Smith, *North Korea*, 63.

61. Smith, *North Korea*, 63.

62. Song, *Human Rights Discourse in North Korea*, 88.

63. Bruce Cumings, *Korea's Place in the Sun: A Modern History* (New York: Norton, 2005), 157.

64. Cumings, *Korea's Place in the Sun*, 231.

65. Yoon, Chung, and An, *2016 White Paper on Religious Freedom in North Korea*, 65.

66. Yoon, Chung, and An, *2016 White Paper on Religious Freedom in North Korea*, 32.

67. Quoted in Yoon, Chung, and An, *2016 White Paper on Religious Freedom in North Korea*, 65.

68. Yoon, Chung, and An, *2016 White Paper on Religious Freedom in North Korea*, 65.

69. "Ali Lameda: A Personal Account of the Experience of a Prisoner of Conscience in the Democratic People's Republic of Korea," January 1, 1979, Index Number ASA 24/002/1979 (London: Amnesty International, 1979). The appendix of this report covers the case of Jacques Sedillot.

70. These cases are discussed in more detail, along with others later in this book. Lameda was in solidary for six years and eventually released in 1975, the same year as Sedillot. Lameda was able to leave the DPRK thanks to Amnesty International's campaign. Sedillot died in Pyongyang a year after his release.

71. "For True Human Rights," *Rodong Shinmun*, June 24, 1995.

72. Cumings, *Korea's Place in the Sun*. See also Human Rights Council, "Report of the Commission of Inquiry on Human Rights in the Democratic People's Republic of Korea," A/HRC/25/63, February 7, 2014, http://undocs.org/A/HRC/25/63; and United Nations General Assembly, "Report of the DPRK Association for Human Rights Studies Submitted to the United Nations General Assembly Security Council," September 15, 2014, A/69/383–S/2014/668, https://digitallibrary.un.org/record/781479/files/A_69_383_S_2014_668-EN.pdf.

73. Bruce Cumings, *The Korean War: A History* (New York: Modern Library, 2010), 39.

2. Famine and Hunger

1. Kim Hyuk, Commission of Inquiry on Human Rights in the Democratic People's Republic of Korea Public Hearings, Seoul, morning session, August 22, 2013, unofficial transcript, 2, 3, 4 of 54. All COI transcripts are found at https://www.ohchr.org/en/hrbodies/hrc/coidprk/pages/publichearings.aspx.

2. Real Stories, "North Korean Orphans Open Up About How They Survive," YouTube, September 19, 2016, https://www.youtube.com/watch?v=cUxIRSdc5y8.

3. ABC News (Australia), "Footage Shows Starving North Korean Children," YouTube, October 6, 2011, https://www.youtube.com/watch?v=6sSw2o2Ujmo.

4. AP Archive, "North Korea—Worsening Famine," YouTube, July 21, 2015 https://www.youtube.com/watch?v=megljY3kWeo.

5. Andrew Natsios attributes this observation to the work of Good Friends, a South Korean Buddhist NGO, and Cortland Robinson, a researcher from Johns Hopkins University who conducted interviews with defectors. The famine "traumatized North Korean society and its political system, and permanently altered the mindset and worldview of the public, who blamed the North Korean government for their predicament." Andrew Natsios, "North Korea's Chronic Food Problem," in *Troubled Transition: North Korea's Politics, Economy, and External Relations*, ed. Choe Sang-Hun, Gi-Wook Shin, and David Straub (Stanford, Calif.: Shorenstein Asia-Pacific Research Center, September 2013), 121.

6. Sandra Fahy, *Marching Through Suffering: Loss and Survival in North Korea* (New York: Columbia University Press, 2015).

7. Fahy, *Marching Through Suffering*, 39.

8. Jang Jin-Sung, *Dear Leader*, trans. Shirley Lee (London: Ebury, 2014), 56.

9. Philip Alston, 1984, president of the committee of Economic Social and Cultural Rights, quoted in *Food and Human Rights in Development*, vol. 1, *Legal and Institutional Dimensions and Selected Topics*, ed. Wenche Barth Eide and Uwe Kracht Sally-Ann Way (Oxford: Intersentia, 2005), 162.

10. General Comment 12 (CESCR), quoted in "The Right to Food," Food and Agriculture Organization of the United Nations, n.d., http://www.fao.org/righttofood/about -right-to-food/en/, my emphasis added.

11. "Special Rapporteur on the Right to Food," United Nations Human Rights Office of the High Commissioner, n.d., https://www.ohchr.org/EN/Issues/Food/Pages/Food Index.aspx.

12. United Nations, Universal Declaration of Human Rights, December 10, 1948, Article 25, http://www.un.org/en/universal-declaration-human-rights/.

13. Robert Malthus, *An Essay on the Principle of Population as It Affects the Future Improvement of Society, with Remarks on the Speculations of Mr. Goodwin, M. Condorcet and Other Writers*, 1st ed. (London: J. Johnson in St Paul's Church-yard, 1798).

14. Stephen Devereux, ed., *The New Famines: Why Famines Persist in an Era of Globalization* (New York: Routledge, 2007), 3, 7.

15. Stephen Devereux, *Theories of Famine: From Malthus to Sen* (Hemel Hempstead, U.K.: Harvester Wheatsheaf, 1993), 35.

16. Tim Dyson and Cormac O Gráda, eds., *Famine Demography: Perspectives from the Past and Present* (Oxford: Oxford University Press, 2002).

17. Robert Dirks, "Social Responses During Severe Food Shortages and Famine [and Comments and Reply]," *Current Anthropology* 21, no. 1 (February 1980): 21–44.

18. Some individuals resist terminal starvation better than others, and these are routinely said to be people who had exposure to starvation before (see Dirks, "Social Responses," 23). Whether this is because they become more adept at famine coping strategies or are biologically more resilient is uncertain.

19. Surviving famine will depend on baseline variables, such as nutritional background, cultural patterns, aggravating factors such as disease or water shortage, and ameliorating factors such as food reserves.

20. Paul Richards, *Coping with Hunger: Hazard and Experiment in an African Rice-Farming System* (London: Allen and Unwin, 1986), 46. The technical language Amartya Sen uses is as follows: "production-based entitlement" (growing food), "trade-based entitlement" (buying food), "own-labour entitlement" (working for food), and "inheritance and transfer entitlement" (being given food by others). Amartya Sen, *Poverty and Famines: An Essay on Entitlement and Deprivation* (Oxford: Clarendon Press,

1981). In Russia in 1922, sociologist and famine survivor Pitirim Sorokin observed six ways to procure food and avoid starvation during the 1921 Russian famine. These were invention; acquisition from other groups by peaceful means; emigration; war and forceful requisition of food from well-fed groups or individuals; redistribution of essential food and riches through criminal ways, organized attacks, revolts, insurrections, and so on; and death—listed as the final means of avoiding starvation. Pitirim Sorokin, *Hunger as a Factor in Human Affairs* (Gainesville, Fla.: University Press of Florida, 1975), 158–59.

21. Amartya Sen, "Famines as Failures of Exchange Entitlements," *Economic and Political Weekly* 11, no. 31–33 (1976): 1273–80.

22. Susan George, *How the Other Half Dies: The Real Reasons for World Hunger* (Middlesex: Penguin, 1977), 206–13. At the time George wrote this, her observation was truly groundbreaking.

23. Amartya Sen, *Development as Freedom* (Oxford: Oxford University Press, 1999), 87, 162, 172.

24. Dirks, "Social Responses," 24; and Sen, *Development as Freedom*, 168.

25. Devereux, *The New Famines*, 7.

26. Stephan Haggard and Marcus Noland, *Famine in North Korea: Markets, Aid, and Reform* (New York: Columbia University Press, 2007), 10.

27. For deeper analysis of Juche, see Brian Reynolds Myers, *North Korea's Juche Myth* (Busan [ROK]: Sthele Press, 2015).

28. After Tzvetan Todorov, *Hope and Memory: Reflections on the Twentieth Century*, trans. David Bellows (London: Atlantic Books, 2003).

29. Kongdan Oh and Ralph C. Hassig, *Through the Looking Glass* (Washington, D.C.: Brookings Institution Press, 2000), 37.

30. Article 19, "Starving in Silence: A Report on Famine and Censorship," April 1, 1990, https://reliefweb.int/report/world/starving-silence-report-famine-and-censorship; Amartya Sen and Jean Drèze, *The Amartya Sen & Jean Drèze Omnibus: Comprising Poverty and Famines, Hunger and Public Action; India: Economic Development and Social Opportunity* (Oxford: Oxford University Press, 1999); Francis D'Sousa "Democracy as a Cure for Famine," *Journal of Peace Research* 31, no. 4 (1994): 369–73; Sen, *Development as Freedom*, 181, 169; and Amartya Sen, "Democracy as a Universal Value," *Journal of Democracy* 10, no. 3 (1999): 3–17.

31. Devereux, *Theories of Famine*; Devereux, *The New Famines*; and Thomas L. Myhrvold-Hanssen, "Democracy, News Media, and Famine Prevention: Amartya Sen and the Bihar Famine of 1966–67," unpublished manuscript, June 2003, https://www.sas.upenn.edu/~dludden/BIHAR1967counterSen.pdf.

32. Shin-Wha Lee, "International Engagement in North Korea's Humanitarian Crisis: The Role of State and Non-State Actors," *East Asia: An International Quarterly* 20, no. 2 (Summer 2003): 82.

33. E.g., Fahy, *Marching Through Suffering*.

34. Sen, *Development as Freedom*, 161, 162–63.

35. E.g., Fahy, *Marching Through Suffering*, 136, 154.

36. Andrew Natsios, Commission of Inquiry on Human Rights in the Democratic People's Republic of Korea Public Hearings, Washington, D.C., October 31, 2013, unofficial transcript, 32–54.

37. Devereux, *The New Famines*.

38. Devereux, *The New Famines*.

39. Devereux, *The New Famines*, 7.

40. Haggard and Noland, *Famine in North Korea*, 215.
41. Jang, *Dear Leader*, 10.
42. "10.2 Human Rights in Times of Emergency," in *International Norms and Standards Relating to Disability*, updated October 2003, United Nations, http://www.un.org/esa /socdev/enable/comp210.htm#10.2.
43. "10.2 Human Rights in Times of Emergency." My emphasis added.
44. For an example of the North Korean government's version of rights, see "Resolution of Meeting of UN Commission on Human Rights Rejected," *KCNA*, April 21, 2005; and for an article published a little closer to when the famine process was under way, see "Another Smear Campaign Against DPRK," *KCNA*, August 4, 1997. See also United Nations General Assembly, "Report of the DPRK Association for Human Rights Studies Submitted to the United Nations General Assembly Security Council," September 15, 2014, A/69/383–S/2014/668, https://digitallibrary.un.org/record/781479 /files/A_69_383_S_2014_668-EN.pdf.
45. Human Rights Council, "Report of the Detailed Findings of the Commission of Inquiry on Human Rights in the Democratic People's Republic of Korea," A/HRC/25 /CRP.1, February 7, 2014. http://daccess-ods.un.org/access.nsf/Get?Open&DS=A/HRC /25/CRP.1&Lang=E, p. 208, para. 688.
46. Alex De Waal, "Famine and Human Rights," *Development in Practice* 1, no. 2 (1991): 77.
47. The Rome Statute of the International Criminal Court, 1998, Article 7, 2b, reads: " 'Extermination' includes the intentional infliction of conditions of life, inter alia the deprivation of access to food and medicine, calculated to bring about the destruction of part of a population." http://legal.un.org/icc/statute/99_corr/cstatute.htm.
48. Rhoda E. Howard-Hassmann, *State Food Crimes* (Cambridge: Cambridge University Press, 2016), 28.
49. Howard-Hassmann, *State Food Crimes*, 3.
50. Food and Agriculture Organization of the United Nations, "Guideline 1.2 FAO," in *The Right to Food: Voluntary Guidelines to Support the Progressive Realization of the Right to Adequate Food in the Context of National Food Security*, adopted November 2004 (Rome: FAO of the UN, 2005), http://www.fao.org/3/a-y7937e.pdf, p. 9.
51. Natsios, *North Korea's Chronic Food Problem*, 124.
52. The United Nations Children's Fund, the World Food Programme, and the Humanitarian Aid department of the European Commission report findings are quoted in Michael Schloms, *North Korea and the Timeless Dilemma of Aid: A Study of Humanitarian Action in Famines* (Berlin: Lit Verlag Münster, 2004), 112.
53. Haggard and Noland, *Famine in North Korea*, 94–95.
54. Natsios, Commission of Inquiry Public Hearings, 22.
55. Kongdan Oh and Ralph Hassig, *The Hidden People of North Korea: Everyday Life in the Hermit Kingdom* (Lanham, Md.: Rowman and Littlefield, 2015).
56. David Morton, "Steep Learning Curves in the DPRK," in *Humanitarian Diplomacy: Practitioners and Their Craft*, ed. Larry Minear and Hazel Smith, 194–214 (New York: United Nations University Press, 2007), 199.
57. Morton, "Steep Learning Curves in the DPRK," 200.
58. Morton, "Steep Learning Curves in the DPRK," 200.
59. Morton, "Steep Learning Curves in the DPRK," 200.
60. Morton, "Steep Learning Curves in the DPRK," 204–5.
61. Several scholars report that the North Korean government denied visas to Korean-speaking aid staff. See, for example, one of the best books reporting on humanitarian work in the DPRK: L. Gordon Flake and Scott Snyder, *Paved with Good Intentions: The NGO Experience in North Korea* (Westport, Conn.: Praeger, 2003). See also Jasper

Becker, *Rogue Regime: Kim Jong Il and the Looming Threat of North Korea* (Oxford: Oxford University Press, 2005).

62. Johan Pottier, *Re-imagining Rwanda: Conflict, Survival and Disinformation in the Late Twentieth Century* (Cambridge: Cambridge University Press, 2002), 54.

63. Sophie Delaunay, "North Korea: The Humanitarian Situation and Refugees," MSF Testimony Delivered to the House Committee on International Relations Subcommittee on East Asia and the Pacific in Washington, D.C., May 1, 2002, https://www.doctorswithoutborders.org/what-we-do/news-stories/research/north-korea-humanitarian-situation-and-refugees.

64. Hugo Slim, "Positioning Humanitarianism in War: Principles of Neutrality, Impartiality and Solidarity," paper presented at the Aspects of Peacekeeping Conference, Royal Military Academy, Sandhurst, U.K., January 1, 1997, http://repository.forcedmigration.org/show_metadata.jsp?pid=fmo:2232.

65. Flake and Snyder, *Paved with Good Intentions*, 33.

66. Flake and Snyder, *Paved with Good Intentions*, 65.

67. Kang Chol-Hwan and Pierre Rigoulot, *The Aquariums of Pyongyang: Ten Years in a North Korean Gulag*, trans. Yair Reiner (New York: Basic Books, 2001), 174–75.

68. Woo Seongji, "North Korea's Food Crisis," *Korea Focus*, May–June (2004), 76.

69. Sue Lautze, "The Famine in North Korea: Humanitarian Responses in Communist Nations," Feinstein International Famine Centre Working Paper, School of Nutrition Science and Policy, Tufts University, June 1997. http://repository.forcedmigration.org/show_metadata.jsp?pid=fmo:1744.

70. World Food Programme 1997, cited in Haggard and Noland, *Famine in North Korea*, 65.

71. Andrew Natsios, "The Politics of Famine in North Korea," United States Institute of Peace, Special Report, August 2, 1999. https://www.usip.org/publications/1999/08/politics-famine-north-korea; and Haggard and Noland, *Famine in North Korea*, 65.

72. Flake and Snyder, *Paved with Good Intentions*; and Haggard and Noland, *Famine in North Korea*, 206.

73. This emergency operation would only target key vulnerable groups in 131 counties in eight provinces: Ryanggang, North Hamgyong, South Hamgyong, Kangwon, North Hwanghae, South Hwanghae, South Pyongan, and Pyongyang. World Food Programme, "Emergency Operation Democratic People's Republic of Korea: 10757.0 — Emergency Assistance to Population Groups Affected by Floods and Rising Food and Fuel Prices," n.d., https://one.wfp.org/operations/current_operations/project_docs/107570.pdf.

74. Scott Snyder, quoted in Marcus Noland, "Famine and Reform in North Korea WP 03-5," *Institute for International Economics*, https://piie.com/publications/wp/03-5.pdf, p. 19.

75. Fiona Terry, "Feeding the Dictator: Special Report: Korea," *Guardian*, August 6, 2001, http://www.guardian.co.uk/world/2001/aug/06/famine.comment.

76. Human Rights Council, "Report of the Detailed Findings," pp. 207–8, para. 282, 683, 684, 688.

77. Howard-Hassmann, *State Food Crimes*, 3.

78. Natsios, "North Korea's Chronic Food Problem," 125.

79. Haggard and Noland, *Famine in North Korea*.

80. Victor Cha, Commission of Inquiry Public Hearings, Washington, D.C., October 31, 2013, p. 11. See also the work of Stephan Haggard and Marcus Noland (*Famine in North Korea*), Daniel Schwekendiek (*A Socioeconomic History of North Korea*), and Sang-Hun Choe, Gi-Wook Shin, and David Straub (*Troubled Transition*).

81. Cha, Commission of Inquiry Public Hearings, 13.

82. FIVIMS (Guidelines for National Food Insecurity and Vulnerability Information and Mapping Systems), quoted in George Kent, *Freedom from Want: The Human Rights to Adequate Food* (Washington, D.C.: Georgetown University Press, 2005), 21. See also Committee on World Food Security, "Guidelines for National Food Insecurity and Vulnerability Information and Mapping Systems (FIVIMS): Background and Principles," Twenty-fourth Session, Rome, June 2–5, 1998, http://www.fao.org/docrep/meeting/W8500e.htm.

83. Kent, *Freedom from Want*, 21.

84. Lawrence Haddad, Eileen Kennedy, and Joan Sullivan, "Choice of Indicators for Food Security and Nutrition Monitoring," *Food Policy* 19, no. 3 (1994): 329.

85. Sun Young Pak, Daniel Schwekendiek, and Hee Kyoung Kim, "Height and Living Standards in North Korea, 1930s–1980s," *Economic History Review* 64 (2011): 142–158.

86. Jeong Eun Kim. "Nutritional State of Children in the Democratic People's Republic of Korea (DPRK): Based on the DPRK Final Report of the National Nutrition Survey 2012," *Pediatric Gastroenterology, Hepatology & Nutrition* 17, no. 3 (2014): 135–39.

87. Kent, *Freedom from Want*, 15.

88. Mary E. Penny, "Severe Acute Malnutrition: Pathophysiology, Clinical Consequences, and Treatment," in *Nutrition in Pediatrics: Basic Science, Clinical Applications*, ed. Christopher Duggan, John B. Watkins, Berthold Koletzko, and W. Allan Walker, 496–557, 5th ed. (Shelton, Conn.: People's Medical, 2016).

89. Maureen M. Black and John P. Ackerman, "Neuropsychological Development," in *Nutrition in Pediatrics: Basic Science, Clinical Applications*, vol. 4, ed. Christopher Duggan, John B. Watkins, and W. Allan Walker, 273–82 (Hamilton, Ont., Can.: BC Decker, 2008), 274.

90. Douglas S. Berkman, Andres G. Lescano, Robert H. Gilman, Sonia L. Lopez, and Maureen M. Black, "Effects of Stunting, Diarrhoeal Disease, and Parasitic Infection During Infancy on Cognition in Late Childhood: A Follow-up Study," *Lancet* 359, no. 9306 (February 2002): 564–71, https://doi.org/10.1016/S0140-6736(02)07744-9; Susan Walker, Sally Grantham-McGregor, Christine A. Powell, and Susan M. Chang, "Effects of Growth Restriction in Early Childhood on Growth, IQ, and Cognition at Age 11 to 12 Years and the Benefits of Nutritional Supplementation and Psychosocial Stimulation," *Journal of Pediatrics* 137 (2000): 36–41, http://dx.doi.org/10.1067/mpd.2000.106227; and M. S. Mendez and L. S. Adair, "Severity and Timing of Stunting in the First Two Years of Life and Affect Performance on Cognitive Tests in Late Childhood," *Journal of Nutrition* 129 (1999): 1555–62.

91. Geoba.se North Korea Data, http://www.geoba.se/country.php?cc=KP&year=2017.

92. Sally Granthan-McGregor, "A Review of Existing Studies of the Effect of Severe Malnutrition on Mental Development," *Journal of Nutrition* 125 (1995): 2223S–38S.

93. Black and Ackerman, "Neuropsychological Development," 277. See also M. Winick, K. K. Meyer, and R. C. Harris, "Malnutrition and Environmental Enrichment by Early Adoption," *Science* 190 (1975): 1173–75.

3. Discrimination and Religious Persecution

1. The broad groupings for Songbun are core (*haeksim*), wavering (*dongyo*), and hostile (*choktae*). Robert Collins, *Marked for Life: Songbun. North Korea's Social Classification System* (Washington, D.C.: Committee for Human Rights in North Korea), 13. https://www.hrnk.org/uploads/pdfs/HRNK_Songbun_Web.pdf.

2. Collins, *Marked for Life*, 17. Details on these departments can be read on pages 16–20 of Collins's report.

3. Charles Armstrong, "Surveillance and Punishment in Postliberation North Korea," *Positions* 3, no. 3 (Winter 1995): 698. See also Patricia Goedde, "Law 'of our own style': The Evolution and Challenges of the North Korean Legal System," *Fordham International Law Journal* 27, no. 4 (2003): 1265–88.

4. Armstrong, "Surveillance and Punishment," 710–11.

5. Armstrong, "Surveillance and Punishment," 710–11.

6. Armstrong, "Surveillance and Punishment," 713. Note also that the widespread global emergence of mass confinement institutions throughout the world was not a replica of a European model but a "synchronous appropriation of a globally circulating idea." See Klaus Mühlhahn, "The Dark Side of Globalization: The concentration Camps in Republic of China in Global Perspective," *World History Connected* 6, no. 1, http://worldhistoryconnected.press.illinois.edu/6.1/muhlhahn.html.

7. Armstrong, "Surveillance and Punishment," 713.

8. United Nations Human Rights Council (UNHRC), *Commission of Inquiry on Human Rights in the Democratic People's Republic of Korea*, February 2014. http://www.ohchr.org/EN/HRBodies/HRC/CoIDPRK/Pages/CommissionInquiryonHRinDPRK.aspx, 717.

9. "Japanese Methods of Prisoner of War Interrogation," Allied Translator and Interpreter Section Supreme Commander for the Allied Powers, Research Report, No. 134, June 1, 1946, http://www.6thinfantry.com.customers.tigertech.net/wp-content/uploads/2011/04/JapaneseTortureTechniques.pdf, p. 3; further details may be found on pages 1001–36 of the "Judgement" International Military Tribunal for the Far East at http://www.ibiblio.org/hyperwar/PTO/IMTFE/index.html.

10. James F. Person, "We Need Help from Outside: North Korean Opposition Movement of 1956," Wilson Center Cold War International History Project, Working Paper #52, August 2006. https://www.wilsoncenter.org/sites/default/files/WP52.pdf.

11. Person, "We Need Help," 34.

12. Sung Yoon Cho, "The Judicial System of North Korea," *Asian Survey* 11, no. 12 (December 1971): 1167–1181.

13. Andrei Lankov, *From Stalin to Kim Il Sung: The Formation of North Korea 1945–1960* (New Brunswick, N.J.: Rutgers University Press, 2002). A concise history of this purge process, up to the present, can be found in Collins, *Marked for Life*, 20–27.

14. Helen-Louise Hunter, *Kim Il-Song's North Korea* (Westport, Conn.: Praeger, 1999), 4, quoted in Collins, *Marked for Life*, 4. The first book in English to identify Songbun is Hunter, *Kim Il-Song's North Korea*. Elsewhere in North Korean parlance, the following terms are used to refer to core, wavering, and hostile: basic stratum, complex stratum, and hostile stratum. Collins, *Marked for Life*, 39–41.

15. Sergey Soukhorukov, "I Escaped North Korea After Famine, Violence," *Sunday Telegraph*, August 8, 2007, http://web.archive.org/web/20070815123438/http://www.telegraph.co.uk/news/main.jhtml?xml=/news/2007/08/05/wnkor105.xml.

16. Collins, *Marked for Life*, 4.

17. Collins, *Marked for Life*, 3.

18. Through this systematic discrimination, North Korea is in violation of the UN Declaration of Human Rights (UNDHR), article 2; the International Covenant on Civil and Political Rights (ICCPR), articles 14 and 27; and the International Covenant on Economic, Social, and Cultural Rights (ICESCR), part 2, article 2. See the United Nations Universal Declaration of Human Rights, article 2, http://www.un.org/en/documents/udhr/.

19. Referenced in Collins, *Marked for Life*, 3n6.

20. Part four of Collins's *Marked for Life* discusses this manual at length.

21. Kim Sang-son and Ri Song-hi, *Resident Registration Project Reference Manual*, ed. Ri Pang-sun (Pyongyang: Social Safety Department Publishing House, 1993); my emphasis added. References to this document are taken from Collins, *Marked for Life*, 28–33. In his reference, Collins states, "Social Safety Department (Sahoe Anjeonbu) is the former designation of North Korea's Ministry of Public Safety."

22. See reference to Kim Dae-hyon, "NK State Security Department Data on Physical Data of 2,100,000 Pyongyang Residents," *Weekly Chosun Magazine*, October 24, 2011. http://weekly.chosun.com/client/news/viw.asp?nNewsNumb=002177100002 &ctcd=C)1, referenced in Collins, *Marked for Life*, 27.

23. Collins, *Marked for Life*.

24. "Chamdaun inkweoneul onghohayeo" [For the protection of true human rights], *Rodong Shinmun*, June 24, 1995. Quoted in Kim Soo-Am, "Conceptions of Democracy and Human Rights in the Democratic People's Republic of Korea," KINU: Korea Institute for National Unification, 2008, 24.

25. Kim, "Conceptions of Democracy," 24.

26. Kim, "Conceptions of Democracy," 23.

27. This mode of thinking was observed among poor communities in the shantytowns of Brazil when anthropologist Nancy Scheper-Hughes conducted her field research. See Nancy Scheper-Hughes, *Death Without Weeping: The Violence of Everyday Life in Brazil* (Berkeley: University of California Press, 1989).

28. Goedde, "Law 'of our own style,'" 1278.

29. Collins, *Marked for Life*, 5.

30. The story of Mr. Kim Yong is illustrative of this, although he did not fraudulently alter his family's history. His book indicates that hereditary identity is checked and rechecked to weed out any past oversights. See Kim Yong and Kim Suk-Young, *The Long Road Home: Testimony of a North Korean Camp Survivor* (New York: Columbia University Press, 2009).

31. Yoon Yeo-sang, Chung Jai-ho, and An Hyunmin, *2016 White Paper on Religious Freedom in North Korea*. (Seoul: NKDB, January 4, 2017), 52–53, available from Database Center for North Korean Human Rights, http://www.nkdb.org/en/library/Books_list.php.

32. Yoon, Chung, and An, *2016 White Paper on Religious Freedom*, 55–56

33. Yoon, Chung, and An, *2016 White Paper on Religious Freedom*, 60. See also DPRK Criminal Law, March 3, 1950, Provision 257, article 21.

34. Institute of North Korean Studies, *Comprehensive Survey 1945–1982* (Seoul: Institute of North Korean Studies, 1983), 1233–34.

35. DPRK Association for Human Rights Studies, "Full Text of the Report of the DPRK Association for Human Rights Studies," September 13, 2014, 72. https://www.ncnk .org/resources/publications/Report_of_the_DPRK_Association_for_Human_Rights _Studies.pdf.

36. Yoon, Chung, and An, *2016 White Paper on Religious Freedom*, 253–54.

37. "Total Denial: Violations of Freedom of Religion or Belief in North Korea," Christian Solidarity Worldwide, September 22, 2016, https://docs-eu.livesiteadmin.com/dc3e323f -351c-4172-800e-4e02848abf80/2016-07-north-korea.pdf, p. 13.

38. Yoon, Chung, and An, *2016 White Paper on Religious Freedom*, 49.

39. Yoon, Chung, and An, *2016 White Paper on Religious Freedom*.

40. Yoon, Chung, and An, *2016 White Paper on Religious Freedom*, 204.

41. Yoon, Chung, and An, *2016 White Paper on Religious Freedom*, 143–44.

42. Hazel Smith, *North Korea: Markets and Military Rule* (Cambridge: Cambridge University Press, 2015), 63.

43. Lorraine Caballero, "North Korea's Photos of 'Fake Churches' Aim to Cover Up Abuse of Christians—Report," *Christian Daily*, January 30, 2018, https://www .christiandaily.com/article/north-koreas-photos-of-fake-churches-aim-to-cover-up -abuse-of-christians-report/61950.htm.

44. Yoon, Chung, and An, *2016 White Paper on Religious Freedom*, 142.

4. Information Control

1. Amartya Sen has abundantly written on the link between open media and basic human rights such as access to food. See Amartya Sen, *Development as Freedom* (Oxford: Oxford University Press, 1999), 184, 188.

2. This is a reference to how North Korean human rights generally are described as "without parallel in the contemporary world" in the UN Commission of Inquiry report of 2014.

3. In 2016 Reporters Without Borders found North Korea to be 179th in the world, second to last, as among the worst in the world for free media. Last ranking is Eritrea. North Korea received the worst ranking for freedom of media, civil liberties, and political rights. Martyn Williams, "DPRK Again Second-to-Last in Press Freedom Ranking," *North Korea Tech*, April 20, 2016, http://www.northkoreatech.org/2016/04 /20/dprk-second-last-press-freedom-ranking/; and Freedom House, "Freedom in the World 2015: North Korea," n.d., https://freedomhouse.org/report/freedom-world/2015 /north-korea.

4. Bob Dietz, "Signs of Change in North Korea," Committee to Protect Journalists, May 17, 2012, https://www.cpj.org/blog/2012/05/signs-of-change-in-north-korea.php.

5. Nat Kretchun and Jane Kim, "A Quiet Opening: North Koreans in a Changing Media Environment," *InterMedia*, May 2012, http://www.intermedia.org/wp-content/uploads /2013/05/A_Quiet_Opening_FINAL_InterMedia.pdf.

6. The report names the Central Scientific and Technological Information Agency, in charge of running the domestic intranet system, Group 109, which tries to control the distribution of foreign media circulating domestically, and Bureau 27, which monitors phones and radio broadcasts. "Enemies of the Internet 2014: Entities at the Heart of Censorship and Surveillance," *Reporters Without Borders*, March 11, 2014. https:// rsf.org/en/news/enemies-internet-2014-entities-heart-censorship-and-surveillance. See also Martyn Williams, "DPRK Organizations Called out for Censorship," *North Korea Tech*, March 13, 2014, https://www.northkoreatech.org/2014/03/13/dprk -organizations-called-out-for-censorship/.

7. Jeong Jin Hwa, UN Commission of Inquiry on Human Rights in the Democratic People's Republic of Korea Public Hearing, afternoon session, August 22, 2013, Seoul, unofficial transcript, p. 4 of 63. Even within prisons and reeducation centers, prisoners are provided with special publications such as *New Start*, a newspaper to be read for two hours each day. Lee Jun Ha, *Reeducation Story* [Kyohwaso iyagi] (Seoul: Shidae Generation [Shidaejŏngshin], 2008), 74.

8. Sandra Fahy, *Marching Through Suffering: Loss and Survival in North Korea* (New York: Columbia University Press, 2015).

9. Yeonmi Park, *In Order to Live: A North Korean Girl's Journey to Freedom*, with Maryanne Vollers (New York: Penguin, 2015), 216–17.

10. DPRK Association for Human Rights Studies, "Report of the DPRK Association for Human Rights Studies," September 15, 2014, https://www.ncnk.org/sites/default/files /content/resources/publications/Report_of_the_DPRK_Association_for_Human _Rights_Studies.pdf, p. 62.

11. North Korea joined the International Covenant on Civil and Political Rights (ICCPR) covenant on September 14, 1981. North Korea tried to withdraw from the ICCPR in 1997, but the covenant does not permit withdrawal. Article 19 of the ICCPR reads:

     1. Everyone shall have the right to hold opinions without interference.

     2. Everyone shall have the right to freedom of expression; this right shall include freedom to seek, receive and impart information and ideas of all kinds, regardless of frontiers, either orally, in writing or in print, in the form of art, or through any other media of his choice.

     3. The exercise of the rights provided for in paragraph 2 of this article carries with it special duties and responsibilities. It may therefore be subject to certain restrictions, but these shall only be such as are provided by law and are necessary:

     (a) For respect of the rights or reputations of others;

     (b) For the protection of national security or of public order (*ordre public*), or of public health or morals.

     http://www.ohchr.org/EN/ProfessionalInterest/Pages/CCPR.aspx.

12. United Nations, Universal Declaration of Human Rights, Article 19, http://www.un .org/en/universal-declaration-human-rights/.

13. "UNHRC: Significant Resolution Reaffirming Human Rights Online Adopted. ORAL REVISIONS of 30 June." Human Rights Council, June 27, 2016. A/HRC/32/L.20, https://www.article19.org/data/files/Internet_Statement_Adopted.pdf. As mentioned in footnote 11, North Korea sought to withdraw from the ICCP in August of 1997. North Korea's human rights situation was brought to the table at the Sub-Commission on Prevention of Discrimination and Protection of Minorities. The subcommission adopted a resolution on human rights in North Korea (the resolution was adopted by a vote of thirteen in favor, nine opposed, and three abstentions). North Korea was criticized for its human rights situation regarding article 13 of the UDHR and article 12 of the ICCPR. The two other countries critiqued were the Congo and Bahrain. See Security Council Resolution 1997/3, "United Nations ESCOR Sub-Committee on Prevention of Discrimination and Protection of Minorities," 49th Session at 114, UN Doc. E/CN.4/Sub.2/1997/50 (1997). "This resolution [raised by a French representative and adopted August 21, 1997] represented the first action by the United Nations on human rights in the DPRK after decades of neglect." David Weissbrodt, Shinobu Garrigues, and Roman Kroke, "An Analysis of the Forty-ninth Session of the United Nations Sub-Commission on Prevention of Discrimination and Protection of Minorities," *Harvard Human Rights Journal* 11 (1998): 230. During the subcommission meetings (which took place over several days) North Korea tried to withdraw from the ICCPR. Kim Yong Nam, then minister for foreign affairs, DPRK, wrote a letter to the UN— dated two days after the resolution was adopted—stating that the ICCPR is connected with "extremely dangerous and hostile acts which encroach upon the sovereignty and dignity of our Republic." North Korea referred to the resolution as a "mere product of the political intrigue of the elements who intend to isolate and stifle our Republic." The letter further elaborates, "The Government of our Republic has exercised its legitimate and just self-defence right." The letter states that the North Korean government provides fundamental freedoms and basic rights on a "level far higher than as required" by the ICCPR.

14. Thae Yong Ho, Keynote address at the Center for Strategic and International Studies conference Beyond Nuclear Diplomacy: A Regime Insider's Look at North Korea, Washington, D.C., October 31, 2017, https://csis-prod.s3.amazonaws.com/s3fs-public/event/171001_Beyond_Nuclear_Diplomacy_transcript.pdf?jJogSGaZruUOmarE1J4.XUfWF9B4.vwm; my emphasis added.

15. Emily B. Landau, "A Nuclear Crisis in Search of a Model: Lessons from Iraq, North Korea, Libya, and Syria," *INSS Insight No. 491*, December 2, 2013, http://www.inss.org.il/publication/a-nuclear-crisis-in-search-of-a-model-lessons-from-iraq-north-korea-libya-and-syria/.

16. Andrei Lankov, "Why Increasing Numbers of Senior Officials Are Fleeing North Korea," *NK News.org*, August 24, 2016. https://www.nknews.org/2016/08/why-increasing-numbers-of-senior-officials-are-fleeing-north-korea/.

17. Fahy, *Marching Through Suffering.*

18. Yong Sub Choi, "North Korea's Hegemonic Rule and Its Collapse," *Pacific Review* 30, no. 5 (2017): 783–800, http://www.tandfonline.com/doi/full/10.1080/09512748.2017.1296885?src=recsys.

19. Andrei Lankov, *The Real North Korea: Life and Politics in the Failed Stalinist Utopia* (Oxford: Oxford University Press, 2015), 42–43.

20. Lankov, *The Real North Korea*, 43.

21. Kim Suk-Young, *Illusive Utopia: Theatre, Film and Everyday Performance in North Korea* (Ann Arbor: University of Michigan Press, 2010), 17.

22. See also Andrei Lankov, *North of the DMZ: Essays on Daily Life in North Korea* (Jefferson, N.C.: McFarland, 2007), 35–36.

23. Seong Hwan Kim and Min Kwon Bae, "North Korean Website Reports on Self-Criticism Sessions Following New Year's Address," *Daily NK*, January 19, 2017, http://www.dailynk.com/english/read.php?cataId=nk01700&num=14321.

24. Ken E. Gause, "Coercison, Control, Surveillance, and Punishment: An Examination of the North Korean Police State," Committee for Human Rights in North Korea, 2012, Washington, D.C., https://www.hrnk.org/uploads/pdfs/HRNK_Ken-Gause_Web.pdf.

25. DPRK Association for Human Rights Studies, "Report of the DPRK Association for Human Rights Studies," 37. See also further elaboration on freedom of speech in North Korea on pages 59–63 of the report.

26. DPRK Association for Human Rights Studies, "Report of the DPRK Association for Human Rights Studies," 59–60; my emphasis added.

27. Hyung-Min Joo, "Hidden Transcripts in Marketplaces: Politicized Discourses in the North Korean Shadow Economy," *Pacific Review* 27, no. 1 (2014): 65–66.

28. Joo, "Hidden Transcripts," 60.

29. United Nations General Assembly, "International Covenant on Civil and Political Rights," December 16, 1966, http://www.ohchr.org/EN/ProfessionalInterest/Pages/CCPR.aspx.

30. DPRK Association for Human Rights Studies, "Report of the DPRK Association for Human Rights Studies," 62.

31. DPRK Association for Human Rights Studies, "Report of the DPRK Association for Human Rights Studies," 62; my emphasis added. Public discourse such as this alone indicates that something terribly pathological is going on in North Korea.

32. A North Korean defector told this to Changyong Choi, a scholar studying information flows in North Korea; see Changyong Choi, "'Everyday Politics' in North Korea," *Journal of Asian Studies* 72, no. 3 (August 2013): 662.

33. Ralph Hassig and Kongdan Oh, *The Hidden People of North Korea: Everyday Life in the Hermit Kingdom* (Lanham, Md.: Rowman & Littlefield, 2009), 134.

34. Joo, "Hidden Transcripts in Marketplaces," 54.

35. Joo, "Hidden Transcripts in Marketplaces," 54–55.

36. Joo, "Hidden Transcripts in Marketplaces," 61.

37. Patrick McEachern, "North Korea's Internal Politics and U.S. Foreign Policy," in *Origins of North Korea's Juche: Colonialism, War, and Development*, ed. Chae-Jong So and Jae-Jung Suh, 145–62 (Lanham, Md.: Lexington Books, 2013).

38. McEachern, "North Korea's Internal Politics." McEachern describes Kim Jong Il's North Korea as a "corporatist" state with "extensive bureaucratic competition" within parts of government (147).

39. McEachern, "North Korea's Internal Politics," 147.

40. Patrick McEachern, *Inside the Red Box: North Korea's Post-totalitarian Politics* (New York: Columbia University Press, 2010).

41. "Traitor Jang Song Thaek Executed," *KCNA*, December 13, 2013. http://www.kcna.co.jp/item/2013/201312/news13/20131213-05ee.html.

42. Thae Yong Ho, "Testimony of Minister Thae, Yong-Ho, House Committee on Foreign Affairs," November 1, 2017. https://docs.house.gov/meetings/FA/FA00/20171101/106577/HHRG-115-FA00-Wstate-Yong-hoT-20171101.pdf, p. 3.

43. Jeong, Commission of Inquiry Public Hearing, 4–5.

44. Fahy, *Marching Through Suffering*, 84, 87–89.

45. Jeong, Commission of Inquiry Public Hearing, 5.

46. Jeong, Commission of Inquiry Public Hearing, 5.

47. Jeong, Commission of Inquiry Public Hearing, 6.

48. Jeong, Commission of Inquiry Public Hearing, 6.

49. Jang Hae Sung, UN Commission of Inquiry on Human Rights in the Democratic People's Republic of Korea Public Hearing, afternoon session, August 22, 2013, Seoul, unofficial transcript, p. 13 of 63.

50. Jang, UN Commission of Inquiry Public Hearing, 11.

51. Jang, UN Commission of Inquiry Public Hearing, 22.

52. Kim Il Sung was born Kim Song Ju on April 15, 1912, in a small village outside of Pyongyang called Namni at the time, now called Mangyungbong. For research on this topic, see Charles K. Armstrong, *The North Korean Revolution, 1945–1950* (Ithaca, N.Y.: Cornell University Press, 2002); Andrei Lankov, *From Stalin to Kim Il-Sung: The Formation of North Korea 1945–1960* (Piscataway, N.J.: Rutgers University Press, 2002); and Andrei Lankov, *Crisis in North Korea: The Failure of De-Stalinization, 1956* (Honolulu: University of Hawai`i Press, 2005). See also Dae-Sook Suh, *Kim Il Sung: The North Korean Leader* (New York: Columbia University Press, 1988).

53. Jang, UN Commission of Inquiry Public Hearing, 12.

54. Jeong, UN Commission of Inquiry Public Hearing, 14. Jeong and Jang were interviewed together during the public hearing.

55. Jeong, UN Commission of Inquiry Public Hearing, 18.

56. High-ranking and "ordinary" DPRK defectors make this claim. See Seong Hwan Kim, "Thae Yong Ho Believes Outside Information Will Topple Regime," *Daily NK*, December 29, 2016, http://www.dailynk.com/english/read.php?cataId=nk00100&num=14280.

57. Thomas Paine, in *The Rights of Man* (1791), wrote, "I smile to myself when I contemplate the ridiculous insignificance into which literature and all the sciences would sink, were they made hereditary." Quoted in Alain de Botton, *Status Anxiety* (New York: Vintage, 2004), 60.

58. "Documentary 'Ineffaceable War Crimes of Japan' English Sub," *Choson Sinbo*, You-Tube video, 37:46, May 28, 2013, https://www.youtube.com/watch?v=RJR-Wzx3E-s. Note the title is also translated as "inerasable," and "war" is omitted in "Documentary 'Inerasable Crimes of Japan' Produced," *KCNA*, November 6, 2005, http://www.kcna.co.jp/item/2005/200511/news11/07.htm.

59. Jang Jin-Sung, *Dear Leader*, translated by Shirley Lee (London: Ebury, 2014), 130.

60. Kim, *Illusive Utopia*, 4.

61. Armstrong, *The North Korean Revolution*, 225.

62. Kim, *Illusive Utopia*, 6.

63. Kim, *Illusive Utopia*, 13.

64. Kim, *Illusive Utopia*, 19. Here Kim is writing about *Yodok Story*, a 2006 musical produced by North Korean defectors in South Korea. See also 299–307.

65. Alzo David-West, "Archetypal Themes in North Korean Literature: Working Notes on Problems and Possibilities," *Jung Journal: Culture & Psyche* 5, no. 1 (2011): 65–80; and Dafna Zur, "Let's Go to the Moon: Science Fiction in the North Korean Children's Magazine Adong Munhak, 1956–1965," *Journal of Asian Studies*, May 2014, 1–25.

66. Ri Wŏn U, *Adong munhak ch'angjak uikil* [The path toward creative writing for children] (Pyo˘ngyang: Kungnip Ch'ulp'ansa, 1956). Referenced in Zur, "Let's Go to the Moon," 17n11.

67. Zur, "Let's Go to the Moon," 17n11. Here Zur sites scholar Yi Yŏng-mi, identifying that Kim Il Sung was influenced by Lenin in beliefs concerning children's literature and political influence. Yi Yŏng-mi, "Pukhan adongmunhakkwa kyoyuk yŏngu" [Study on North Korean children's literature and education], 227, in *Han'guk munhak ironkwa pip'yŏng* 30, no. 10.1 (2006): 225–57.

68. Dafna Zur, "The Korean War in Children's Picture Books of the DPRK," in *Exploring North Korean Arts*, ed. Rüdiger Frank (Wien: University of Vienna Press, 2011), 166–88.

69. Zur, "The Korean War in Children's Picture Books," 168.

70. Immanuel Kim, "Problems with Institutionalizing the April 15 Literary Production Unit," *Korea Journal* 56, no. 1 (Spring 2016): 155.

71. Rüdiger Frank, "The Political Economy of North Korean Arts," in *Exploring North Korean Arts*, ed. Rüdiger Frank, 9–30 (Wien: University of Vienna Press, 2011), 21.

72. Jang, *Dear Leader*, 208.

73. "The Right to Write: The Bittersweet Liberty of a North Korean Writer in Exile," International Publishers Association, September 28, 2016, http://www.internationalpublishers.org/freedom-to-publish/freedom-to-publish-news/434-the-right-to-write-the-bittersweet-liberty-of-a-north-korean-writer-in-exile.

74. Brian R. Myers, "Knocking on the Great Gate: The 'Strong and Prosperous Country' Campaign in North Korean Propaganda," in *Exploring North Korean Arts*, ed. Rüdiger Frank, 72–87 (Wien: University of Vienna Press, 2011). See also Gi-wook Shin, *Ethnic Nationalism in Korea: Genealogy, Politics, and Legacy* (Stanford, Calif.: Stanford University Press, 2006).

75. "The Right to Write."

76. "The Right to Write."

77. Omoniwa adul Adong Munhak, September 2005, 3, quoted in Zur, "The Korean War in Children's Picture Books," 167.

78. *Democratic People's Republic of Korea*, no. 66, Juche 95, no. 6 (2006): 15.

79. "New Documentary Film Produced," *KCNA*, December 31, 2008, http://www.kcna.co.jp/item/2008/200801/news01/01.htm.

80. Park, *In Order to Live.*

81. "Korean Children's Union, Success to Revolution," *KCNA*, June 7, 2007, http://www
    .kcna.co.jp/item/2007/200706/news06/07.htm.

82. "DPRK Inphung Secondary School Renamed Han Hyon Gyong Secondary School,"
    KCNA, July 17, 2012, http://www.kcna.co.jp/item/2012/201207/news17/20120717-18ee
    .html; my emphasis added.

83. "Kim Jong Un Sends Autographs to Officials, Workers and Children," *KCNA*, June
    29, 2012, http://www.kcna.co.jp/item/2012/201206/news29/20120629-13ee.html.

84. Kim Soo Am, UN Commission of Inquiry on Human Rights in the Democratic Peo-
    ple's Republic of Korea Public Hearing, afternoon session, August 21, 2013, Seoul,
    unofficial transcript, 53–55. This quotation is slightly edited for readability; the origi-
    nal meaning is not altered.

85. Mina Yoon, "When a Goat and Pig Decided to Join the North Korean Army," *NK
    News*, November 13, 2013, https://www.nknews.org/2013/11/when-a-goat-and-pig
    -decided-to-join-the-north-korean-army/.

86. Jon Henley, "Meet Srdja Popovic, the Secret Architect of Global Revolution," *Guard-
    ian*, March 8, 2015, https://www.theguardian.com/world/2015/mar/08/srdja-popovic
    -revolution-serbian-activist-protest.

87. Audre Lorde, "The Master's Tools Will Never Dismantle the Master's House," in *This
    Bridge Called My Back: Writings by Radical Women of Color*, ed. Cherrie Moraga and
    Gloria Anzaldúa, 94–97 (New York: Kitchen Table Press, 1983).

88. For a study on this in the case of Syria, see Lisa Wedeen, "Ideology and Humor in
    Dark Times: Notes from Syria," *Critical Inquiry* 39 (Summer 2013): 841–73, https://
    misr.mak.ac.ug/sites/default/files/events/CRITICAL%20INQUIRY,%20final%20
    copy.pdf.

89. Joo, "Hidden Transcripts in Marketplaces," 65–66.

5. Forbidding the Foreign

1. Quoted in Jang Jin-Sung, *Dear Leader*, trans. Shirley Lee (London: Elbury, 2014), 261.

2. Nat Kretchun and Jane Kim, "A Quiet Opening: North Koreans in a Changing Media
   Environment," *InterMedia*, May 2012. http://www.intermedia.org/wp-content/uploads
   /2013/05/A_Quiet_Opening_FINAL_InterMedia.pdf.

3. The television was mostly Chinese, Yanji TV (due to geographic distribution), and in
   the southern part of North Korea, the Korean Broadcasting Station (KBS) could be
   viewed. Kretchun and Kim, "A Quiet Opening," 12.

4. Jieun Baek, *North Korea's Hidden Revolution: How the Information Underground Is
   Transforming a Closed Society* (New Haven, Conn.: Yale University Press, 2016), 130.

5. Kretchun and Kim, "A Quiet Opening," 13.

6. Kretchun and Kim, "A Quiet Opening," 17.

7. Kretchun and Kim, "A Quiet Opening," 39.

8. Kretchun and Kim, "A Quiet Opening," 39.

9. Nat Kretchun, Catherine Lee, and Seamus Tuohy, "Compromising Connectivity:
   Information Dynamics Between the State and Society in a Digitizing North Korea,"
   InterMedia, 2017, http://www.intermedia.org/wp-content/uploads/2017/02/Compro
   mising-Connectivity-Final-Report_Soft-Copy.pdf.

10. Kretchun and Kim, "A Quiet Opening," 30–31.

11. Kretchun and Kim, "A Quiet Opening," 33.

12. Holger Lutz Kern and Jens Hainmueller, "Opium for the Masses: How Foreign Media Can Stabilize Authoritarian Regimes," *Political Analysis* 17, no. 4 (2009): 377–99, https://doi.org/10.1093/pan/mpp017.

13. Kretchun and Kim, "A Quiet Opening."

14. Kretchun and Kim, "A Quiet Opening."

15. The group Rimjin-gang works with covert North Korea–based citizen journalists. Their website can be accessed here: http://www.asiapress.org/rimjin-gang/.

16. Quoted in Baek, *North Korea's Hidden Revolution*, 160.

17. Baek, *North Korea's Hidden Revolution*, 160.

18. Mi Ae Taylor and Mark E. Manyin, "Non-Governmental Organizations' Activities in North Korea," Congressional Research Service, March 25, 2011, https://fas.org/sgp/crs/row/R41749.pdf.

19. Words attributed to Kim Jong Il by DPRK official Jang Yong-sun, quoted in Chris Green, "Wrapped in a Fog: On the DPRK Constitution and the Ten Principles," in *Change and Continuity in North Korean Politics*, ed. Adam Cathcart, Robert Winstanley-Chesters, and Christopher K. Green (New York: Routledge, 2017), 24.

20. Jang identifies in his book three diplomatic tools of engagement formally set by Kim Jong Il: "The US will buy any lie, as long as it is logically presented. Japan is susceptible to emotional manipulation," and "South Korea can be ignored or blackmailed." Jang, *Dear Leader*, 253.

21. Choe Sang-Hun, "North Korean Defector Says Kim Jong-Un's Control Is Crumbling," *New York Times*, January 25, 2017. https://www.nytimes.com/2017/01/25/world/asia/north-korea-defector.html.

22. Thae Yong Ho, "Testimony of Minister Thae, Yong-Ho, House Committee on Foreign Affairs," November 1, 2017, https://docs.house.gov/meetings/FA/FA00/20171101/106577/HHRG-115-FA00-Wstate-Yong-hoT-20171101.pdf, 2.

23. Thae, "Testimony of Minister Thae," 3.

24. The fact that Thae Yong Ho was able to defect with his wife and two sons is truly exceptional. It is also a testament to how much he was trusted by the government.

25. Former diplomat Thae lived in the United Kingdom for ten years, earning the trust of the DPRK regime for his loyalty. It was rare that he would have both of his children with him abroad. This is one of the reasons he gave for the timing of his defection. Thae's family who remain in North Korea will be used in one of two ways. Either they will be purged to a prison camp or they will appear in state media as tools of propaganda. Elise Hu, "North Korean Defector: Information Flow Will Help Bring Down Kim Jong Un," *NPR*, January 26, 2017. http://www.npr.org/sections/parallels/2017/01/26/511745886/north-korean-defector-information-flow-will-help-bring-down-kim-jong-un.

26. Eventually, Kim Hyun Hee confessed. Her memoir is a gripping narrative about North Korean psychological operations. Kim Hyun Hee, *Tears of My Soul* (New York: Morrow, 1993).

27. Oliver Holmes, "Kim Jong-nam's Body Targeted in Morgue Break-In, Say Police," *Guardian*, February 22, 2017, https://www.theguardian.com/world/2017/feb/22/kim-jong-nams-body-targeted-in-morgue-break-in; and Oliver Holmes, Tom Phillips, and Agencies, "Kim Jong-nam Killed by VX Nerve Agent, a Chemic Weapon, Say Malaysian Police," *Guardian*, February 24, 2017, https://www.theguardian.com/world/2017/feb/24/kim-jong-nam-north-korea-killed-chemical-weapon-nerve-agent-mass-destruction-malaysian-police.

28. "Korean Jurists Committee Hits out at Malaysian Side's Unfriendly Attitude," *KCNA*, February 23, 2017, http://www.kcna.co.jp/index-e.htm.

29. Information about Asia Press's work on *Rimjin-gang* can be found here: "About Our Team: ASIAPRESS and Rimjin-gang," June 27, 2012, http://www.asiapress.org/rimjin-gang/2012/06/about-rimjin-gan/about_our_team_-_asiapress_and_rimjin-gang/.

30. Scott Thomas Bruce, "Information Technology and Social Controls in North Korea," Korea Economic Institute of America, Academic Paper Series, January 28, 2014, http://www.keia.org/sites/default/files/publications/2014_aps_scottbruce.pdf, 3.

31. Kevin Stahler, "New Research on Cell Phone Use in North Korea," *North Korea: Witness to Transformation* (blog), March 7, 2014, http://blogs.piie.com/nk/?p=12941.

32. For an excellent and detailed analysis of mobile phone use, official and unofficial, in North Korea, see Kim Yonho, "Cell Phones in North Korea," *Voice of America*, 2014, https://38north.org/wp-content/uploads/2014/03/Kim-Yonho-Cell-Phones-in-North-Korea.pdf, 14.

33. Yonho, "Cell Phones in North Korea," 29, 13.

34. Hyun-Jung Ryu, "A Study on North Korea's Dual Network of Mobil Telecommunications System Using Actor-Network Theory" [in Korean] (M.A. thesis, University of North Korean Studies, 2012), referenced in Kim, "Cell Phones in North Korea," 25. There are reports that international calls can be made from North Korea directly. A Chinese businessman whom Kim Yonho interviewed was able to use his Chinese phone with a SIM card bought in Pyongyang to call Seoul using a Chinese roaming service; see Kim, "Cell Phones in North Korea," 26.

35. Heather A. Horst and Daniel Miller, *The Cell Phone: An Anthropology of Communication* (Oxford: Berg, 2006), 114.

36. Sirpa Tenhunen, "Mobile Technology in the Village: ICTs, Culture, and Social Logistics in India," *Journal of the Royal Anthropological Institute* 14 (2008): 515–34.

37. Anthony Giddens, *The Consequences of Modernity* (Cambridge, U.K.: Polity, 1990), 18.

38. Shin Junshik, "North Koreans' Speech Shortening" [in Korean], *New Focus*, December 18, 2014, http://www.newfocus.co.kr/client/news/viw.asp?cate=M1004&nNewsNumb=20141215201.

39. Kang Mi-jin, "North Korean 'Executed for Communication with the Outside World,'" *Guardian*, May 23, 2014, http://www.theguardian.com/world/2014/may/23/north-korean-executed-for-communicating-with-outside-world.

40. As Alexandre Y. Mansourov states, "North Korea has transitioned from a panopticon of total control to a voluntary compliance system where the government makes an example of a select group to try and force the rest of the country to stay in line." Alexandre Y. Mansourov, "North Korea on the Cusp of Digital Transformation," *Nautilus Institute Special Report*, October 2011, http://nautilus.org/wp-content/uploads/2011/12/DPRK_Digital_Transformation.pdf, 20.

41. Danielle Chubb, *Contentious Activism and Inter-Korean Relations* (New York: Columbia University Press, 2014), 186.

42. Referenced in Chubb, *Contentious Activism*, 187.

43. Chubb, *Contentious Activism*, 187.

44. Free North Korea Radio does have a series called "Letters Home," but these are anonymously addressed letters that cannot be too direct for fear of reprisals to family or friends, or to the letter-writers themselves.

45. See, for example, Vicente L. Rafael, "The Cell Phone and the Crowd: Messianic Politics in the Contemporary Philippines," *Public Culture* 15, no. 3 (2003): 399–425.

46. See Laura Kunreuther, "Technologies of the Voice: FM Radio, Telephone, and the Nepali Diaspora in Kathmandu," *Cultural Anthropology* 21, no. 3 (2006): 323–53.

47. Database Center for North Korean Human Rights (NKDB), "2010 North Korean Defectors' Economic Activity" [Pukhani taljumin kyunjae hwaldong donghyang: chiop, silop, soduk] (Seoul: NKDB, 2010), 109.

48. The NGO rescues North Korean children, people with disabilities, and women, helping them to reach South Korea, but it also sends radiobroadcasts into the DPRK; see the NAUH website: http://www.nauh.or.kr/main/main.php.

49. Baek, *North Korea's Hidden Revolution*, 148.

50. Sheena Chestnut Greitens, "Authoritarianism Online: What Can We Learn from Internet Data in Nondemocracies?" *PS: Political Science & Politics* 46, no. 2 (2013): 262–70.

51. Seva Gunitsky, "Corrupting the Cyber-Commons: Social Media as a Tool of Autocratic Stability," *Perspectives on Politics*, 2015: 42–54, http://individual.utoronto.ca/seva/corrupting_cybercommons.pdf.

52. Gunitsky, "Corrupting the Cyber-Commons," 52–53.

6. Control of Movement

1. "Suspected North Korean Defector Found in Japan, Say Reports," *Asia Times*, July 17, 2016, http://atimes.com/2016/07/suspected-north-korean-defector-found-in-japan-reports/.

2. MilitaryNotes, "North Korea: The Most Daring Escape Captured on Camera," YouTube video, November 22, 2017, https://www.youtube.com/watch?v=bYKNJ--GHGU.

3. Arguably there are other times when the state was "caught on camera," such as when Kim Jong Nam was assassinated in Kuala Lumpur International Airport on February 13, 2017. I thank Hyun Song for this observation. That murder case has yet to be attributed to the DPRK. As for the DMZ, several other individuals have crossed, but it is exceptionally rare. In March 1967 Lee Su-geun, vice president of the KCNA, crossed under a hail of bullets. There might be video footage of that defection and his comrades' attempts to kill him, but to my knowledge that footage is not in the public domain. Senior Lieutenant Byon Yong-Kwan defected across the JSA in February 1998. In September of 2007 another soldier crossed the JSA, but it was not disclosed to the public. "North Korean Soldier Shot While Defecting at the JSA in Panmunjeom," *Hankyoreh*, November 14, 2017, http://english.hani.co.kr/arti/english_edition/e_northkorea/818985.html.

4. U.S. Department of State, *Armistice in Korea: Selected Statements and Documents* (Washington, D.C.: Government Printing Office, 1953).

5. UNHRC, *Commission of Inquiry on Human Rights in the Democratic People's Republic of Korea*, February 7, 2014, https://www.ohchr.org/Documents/HRBodies/HRCouncil/CoIDPRK/Report/A.HRC.25.CRP.1_ENG.doc, para. 402, 403, pp. 112–13.

6. Kim Jong Il, *On Strengthening Socialist Lawful Life* (Pyongyang: Korean Workers' Party Publishers, 1989), 11. Quoted in Dong-ho Han, Soo Kim, Kyu Lee, Keum Lee, and Jeong Cho, *White Paper on Human Rights in North Korea* (Seoul: Korea Institute for National Unification, 2014), 85, http://www.kinu.or.kr/pyxis-api/1/digital-files/a55edee1-5640-41b9-845d-89fd3dfc9509.

7. Han et al., *White Paper on Human Rights*, 102. This white paper suggests that shoot-to-kill dates back to the 1980s.

8. This is an echo of biopower explored in the work of Giorgio Agamben and Michel Foucault.

9. Lijiang Zhu, "The Hukou System of the People's Republic of China: A Critical Appraisal Under International Standards of Internal Movement and Residence," *Chinese Journal of International Law* 2 (2003): 519–66; and Pan Xiaoling, "Precious Pyongyang's Household Registration," *Southern Weekly* (2011).

10. Zhongdong Ma and Donglin Zeng, "Population and Internal Migration in North Korea Since 2000," *Eurasian Geography and Economics* 56, no. 4 (2015): 464.

11. North Korea has attracted foreign investment and technology through the establishment of special economic zones and special administrative regions. There are nineteen special economic zones that have helped to improve North Korea's economy, including Rason SEZ, established early 1990s; Sinuiju SAR, established 2002 to initialize market reform; Mount Kumgang Tourist Region, established 2002 for tourism; and Kaesong Industrial Region, established 2002 for collaborative projects with South Korea. Hundreds of ROK companies in the Kaesong Industrial Park employed around seven thousand people in 2006 and forty-six thousand in 2011. See Norimitsu Onishi, "South Brings Capitalism, Well Isolated, to North Korea," *New York Times*, July 18, 2006; and Charles Scanlon, "North Korea's Resort Seizure Ends Project of Hope," *BBC News*, August 22, 2011. Local officials select young women from regions close to these zones for work. The work is focused on making cosmetics, clothes, and shoes. Ma and Zeng, "Population and Internal Migration."

12. Courtland Robinson, "Famine in Slow Motion: A Case Study of Internal Displacement in the Democratic People's Republic of Korea," *Refugee Survey Quarterly* 19, no. 2 (2000): 121–22. In late September 1997 North Korea set up feeding centers where wandering children were gathered up and held.

13. Han et al., *White Paper on Human Rights*, 242. The storm corps are squads of soldiers from the Escort Bureau of the Korean People's Army, the State Security Department, Kim Il Sung Military University, Security Cadre Training Center, Politics University of the MPS, and the National Defense University.

14. Alexey Eremenko, "Russia Moves to Send North Korean Refugees Back Home to Uncertain Fate," *Moscow Times*, November 4, 2014, http://www.themoscowtimes.com/news/article/russia-movesto-send-north-korean-refugees-back-home-to-uncertain-fate/511179.html.

15. Kim Soo-Am, "The North Korean Penal Code, Criminal Procedures, and Their Actual Applications," Korea Institute for National Unification Studies Series 06-01, 2006, 6.

16. Han et al., *White Paper on Human Rights*, 113.

17. Lee Jin-a, "Pastor Slain Near China N-Korea Border," *Korea Times*, May 2, 2016, http://www.koreatimes.co.kr/www/news/nation/2016/05/485_203854.html.

18. Joel R. Charny, "North Koreans in China: A Human Rights Analysis," *International Journal of Korean Unification Studies* 13, no. 2 (2004): 75–97.

19. Charney, "North Koreans in China," 93.

20. Luke Lee, "Internally Displaced Persons and Refugees: Toward a Legal Synthesis?" *Journal of Refugee Studies* 9, no. 1 (1996): 27–42.

21. Hazel Smith, "Explaining North Korean Migration to China," North Korea International Documentation Project E-Dossier #11, September 2012, Woodrow Wilson International Center for Scholars, https://www.wilsoncenter.org/publication/explaining-north-korean-migration-to-china; and Zhihua Shen and Yafeng Xia, "Contested Border: A Historical Investigation into the Sino-Korean Border Issue, 1950–1964," *Asian Perspective* 37, no. 1 (January–March 2013).

22. Smith, "Explaining North Korean Migration to China," 1.
23. "Document No. 4: Investigative Report from the 4th Bureau of the Ministry of Public Security on the Outflow of Border Residents, 9 May 1961," in *Explaining North Korean Migration to China: E-Dossier #11*, introduction by Hazel Smith, September 2012, Woodrow Wilson International Center for Scholars, North Korea International Documentation Project, https://www.wilsoncenter.org/sites/default/files/NKIDP_eDossier _11_Explaining_North_Korean_Migration_to_China_1.pdf.
24. Smith, "Explaining North Korean Migration to China," 1–2.
25. "Document No. 10: Protocol Between the PRC Ministry of Public Security and the DPRK Social Safety Ministry for Mutual Cooperation in Safeguarding National Security and Social Order in Border Areas, 9 June 1964," in *Explaining North Korean Migration to China: E-Dossier #11*, introduction by Hazel Smith, September 2012, Woodrow Wilson International Center for Scholars, North Korea International Documentation Project, https://www.wilsoncenter.org/sites/default/files/NKIDP_eDossier _11_Explaining_North_Korean_Migration_to_China_1.pdf.
26. The 1986 protocol is called the Mutual Cooperation Protocol for the Work of Maintaining National Security and Social Order in the Border Areas. It is available at http://www.nkfreedom.org/UploadedDocuments/NK-China-bilateral_treaty.pdf.
27. Mutual Cooperation Protocol.
28. See Article 2, no. 3, of the International Covenant on Economic, Social and Cultural Rights, https://www.ohchr.org/en/professionalinterest/pages/cescr.aspx.
29. "DPRK Defectors in China Secret Exposed: They Go Through 2 Routes to Go to S. Korea," *V.Ifeng.com Phoenix TV News*, October 21, 2014.
30. Stephan Haggard and Marcus Noland, "The North Korean Refugees as a Human Rights Issue," in *The North Korean Refugee Crisis: Human Rights and International Responses*, eds. Stephan Haggard and Marcus Noland (Washington, D.C.: U.S. Committee for Human Rights in North Korea, 2006), 10.
31. Joshua Kurlantzick and Jana Mason, "North Korean Refugees: The Chinese Dimension," in *The North Korean Refugee Crisis: Human Rights and International Response*, eds. Stephan Haggard and Marcus Noland (Washington, D.C.: U.S. Committee for Human Rights in North Korea, 2006).
32. Erika Feller, Volker Türk, and Frances Nicholson, *Refugee Protection in International Law: UNHCR's Global Consultations on International Protection* (Cambridge: Cambridge University Press, 2003), 118.
33. Emma Haddad, "The Refugee: The Individual Between Sovereigns," *Global Society* 17, no. 3 (2003): 309.
34. Jiyoung Song, "The Complexity of North Korean Migration," *Asia Pacific Memo*, no. 229 (June 6, 2013), http://apm.iar.ubc.ca/the-complexity-of-north-korean -migration/.
35. Lawrence Preuss, cited in Hannah Arendt, *Imperialism: Part Two of "The Origins of Totalitarianism"* (New York: Harcourt, Brace, & World, 1968), 164n36.
36. Giorgio Agamben, *Homo sacer: Sovereign Power and Bare Life*, trans. Daniel Heller-Roazen (Stanford, Calif.: Stanford University Press, 1998), 75.
37. "29 North Korean Defectors Burst into Japanese School in Beijing," *Radio Free Asia*, September 1, 2004, https://www.rfa.org/english/news/noko_schooldefect090104 -20040901.html.
38. Choe Sang-Hun, "Nine North Koreans Escape to Vietnam," *New York Times*, September 24, 2009, http://www.nytimes.com/2009/09/25/world/asia/25korea.html.

39. "North Korean Refugee Developments," WikiLeaks, June 29, 2006, Canonical ID: 06BANGKOK3842_a, https://WikiLeaks.org/plusd/cables/06BANGKOK3842_a.html.

40. Human Rights Watch, "Appendix B: Letter from Chinese Ministry of Foreign Affairs to Foreign Embassies, May 31, 2002," https://www.hrw.org/reports/2002/northkorea/norkor1102-06.htm. See also "The Invisible Exodus: North Koreans in the People's Republic of China," *Human Rights Watch* 14, no. 8 (November 2002), https://www.hrw.org/reports/2002/northkorea/norkor1102.pdf.

41. North Korea Freedom Coalition, "2013 Update 'The List' of North Korean Refugees and Humanitarian Workers Seized by Chinese Authorities," http://www.nkfreedom.org/UploadedDocuments/2013.12.10_THE_LIST_ENGLISH.pdf, 14.

42. North Korea Freedom Organization, "2013 Update 'The List,'" 16, and other places.

43. Rhoda Margesson, Emma Chanlett-Avery, and Andorra Bruno, *North Korean Refugees in China and Human Rights Issues: International Response and U.S. Policy Options.* CRS Report for Congress RL34189 (Washington, D.C.: Congressional Research Service, 2007).

44. Kelly M. Greenhill, *Weapons of Mass Migration: Forced Displacement, Coercion, and Foreign Policy*, Cornell Studies in Security Affairs (Ithaca, N.Y.: Cornell University Press, 2010), 229.

45. A leaked report from China's main state-owned telecommunications company appeared on Weibo, a microblogging site, stating that a county along the border with North Korea was preparing camps, anticipating an outflow of people as North Korea and the United States exchanged threats in late 2017. Jane Perlez, "Fearing the Worst, China Plans Refugee Camps on North Korean Border," *New York Times*, December 11, 2017, https://www.nytimes.com/2017/12/11/world/asia/china-north-korea-border.html; Greenhill, *Weapons of Mass Migration*, 243–44; and rbaker@stratfor.com, email to analysts@stratfor.com, astrid.edwards@stratfor.com, "RE: [OS] Thailand: Thais Struggle with Refugee Influx," Wikileaks, May 18, 2007, Global Intelligence Files, email ID: 324213, https://wikileaks.org/gifiles/docs/32/324213_re-os-thailand-thais-struggle-with-refugee-influx-.html. rbaker@stratfor.com writes to analysts@stratfor.com and astrid.edwards@stratfor.com, saying, "many more are defecting now, not because things are worse, but because the groups out to crash the dprk regime are sponsoring massive church efforts to get these folks to go to ROK."

46. Malcolm Moore, "China Defends Policy of Sending Back North Korean Defectors," *Daily Telegraph*, February 19, 2014.

47. Eunyoung Choi, "North Korean Women's Narratives of Migration: Challenging Hegemonic Discourses of Trafficking and Geopolitics," *Annals of the Association of American Geographers* 104, no. 2 (2014): 271–79; and Yoonok Chang, Stephan Haggard, and Marcus Noland, *Migration Experiences of North Korean Refugees: Survey Evidence from China*, Working Paper series WP 08-4 (Washington, D.C.: Peterson Institute for International Economics, 2008).

48. Emilie M. Hafner-Burton, "Sticks and Stones: Naming and Shaming the Human Rights Enforcement Problem," *International Organization* 62 (Fall 2008): 689–716.

49. Smith, "Explaining North Korean Migration to China."

50. "The Invisible Exodus."

51. Hannah Arendt, *Origins of Totalitarianism* (San Diego: Harcourt Brace, 1976 [1951]), 295–96.

52. Arendt, *Origins of Totalitarianism*, 286.

53. Arendt, *Origins of Totalitarianism*, 286.

54. Agamben, *Homo sacer*, 28.

55. Andrei Lankov, "North Korean Refugees in Northeast China," *Asian Survey* 44, no. 6 (November/December 2004): 856.

56. Bela Hovy, "Human Rights and Citizenship: The Need for Better Data and What to Do About It," in *Children Without a State: A Global Human Rights Challenge*, ed. Jacqueline Bhabha (Cambridge, Mass.: MIT Press, 2011), 89.

57. Jacqueline Bhabha, preface to Bhabha, ed., *Children Without a State*, xiii.

58. Bhabha, preface to *Children Without a State*, xi.

59. Human Rights Council, "Report of the Detailed Findings of the Commission of Inquiry on Human Rights in the Democratic People's Republic of Korea," A/HRC/25 /CRP.1, February 7, 2014, http://daccess-ods.un.org/access.nsf/Get?Open&DS=A/HRC /25/CRP.1&Lang=E, p. 169, para. 560.

60. Human Rights Council, "Report of the Detailed Findings," p. 167, para. 551.

61. Brad K. Blitz, "Neither Seen nor Heard: Compound Deprivation Among Stateless Children." In Bhabha, ed., *Children Without a State*, 65.

62. Christina O. Alfirev, "Volatile Citizenship or Statelessness? Citizen Children of Palestinian Descent and the Loss of Nationality in Israel," in Bhabha, ed., *Children Without a State*, 69.

63. "What Items Must North Korean Defectors Take on Their Journey?" *New Focus International*, February 28, 2013.

64. "North Korean Refugees Embark on Blind Journey to Freedom," *New Focus International*, June 19, 2013.

65. Kristen Di Martino, "China: Ensuring Equal Access to Education and Health Care for Children of Internal Migrants," in Bhabha, ed., *Children Without a State*, 279–305. See also Gerison Lansdown, "Children's Welfare and Children's Rights," in *Children in Society: Contemporary Theory, Policy and Practice*, ed. Pam Foley, Jeremy Roche, and Stan Tucker, 143–56 (New York: Palgrave Macmillan, 2001); Onora O'Neill, "Children's Rights and Children's Lives," *Ethnics* 98, no. 3 (1988); and Elizabeth F. Cohen, "Neither Seen nor Heard: Children's Citizenship in Contemporary Democracies," *Citizenship Studies* 9, no. 2 (2005).

66. China's Nationality Law, Zhōnghuá Rénmín Gònghéguó Guójí Fǎ, adopted by the National People's Congress on September 10, 1980, includes eighteen articles that broadly explain China's citizenship policies.

67. Lankov, "North Korean Refugees in Northeast China," 856; Hong Soon-Do, "50,000–200,000 N. Korean Defectors Estimated to Be Residing in China," *Huffington Post*, June 7, 2016; and Jenna Yoojin Yun, "30,000 North Korean Children Living in Limbo in China," *Guardian*, February 5, 2016, https://www.theguardian.com/world/2016/feb /05/north-koreas-stateless-children.

68. Refugees International, "Acts of Betrayal: The Challenge of Protecting North Koreans in China," Relief Web, May 12, 2005, https://reliefweb.int/report/democratic -peoples-republic-korea/acts-betrayal-challenge-protecting-north-koreans-china-0.

69. James D. Seymour, "China: Background Paper on the Situation of North Koreans in China," Commissioned by the United Nations High Commissioner for Refugees, Protection Information Section, January 2005, http://nautilus.org/wp-content/uploads /2011/12/0527A_Seymour.pdf, 16.

70. Roberta Cohen, "Admitting North Korean Refugees to the United States," Brookings, September 20, 2011, https://www.brookings.edu/opinions/admitting-north-korean -refugees-to-the-united-states-obstacles-and-opportunities/.

71. Ministry of Unification, 2014 statistics on North Koreans arriving in South Korea [in Korean], available at: http://www.unikorea.go.kr/content.do?cmsid=1440.

72. See Oliver Hotham, "Work Visas for North Koreans Going to China up 17.2%," *NK News*, April 15, 2014, http://www.nknews.org/2014/01/work-visas-for-north-koreans-going-to-china-up-17-2/.

73. Sandra Fahy, *Marching Through Suffering: Loss and Survival in North Korea* (New York: Columbia University Press, 2015).

74. Refugees International, "Acts of Betrayal," 14.

75. Stephan Haggard and Marcus Noland, eds., *The North Korean Refugee Crisis: Human Rights and International Response* (Washington, D.C.: U.S. Committee for Human Rights in North Korea, 2006).

76. "North Korean Border Guards Flee to China," *Telegraph*, December 15, 2011, https://www.telegraph.co.uk/news/worldnews/asia/northkorea/8957669/North-Korean-border-guards-flee-to-China.html.

77. Crisis Group International, "Perilous Journeys: The Plight of North Koreans in China and Beyond," *Crisis Group Asia Report No. 122*, October 26, 2006, https://web.archive.org/web/20070927012303/http://www.nautilus.org/fora/security/0694IGC.pdf, 17.

78. Song, "The Complexity of North Korean Migration."

79. Yeonmi Park, *In Order to Live: A North Korean Girl's Journey to Freedom*, with Maryanne Vollers (New York: Penguin, 2015), 154.

80. Park, *In Order to Live*, 204.

81. Anthony W. Rinna, "Ulan Bator's Small Country Diplomacy: The Case of North Korea," *SINO-NK*, June 22, 2015, http://sinonk.com/2015/06/22/ulan-bators-small-country-diplomacy-the-case-of-north-korea/.

82. James Brooke, "Refugee Plan for Mongolia Adds to Dispute on North Korea," *New York Times*, September 28, 2003, http://www.nytimes.com/2003/09/28/world/refugee-plan-for-mongolia-adds-to-dispute-on-north-korea.html.

83. Migeddorj Batchimeg "Mongolia's DPRK Policy: Engaging North Korea," *Asian Survey* 46, no. 2 (March/April 2006): 285.

84. Constitution of Mongolia, Article 18.4, quoted in UNHCR "Universal Period Review: Mongolia," August 2014, http://www.refworld.org/pdfid/553a28474.pdf, 1.

85. Constitution of Mongolia, Article 7.3.3, quoted in UNHCR "Universal Period Review: Mongolia."

86. Batchimeg, "Mongolia's DPRK Policy," 285.

87. David L. Caprara, Katharine H. S. Moon, and Paul Park, "Mongolia: Potential Mediator between the Koreas and Proponent of Peace in Northeast Asia," Brookings, January 20, 2015, https://www.brookings.edu/opinions/mongolia-potential-mediator-between-the-koreas-and-proponent-of-peace-in-northeast-asia/.

88. Batchimeg, "Mongolia's DPRK Policy," 284–85.

89. Batchimeg, "Mongolia's DPRK Policy," 285.

90. Batchimeg, "Mongolia's DPRK Policy," 285.

91. James Brooke, "Mongolia Under Pressure to Serve as Haven for Refugees," *New York Times*, November 22, 2004, http://www.nytimes.com/2004/11/21/world/asia/mongolia-under-pressure-to-serve-as-haven-for-refugees.html.

92. Ben Paviour and Kuch Naren, "North Korean Attackers Sent to Cambodia, Paper Reports," *Cambodia Daily*, July 28, 2016, https://www.cambodiadaily.com/news/north-korean-attackers-sent-to-cambodia-paper-reports-115985/.

93. "US Concern After Cambodia Deports 20 Chinese Uighurs," *BBC*, December 20, 2009, http://news.bbc.co.uk/2/hi/8422022.stm; and "Cablegate: North Korean Refugee

Held in Mondolkiri Province," Scoop Independent News, WikiLeaks, November 22, 2006. Ref: 06PHNOMPENH2072, http://www.scoop.co.nz/stories/WL0611/S01144.htm.

94. "North Korean Waitress in Phnom Penh Reportedly Defects to South Korea," February 7, 2012, *Asiapundits.com*, https://www.asiapundits.com/regions/korea/update-north-korean-waitress-in-phnom-penh-reportedly-defects-to-south-korea/.

95. "Guidance Regarding Two North Korean Sisters in Cambodia," Wikileaks, June 7, 2005, Canonical ID: 05BANGKOK3744_a, https://WikiLeaks.org/plusd/cables/05BANGKOK3744_a.html. See also "Embassy Discussions with RTG on Hmong and North Korean Refugee Issues," Wikileaks, July 9, 2007, Canonical ID: 07BANGKOK3755_a, https://WikiLeaks.org/plusd/cables/07BANGKOK3755_a.html.

96. "Diplomatic Note from Permanent Mission of Thailand to the United Nations Office, Geneva, Response to Lawyers Committee for Human Rights Questionnaire on Detention of Asylum Seekers," Lawyers' Committee for Human Rights, February 22, 2002.

97. Human Rights Watch, "Ad Hoc and Inadequate: Thailand's Treatment of Refugees and Asylum Seekers," September 12, 2012, https://www.hrw.org/report/2012/09/12/ad-hoc-and-inadequate/thailands-treatment-refugees-and-asylum-seekers. See also os@stratfor.com, email to intelligence@stratfor.com, "Thailand Accused of Deliberate Abuses of N Koreans" WikiLeaks, September 18, 2007, Global Intelligence Files, email ID: 377185, https://WikiLeaks.org/gifiles/docs/37/377185_-os-thailand-thailand-accused-of-deliberate-abuses-of.html.

98. "North Korean Refugee Developments."

99. "North Korean Refugee Developments."

100. Sarah Kim, "North Orders Terror Strikes on South Koreans," *Korea JoongAng Daily*, July 27, 2016, http://koreajoongangdaily.joins.com/news/article/article.aspx?aid=3021812.

101. Stimmekoreas, "North Korean Restaurant Workers Abducted by South Korea! [English]," YouTube video, 8:01. April 29, 2016, https://www.youtube.com/watch?v=IAkXVO24ZXw.

102. "DPRK Refugee Incidents in Vietnam," WikiLeaks, October 14, 2003, Canonical ID: 03HANOI2617_a, https://WikiLeaks.org/plusd/cables/03HANOI2617_a.html.

103. Barbara Demick, "Rescue Yields Repercussions for South Korea," *Los Angeles Times*, August 28, 2004, http://articles.latimes.com/2004/aug/28/world/fg-defect28.

104. "Thailand Accused of Deliberate Abuses of N Koreans," WikiLeaks, September 18, 2007, email ID: 377185, https://WikiLeaks.org/gifiles/docs/37/377185_-os-thailand-thailand-accused-of-deliberate-abuses-of.html.

105. Justin McCurry, "Fears for North Korean Refugees Who May 'Face Death' if Returned by China," *Guardian*, November 25, 2015, https://www.theguardian.com/world/2015/nov/25/fears-for-north-korean-refugees-who-may-face-death-if-returned-by-china.

106. McCurry, "Fears for North Korean Refugees"; and "DPRK Refugee Incidents in Vietnam."

107. "Activist: 64 N. Korean Defectors Held by Myanmar Rebels," *Dong-a Ilbo*, July 13, 2013, http://english.donga.com/List/3/all/26/406601/1.

108. "Burma: Visit of DPRK Vice Foreign Minister," WikiLeaks, November 19, 2008, Canonical ID: 08RANGOON901_a, https://WikiLeaks.org/plusd/cables/08RANGOON901_a.html.

109. "Burma: Visit of DPRK Vice Foreign Minister."

110. "GRP Grants Permission to Process North Korean Refugee," WikiLeaks, December 21, 2006, Canonical ID: 06MANILA5062_a, https://WikiLeaks.org/plusd/cables/06MANILA5062_a.html.

111. "GRP Grants Permission to Process."
112. UNHCR, "Protecting Refugees: Questions and Answers," February 1, 2002, https://www.unhcr.org/publications/brochures/3b779dfe2/protecting-refugees-questions-answers.html.
113. United Nations General Assembly, "The Problem of Manifestly Unfounded or Abusive Applications for Refugee Status or Asylum, No. 30 (XXXIV)—1983," October 20, 1983, recommendation (i), https://www.unhcr.org/excom/exconc/3ae68c6118/problem-manifestly-unfounded-abusive-applications-refugee-status-asylum.html.
114. Niraj Nathwani, *Rethinking Refugee Law* (Boston: Martinus Nijoff Publishers, 2003), 44.

7. Prison Camps, Torture, and Execution

1. Jee Heon A, Commission of Inquiry on Human Rights in the Democratic People's Republic of Korea, Public Hearings, Seoul, afternoon session, August 20, 2013, unofficial transcript, 53. Clarification added with Korean audio of testimony. All COI transcripts are found at https://www.ohchr.org/en/hrbodies/hrc/coidprk/pages/publichearings.aspx.
2. Article 28, "Principal Punishments and Supplementary Punishments," of the Criminal Law of the Democratic People's Republic of Korea, trans. Sang hyup Lee, Hyeong Su Park, Kyung Eun Ha, Markus Simpson Bell, Lillian Lee, and Andrew Wolman (Seoul: Citizens' Alliance for North Korean Human Rights, 2009), https://www.hrnk.org/uploads/pdfs/The%20Criminal%20Law%20of%20the%20Democratic%20Republic%20of%20Korea_2009_%20(1).pdf.
3. U.S. Department of State, "Korea, Democratic People's Republic of: Tier 3," in *Trafficking in Persons Report, 2016* (Washington, D.C.: Government Publishing Office, June 2016), 228, https://www.state.gov/documents/organization/258876.pdf.
4. Human Rights Watch, "UN: North Korea Exploiting Children," February 8, 2017, https://www.hrw.org/news/2017/02/08/un-north-korea-exploiting-children
5. Kim Hyuk, Commission of Inquiry on Human Rights in the Democratic People's Republic of Korea Public Hearings, Seoul, morning session, August 22, 2013, unofficial transcript, 18 of 54.
6. Michel Foucault, *Discipline and Punish: The Birth of the Prison*, trans. Alan Sheridan (London: Penguin, 1977), 24.
7. Foucault, *Discipline and Punish*, 30, 31.
8. Brian Reynolds Myers, *The Cleanest Race: How North Koreans See Themselves and Why It Matters* (New York: Melville House, 2010).
9. Human Rights Council, "Report of the Detailed Findings of the Commission of Inquiry on Human Rights in the Democratic People's Republic of Korea," A/HRC/25/CRP.1, February 7, 2014. http://daccess-ods.un.org/access.nsf/Get?Open&DS=A/HRC/25/CRP.1&Lang=E, para. 432.
10. Human Rights Council, "Report of the Detailed Findings," para. 426.
11. Human Rights Council, "Report of the Detailed Findings," para. 428.
12. Human Rights Council, "Report of the Detailed Findings," paras. 428–30.
13. The People's Safety Enforcement Law (1992), Article 50(3), in Human Rights Council, "Report of the Detailed Findings," para. 433.
14. Human Rights Council, "Special Rapporteurs on Torture and Other Cruel, Inhuman and Degrading Treatment," February 1, 2013, A/HRC/22/53, https://www.ohchr.org/Documents/HRBodies/HRCouncil/RegularSession/Session22/A.HRC.22.53_English

.pdf, para. 48; and Human Rights Council, "Promotion and Protection of All Human Rights, Civil, Political, Economic, Social and Cultural Rights, Including the Right to Development." A/HRC/7/3, January 15, 2008, https://documents-dds-ny.un.org/doc/UNDOC/GEN/G08/101/61/PDF/G0810161.pdf?OpenElement, para. 69. See also Human Rights Committee, "CCPR General Comment No. 28: Article 3 (The Equality of Rights Between Men and Women)," CCPR/C/21/Rev.1/Add.10, https://www.refworld.org/docid/45139c9b4.html, para. 11.

15. Young Jeon Shin, "The Characteristics of Korea's Eugenic Movement in the Colonial Period Represented in the Bulletin, Woosaeng," *Korea Journal of Medical History* 15, no. 2 (2006): 133–55.

16. Ji Seong Ho, Commission of Inquiry on Human Rights in the Democratic People's Republic of Korea Public Hearings, Seoul, morning session, August 22, 2013, unofficial transcript, 29 of 54.

17. Ji, COI Public Hearings, 29.

18. Chris Green, "Wrapped in a Fog: On the DPRK Constitution and the Ten Principles," in *Change and Continuity in North Korean Politics*, ed. Adam Cathcart, Robert Winstanley-Chesters, and Christopher K. Green (New York: Routledge, 2017), 24.

19. Kim Suk-Young, *Illusive Utopia: Theatre, Film and Everyday Performance in North Korea* (Ann Arbor: University of Michigan Press, 2010), 4 and other places.

20. Ji, COI Public Hearings, 29.

21. This is a paraphrase of François Furet's "illusion resists the knowledge of facts." François Furet, *The Passing of an Illusion: The Idea of Communism in the Twentieth Century*, trans. Deborah Furet (Chicago: University of Chicago Press, 1999), 143, quoted in Claude Lefort, *Communism and the Dilemmas of Democracy* (New York: Columbia University Press, 1999), 91.

22. Charles Armstrong, "Surveillance and Punishment in Postliberation North Korea," *Positions* 3, no. 3 (Winter 1995): 715.

23. Ji, COI Public Hearings, 26. Testimony edited for clarity. Meaning has not been altered. In his account, Ho uses the Korean word "*jagil*," which refers to gravel.

24. Citizens' Alliance for North Korean Human Rights (NKHR), *Status of Women's Rights in the Context of Socio-Economic Changes in the DPRK* (Seoul: NKHR, 2013).

25. Ji, COI Public Hearings, 30.

26. The PRC didn't have a penal code until 1979, according to Balazs Szalontai, *Kim Il Sung in the Khrushchev Era: Soviet-DPRK Relations and the Roots of North Korean Despotism, 1953–1964* (Stanford, Calif.: Stanford University Press, 2005), 24.

27. Szalontai, *Kim Il Sung in the Khrushchev Era*, 24.

28. Szalontai, *Kim Il Sung in the Khrushchev Era*, 24.

29. Szalontai, *Kim Il Sung in the Khrushchev Era*, 80.

30. Szalontai, *Kim Il Sung in the Khrushchev Era*, 213.

31. Giorgio Agamben, *Means Without End: Notes on Politics*, trans. Vincenzo Binetti and Cesare Casarino (Minneapolis: University of Minnesota Press, 2000), 39–40.

32. Agamben, *Means Without End*, 39–40.

33. Patrick McEachern, "North Korea's Internal Politics and U.S. Foreign Policy," in *Origins of North Korea's Juche: Colonialism, War, and Development*, ed. Chae-Jong So and Jae-Jung Suh (Lanham, Md.: Lexington Books, 2013), 145–62.

34. Also referred to as the "Ten Principles," and the "Ten Principles for the Establishment of One-Ideology System." Further details on these principles and how they impact children's education can be found in Robert M. Collins and Amanda Mortwedt Oh, *From Cradle to Grave: The Path of the Korean Innocents* (Washington, D.C.:

Committee for Human Rights in North Korea, 2017), https://www.hrnk.org/uploads/pdfs/Collins_Cradle_to_Grave_WEB_FINALFINAL.pdf.

35. For further details on the Organization and Guidance Department, see Jang Jin-Sung, *Dear Leader*, trans. Shirley Lee (London: Ebury, 2014), 132–39. See also Robert Collins, *Pyongyang Republic: North Korea's Capital of Human Rights Denial* (Washington, D.C.: Committee for Human Rights in North Korea, 2016), 112–17.

36. Robert Collins, *Marked for Life: Songbun, North Korea's Social Classification System* (Washington, D.C.: Committee for Human Rights in North Korea, 2012), https://www.hrnk.org/uploads/pdfs/HRNK_Songbun_Web.pdf, 15.

37. Green, "Wrapped in a Fog," 28–31.

38. "What Are the 'Ten Principles?'" *Daily NK*, August 9, 2013, https://www.dailynk.com/english/read.php?cataId=nk02900&num=10829.

39. Jang Hae Sung, Commission of Inquiry on Human Rights in the Democratic People's Republic of Korea Public Hearings, Seoul, afternoon session, August 22, 2014, Seoul, unofficial transcript, p. 13 of 63.

40. For more details on North Korea's early court system, see Sung Yoon Cho, "The Judicial System in North Korea," *Asian Survey* 11, no. 12 (December 1971): 1168.

41. Kim Il Sung, *Selected Works*, 1:384, quoted in Cho, "The Judicial System in North Korea," 1180.

42. United Nations General Assembly, "International Covenant on Civil and Political Rights," December 19, 1966, http://www.ohchr.org/EN/ProfessionalInterest/Pages/CCPR.aspx.

43. After Alexander Paterson, *Paterson on Prisons: Being the Collected Papers of Sir Alexander Paterson*, ed. S. K. Ruck (London: F. Muller, 1951), 13.

44. See Human Rights Council, "Report of the Detailed Findings," sections IV.E.3 and IV.E.4, for a more detailed description of conditions in political and ordinary prisons.

45. Human Rights Council, "Report of the Detailed Findings," para. 689.

46. For example, Article 6 (the right to life), Article 7 (freedom from torture and cruel, inhuman or degrading treatment), Article 9 (right to liberty and security of the person), Article 10 (humane treatment of detainees), and Article 14 (right to a fair trial) are all violated in this process.

47. The DPRK is in violation of Article 6 (right to life), Article 37 (freedom from torture and unlawful deprivation of liberty), and Article 40 (treatment in detention) of the Convention on the Rights of the Child. Human Rights Council, "Report of the Detailed Findings."

48. Lee Jun Ha, *Reeducation Story* [Kyohwaso iyagi] (Seoul: Shidae Generation Publishing [Shidaejŏngshin], 2008), 156, 191.

49. Ahn Myong Chul, Commission of Inquiry on Human Rights in the Democratic People's Republic of Korea Public Hearings, Seoul, afternoon session, August 21, 2013, unofficial transcript, p. 10 of 55. It is unclear from Ahn's testimony if these children were in the camp because they had inherited the crimes of their parents or if they were born in the prison camp. Several camps have facilities for educating children in basic reading, writing, and math.

50. Lee, *Reeducation Story*, 118.

51. Lee, *Reeducation Story*, 140.

52. Lee, *Reeducation Story*, 160, 163.

53. Lee, *Reeducation Story*, 234.

54. DPRK Criminal Law (2009), Article 30, § 2, "Life and Limited Term of Reform Through Labor," available from Citizens' Alliance for North Korean Human Rights,

trans. Sang hyup Lee, Hyeong Su Park, Kyung Eun Ha, Markus Simpson Bell, Lillian Lee, and Andrew Wolman, https://www.hrnk.org/uploads/pdfs/The%20Criminal%20 Law%20of%20the%20Democratic%20Republic%20of%20Korea_2009_%20(1).pdf.

55. Jeong Kwang Il, Commission of Inquiry on Human Rights in the Democratic People's Republic of Korea Public Hearings, Seoul, morning session, August 21, 2013, unofficial transcript, p. 50 of 63. Emphasis added.

56. Kim Eun Cheol, Commission of Inquiry on Human Rights in the Democratic People's Republic of Korea Public Hearings, Seoul, morning session, August 21, 2013, unofficial transcript, p. 32 of 63.

57. Kim, COI Public Hearings, 43.

58. Kim, COI Public Hearings, 43.

59. K. Tokyo, Commission of Inquiry on Human Rights in the Democratic People's Republic of Korea Public Hearings, Seoul, afternoon session, August 30, 2013, unofficial transcript, p. 30 of 36.

60. Ahn, COI Public Hearings, 2–3.

61. Ahn, COI Public Hearings, 5–6. NB: The transcript reads "tried to emulate the bunker buster" but the audio is "eliminate."

62. Yoon Yeo-sang, Jae-eun Lee, and Sun-young Han, *Political Prison Camps in North Korea Today* (Seoul: NKDB, July 20, 2011), 247.

63. The international organization is possibly Amnesty International. In 1993 they published a report that identified several political prison camps in North Korea, evidenced by testimony from former escaped prisoners. Amnesty International, *Amnesty International Annual Report 1993*, POL 10/0001/1993 (London: Amnesty International Publications, 1993), 180–81, https://www.amnesty.org/en/documents /pol10/0001/1993/en/.

64. Ahn, COI Public Hearings, 8.

65. Ahn, COI Public Hearings, 8.

66. Ahn, COI Public Hearings, 8.

67. Ahn, COI Public Hearings, 8.

68. Ahn, COI Public Hearings, 9.

69. Ahn, COI Public Hearings, 11.

70. Article 29 of the DPRK Criminal Law ("Death Penalty") states that public execution cannot be carried out on pregnant women.

71. Ahn, COI Public Hearings, 8–9.

72. Ahn, COI Public Hearings, 9.

73. Ahn, COI Public Hearings, 10.

74. Lee, *Reeducation Story*, 39.

75. Human Rights Council, "Report of the Detailed Findings," para. 700.

76. Under Secretary of State for Civilian Security, Democracy, and Human Rights, "Korea, Democratic People's Republic of: Tier 3," 228.

77. Under Secretary of State for Civilian Security, Democracy, and Human Rights, "Korea, Democratic People's Republic of: Tier 3," 228.

78. Stephan Haggard and Marcus Noland, "Repression and Punishment in North Korea: Survey Evidence of Prison Camp Experiences," *East-West Center Working Papers: Politics, Governance, and Security Series*, no. 20, October 2009, https://www .eastwestcenter.org/system/tdf/private/pswp020.pdf?file=1&type=node&id=32365.

79. Marcus Noland and Stephan M. Haggard, "Reform from Below: Behavioral and Institutional Change in North Korea," *Journal of Economic Behavior & Organization* 73, no. 2 (February 2010): 133–52, https://doi.org/10.1016/j.jebo.2009.09.009.

80. Lee, *Reeducation Story*, 127.
81. Lee, *Reeducation Story*, 53.
82. Lee, *Reeducation Story*, 41.
83. Lee, *Reeducation Story*, 75.
84. Lee, *Reeducation Story*, 148.
85. Ahn, COI Public Hearings, 11.
86. Ahn, COI Public Hearings, 11.
87. Ahn, COI Public Hearings, 11.
88. Ahn, COI Public Hearings, 11.
89. DPRK Criminal Law, Article 12, "Treatment of Offender Who Commits Socially Dangerous Acts in a State of Mental Disorder." Suicide as a crime does not appear in the DPRK Criminal Law.
90. Ahn, COI Public Hearings, 12–13.
91. Human Rights Council, "Report of the Detailed Findings," para. 694.
92. Human Rights Council, "Report of the Detailed Findings," para. 694. See also note 1013, which cites the DPRK Code of Criminal Procedure, Articles 160, 180, and 182. See also statements by the delegation of the DPRK before the Human Rights Committee, as reflected in the Summary Record of the 1946th Meeting, July 20, 2011, CCPR/C/SR.1946, para. 20.
93. Korean Bar Association, *2012 White Paper on Human Rights in North Korea* (Seoul: Korean Bar Association, 2013), 203.
94. Human Rights Council, "Report of the Detailed Findings," para. 699, note 1021.
95. Korean Bar Association, *2012 White Paper*, 202.
96. Human Rights Council, "Report of the Detailed Findings," para. 695.
97. Lee, *Reeducation Story*.
98. Human Rights Council, "Report of the Detailed Findings," para. 696.
99. Kim Young Soon, Commission of Inquiry on Human Rights in the Democratic People's Republic of Korea Public Hearings, Seoul, morning session, August 21, 2013, unofficial transcript, 9 of 63.
100. Kim Hyuk, Commission of Inquiry on Human Rights in the Democratic People's Republic of Korea Public Hearings, Seoul, morning session, August 22, 2013, unofficial transcript, 11–12 of 54. This quotation is slightly edited for readability; the original meaning is not altered.
101. Ahn, COI Public Hearings, 4–5.
102. Ahn, COI Public Hearings, 16.
103. DPRK Criminal Law, Article 30, "Life and Limited Term of Reform Through Labor."
104. Kim Eun Cheol, Commission of Inquiry on Human Rights in the Democratic People's Republic of Korea Public Hearings, Seoul, morning session, August 21, 2013, unofficial transcript, p. 28 of 63, https://www.ohchr.org/en/hrbodies/hrc/coidprk/pages/publichearings.aspx.
105. DPRK Criminal Law, Article 11, "Age of Criminal Responsibility": "Criminal responsibility shall be imposed only on offenders who are over 14 years of age when they commit an offence."
106. FIDH, *The Death Penalty in North Korea: In the Machinery of a Totalitarian State*, n.d., https://www.fidh.org/IMG/pdf/en-report-northkorea-high-resolution.pdf, 23.
107. D. S. Choi, "Economic Crisis and Shift in Political System in North Korea," *Collection of Treatises on Unification* 25 (2007): 101–23. Referenced in Woo-Teak Jeon, Shi-Eun Yu, Young-A Cho, and Jin-Sup Eom, "Traumatic Experiences and Mental Health of

North Korean Refugees in South Korea," *Psychiatry Investigation* 5, no. 4 (2008): n22, https://dx.doi.org/10.4306%2Fpi.2008.5.4.213.

108. Database Center for North Korean Human Rights (NKDB), *White Paper on North Korean Human Rights 2016* (Seoul: NKDB, October 10, 2016), 111–22, http://www .nkdb.org/en/library/Books_list.php.

109. Jeon et al., "Traumatic Experiences and Mental Health," 251.

110. International Federation for Human Rights (FIDH), *The Death Penalty in North Korea: In the Machinery of a Totalitarian State* (Paris: FIDH, May 2013), 4, https:// www.fidh.org/IMG/pdf/en-report-northkorea-high-resolution.pdf.

111. FIDH, *The Death Penalty in North Korea*, 13. The following sections related to the UN Special Rapporteur mandate on executions are also drawn from this report, 14–15.

112. Human Rights Committee, "Concluding Observations of the Human Rights Committee: Nigeria," CCPR/C/79/Add.65, July 24, 1996, para. 282. http://hrlibrary.umn .edu/hrcommittee/57nig4.htm.

113. Human Rights Council, "Report of the Special Rapporteur on Extrajudicial, Summary or Arbitrary Executions, Philip Alston," A/HRC/14/24, May 20, 2010, https:// www2.ohchr.org/english/bodies/hrcouncil/docs/14session/A.HRC.14.24.Add6.pdf, paras. 50, 51(a).

114. FIDH, *The Death Penalty in North Korea*, 14.

115. Human Rights Council, "Report of the Special Rapporteur on the Situation of Human Rights in the Democratic People's Republic of Korea, Marzuki Darusman," A/HRC/22/57, February 1, 2013, https://www.ohchr.org/Documents/HRBodies/HR Council/RegularSession/Session22/A.HRC.22.57_English.pdf, para. 6(g).

116. Jang, *Dear Leader*, 58.

117. Foucault, *Discipline and Punish*, 48–49.

118. Jang, *Dear Leader*, 70.

119. The acronym ZPU refers to antiaircraft machine guns that are mounted on a small vehicle, from the Russian зенитная пулемётная установка.

120. Greg Scarlatoiu and Joseph Bermudez Jr., "Unusual Activity at the Kanggon Military Training Area in North Korea: Evidence of Execution by Anti-Aircraft Machine Guns?" Committee for Human Rights in North Korea, *HRNK Insider*, April 29, 2015, http://www.hrnkinsider.org/2015/04/unusual-activity-at-kanggon-military.html. To avoid destroying objects behind the targets, the ZPUs could have used proximity ammunition, which would have exploded the moment they reached the target, not passing through it as other ammunition would.

121. Scarlatoiu and Bermudez, "Unusual Activity," 2.

122. It is certain that a person shot by several ZPU-4s would be pulverized to the point of having little left. The *New York Times* reported that Ri Ryong-ha and Jang Su-gil, deputies of Jang, were "torn apart by antiaircraft machine guns, according to South Korea's National Intelligence Service. The executioners then incinerated their bodies with flame throwers." Choe Sang-Hun, "In Hail of Bullets and Fire, North Korea Killed Official Who Wanted Reform," *New York Times*, March 12, 2016, https://www .nytimes.com/2016/03/13/world/asia/north-korea-executions-jang-song-thaek.html.

123. "Traitor Jang Song Thaek Executed," *KCNA*, December 13, 2013, http://www.kcna.co .jp/item/2013/201312/news13/20131213-05ee.html.

124. Ra Jong-yil's biography was reportedly titled *Son-in-Law of a Theocracy* at the time of the *New York Times* article. Ra is quoted in Choe Sang-Hun, "In Hail of Bullets and Fire." See also Ra Jong-yil, *Jang Song-Taek-ui gil* [The road of Jang Song Taek] (Seoul: Ama, 2016).

125. Alexandre Mansourov, "North Korea: The Dramatic Fall of Jang Song Thaek," *38 North*, December 9, 2013, http://38north.org/2013/12/amansourov120913; emphasis added.

126. "North Korea Executes Kim Jung-Un's Uncle," *Telegraph*, YouTube, December 13, 2013, https://www.youtube.com/watch?v=qrKIsPEjdw8.

127. Hwang Min, former agriculture minister, and Ri Young-Jin, a senior official in the education ministry, were executed by antiaircraft guns in August 2016. Justin McCurry, "North Korea Executes Officials with Anti-Aircraft Gun in New Purge—Report," *Guardian*, August 30, 2016, https://www.theguardian.com/world/2016/aug/30/north-korea-reportedly-executes-officials-anti-aircraft-gun-purge. Hyon Yong-Chol was executed for allegedly dozing off during a meeting. Justin McCurry and agencies in Seoul, "North Korea Defence Chief Reportedly Executed with Anti-Aircraft Gun," *Guardian*, May 13, 2016, https://www.theguardian.com/world/2015/may/13/north-korean-defence-minister-executed-by-anti-aircaft-gun-report.

128. "Senior North Korean Diplomat Says Kim Jong-Un's Executed Uncle Was Killed Because of 'Tremendous Crimes Against the Country' (but That His Other Relatives Are Probably Still Alive)," *Daily Mail*, January 30, 2014, http://www.dailymail.co.uk/news/article-2548843/Senior-North-Korean-diplomat-says-Kim-Jong-uns-executed-uncle-killed-tremendous-crimes-against-country-relatives-probably-alive-well.html.

129. Jang, *Dear Leader*, 175. Moon Sung-sul, general secretary of the Workers' Party Headquarters, then the third-most-senior person in the country after Kim Il Sung and Kim Jong Il, was accused of espionage by Jang Song-thaek. He was tortured and beaten to death. Several other high-ranking cadres were executed.

130. "'Jang Song-Thaek's Execution' Reported to the ICC by NKSC," *New Focus International*, February 14, 2017, https://policy.dfns.net/2017/02/14/jang-song-thaek-execution-reported-to-the-icc-by-nksc/.

131. Stephan Haggard, "Slave to the Blog: Trojan Horse Edition," *North Korea: Witness to Transformation* (blog), April 13, 2015, Peterson Institute for International Economics https://piie.com/blogs/north-korea-witness-transformation/slave-blog-trojan-horse-edition. See also "Exclusive: North Korea's State Security and People's Security Ministries Implement '9.8 Measures,'" *New Focus International*, April 12, 2015.

132. "Exclusive: North Korea's State Security."

133. "Exclusive: North Korea's State Security."

134. Haggard, "Slave to the Blog."

135. North Korean Human Rights Archives, *White Paper on North Korean Human Rights, 2008* (Seoul: NKDB, 2008), 116, http://www.nkdb.org/en/main.php.

8. Exporting Rights Violations

1. Kang Jin-kyu, "Pyongyang's Flying Doctors Pull in $15M a Year: NIS," *Korea Joongang Daily*, November 25, 2015. http://koreajoongangdaily.joins.com/news/article/Article.aspx?aid=3011968.

2. Yoon Yeo-sang and Lee Seung-Ju, "North Korea's Export Laborer's Status and Human Rights Situation" (Seoul: Database Center for North Korean Human Rights, January 2015), 25.

3. Alain Devalpo, "North Korean Slaves," *Le Monde Diplomatique*, April 8, 2006, https://mondediplo.com/2006/04/08koreanworkers; Andrew Higgins, "In Siberia's Last Gulag," *Independent*, June 26, 1994, http://www.independent.co.uk/arts-entertainment/in-siberias-last-gulag-conditions-in-north-koreas-russian-logging-camps

-originally-built-for-1425245.html; and U.S. Department of State, *Trafficking in Persons Report 2009* (Washington, D.C.: U.S. Department of State, 2009), http://www.state.gov/documents/organization/123357.pdf, 228.

4. Yoon Yeo-sang and Lee Seung-Ju, "Human Rights and North Korea's Overseas Laborers: Dilemmas and Policy Challenges" (Seoul: Database Center for North Korean Human Rights, May 8, 2015), 14.

5. Marte Boonen, Klara Boonstra, Remco Breuker, Christine Chung, Imke van Gardigen, Kim Kwang-cheol, Oh Kyuwook, and Anoma van der Veere, *North Korean Forced Labour in the EU, the Polish Case: How the Supply of a Captive DPRK Workforce Fits Our Demand for Cheap Labour*, Leiden Asia Centre, Findings from the Slaves to the System Project, July 6, 2016, http://leidenasiacentre.nl/wp-content/uploads /2017/06/rapport-slaves.pdf, 41.

6. Greg Scarlatoiu, "The Rime of the Juche Mariner: North Korean Sailors and Fishermen Dispatched Overseas Through Montevideo, Uruguay," *HRNK Insider*, June 22, 2016. http://www.hrnkinsider.org/2016/06/the-rime-of-juche-mariner-north-korean .html.

7. Scarlatoiu, "The Rime of the Juche Mariner."

8. Marcus Noland, "Rust Buckets of the World Unite! You Don't Want to Be a North Korean Sailor," Peterson Institute of International Economics, *North Korea: Witness to Transformation* (blog), June 20, 2016. https://piie.com/blogs/north-korea-witness -transformation/rust-buckets-world-unite. Noland makes a striking observation in this article about South Korea being the country with the best record on the Tokyo MOU scorecard. The summary data for 2013–2015 shows that the DPRK is the sixth-worst country, firmly on the Tokyo MOU blacklist with 669 inspections and 98 detentions. For context, consider that ships inspected and found to have as many as twenty deficiencies still do not reach the threshold for detention. Tokyo MOU Secretariat, *Annual Report on Port State Control in the Asia-Pacific Region*, 2015, http:// www.tokyo-mou.org/doc/ANN15.pdf. Leo Byrne states that, of 244 ship inspections in 2015, there were nearly 200 deficiencies. Leo Byrne, "Papers Please: N. Korean Ships Fare Poorly on Inspections," *NKNews.org*, November 5, 2015, https://www .nknews.org/2015/11/papers-please-n-korean-ships-fare-poorly-on-inspections/.

9. Between January 1, 2017, and February 1, 2018, thirty-two ships sailing under the DPRK flag were detained. For instance, *Sa Hyang San*, call sign HMYX7, had thirty-one deficiencies, the most egregious of which concerned radio communications, fire safety, and safety of navigation. See the Port State Control Committee PSC Database, http://www.tokyo-mou.org/inspections_detentions/psc_database.php.

10. Shin Chang-Hoon and Go Myung-Hyun, "Beyond the UN COI Report on Human Rights in North Korea," Asan Institute for Policy Studies, November 4, 2014. http:// en.asaninst.org/contents/asan-report-beyond-the-coi-dprk-human-rights-report/.

11. United Nations General Assembly, "Report of the Special Rapporteur on the Situation on Human Rights in the Democratic People's Republic of Korea," September 8, 2015, UN Doc. A/70/362, http://undocs.org/A/70/362.

12. Boonen et al., *North Korean Forced Labour in the EU*.

13. Scarlatoiu, "The Rime of the Juche Mariner."

14. Chan Hong Park, "North Korean Overseas Laborers in Russia" (Seoul: Database Center for North Korean Human Rights, 2016), 55–56.

15. Boonen et al., *North Korean Forced Labour in the EU*, 42. See also Vladimír Křivka, "Šít a žít ve jménu vůdce" *Týden.cz* (n.d.), http://t.tyden.cz/tema/sit-a-zit-ve-jmenu -vudce_2245.html.

16. Poppy McPherson, "The Curious Case of North Korea's Overseas Doctors," *Diplomat*, April 10, 2015, http://thediplomat.com/2015/04/the-curious-case-of-north-koreas -overseas-doctors/.

17. Joshua Lipes, "China Deports North Korean Workers Forced into Sex Trade," *Radio Free Asia*, June 12, 2014, http://www.rfa.org/english/news/korea/deportation-06122 014162010.html.

18. Chang Jae-soon, "Mass Defection of N.K. Restaurant Workers Shows China's Frustration with Pyongyang: U.S. Envoy," *Yonhap News Agency*, May 3, 2016, http://eng lish.yonhapnews.co.kr/search1/2603000000.html?cid=AEN20160503000500315.

19. Alexey Eremenko, "Решения, принятые на заседании Правительства 16 октября 2014 года" [Decisions taken at the government meeting on October 16, 2014], *Moscow Times*, October 17, 2014, http://government.ru/news/15262/.

20. Vera Vasilyeva, "Human Rights Activists: 'To prevent the extradition of refugees to North Korea,'" *Human Rights in Russia*, November 26, 2014; and Civic Assistance Committee, "Agreement with DPRK Is a Sham for Our Country," November 27, 2014, http://refugee.ru/news/soglashenie-s-kndr-pozor-dlya-nashej-strany/.

21. "Russia and the DPRK Will Sign an Agreement on the Prevention of Dangerous Military Activities," *Interfax*, In the World, June 23, 2015, http://www.interfax.ru/world /449075. All procedures about extradition between Russia and DPRK are fixed in the Treaty on Mutual Legal Assistance in Criminal Matters, December 16, 1957, http:// www.arbitr.ru/_upimg/5D060A8FD6C9D0615E98E2BEC8209D35_sssr_kndr_1957.pdf.

22. United Nations Security Council, Resolution 1718, Non-proliferation/Democratic People's Republic of Korea, S/RES/1718 (October 14, 2006), http://unscr.com/en/reso lutions/1718.

23. Czech Republic, "Part 1 of 111: Seventh Annual Anti-Trafficking Report—Czech Republic," February 28, 2007, WikiLeaks, Canonical ID: 07PRAGUE200_a, https:// wikileaks.org/plusd/cables/07PRAGUE200_a.html.

24. Czech Republic, "North Korean Laborers in the Czech Republic," November 9, 2006, WikiLeaks, Canonical ID: 06PRAGUE1400_a, https://wikileaks.org/plusd/cables /06PRAGUE1400_a.html.

25. For example, Labor Inspector General Rudolf Hahn noted that if workers were not permitted to watch TV or listen to the radio, such concerns were "outside of the legal mandate that labor inspectors have to investigate." Czech Republic, "North Korean Laborers in the Czech Republic."

26. Czech Republic, "North Korean Laborers in the Czech Republic."

27. Yoon and Lee, "Human Rights and North Korea's Overseas Laborers," 5.

28. Yoon and Lee, "Human Rights and North Korea's Overseas Laborers," 5.

29. Scarlatoiu, "The Rime of the Juche Mariner."

30. "Mongolia: Tier 2," in U.S. Department of State, *Trafficking in Persons Report 2016* (Washington, D.C.: Government Publishing Office, June 2016), 273, https://www .state.gov/documents/organization/258876.pdf.

31. U.S. Department of State, *Trafficking in Persons Report 2016*, 274.

32. U.S. Department of State, *Trafficking in Persons Report 2016*, 233.

33. U.S. Department of State, *Trafficking in Persons Report 2016*, 233.

34. "Korea, Democratic People's Republic of: Tier 3," in U.S. Department of State, *Trafficking in Persons Report 2016*, 228.

35. Yoon and Lee, "Human Rights and North Korea's Overseas Laborers," 16.

36. Yoon and Lee, "Human Rights and North Korea's Overseas Laborers," 14.

37. Boonen et al., *North Korean Forced Labour in the EU*, 57.

38. Boonen et al., *North Korean Forced Labour in the EU*, 16–17.
39. Boonen et al., *North Korean Forced Labour in the EU*, 44.
40. Boonen et al., *North Korean Forced Labour in the EU*, 44. See also Scarlatoiu, "The Rime of the Juche Mariner."
41. Boonen et al., *North Korean Forced Labour in the EU*, 43.
42. Boonen et al., *North Korean Forced Labour in the EU*, 47.
43. This is the description used by Thae Young Ho, the high-ranking diplomat who defected from North Korea's London embassy in 2016.
44. Boonen et al., *North Korean Forced Labour in the EU*, 18.
45. Boonen et al., *North Korean Forced Labour in the EU*, 49–50.
46. Boonen et al., *North Korean Forced Labour in the EU*, 45.
47. Yoon and Lee, "Human Rights and North Korea's Overseas Laborers," 20.
48. South Korea, "DPRK Defector Personifies Materialistic Motives for Defection," April 17, 2007, WikiLeaks, Canonical ID: 07SEOUL1108_a, https://wikileaks.org/plusd/cables/07SEOUL1108_a.html.
49. United Nations Security Council, Resolution 2321 (2016), S/RES/2321 (November 30, 2016), http://undocs.org/S/RES/2321(2016). This resolution came about as a result of, among other violated resolutions, DPRK's nuclear test on September 9, 2016, which was a violation of resolutions 1718 (2006), 1874 (2009), 2087 (2013), 2094 (2013), and 2270 (2016). Resolution 2321 does not restrict North Korean export of citizens for labor. It does, however, express "concern that DPRK nationals are sent to work in other states for the purpose of earning hard currency that the DPRK uses for its nuclear and ballistic missile programs" (para 34) and "concern that bulk cash may be used to evade measures imposed by the Security Council, and *calls upon* Member States to be alert to this risk" (para 35, emphasis in original). This resolution also recalls the Vienna Convention on Diplomatic Relations of 1961 restricting diplomatic agents from practice of professional or commercial activity that is personally profit generating (para 17). Subsequent resolution S/RES/2371 (2017) bans the hiring and paying of additional DPRK laborers used to generate foreign export earnings. See United Nations Security Council, Resolution 2371 (2017), S/RES/2371 (August 5, 2017), http://unscr.com/en/resolutions/2371.
50. UN Security Council, Resolution 2371.
51. Yoon and Lee, "Human Rights and North Korea's Overseas Laborers," 24.
52. Yoon and Lee, "Human Rights and North Korea's Overseas Laborers," 24, 26.
53. Yoon and Lee, "Human Rights and North Korea's Overseas Laborers," 29.
54. Yoon and Lee, "Human Rights and North Korea's Overseas Laborers," 28.
55. Boonen et al., *North Korean Forced Labour in the EU*, 44.
56. Boonen et al., *North Korean Forced Labour in the EU*, 46.
57. Boonen et al., *North Korean Forced Labour in the EU*, 21.
58. Pictures of the notebooks, along with translations, can be found in Scarlatoiu, "The Rime of the Juche Mariner."
59. Boonen et al., *North Korean Forced Labour in the EU*, 48.
60. Boonen et al., *North Korean Forced Labour in the EU*, 49.
61. Boonen et al., *North Korean Forced Labour in the EU*, 58.
62. However, see Remco Breuker and Imke van Gardingen, eds., *People for Profit: North Korean Forced Labour on a Global Scale* (Leiden: Leiden Asia Centre, Leiden, 2018), http://humantraffickingsearch.org/resource/people-for-profit/; and *Dollar Heroes* (video), *BBC*, October 18, 2018 https://www.bbc.co.uk/programmes/po6nwwfv.
63. Breuker and van Gardingen, *People for Profit*, 41.

64. This is according to Kim T'aesan, manager of 150 North Korean women sent to the Czech Republic from 2000–2002, in Breuker and van Gardingen, *People for Profit*, 42.

65. Boonen et al., *North Korean Forced Labour in the EU*, 43.

66. Quoted in Boonen et al., *North Korean Forced Labour in the EU*, 43.

67. Boonen et al., *North Korean Forced Labour in the EU*, 47.

68. Boonen et al., *North Korean Forced Labour in the EU*, 27.

69. Czech Republic, "North Korean Laborers in the Czech Republic," November 9, 2006, WikiLeaks, Canonical ID: 06PRAGUE1400_a, https://wikileaks.org/plusd/cables /06PRAGUE1400_a.html.

70. Czech Republic, "North Korean Laborers in the Czech Republic."

71. Paweł Strawiński, "Niewolnicy Kima znad Wisły," *Onet.biznes*, June 15, 2016, http:// biznes.onet.pl/praca/prawo-pracy/pracownicy-z-korei-polnicnej-w-polsce-niew olnicy-kima-znad-wisly/yb51zf. See also Boonen et al., 35.

72. Boonen et al., *North Korean Forced Labour in the EU*, 23.

73. Julian Ryall, "Polish Firms Employing North Korean 'Slave Labourers' Benefit from EU Aid," *Telegraph*, May 31, 2016, http://www.telegraph.co.uk/news/2016/05/31/polish -firms-employing-north-korean-slave-labourers-benefit-from/.

74. Boonen et al., *North Korean Forced Labour in the EU*, 23.

75. Teodora Gyupchanova, "Labor and Human Rights Conditions of North Korean Workers Dispatched Overseas: A Look at the DPRK Exploitative Practices in Russia, Poland, and Mongolia," *Cornell International Law Journal* 51 (2018): 190–91, 204.

76. Boonen et al., *North Korean Forced Labour in the EU*, 65.

77. Gyupchanova, "Labor and Human Rights Conditions," 205.

78. Emilie M. Hafner-Burton, "Sticks and Stones: Naming and Shaming the Human Rights Enforcement Problem," *International Organization* 62 (Fall 2008): 689–716.

79. Yoon and Lee, "Human Rights and North Korea's Overseas Laborers," 23. This was as recently as 2010.

80. Currently the only online reference available for this story is here: "Guinée équatoriale: Un goulag nord-coréen à Santiago," *Le Temps d'Algerie*, November 30 https:// www.djazairess.com/fr/letemps/180173. The link embedded in the article is broken, and the newspaper archive provides no story related to "goulag nord-coréen à Santiago."

81. "Santiago de Baney un municipio lleno de misterio y presos norte-coreanos," *Diario Rombe* [Guinea Ecuatorial], June 1, 2014, http://diariorombe.es/santiago-de-baney -un-municipio-lleno-de-misterio-y-presos-norte-coreanos/.

82. North Korea has worked closely with governments in the past training militia soldiers. For example, during the Dhofar Rebellion (Omani Civil War) the DPRK provided training in sabotage and assassination for at least twenty NDFLOAG operatives within North Korea. The NDFLOAG (National Democratic Front for the Liberation of Oman and the Arabian Gulf) was a branch of the People's Revolution Movement, a movement formed by breakaway groups of ten gulf members of the Arab Nationalist Movement. Groups trained by the communist bloc posed a serious internal threat to Oman. The group was trained in counterinsurgency against the Sultanate. North Korea also trained Dhofar Liberation Front guerrillas. John Graham Collection 3/8, Notes on Current State of Subversive Organisations in Northern Oman, October 31, 1971, Middle East Center, St. Anthony's College, Oxford University.

83. Albert Hong, "Equatorial Guinea and North Korean Prison Activities," *Radio Free Asia*, May 9, 2016, http://www.rfa.org/korean/in_focus/prisoner-05092016150403.html.

84. Hamish MacDonald, "Equatorial Guinea Calls for Suspension of North Korean Business Dealings: MFA," *NKNews.org*, January 25, 2018, https://www.nknews.org/2018 /01/equatorial-guinea-bringing-an-end-to-north-korean-business-dealings-mfa/.

85. Albert Hong, "Tanzania Shutters Two North Korean Medical Clinics," *Radio Free Asia*, April 19, 2016, http://www.rfa.org/english/news/korea/tanzania-shutters-two -04192016143509.html.

86. Kang, "Pyongyang's Flying Doctors."

87. Joshua Lipes, "Exporting Fakes? North Korean Clinics Hawk Questionable Medical Care to Tanzania," *Radio Free Asia*, special investigation, 2015, http://www.rfa.org/eng lish/news/special/nkinvestigation/tanzania.html.

88. Hong, "Tanzania Shutters Two North Korean Medical Clinics."

89. Mohammed Abubakar, "Attackers Kill 3 North Korean Doctors in Nigeria," *Associated Press*, February 11, 2013, https://www.yahoo.com/news/attackers-kill-3-north -korean-doctors-nigeria-133426830.html?ref=gs.

90. McPherson, "The Curious Case."

91. Kang Soo Jeong, "N. Korean Doctors in Libya Caught Smuggling Gold and Medical Supplies," *Daily NK*, June 12, 2015, http://www.dailynk.com/english/read.php?num =13270&cataId=nk00100.

92. Lipes, "Exporting Fakes?"

93. See especially the case of Gabriel Shayo, a nineteen-year-old former soccer prodigy featured in the May 2015 article in the Swahili-language daily *Nipashe*, cited in Lipes, "Exporting Fakes?"

94. Lipes, "Exporting Fakes?"

95. Lipes, "Exporting Fakes?"

96. McPherson, "The Curious Case." These two doctors may be the men who reportedly died of heart attacks in early 2016. Justin McCurry, "The Intriguing Deaths of Two North Korean Doctors in Cambodia," *Guardian*, January 5, 2016, https://www.theg uardian.com/world/2016/jan/05/two-north-korean-doctors-die-cambodia-intrigue.

97. Benjamin Young, "A Revolutionary State: North Korea's Support of Non-State Actors, Past Policies and Future Issues," Korea Economic Institute of America, *On Korea* Academic Paper Series, October 5, 2017, http://www.keia.org/sites/default/files/publi cations/kei_aps_young_final.pdf.

98. Sheena Chestnut, "Illicit Activity and Proliferation: North Korean Smuggling Networks," *International Security* 32, no. 1 (Summer 2007): 80–111; and Sheena Chestnut Greitens, *Illicit: North Korea's Evolving Operations to Earn Hard Currency* (Washington, D.C.: Committee for Human Rights in North Korea, 2014), https://www.hrnk .org/uploads/pdfs/SCG-FINAL-FINAL.pdf.

99. United Nations Security Council, "Report of the Panel of Experts Established Pursuant to Resolution 1874 (2009)," March 5, 2018, S/2018/171, https://www.securitycoun cilreport.org/atf/cf/%7B65BFCF9B-6D27-4E9C-8CD3-CF6E4FF96FF9%7D/s_2018 _171.pdf.

100. United Nations Security Council, "Report of the Panel of Experts."

9. From the Mouths of Foreign Nationals

1. Stephan Haggard, "Arturo Pierre Martinez," PIIE, *North Korea: Witness to Transformation* (blog), December 15, 2014, http://blogs.piie.com/nk/?p=13698; see also the "Previous Posts on the Detainees" section of this blog post.

2. Haggard, "Arturo Pierre Martinez." Haggard writes that Martinez's mother reported that Martinez had fled from a psychiatric hospital only a few days before arriving illegally in North Korea.

3. Arturo Pierre Martinez, quoted in "US Citizen Interviewed in DPRK," *KCNA*, December 14, 2014, http://www.kcna.co.jp/item/2014/201412/news14/20141214-20ee.html. For an analysis of several detainees' cases, see Haggard, "Arturo Pierre Martinez."

4. Kenneth Bae, *Not Forgotten: The True Story of My Imprisonment in North Korea*, with Mark Tabb (Nashville, Tenn.: W Publishing Group, 2016), 128.

5. Jane Perlez, "Merrill Newman, U.S. Veteran Who Was Held in North Korea, Tells His Story," *New York Times*, December 11, 2014. http://www.nytimes.com/2014/12/12/world/asia/merrill-newman-us-veteran-who-was-held-in-north-korea-tells-his-story.html.

6. Charles Robert Jenkins, *The Reluctant Communist: My Desertion, Court-Martial, and Forty-Year Imprisonment in North Korea*, with Jim Frederick (Berkeley: University of California Press, 2008), xxxii.

7. Jenkins, *The Reluctant Communist*, 20, 21.

8. Jenkins, *The Reluctant Communist*, 50.

9. Jenkins, *The Reluctant Communist*, xxi.

10. David W. Brown, "5 Americans Who Defected to North Korea," *Mental Floss*, April 15, 2013, http://mentalfloss.com/article/50095/5-americans-who-defected-north-korea.

11. Anna Fifield, "An American GI Defected to North Korea. Now His Sons Are Propaganda Stars," *Washington Post*, May 25, 2016, https://www.washingtonpost.com/news/worldviews/wp/2016/05/25/the-north-korean-born-sons-of-an-american-defector-speak-in-korean/.

12. Jenkins, *The Reluctant Communist*, x.

13. "The Motherland of 'Kim Il Sung Award' Winner," *Dong-A Ilbo*, October 1, 2014, http://english.donga.com/List/3/all/26/409193/1.

14. Fifield, "An American GI Defected to North Korea."

15. Bruce Cumings, *Korea's Place in the Sun: A Modern History* (New York: Norton, 2005), 404.

16. Benjamin Young, "'Our Common Struggle Against our Common Enemy': North Korea and the American Radical Left," North Korea International Documentation Project (NKIDP) E-Dossier #14, February 2013, https://www.wilsoncenter.org/sites/default/files/NKIDP_eDossier_14_North_Korea_and_the_American_Radical_Left.pdf.

17. Young, "'Our Common Struggle,'" 2.

18. Young, "'Our Common Struggle.'"

19. Benjamin Young, "A Revolutionary State: North Korea's Support of Non-State Actors, Past Policies and Future Issues," Korea Economic Institute of America, Academic Paper Series, October 5, 2017, http://www.keia.org/sites/default/files/publications/kei_aps_young_final.pdf; and Jed Lea-Henry, Korea Now Podcast, "#10—Ben Young—'Friends in Strange Places—Cold War Allies' (2018), https://player.fm/series/the-korea-now-podcast/the-korea-now-podcast-10-ben-young-friends-in-strange-places-cold-war-allies.

20. Charles K. Armstrong, "*Juche* and North Korea's Global Aspirations," NKIDP Working Paper No. 1 (Washington, D.C.: Woodrow Wilson Center, April 2009), https://www.wilsoncenter.org/sites/default/files/NKIDP_Working_Paper_1_Juche_and_North_Koreas_Global_Aspirations_web.pdf.

21. Young, "Our Common Struggle."

22. Adrian Buzo, *The Guerilla Dynasty: Politics and Leadership in North Korea* (Boulder, Colo.: Westview, 1999), 265.

23. "Ali Lameda: A Personal Account of the Experience of a Prisoner of Conscience in the Democratic People's Republic of Korea," Index Number ASA 24/002/1979 (Amnesty International, 1979), 11, https://www.amnesty.org/en/documents/ASA24/002/1979/en/.

24. "Ali Lameda," 12.
25. "Ali Lameda," 15.
26. "Ali Lameda," 15.
27. "Ali Lameda," 15.
28. "Ali Lameda," 16.
29. "Ali Lameda," 16.
30. Index on Censorship, "From a North Korean Jail," June 1979, pp. 46–49, extracted from "Ali Lameda," 49.
31. Venezuela, "Release of Venezuelan Imprisoned in North Korea," September 12, 1974, 19:52 (Thursday), WikiLeaks, Canonical ID: 1974CARACA09008_b, https://wikileaks.org/plusd/cables/1974CARACA09008_b.html.
32. Venezuela, "Venezuela Recognizes North Korea," October 29, 1974, 20:35 (Tuesday), WikiLeaks, Canonical ID: 1974CARACA10720_b, https://wikileaks.org/plusd/cables/1974CARACA10720_b.html.
33. Venezuela, "Venezuelan Imprisoned in North Korea," September 27, 1974, 15:26 (Friday), WikiLeaks, Canonical ID: 1974CARACA09600_b, https://wikileaks.org/plusd/cables/1974CARACA09600_b.html.
34. "Ali Lameda," appendix I: Jacques Sedillot, 22.
35. "Ali Lameda," 22.
36. "Ali Lameda," 23.
37. "Ali Lameda," 24.
38. *William Thomas Massie, et al. v. Government of the Democratic People's Republic of Korea,* Civil Action 06-00749 (HHK), https://cases.justia.com/federal/district-courts/district-of-columbia/dcdce/1:2006cv00749/120360/14/0.pdf.
39. Several legal cases have found the DPRK liable for terrorism related to the *Pueblo*. *Massie v. DPRK* (D.D.C. December 30, 2008). Mitchell Silberber & Knupp LLP is representing one hundred plaintiffs concerning the capture of the eighty-two men (*John Doe A-1 et al. v. Democratic People's Republic of Korea*). "Mitchell Silberberg & Knupp Represents Plaintiffs in Terrorism Case Against North Korea," press release, February 5, 2018, https://www.msk.com/newsroom-headlines-261.
40. James Griffiths, "How the Seizure of a US Spy Ship by North Korea Nearly Sparked Nuclear War," *CNN*, January 21, 2018, https://edition.cnn.com/2018/01/20/asia/north-korea-uss-pueblo-intl/index.html.
41. "316. Telegram from the Embassy in Korea to the Department of State," National Archives and Records Administration, RG 59, Central Files 1967–69, POL 33–6 KOR N–US. Secret; Immediate; Nodis; Cactus. *Foreign Relations of the United States, 1964–1968,* vol. 29, part 1, Korea, https://history.state.gov/historicaldocuments/frus1964-68v29p1/d316.
42. "Inquiry into the USS Pueblo and EC-121 Plane Incidents," report of the Special Subcommittee on the USS *Pueblo*, Committee on Armed Services House of Representatives, ninety-first Congress, first session, July 28, 1969, NSA 09-14-2012 FOIA Case #40722, p. 1629, https://www.nsa.gov/news-features/declassified-documents/uss-pueblo/assets/files/congressional-actions/Inquiry_into_the_USS_Pueblo.pdf.
43. "Press Conference: Reporters from Many Countries of the World Meet Crewmen of the U.S. Imperialist Armed Spy Ship 'Pueblo,'" Korean Central News Agency (Pyongyang: DPRK, 1969).
44. "Excerpts from Bucher's Final Confession," USSPueblo.org, USS Pueblo (AGER-2) Prisoners, http://www.usspueblo.org/Prisoners/Pete_Final_Confession.html. The "confession" makes for humorous reading.

Our first stop was Hawaii where I visited the kingpin of all provocateurs, including spies. None other than Fleet General Barney Google. He was all I had been told, sly, cunning, closed mouthed, bulbous nosed, smelling of musty top secrets and some foul smelling medicine that kept him going twenty hours a day in pursuit of the perfect spy mission. He talked haltingly with me but persuasively about our forthcoming mission. "By God, Bucher, I want you to get in there and be elusive, spy them out, spy out their water, look sharp for signs of electronic saline water traps. You will be going to spy out the DPRK. By the sainted General Bullmoose we must learn why they are so advanced in the art of people's defense."

45. Central Intelligence Agency, Intelligence Information Cable, September 12, 1969, "Reactions of Pueblo Crew Members at Press Conference on 12 September," https://nsarchive2.gwu.edu/NSAEBB/NSAEBB453/docs/doc22.pdf.

46. Mitchell Learner, Jong-Dae Shin, and Eliza Gheorghe, "New Romanian Evidence on the Blue House Raid and the USS Pueblo Incident," E-Dossier #5, Woodrow Wilson International Center for Scholars, North Korea International Documentation Project, March 2012, https://www.wilsoncenter.org/sites/default/files/NKIDP_eDossier_5_The_Blue_House_Raid_and_the_Pueblo_Incident.pdf.

47. Stephan Haggard, "Mike Chinoy on Merrill Newman," PIIE, *North Korea: Witness to Transformation* (blog), December 17, 2014, https://piie.com/blogs/north-korea-witness-transformation/mike-chinoy-merrill-newman.

48. Perlez, "Merrill Newman."

49. "Apology of U.S. Citizen for His Hostile Acts in DPRK," *KCNA*, November 30, 2013, http://www.kcna.co.jp/item/2013/201311/news30/20131130-11ee.html.

50. "Apology of U.S. Citizen." In Korean, the title is "Detained US Citizen's Written Apology," *KCNA*, http://www.kcna.co.jp/index-k.htm.

51. jonnydopplr, "Merrill Newman, American Vet Held in N. Korea, Reads 'Apology Letter,'" YouTube, November 29, 2013, https://www.youtube.com/watch?v=ShpW9qCuwGE.

52. Stephan Haggard, "Detainee Update: Otto Warmbier," PIIE, *North Korea: Witness to Transformation* (blog), March 8, 2016, https://piie.com/blogs/north-korea-witness-transformation/detainee-update-otto-warmbier.

53. Ben Tinker, "What an Autopsy May (or May Not) Have Revealed About Otto Warmbier's Death," *CNN*, June 22, 2017, https://edition.cnn.com/2017/06/21/health/otto-warmbier-autopsy/index.html.

54. Warmbier was Jewish. However, Jewish law does not have a strict prohibition against autopsy as long as it is carried about by a pathologist familiar with halacha. Rabbi Abner Weiss, "Autopsies and Jewish Law: An Orthodox Perspective," My Jewish Learning, n.d., https://www.myjewishlearning.com/article/autopsies-and-jewish-law/.

55. Hamilton County Coroner's Office, Death Record, Case No. CC17-02221, Otto Fredrick Warmbier, University of Cincinnati Medical Center, https://assets.documentcloud.org/documents/4063097/Warmbierpathologyreport.pdf.

56. "Otto Warmbier 'Was Brutalised by Pariah N Korea,' Parents Say," *BBC*, June 14, 2017, http://www.bbc.com/news/world-asia-40271202.

57. "Identifying Marks and Scars," in Hamilton County Coroner's Office, Death Record, Case No. CC17-02221, Otto Fredrick Warmbier.

58. "Report on Bill Clinton's Visit to DPRK Made Public," *KCNA*, August 5, 2009, http://www.kcna.co.jp/item/2009/200908/news05/20090805-01ee.html.

59. "Report on Bill Clinton's Visit."

60. Nate Thayer, "Matthew Miller's Excellent Adventure in North Korea," *NK News*, November 14, 2014, https://www.nknews.org/2014/11/matthew-millers-excellent-adventure-in-north-korea/.

61. Rick Gladstone, "Kenneth Bae, Longest-Held U.S. Prisoner of North Korea, Reveals Details of Ordeal," *New York Times*, May 2, 2016, https://www.nytimes.com/2016/05/03/world/asia/kenneth-bae-longest-held-us-prisoner-of-north-korea-reveals-details-of-ordeal.html.

62. "Korean-American Spy Arrestee Interviewed in Pyongyang," Korean Central Television, March 25, 2016; and "Korean-American Sentenced to 10 Years of Hard Labor," *KCNA*, April 29, 2016, http://www.kcna.co.jp/item/2016/201604/news29/20160429-23ee.html.

63. "Report on Bill Clinton's Visit."

64. Brad Williams and Erik Mobrand, "Explaining Divergent Responses to the North Korean Abductions Issue in Japan and South Korea," *Journal of Asian Studies* 69, no. 2 (May 2010): 507–36. See especially pages 519–21 for details on how the abduction issue was used to generate nationalist goals.

65. For more information on the history of the abduction issue, see Williams and Mobrand, "Explaining Divergent Responses."

66. For more details about each of the Japanese nationals abducted and the 1960s Red Army Faction of the "Yodogō" hijacking, see Patricia G. Steinhoff, "Kidnapped Japanese in North Korea: The New Left Connection," *Journal of Japanese Studies* 30, no. 1 (Winter 2004): 123–42.

67. Williams and Mobrand, "Explaining Divergent Responses," 509.

68. Robert Boynton, *The Invitation Only Zone: The True Story of North Korea's Abduction Project* (New York: Farrar, Straus and Giroux, 2016).

69. Eric Johnston, "The North Korea Abduction Issue and Its Effect on Japanese Domestic Politics," JPRI Working Paper No. 101, June 2004, http://www.jpri.org/publications/workingpapers/wp101.html.

70. Johnston, "The North Korea Abduction Issue."

71. Ushio Shioda, "Abe Shinzō no Jitsuryoku" [Abe Shinzō's power], *Ronza*, July 2006, 128.

72. David Cyranoski, "DNA Is Burning Issue as Japan and Korea Clash over Kidnaps," *Nature* 433, 445 (February 3, 2005), http://www.nature.com/nature/journal/v433/n7025/full/433445a.html.

73. Headquarters for the Abduction Issue, Government of Japan, "Abductions of Japanese Citizens by North Korea," n.d., http://www.rachi.go.jp/en/shisei/taisaku/.

74. A total of 3,835 South Koreans have been abducted to North Korea; of these, 3,319 have escaped or were released, and 516 remain in North Korea. For more details, see Go Myong-Hyun and Ben Forney, "Kidnapping as Foreign Policy: North Korea's History of State Sponsored Abductions," *Asan Institute for Policy Studies*, April 11, 2018.

75. Richard J. Samuels, "Kidnapping Politics in East Asia," *Journal of East Asian Studies* 10, no. 3 (2010): 363–95; Celeste Arrington, "The Abductions Issue in Japan and South Korea: Ten Years after Pyongyang's Admission," *International Journal of Korean Studies* 108 (Spring 2013): 108–39, http://www.icks.org/data/ijks/1482461222_add_file_6.pdf; Hyung Gu Lynn, "Vicarious Traumas: Television and Public Opinion in Japan's North Korea Policy," *Pacific Affairs* 79, no. 3 (2006): 483–508.

76. Mark Jenkins, "A Korean Celebrity Couple Kidnapped by Kim Jong Il: 'The Lovers and the Despot,'" *NPR*, September 22, 2016, https://www.npr.org/2016/09/22/494908429/a-korean-celebrity-couple-kidnapped-by-kim-jong-il-the-lovers-and-the-despot.

77. Arrington, "The Abductions Issue," 115.

78. Samuels, "Kidnapping Politics in East Asia," 12. The Korean War Abductee Family Union's approximation differs from that of Go and Forney, "Kidnapping as Foreign Policy."

79. "South Korea's Unforgotten," *Radio Free Asia*, July 22, 2009, http://www.refworld.org /docid/4a842f0ac.html.

80. Samuels, "Kidnapping Politics in East Asia," 12.

81. Adam Cathcart, Christopher Green, and Steven Denny, "How Authoritarian Regimes Maintain Domain Consensus: North Korea's Information Strategies in the Kim Jong Un Era," *Review of Korean Studies* 17, no. 2 (December 2014): 154.

82. Cathcart, Green, and Denny, "How Authoritarian Regimes," 154.

83. Greg Scarlatoiu, Jana Johnson, and Miran Song, "Re-Defection to North Korea: Exaggeration or the Beginning of a Trend?" *NK News*, January 24, 2013, https://www.nknews .org/2013/01/re-defection-to-north-korea-exaggeration-or-the-beginning-of-a-trend/.

84. Referenced in Justin McCurry, "The Defector Who Wants to Go Back to North Korea," *Guardian*, April 22, 2014, https://www.theguardian.com/world/2014/apr/22 /defector-wants-to-go-back-north-korea.

85. McCurry, "The Defector Who Wants to Go Back."

86. "Another DPRK Kidnapping or Another Re-Defection?" *New Focus International*, May 22, 2013.

87. Chico Harlan, "North Korean Defector Manipulated into Returning, Claim Friends in Seoul," *Guardian*, October 2, 2012, https://www.theguardian.com/world/2012/oct /02/north-korea-defector-family-blackmail.

88. McCurry, "The Defector Who Wants to Go Back."

89. Justin McCurry, "North Korea Claims Propaganda Win After Exiled Woman Returns," *Guardian*, June 29, 2012, https://www.theguardian.com/world/2012/jun/29 /north-korea-defector-returns-south; and horacelu, "Watch: North Korean Defector Returns to the DPRK and Tells of the Evil South," *Shanghaiist*, May 5, 2018, http:// shanghaiist.com/2012/06/29/watch_north_korean_defector_returns.php. The defector speaks about South Korea being the only country in the world that has websites dedicated to suicide. However, see Shuichi Katsuragawa, "Family and Group Suicide in Japan: Cultural Analysis," *World Cultural Psychology Research Review* 4, no. 1 (January 2009): 28–32, http://www.wcprr.org/wp-content/uploads/2013/09/2009.01 .2832.pdf. See also Shibuya T., "Shall We Die Tomorrow? A Shinjyu Story of Seven People with Internet" [Japanese] (Tokyo: Gentosha-bunko, 2007).

90. Ahlam Lee, *North Korean Defectors in a New and Competitive Society: Issues and Challenges in Resettlement, Adjustment and the Learning Process* (Lanham, Md.: Lexington, 2016).

91. Leslie Young, "Meet Ellie Cha, the North Korean Defector Working on Parliament Hill," *Global News*, November 5, 2017, https://globalnews.ca/news/3839951/north-korean -defector-ellie-cha/.

92. Scarlatoiu, Johnson, and Song, "Re-Defection to North Korea."

93. Scarlatoiu, Johnson, and Song, "Re-Defection to North Korea."

94. "Arrested Terrorist Interviewed," *KCNA*, July 19, 2012, http://www.kcna.co.jp/item /2012/201207/news19/20120719-08ee.html. A video of the conference can be seen at "Terrorista arrestado Jon Yong Chol se entrevista con medios de prensa," YouTube, https://www.youtube.com/watch?v=NpMemd1N9BM.

95. Images are from SinoNK.com via Uriminzokkiri. Adam Cathcart and Brian Gleason, "North Korean Claims of Terrorism from Inside Chinese Territory: An Annotated

Analysis," *SinoNK*, August 14, 2012, http://sinonk.com/2012/08/14/north-korean
-claims-of-terrorism-from-inside-chinese-territory-an-annotated-analysis/.

96. McCurry, "North Korea Claims Propaganda Win"; and horacelu, "Watch: North Korean Defector Returns."

97. "Pak Jong Suk's Family Enjoys Happy Life in Pyongyang," *KCNA*, July 12, 2012, http://www.kcna.co.jp/item/2012/201207/news10/20120710-22ee.html.

98. Kwon Hyo-jin and Kang Mi-jin, "North Korea Releases Video of Defectors Forced to Return," *Guardian*, December 11, 2014, https://www.theguardian.com/world/2014/dec/11/north-korea-releases-video-defectors-forced-return; and "Round-table Talks Held with Teenagers Who Came Back to DPRK," *KCNA*, June 20, 2013, http://www.kcna.co.jp/item/2013/201306/news20/20130620-20ee.html.

99. Paula Hancocks and KJ Kwon, "Defectors Agonizingly Close to Freedom Sent Back to North Korean Nightmare," *CNN*, October 4, 2013, http://edition.cnn.com/2013/09/30/world/asia/north-korea-laos-defectors-hancocks/.

100. "Round-Table Talks Held with Teenagers."

101. Choe Sang-hun, "North Korea Threatens South Korea over 13 Defectors," *New York Times*, April 12, 2016, http://www.nytimes.com/2016/04/13/world/asia/north-korea-threatens-south-korea-over-13-defectors.html.

102. Choe Sang-hun, "North Korea Proposes Having 13 Defectors to the South Meet with Relatives," *New York Times*, April 21, 2016, http://www.nytimes.com/2016/04/22/world/asia/north-korea-defectors-relatives.html; and Choe, "North Korea Threatens South."

103. Choe Sang-Hun, "North Korean Defector in South Seeks Vietnam's Help to Return Home," *New York Times*, March 7, 2016, http://www.nytimes.com/2016/03/08/world/asia/north-korean-defector-in-south-seeks-vietnams-help-to-return-home.html.

104. James Rothwell, "North Korean Defector Returns Home After 16 Years and Rips Up Her Memoirs on Camera," *Telegraph*, January 21, 2016, http://www.telegraph.co.uk/news/worldnews/asia/northkorea/12112246/North-Korean-defector-returns-home-after-16-years-and-rips-up-her-memoirs-on-camera.html.

105. StimmeKoreas, "North Korean Defectors Return After 4 Years in South Korea!" You-Tube video, 3:20, November 9, 2012, https://www.youtube.com/watch?v=x139pGGR_40.

106. Scarlatoiu, Johnson, and Song, "Re-Defection to North Korea."

107. Scarlatoiu, Johnson, and Song, "Re-Defection to North Korea."

108. Referencing Spinoza. Giorgio Agamben, *Means Without End: Notes on Politics*, trans. Vincenzo Binetti and Cesare Casarino (Minneapolis: University of Minnesota Press, 2000), 128.

109. Elaine Scarry, *The Body in Pain: The Making and Unmaking of the World* (New York: Oxford University Press, 1985), 14.

110. Scarry, *The Body in Pain*, 182.

111. Scarry, *The Body in Pain*, 14.

10. The State News Strikes Back

1. Thomas Risse, Stephen C. Ropp, and Kathryn Sikkink, eds., *The Power of Human Rights: International Norms and Domestic Change* (Cambridge: Cambridge University Press, 1999), 23.

2. On September 21, 2015, at the 16th Meeting 30th Regular Session of the Human Rights Council, Kim Yong-Ho, representative of the DPRK, addressed the panel stating that

the United Nations should follow a proverb common in North Korea: "mind your own business." Felixius Dzerzhinsky, "North Korea on Human Rights, UN 150921," YouTube video, 4:47, September 21, 2015, https://www.youtube.com/watch?v=WpbX vlkwcnk.

3. The *Rodong Shinmun* is accessible at http://www.rodong.rep.kp/ko/.

4. KCNA Watch, "Open Questionnaire of DPRK Institute of International Studies," *Rodong Sinmun*, August 12, 2016, https://kcnawatch.co/newstream/1530454241 -789560501/open-questionnaire-of-dprk-institute-of-international-studies/. North Korea does not reference any documentation. However, further reading on the topic of the United States "humanitarian" invasion of Iraq can be found here: Human Rights Watch, "War in Iraq: Not a Humanitarian Intervention," January 25, 2004, https://www.hrw.org/news/2004/01/25/war-iraq-not-humanitarian-intervention.

5. "Korean Central News Agency Hits Commission of Inquiry Report," *KCNA*, February 28, 2014.

6. "News Analysis on Poor Human Rights Records in US," *KCNA*, April 30, 2014, http:// www.kcna.co.jp/item/2014/201404/news30/2014-0430-23ee.html.

7. Matt Ford, "Is North Korea Right About U.S. Human-Rights Abuses?" *Atlantic*, May 4, 2014, https://www.theatlantic.com/international/archive/2014/05/is-north -korea-right-about-us-human-rights-abuses/361589/.

8. "White Paper on Human Rights Situation in U.S. in 2016," *KCNA*, March 15, 2017, http://www.kcna.co.jp/item/2017/201703/news15/20170315-21ee.html.

9. "Monstrous Crimes Committed by U.S. Against Koreans Blasted," *KCNA*, May 5, 2014, http://www.kcna.co.jp/item/2014/201405/news05/20140505-17ee.html.

10. "US Soldier Jailed for Rape in South Korea," *BBC*, November 1, 2011, http://www.bbc .com/news/world-asia-pacific-15533011.

11. "West's Anti-DPRK Human Rights Abuses Rejected by Bulgarian Paper," *KCNA*, July 20, 2014, http://www.kcna.co.jp/item/2014/201407/news20/20140720-05ee.html.

12. "KCNA Commentary Discloses Absurdity of U.S. 'Human Rights' Racket Against DPRK," *KCNA*, March 11, 2015, http://www.kcna.co.jp/item/2015/201503/news11 /20150311-17ee.html; emphasis added.

13. The visit took place in 2003. See a copy of the article here: Christopher Black, "North Korea: The Grand Deception Revealed," *WikiSpooks*, last modified March 10, 2017, https://wikispooks.com/wiki/Document:North_Korea_-_The_Grand_Deception _Revealed.

14. Christopher Black, "North Korea, the UN, and War Propaganda," *New Eastern Outlook*, November 30, 2014, https://journal-neo.org/2014/11/30/north-korea-the-un-and -war-propaganda-2/. The full text is republished in "Article Posted on Online Magazine of Russia," *KCNA*, December 5, 2014, http://www.kcna.co.jp/item/2014/201412 /news05/20141205-24ee.html.

15. Joshua Stanton, "Guild of Liars, Part 2: North Korean Refugees Expose the Lies of the National Lawyers' Guild," *One Free Korea* (blog), September 30, 2006, https:// freekorea.us/2006/09/30/guild-of-liars-part-2-north-korean-refugees-expose-the -lies-of-the-national-lawyers-guild/.

16. Sarah Grant, "Watch John Oliver Break Down Trump's Three Dangerous Manipulation Tactics," *Rolling Stone*, November 13, 2017, https://www.rollingstone.com/tv/news /john-oliver-breaks-down-trumps-dangerous-speaking-tactics-w511598.

17. Elisabeth R. Anker, *Orgies of Feeling: Melodrama and the Politics of Freedom* (Durham, N.C.: Duke University Press, 2014).

18. This is inspired by the work of Sara Ahmed, *The Cultural Politics of Emotion* (Edinburgh: Edinburgh University Press, 2004).

19. "Kim Jung Un Inspects Dental Hygiene Supplies Factory," *Pyongyang Times*, November 25, 2017.

20. After the work of Sara Ahmed, "The Politics of Fear in the Making of Worlds," *Qualitative Studies in Education* 16, no. 3 (May–June 2003): 377–98.

21. Statement by H. E. Mr. Ri su Young, Minister for Foreign Affairs of the Democratic People's Republic of Korea at the General Debate of the 70th Session of the UN General Assembly, New York, October 1, 2015, p. 5: "[The DPRK] establishes the equation that the UN equals the United States as the US troops are just the 'UN forces' on the Korean peninsula."

22. "U.S. 'Human Rights' Racket Against DPRK's Sovereignty Is Doomed to Failure: KCNA Report," *KCNA*, March 26, 2014, http://www.kcna.co.jp/item/2014/201403 /news26/20140326-17ee.html.

23. Neta C. Crawford, "The Passion of World Politics: Propositions on Emotion and Emotional Relationships," *International Security* 24, no. 4 (Spring 2000): 132.

24. Rose McDermott, "Experimenting with Emotions," in *Emotions, Politics and War*, ed. Linda Åhäll and Thomas Gregory (London: Routledge, 2015), 100.

25. Jennifer S. Lerner and Dacher Keltner, "Fear, Anger, and Risk," *Journal of Personality and Social Psychology* 81 no. 1 (2001): 146, http://dx.doi.org/10.1037//O022-3514.81.1 .146; and Jennifer S. Lerner, Roxana M. Gonzales, Deborah A. Small, and Baruch Fischhoff, "Effects of Fear and Anger on Perceived Risks of Terrorism: A National Field Experiment," *Psychological Science* 14 no. 2 (2003): 144–50, http://dx.doi.org/10 .1111/1467-9280.01433.

26. Anker, *Orgies of Feeling*, 2.

11. North Korea's Rhetoric of Denial at the United Nations

1. Ja Song Nam, "Letter Dated 15 March 2014 from the Permanent Representative of the Democratic People's Republic of Korea to the United Nations Addressed to the President of the Security Council," March 17, 2014, S/2014/194.

2. United Nations, "No. 14668 Multilateral International Covenant on Civil and Political Rights, Adopted by the General Assembly of the United Nations on 19 December 1966," *United Nations Treaty Series*, vol. 999, no. I-14668, https://treaties.un.org /doc/publication/unts/volume%20999/volume-999-i-14668-english.pdf.

3. Jiyoung Song, *Human Rights Discourse in North Korea: Post-Colonial, Marxist and Confucian Perspectives* (New York: Routledge, 2014). See also Robert Weatherly and Song Jiyoung, "The Evolution of Human Rights Thinking in North Korea," *Journal of Communist Studies and Transition Politics* 24, no. 2 (June 2008): 272–96, https://doi .org/10.1080/13523270802003111.

4. Weatherly and Song, "The Evolution of Human Rights," 273.

5. Weatherly and Song, "The Evolution of Human Rights," 290.

6. Weatherly and Song, "The Evolution of Human Rights," 279.

7. Kim Jong Il, "Socialism Is Science," *Rodong Shinmun*, November 4, 1994, quoted in Weatherly and Song, "The Evolution of Human Rights," 280.

8. Weatherly and Song, "The Evolution of Human Rights," 283.

9. Weatherly and Song, "The Evolution of Human Rights," 283.

10. Quoted in Weatherly and Song, "The Evolution of Human Rights," 286.

11. Thomas Risse, Stephen C. Ropp, and Katheryn Sikkink, eds., *The Power of Human Rights: International Norms and Domestic Change* (Cambridge: Cambridge University Press, 2007); and Thomas Risse, Stephen C. Ropp, and Katheryn Sikkink, eds., *The Persistent Power of Human Rights: From Commitment to Compliance* (Cambridge: Cambridge University Press, 2013).

12. "ID Commission of Inquiry on DPRK—14th Meeting 24th Regular Session of Human Rights Council," September 17, 2013, UN Web TV. Kirby speaks and addresses the absence of the DPRK in research at 1:26:15 in the video. http://webtv.un.org/watch/id -commission-of-inquiry-on-dprk-14th-meeting-24th-regular-session-of-human -rights-council/2677214609001.

13. Kim In Ryong, "Kim In Ryong (DPRK) on Human Rights—Press Conference (13 December 2016)," UN Web TV video, 25:49, http://webtv.un.org/watch/kim-in-ryong -dprk-on-human-rights-press-conference-13-december-2016/5246257589001/?term =&lan=original. Kim Yong Ho, as representative of the DPRK, speaks at 00:17:39.

14. "ID Commission of Inquiry on DPRK—31st Meeting 25th Regular Session of Human Rights Council," UN Web TV, video, 02:45:24, March 17, 2014, http://webtv.un.org /watch/id-commission-of-inquiry-on-dprk-31st-meeting-25th-regular-session-of-human -rights-council/3350537719001/?term=&page=2. So Se Pyong speaks at 00:16:46—all quotes are taken from this portion of the DPRK representative's response.

15. Michael Kirby and Kim Song, "Epic Exchange Between Justice Kirby and DPRK Councillor Kim Song," Michaelkirby.com, February 2016, http://www.michaelkirby.com.au /content/epic-exchange-between-justice-kirby-and-dprk-councillor-kim-song-1.

16. An Myong Hun, "North Korea News Conference at United Nations," YouTube video, 31:46. January 15, 2015, https://www.youtube.com/watch?v=evpTxoJvzYM.

17. Jang Jin-Sung, "The Market Shall Set North Korea Free," *New York Times*, April 27, 2013, http://www.nytimes.com/2013/04/27/opinion/global/The-Market-Shall-Set-North -Korea-Free.html.

18. Quoted in Choi Sun-young, Yang Jina, Song Hanna, and Lee Na-kyeong, *United Nations Universal Periodic Review and the DPRK: Monitoring of North Korea's Implementation of Its Recommendations* (Seoul: NKDB, 2017), 8.

19. The event was held in New York on April 30, 2015, in a conference room as a member-state-run event, not a UN-organized event. Martyn Williams, "More on UN Meeting, Silencing of DPRK Microphone," *North Korea Tech*, May 2, 2015, http://www.north koreatech.org/2015/05/02/more-on-un-meeting-silencing-of-dprk-microphone/.

20. Joseph Kim's book about his experience came out the same year as this event. Joseph Kim, *Under the Same Sky: From Starvation in North Korea to Salvation in America*, with Stephan Talty (New York: Houghton Mifflin Harcourt, 2015).

21. Samantha Power, "Remarks at a Panel Discussion on Human Rights Abuses in North Korea, 'Victims' Voices: A Conversation on North Korean Human Rights,'"April 30, 2015, http://webtv.un.org/watch/victims'-voices-a-conversation-on-north-korean-human -rights/4207187028001.

22. Y. Kim, "North Korea on Human Rights, UN 150921," YouTube video, 4:47, September 21, 2015, https://www.youtube.com/watch?v=WpbXvlkwcnk.

23. Every year the General Assembly elects five nonpermanent members for the two-year term to sit on the Security Council. The seats are distributed on a regional basis and elected according to regulations of the General Assembly. The region seats are distributed as follows: five for African and Asian states, one for Eastern European states, two for the Latin American and Caribbean states, and two for Western European

and other states. See United Nations, "General Assembly Resolution 1991 (XVIII)," December 17, 1963, http://www.un.org/en/ga/search/view_doc.asp?symbol=A/RES /1991(XVIII).

24. Felixius Dzerzhinsky, "North Korea on Human Rights, UN 150921," YouTube, September 21, 2015, https://www.youtube.com/watch?v=WpbXvlkwcnk.

25. Dzerzhinsky, "North Korea on Human Rights, UN 150921."

26. Dzerzhinsky, "North Korea on Human Rights, UN 150921."

27. Kim In Ryong, "Kim In Ryong (DPRK) Press Conference (15 November 2016)," UN Web TV, 23:59, http://webtv.un.org/watch/kim-in-ryong-dprk-press-conference-15 -november-2016/5211267770001.

28. Jonathan T. Chow, "North Korea's Participation in the Universal Periodic Review of Human Rights," *Australian Journal of International Affairs* 71, no. 2 (2017): 12.

29. Kim, "Kim In Ryong (DPRK) Press Conference (15 November 2016)."

30. Kim, "Kim In Ryong (DPRK) on Human Rights—Press Conference (13 December 2016)".

31. United Nations Security Council, "The Situation in the Democratic People's Republic of Korea," S/PV.7830, December 9, 2016, http://www.securitycouncilreport.org/atf/cf /%7B65BFCF9B-6D27-4E9C-8CD3-CF6E4FF96FF9%7D/s_pv_7830.pdf.

32. "DPRK Foreign Ministry Spokesman Hits Out at U.S.-Sponsored Anti-DPRK 'Human Rights' Farce at UNSC," *KCNA*, December 11, 2016, http://www.kcna.co.jp /item/2016/201612/news11/20161211-14ee.html.

33. "DPRK Association for Human Rights Studies Forwards Open Questionnaire to UN," *KCNA*, November 23, 2016, http://www.kcna.co.jp/item/2016/201611/news23 /20161123-29ee.html.

34. "Association for Human Rights Studies: UN's 'North Korea Human Rights Report' an Operation of National Terror," *KCNA*, November 23, 2016, http://www.kcna.co.jp /index-k.htm.

35. Shin Chang-Hoon and Myong-Hyun Go, "Beyond the UN COMMISSION Report on Human Rights in North Korea," Asan Institute for Policy Studies, November 3, 2014, http://en.asaninst.org/contents/asan-report-beyond-the-coi-dprk-human-rights -report/; Marte Boonen, Klara Boonstra, Remco Breuker, Christine Chung, Imke van Gardigen, Kim Kwang-cheol, Oh Kyuwook, and Anoma van der Veere, *North Korean Forced Labour in the EU, the Polish Case: How the Supply of a Captive DPRK Workforce Fits Our Demand for Cheap Labour* (Leiden Asia Centre, Findings from the Slaves to the System Project, July 6, 2016), http://leidenasiacentre.nl/wp-content/uploads /2017/06/rapport-slaves.pdf; Chan Hong Park, "Conditions of Labor and Human Rights: North Korean Overseas Laborers in Russia" (Seoul: Database Center for North Korean Human Rights, 2016); and Yoon Yeo-sang and Lee Seung-Ju, "Human Rights and North Korea's Overseas Laborers: Dilemmas and Policy Challenges" (Seoul: Database Center for North Korean Human Rights, May 8, 2015).

36. "Park Geun Hye Censured as Root Cause of Disasters of Nation," *KCNA*, May 2, 2014, http://www.kcna.co.jp/item/2014/201405/news02/20140502-22ee.html.

37. "KCNA Commentary Slams Artifice by Political Swindlers," *KCNA*, April 22, 2014, http://www.kcna.co.jp/item/2014/201404/news22/20140422-02ee.html.

38. "KCNA Commentary Slams Artifice."

39. Kim, "Kim In Ryong (DPRK) on Human Rights—Press Conference (13 December 2016)."

40. Martyn Williams, "DPRK UN Ambassador Takes Questions, Gives Advice," *North Korea Tech*, January 26, 2014, http://www.northkoreatech.org/2014/01/26/dprk-un -ambassador-takes-questions-gives-advice/.

41. Examples of the leaflets that are sent can be found here: "How Propaganda Flyers Try to Win Over N. Koreans," *Chosun Ilbo*, October 16, 2014, http://english.chosun.com /site/data/html_dir/2014/10/16/2014101600781.html. See also Kwon Hyo-jin, "North Korea Calls Anti-Government Leaflet Drop 'Grave Provocation,'" *Guardian*, September 25, 2014, http://www.theguardian.com/world/2014/sep/25/north-korea-condemns -anti-government-leaflets.

42. Ri Su Yong, "North Korean Foreign Minister at UN General Assembly (English)," YouTube video. 17:02, at 13:32, https://www.youtube.com/watch?v=Ys56r7IleWY.

43. United Nations General Assembly, "Report of the DPRK Association for Human Rights Studies Submitted to the United Nations General Assembly Security Council." September 15, 2014, A/69/383–S/2014/668. https://undocs.org/A/69/383.

44. "Report of the DPRK Association for Human Rights Studies," 23, 24; emphasis added.

45. See pages 59, 60, 61, 63, 85, 86, 102, and 104 of "Report of the DPRK Association for Human Rights Studies."

46. "Report of the DPRK Association for Human Rights Studies," 85; emphasis added.

47. "Report of the DPRK Association for Human Rights Studies," 86; emphasis added.

48. "Report of the DPRK Association for Human Rights Studies," 102; emphasis added.

49. "Report of the DPRK Association for Human Rights Studies," 104; emphasis added.

50. "World's Poorest Human Rights Record in S. Korea Disclosed," *KCNA*, April 29, 2014, http://www.kcna.co.jp/item/2014/201404/news29/2014-0429-12ee.html.

51. "China's State Council on Human Rights Situation in U.S.," *KCNA*, March 13, 2014, http://www.kcna.co.jp/item/2014/201403/news13/20140313-14ee.html.

52. "KCNA Terms U.S. Worst Human Rights Abuser," *KCNA*, March 7, 2014, http://www .kcna.co.jp/item/2014/201403/news07/20140307-16ee.html.

53. "Report of the DPRK Association for Human Rights Studies," 59–60.

54. "Report of the DPRK Association for Human Rights Studies," 61.

55. "Report of the DPRK Association for Human Rights Studies," 63.

56. "KCNA Terms U.S. Worst Human Rights Abuser."

57. "U.S. 'Human Rights' Racket Against DPRK's Sovereignty Is Doomed to Failure: KCNA Report," *KCNA*, March 26, 2014, http://www.kcna.co.jp/item/2014/201403 /news26/20140326-17ee.html.

58. Jang Il Hun's name has also been romanized as Jung Il Hoon. Video of this "conversation" makes for fascinating watching. Jang Il Hun, "Ambassador Jang Il-Hun on Human Rights in North Korea," *Council on Foreign Relations*, October 20, 2014, http:// www.cfr.org/north-korea/ambassador-jang-il-hun-human-rights-north-korea/p35758; video available at YouTube, https://www.youtube.com/watch?v=iBKXTDmhFGA (minutes refer to the YouTube video).

59. Jang, "Ambassador Jang Il-Hun on Human Rights."

60. Jang, "Ambassador Jang Il-Hun on Human Rights," video at 40:52; emphasis added.

61. On September 2014, Minjok Tongshin—a pro-DPRK group in the United States— also referenced a senior official identifying reform camps.

62. Sandra Fahy, *Marching Through Suffering: Loss and Survival in North Korea* (New York: Columbia University Press, 2015), 86–87.

63. The performative aspect of speaking is captured most clearly in the work of John L. Austin, *How to Do Things with Words* (Oxford: Clarendon Press, 1962).

64. Jang, "Ambassador Jang Il-Hun on Human Rights," video, 42:58; emphasis added.

65. Martyn Williams, "Victims' Voices: A Conversation on North Korean Human Rights," YouTube video, 1:32:19, May 1, 2015, https://www.youtube.com/watch?v=2V-TP BXB-F8.

66. Fahy, *Marching Through Suffering.*
67. Power, "Remarks at a Panel Discussion."
68. Ri Song Chol, "Statement Made by Mr. Ri Song Chol, Counsellor of the Permanent Mission of the Democratic People's Republic of Korea (DPRK) to the United Nations at the 'Panel Discussion' Organized by the US and South Korea on 30 April 2015," Press Release, No. 11/04/15, April 30, 2015, https://www.scribd.com/doc/263669008 /North-Korea-Speech-at-UN-Event-US-Said-Turn-Off-the-Mic-So-Here.
69. Ri Song Chol, "Statement Made by Mr. Ri Song Chol."
70. In the report his name is spelled Sin Tong Hyok.
71. Cara Ana, "North Korea to UN: Human Rights Resolution Is Illegal," *Daily Mail*, February 4, 2015, https://www.dailymail.co.uk/wires/ap/article-2940025/North-Korea -UN-Human-rights-resolution-illegal.html.
72. Yi Han-yong, *Kim Jong-il's Royal Family* (Seoul: Sidae Jeongsin, 2005).

12. Broadcasting Denial

1. Multiple media outlets reported on this letter, including the DPRK. See, for example, KH Digital 2, "N. Korea Sends Letter to UN Chief Demanding Repatriation of Women 'Abducted' by S. Korea," *Korea Herald*, January 31, 2017, http://www.korea herald.com/view.php?ud=20170131000914. To my knowledge it does not appear in the UN document record, suggesting that no such letter was ever sent.
2. "Letter of the 12 Allured and Kidnapped Girls' Families to the UN Secretary-General, President of the UN Human Rights Council and High Commissioner for Human Rights," tv.uriminzokkiri, March 9, 2017, http://www.uriminzokkiri.com/itv/index .php?ppt=lie_human&no=33279.
3. Andrei Lankov, *Crisis in North Korea: The Failure of De-Stalinization* (Honolulu: University of Hawai`i Press, 2005), 192–94.
4. "Terrible Human Wreck Who Steals a Person's Name and Career," tv.uriminzokkiri, September 11, 2015, http://www.uriminzokkiri.com/itv/index.php?ppt=lie_human&no =25376.
5. "Human Rights—Lies and Truth," tv.uriminzokkiri, http://www.uriminzokkiri.com /itv/index.php?ppt=lie_human.
6. Dozens of videos were up by the end of 2013. See Adam Cathcart, Christopher Green, and Steven Denny, "How Authoritarian Regimes Maintain Domain Consensus: North Korea's Information Strategies in the Kim Jong Un Era," *Review of Korean Studies* 17, no. 2 (December 2014): 145–78.
7. Hannah Arendt, "Truth and Politics," *New Yorker*, February 25, 1967, https://www .newyorker.com/magazine/1967/02/25/truth-and-politics; my emphasis.
8. Arendt, "Truth and Politics."
9. The testimony of Shin Dong Hyuk on political prison camps is at 00:12:36–02:11:30. Shin Dong Hyuk, "Commission of Inquiry on Human Rights in the DPRK—Seoul Public Hearing Day 1 (pm) 20 August." UN Web TV, 3:47:02, August 20, 2013, http:// webtv.un.org/search/commission-of-inquiry-on-human-rights-in-the-dprk-seoul -public-hearing-day-1-pm-20-august/2668611257001?term=%EA%B3%B5%EC%B2% AD%ED%9A%8C.
10. The North Korean documentary romanizes Shin Dong Hyuk's name as Sin Tong Hyok. "Who Is Sin Tong Hyok?" tv.uriminzokkiri.com, part 1, March 4, 2017, http:// www.uriminzokkiri.com/itv/index.php?ppt=lie_human&no=33226; and part 2,

March 5, 2017, http://www.uriminzokkiri.com/itv/index.php?ppt=lie_human&no=33227.

11. Allan Sekula, "On the Invention of Photographic Meaning," in *Thinking Photography*, ed. Victor Burgin (London: Palgrave Macmillan, 1982), 84–109.

12. Sekula, "On the Invention of Photographic Meaning," 87.

13. Marcus Banks, *Visual Methods in Social Research* (London: Sage, 2001), 65.

14. "Who Is Sin Tong Hyok?" tv.uriminzokkiri.com, part 1.

15. Maryanne Vollers, "The Woman Who Faces the Wrath of North Korea," *Guardian*, March 15, 2015, http://www.theguardian.com/world/2015/mar/15/park-yeon-mi-north-korea-defector. Yeonmi Park's book is titled *In Order to Live: A North Korean Girl's Journey to Freedom* (New York: Penguin, 2015).

16. Judith Herman, *Trauma and Recovery: The Aftermath of Violence—from Domestic Abuse to Political Terror* (New York: Basic Books, 1997).

17. This observation is inspired by the work of Eleni Coundouriotis, "'You only have your word': Rape and Testimony," *Human Rights Quarterly* 35, no. 2 (May 2013): 365–85.

18. See "Who Is Sin Tong Hyok?" tv.uriminzokkiri.com, part 1, March 4, 2017, http://www.uriminzokkiri.com/itv/index.php?ppt=lie_human&no=33226; and part 2, March 5, 2017, http://www.uriminzokkiri.com/itv/index.php?ppt=lie_human&no=33227. A third video was uploaded February 2, 2015, by stimmekoreas, "North Korean Eye Witness on Shin Dong Hyuk & 'Escape from Camp 14,'" https://www.youtube.com/watch?v=J6whpUIFtSY.

19. See 5:56 of the YouTube video posted by *Cihiribey Japene* on March 23, 2016: "uriminjokkiri vs t'albukcha pakyŏnmi ch'uaksangŭl tashigŭm p'ahech'yŏ ponda" ["Our people vs. defector Yeonmi Park, digging up the beast again"], https://www.youtube.com/watch?v=__sIBm8eH3A; and John Power, "North Korean Defectors and Their Skeptics," *Diplomat*, October 29, 2014, https://thediplomat.com/2014/10/north-korea-defectors-and-their-skeptics/.

20. "Our people vs. defector Yeonmi Park"; and Power, "North Korean Defectors."

21. Mary Ann Jolley, "The Strange Tale of Yeonmi Park," *Diplomat*, December 20, 2014, https://thediplomat.com/2014/12/the-strange-tale-of-yeonmi-park/.

22. Chang Hao Jin, "We Reveal, Once Again, the True Identity of the Human Trash, Sin Tong Hyok," YouTube, March 11, 2015, https://www.youtube.com/watch?v=xbd4TqipHYk.

23. For example,

> In April 2012, North Korean agent An Hak-young was sentenced to four years imprisonment by a South Korean court for plotting to assassinate outspoken anti-Pyongyang activist Park Sang-hak with a poison-tipped needle. In August 2011, a South Korean evangelical Christian pastor, Patrick Kim died after collapsing in the Chinese border city of Dandong. South Korea said Kim was likely attacked by a North Korean agent using a poisoned needle. Kim had helped North Korean defectors escape to China. Two days later, in another Chinese city, a pastor who had helped defectors, Gahng Ho-bin, was stabbed in the neck with what was believed to be a poisoned knife. South Korean authorities accused the North in this attack as well. Gahng survived. In July 2010, two agents of the North Korean General Reconnaissance Bureau, the regime's spy agency, were arrested and pleaded guilty before a South Korean court to attempting to assassinate high-level defector Hwang Jang-Yop, who was residing in South Korea. Kim Myung-ho and Do Myung-kwan were sentenced to

10 years in jail. In October 2008, a North Korean woman was convicted by a South Korean court for plotting to kill South Korean intelligence agents with poisoned needles.

Robert Windrem, Ken Dilanian, and Abigail Williams, "North Korea Has a History of Assassination Attempts on Foreign Soil," *NBC News*, November 21, 2017, https://www.nbcnews.com/news/north-korea/north-korea-has-history-assassination -attempts-foreign-soil-n823016.

24. Sandra Fahy, *Marching Through Suffering: Loss and Survival in North Korea* (New York: Columbia University Press, 2015).

25. Elaine Scarry, *The Body in Pain: The Making and Unmaking of the World* (New York: Oxford University Press, 1985).

26. Emphasis in the original. Lauren Berlant, "The Epistemology of State Emotion," in *Dissent in Dangerous Times*, ed. Austin Sarat (Ann Arbor: University of Michigan Press, 2005), 47.

27. Berlant, "The Epistemology of State Emotion," 47.

28. In his work *On the Art of Cinema*, it appears 355 times. There is also a chapter focused entirely on emotion titled, "The Director Should Clearly Define Emotions." Kim Jong Il, *On the Art of Cinema* (Pyongyang: Foreign Language Publishing House, 1989).

29. Kim Jong Il, *The Cinema and Directing* (Pyongyang: Foreign Languages Publishing House, 1987), 33, http://www.korea-dpr.info/lib/209.pdf.

30. Kim, *The Cinema and Directing*, 36.

31. In contemporary documentary there are creative and dynamic methods of storytelling. Karina Longworth, "Charlie Chaplin, 'the Peace-Monger,'" *Slate*, March 30, 2016, http://www.slate.com/articles/podcasts/you_must_remember_this/2016/03/charlie _chaplin_and_the_blacklist_and_the_making_of_monsieur_verdoux.html.

32. Personal communication with the artist, March 29, 2016.

33. Garth S. Jowett and Victoria O'Donnell, *Propaganda and Persuasion*, 2nd ed. (Newbury Park, Calif.: Sage, 1992), 122–54.

34. In a one-minute segment I cut from the DPRK documentary about Jeong Kwang Il (aka Chung Kwang Il, Jung Gwang Il), you can count seven points where the footage was clipped and joined, along with changes in light and voice tone. See Oliver Hotham, "Sandra Fahy Clip—NK News," YouTube video, 0:59, September 14, 2016, https://www .youtube.com/watch?v=Jqcjv7wcajQ.

35. Thomas Risse, Stephen C. Ropp, and Katheryn Sikkink, eds., *The Power of Human Rights: International Norms and Domestic Change* (Cambridge: Cambridge University Press, 1999); and Thomas Rissse, Stephen C. Ropp, and Katheryn Sikkink, eds., *The Persistent Power of Human Rights: From Commitment to Compliance* (Cambridge: Cambridge University Press, 2013).

36. "North Koreans Protest Against UN Resolution on Human Rights," Associated Press in Pyongyang, November 25, 2014, https://www.theguardian.com/world/2014/nov/25 /-sp-north-korea-protest-un-resolution-human-rights.

37. "DPRK Protests Against UN Resolution on Human Rights" YouTube video, 0:48, *GCTN*, November 25, 2014, https://www.youtube.com/watch?v=bd-YHFCC5GQ.

38. Risse, Ropp, and Sikkink, *The Power of Human Rights*, 23.

39. The original link for this broadcast was removed from YouTube. However, a clip can be viewed here: Sandra Fahy, "DPRK 8 o'Clock News November 25, 2014," YouTube video, 3:06, April 4, 2018, https://www.youtube.com/watch?v=VAHZH 5HX4jU.

40. See United Nations General Assembly, "Report of the DPRK Association for Human Rights Studies Submitted to the United Nations General Assembly Security Council," September 15, 2014, A/69/383–S/2014/668, https://undocs.org/A/69/383.

41. "Russian News Identifies North Korea's Rights Are Guaranteed at the Highest Level," [Rossiyashinmun chosŏnŭn in'gwŏni ch'oesangŭi sujunesŏ pojangdoenŭn nararago sogae], *KCNA*, October 31, 2014, http://www.kcna.co.jp/calendar/2014/10/10-31/2014 -1031-006.html.

42. "Russian News Identifies."

43. "Do You Know North Korea?" *KCNA*, Rokhwa Press, YouTube video. The original link was removed by YouTube. A clip can be viewed at Fahy, "DPRK 8 o'Clock News."

44. "Rokhwa Press, Our Country Affairs Viewed from Other Nations," *KCNA*, YouTube video [no longer available].

45. "Juche 103 (2014) November 11. Central Television 5 o'Clock News," YouTube video [no longer available].

46. "Juche 103 (2014) November 11."

47. "Juche 103 (2014) November 24, Central Television, 8 o'Clock News," YouTube video [no longer available].

48. "Juche 103 (2014) November 24."

49. "Juche 103 (2014) November 24."

50. The original link for this broadcast was removed from YouTube. However, a clip can be viewed here: Fahy, "DPRK 8 o'Clock News.

51. The original link for this broadcast was removed from YouTube. However, a clip can be viewed at Fahy, "DPRK 8 o'Clock News."

52. The original link for this broadcast was removed from YouTube. However, a clip can be viewed at Fahy, "DPRK 8 o'Clock News."

53. "We Reveal the True Nature of the Report on Human Rights in North Korea," November 19, 2014, http://www.uriminzokkiri.com/itv/index.php?ppt=lie_human&no=21764.

54. "We Reveal the True Nature."

55. "North Korea Defends Human Rights Record," *CNN*, June 30, 2015, YouTube video, 3:01, https://www.youtube.com/watch?v=eS3-8ErBYpQ.

56. "North Korean Families Plead for Defectors to Return," *CNN*, May 11, 2016, YouTube video, 2:44, https://www.youtube.com/watch?v=yo2h-UAp5Lw.

57. After Mladen Dolar, *A Voice and Nothing More* (Cambridge, Mass.: MIT Press, 2006).

58. "North Korean Families Plead for Defectors to Return," *CNN*, May 11, 2016, https:// edition.cnn.com/videos/world/2016/05/11/north-korea-defector-families-pkg-ripley .cnn/video/playlists/top-news-videos/.

59. Michael Kirby, foreword to *The United Nations Universal Periodic Review and the DPRK: Monitoring of North Korea's Implementation of Its Recommendations* (Seoul: NKDB, 2017), 7.

60. See "About the Media Lab," https://lab.witness.org/about/.

61. Aleksandr I. Solzhenitsyn, *The Gulag Archipelago 1918–1956: An Experiment in Literary Investigation* (New York: HarperCollins, 2002), 13.

62. The videos and transcripts of the public hearings of the Commission of Inquiry are available at http://www.ohchr.org/EN/HRBodies/HRC/CoIDPRK/Pages/PublicHear ings.aspx.

63. Sam Gregory, "Cameras Everywhere: Ubiquitous Video Documentation of Human Rights, New Forms of Video Advocacy, and Considerations of Safety, Security, Dignity and Consent," *Journal of Human Rights Practice* 2, no. 2 (2010): 191–207, https:// doi.org/10.1093/jhuman/huq002.

Conclusion: Ascent

1. Hannah Arendt, *Between Past and Future: Eight Exercises in Political Thought* (London: Viking, 1968), 308.
2. Reuters, "North Korea Human Rights Remain Dire After Year of Work," *VOA*, East Asia, January 11, 2019, https://www.voanews.com/a/north-korea-human-rights-remain-dire/4738466.html.
3. Security Council Report, Monthly Forecast, February 2019, p. 20, https://www.security councilreport.org/atf/cf/%7B65BFCF9B-6D27-4E9C-8CD3-CF6E4FF96FF9%7D/2019_02_forecast.pdf.
4. The exact location is withheld for safety.

BIBLIOGRAPHY

Abubakar, Mohammed. "Attackers Kill 3 North Korean Doctors in Nigeria." *Associated Press*, February 11, 2013. https://www.yahoo.com/news/attackers-kill-3-north-korean -doctors-nigeria-133426830.html?ref=gs.

Agamben, Giorgio. *Homo sacer: Sovereign Power and Bare Life*. Trans. Daniel Heller-Roazen. Stanford, Calif.: Stanford University Press, 1998.

——. *Means Without End: Notes on Politics*. Trans. Vincenzo Binetti and Cesare Casarino. Minneapolis: University of Minnesota Press, 2000.

Ahmed, Sara. *The Cultural Politics of Emotion*. Edinburgh: Edinburgh University Press, 2004.

——. "The Politics of Fear in the Making of Worlds." *Qualitative Studies in Education* 16, no. 3 (May–June 2003): 377–98.

Alfirev, Christina O. "Volatile Citizenship or Statelessness? Citizen Children of Palestinian Descent and the Loss of Nationality in Israel." In *Children Without a State: A Global Human Rights Challenge*, ed. Jacqueline Bhabha, 67–88. Cambridge, Mass.: MIT Press, 2011.

"Ali Lameda: A Personal Account of the Experience of a Prisoner of Conscience in the Democratic People's Republic of Korea." Index Number ASA 24/002/1979. London: Amnesty International, 1979.

Amnesty International. *Amnesty International Annual Report 1993*. POL 10/0001/1993. London: Amnesty International Publications, 1993. https://www.amnesty.org/en/docu ments/pol10/0001/1993/en/.

An Myong Hun. "North Korea News Conference at United Nations." YouTube video, 31:46. January 15, 2015. https://www.youtube.com/watch?v=evpTxoJvzYM.

Anker, Elisabeth R. *Orgies of Feeling: Melodrama and the Politics of Freedom*. Durham, N.C.: Duke University Press, 2014.

Arendt, Hannah. *Between Past and Future: Eight Exercises in Political Thought*. London: Viking, 1968.

——. *Imperialism: Part Two of "The Origins of Totalitarianism."* New York: Harcourt, Brace, & World, 1968.

——. *Origins of Totalitarianism.* San Diego: Harcourt Brace, 1976. First published 1951.

——. "Truth and Politics." *New Yorker,* February 25, 1967. https://www.newyorker.com /magazine/1967/02/25/truth-and-politics.

Armstrong, Charles. "*Juche* and North Korea's Global Aspirations." NKIDP Working Paper No. 1 (Washington, D.C.: Woodrow Wilson Center, April 2009). https://www .wilsoncenter.org/sites/default/files/NKIDP_Working_Paper_1_Juche_and_North _Koreas_Global_Aspirations_web.pdf.

——. *The North Korean Revolution, 1945–1950.* Ithaca, N.Y.: Cornell University Press, 2002.

——. "Surveillance and Punishment in Postliberation North Korea." *Positions* 3, no. 3 (Winter 1995).

Arrington, Celeste. "The Abductions Issue in Japan and South Korea: Ten Years After Pyongyang's Admission." *International Journal of Korean Studies* 108 (Spring 2013): 108–39. http://www.icks.org/data/ijks/1482461222_add_file_6.pdf.

Austin, John L. *How to Do Things with Words.* Oxford: Clarendon, 1962.

Bae, Kenneth. *Not Forgotten: The True Story of My Imprisonment in North Korea,* with Mark Tabb. Nashville, Tenn.: W Publishing Group, 2016.

Baek, Jieun. *North Korea's Hidden Revolution: How the Information Underground Is Transforming a Closed Society.* New Haven, Conn.: Yale University Press, 2016.

Banks, Marcus. *Visual Methods in Social Research.* London: Sage, 2001.

Batchimeg, Migeddorj. "Mongolia's DPRK Policy: Engaging North Korea." *Asian Survey* 46, no. 2 (March/April 2006): 275–97.

Becker, Jasper. *Rogue Regime: Kim Jong Il and the Looming Threat of North Korea.* Oxford: Oxford University Press, 2005.

Berkman, Douglas S., Andres G. Lescano, Robert H. Gilman, Sonia L. Lopez, and Maureen M. Black. "Effects of Stunting, Diarrhoeal Disease, and Parasitic Infection During Infancy on Cognition in Late Childhood: A Follow-Up Study." *Lancet* 359, no. 9306 (February 2002): 564–71. https://doi.org/10.1016/S0140-6736(02)07744-9.

Berlant, Lauren. "The Epistemology of State Emotion." In *Dissent in Dangerous Times,* ed. Austin Sarat, 46–78. Ann Arbor: University of Michigan Press, 2005.

Bhabha, Jacqueline, ed. *Children Without a State: A Global Human Rights Challenge.* Cambridge, Mass.: MIT Press, 2011.

——. "From Citizen to Migrant: The Scope of Child Statelessness in the Twenty-First Century." In *Children Without a State: A Global Human Rights Challenge,* ed. Jacqueline Bhabha, 1–40. Cambridge, Mass.: MIT Press, 2011.

Black, Christopher. "North Korea: The Grand Deception Revealed." *WikiSpooks,* last modified March 10, 2017. https://wikispooks.com/wiki/Document:North_Korea_-_The_Grand _Deception_Revealed.

——. "North Korea, the UN, and War Propaganda." *New Eastern Outlook,* November 30, 2014. https://journal-neo.org/2014/11/30/north-korea-the-un-and-war-propaganda-2/.

Black, Maureen M., and John P. Ackerman. "Neuropsychological Development." In *Nutrition in Pediatrics: Basic Science, Clinical Applications,* vol. 4, ed. Christopher Duggan, John B. Watkins, and W. Allan Walker. Hamilton, Ontario: BC Decker, 2008.

Blitz, Brad K. "Neither Seen nor Heard: Compound Deprivation Among Stateless Children." In *Children Without a State: A Global Human Rights Challenge,* ed. Jacqueline Bhabha, 43–66. Cambridge, Mass.: MIT Press, 2011.

Boonen, Marte, Klara Boonstra, Remco Breuker, Christine Chung, Imke van Gardigen, Kim Kwang-cheol, Oh Kyuwook, and Anoma van der Veere. *North Korean Forced*

Labour in the EU, the Polish Case: How the Supply of a Captive DPRK Workforce Fits Our Demand for Cheap Labour. Leiden Asia Centre, Findings from the Slaves to the System Project, July 6, 2016. http://leidenasiacentre.nl/wp-content/uploads/2017/06/rapport-slaves.pdf.

Boynton, Robert. *The Invitation Only Zone: The True Story of North Korea's Abduction Project.* New York: Farrar, Straus and Giroux, 2016.

Breuker, Remco, and Imke van Gardingen, eds. *People for Profit: North Korean Forced Labour on a Global Scale.* Leiden: Leiden Asia Centre, Leiden, 2018. http://humantrafficking search.org/resource/people-for-profit/.

Brooke, James. "Mongolia Under Pressure to Serve as Haven for Refugees." *New York Times,* November 22, 2004. http://www.nytimes.com/2004/11/21/world/asia/mongolia-under-pressure-to-serve-as-haven-for-refugees.html.

——. "Refugee Plan for Mongolia Adds to Dispute on North Korea." *New York Times,* September 28, 2003. http://www.nytimes.com/2003/09/28/world/refugee-plan-for-mongolia-adds-to-dispute-on-north-korea.html.

Brown, David W. "5 Americans Who Defected to North Korea." *Mental Floss,* April 15, 2013. http://mentalfloss.com/article/50095/5-americans-who-defected-north-korea.

Bruce, Scott Thomas. "Information Technology and Social Controls in North Korea." Korea Economic Institute of America, Academic Paper Series, January 28, 2014. http://www.keia.org/sites/default/files/publications/2014_aps_scottbruce.pdf.

Buzo, Adrian. *The Guerilla Dynasty: Politics and Leadership in North Korea.* Boulder, Colo.: Westview, 1999.

Byrne, Leo. "Papers Please: N. Korean Ships Fare Poorly on Inspections." *NKNews.org,* November 5, 2015. https://www.nknews.org/2015/11/papers-please-n-korean-ships-fare-poorly-on-inspections/.

Caballero, Lorraine. "North Korea's Photos of 'Fake Churches' Aim to Cover Up Abuse of Christians—Report." *Christian Daily,* January 30, 2018. https://www.christiandaily.com/article/north-koreas-photos-of-fake-churches-aim-to-cover-up-abuse-of-christians-report/61950.htm.

Caprara, David L., Katharine H. S. Moon, and Paul Park. "Mongolia: Potential Mediator Between the Koreas and Proponent of Peace in North Koreas Asia." Brookings, January 20, 2015. https://www.brookings.edu/opinions/mongolia-potential-mediator-between-the-koreas-and-proponent-of-peace-in-northeast-asia/.

Cara, Ana. "North Korea to UN: Human Rights Resolution Is Illegal." *Daily Mail,* February 4, 2015. https://www.dailymail.co.uk/wires/ap/article-2940025/North-Korea-UN-Human-rights-resolution-illegal.html.

Cathcart, Adam, Christopher Green, and Steven Denny. "How Authoritarian Regimes Maintain Domain Consensus: North Korea's Information Strategies in the Kim Jong Un Era." *Review of Korean Studies* 17, no. 2 (December 2014): 145–78.

Cha, Victor. "North Korea's Economic Reforms and Security Intentions." Testimony of Dr. Victor D. Cha to the United States Senate, March 2, 2004. https://nautilus.org/pub lications/books/dprkbb/transition/dprk-briefing-book-north-koreas-economic-reforms-and-security-intentions/.

Chang Hao Jin. "We Reveal, Once Again, the True Identity of the Human Trash, Sin Tong Hyok." YouTube, March 11, 2015. https://www.youtube.com/watch?v=xbd4T qipHYk.

Chang Jae-soon. "Mass Defection of N.K. Restaurant Workers Shows China's Frustration with Pyongyang: U.S. Envoy." *Yonhap News Agency,* May 3, 2016. http://english.yonhapnews.co.kr/search1/2603000000.html?cid=AEN20160503000500315.

Chang, Yoonok, Stephan Haggard, and Marcus Noland. *Migration Experiences of North Korean Refugees: Survey Evidence from China.* Working Paper series WP 08-4. Washington, D.C.: Peterson Institute for International Economics, 2008.

Charny, Joel R. "North Koreans in China: A Human Rights Analysis." *International Journal of Korean Unification Studies* 13, no. 2 (2004): 75–97.

Chestnut, Sheena. "Illicit Activity and Proliferation: North Korean Smuggling Networks." *International Security* 32, no. 1 (Summer 2007): 80–111.

Cho, Sung Yoon. "The Judicial System in North Korea." *Asian Survey* 11, no. 12 (December 1971): 1167–81.

Choe Sang-Hun. "In Hail of Bullets and Fire, North Korea Killed Official Who Wanted Reform." *New York Times,* March 12, 2016. https://www.nytimes.com/2016/03/13/world/asia/north-korea-executions-jang-song-thaek.html.

——. "Nine North Koreans Escape to Vietnam." *New York Times,* September 24, 2009. http://www.nytimes.com/2009/09/25/world/asia/25korea.html.

——. "North Korea Proposes Having 13 Defectors to the South Meet with Relatives." *New York Times,* April 21, 2016. http://www.nytimes.com/2016/04/22/world/asia/north-korea-defectors-relatives.html.

——. "North Korea Threatens South Korea over 13 Defectors." *New York Times,* April 12, 2016. http://www.nytimes.com/2016/04/13/world/asia/north-korea-threatens-south-korea-over-13-defectors.html.

——. "North Korean Defector Says Kim Jong-Un's Control Is Crumbling." *New York Times,* January 25, 2017. https://www.nytimes.com/2017/01/25/world/asia/north-korea-defector.html.

——. "North Korean Defector in South Seeks Vietnam's Help to Return Home." *New York Times,* March 7, 2016. http://www.nytimes.com/2016/03/08/world/asia/north-korean-defector-in-south-seeks-vietnams-help-to-return-home.html.

Choi, Changyong. "'Everyday Politics' in North Korea." *Journal of Asian Studies* 72, no. 3 (August 2013): 655–73.

Choi, Changyong, and Jess Lecy. "A Semantic Network Analysis of Changes in North Korea's Economic Policy." *Governance* 25, no. 4 (2012): 589–616.

Choi, D. S. "Economic Crisis and Shift in Political System in North Korea." *Collection of Treatises on Unification* 25 (2007): 101–23.

Choi, Eunyoung. "North Korean Women's Narratives of Migration: Challenging Hegemonic Discourses of Trafficking and Geopolitics." *Annals of the Association of American Geographers* 104, no. 2 (2014): 271–79.

Choi Sun-young, Yang Jina, Song Hanna, and Lee Na-kyeong. *United Nations Universal Periodic Review and the DPRK: Monitoring of North Korea's Implementation of Its Recommendations.* Seoul: NKDB, 2017.

Choi, Yong Sub. "North Korea's Hegemonic Rule and Its Collapse." *Pacific Review* 30, no. 5 (2017): 783–800. http://www.tandfonline.com/doi/full/10.1080/09512748.2017.1296885?src=recsys.

Chow, Jonathan T. "North Korea's Participation in the Universal Periodic Review of Human Rights." *Australian Journal of International Affairs* 71, no. 2 (2017): 1–18.

Chubb, Danielle. *Contentious Activism and Inter-Korean Relations.* New York: Columbia University Press, 2014.

Citizens' Alliance for North Korean Human Rights (NKHR). *Status of Women's Rights in the Context of Socio-Economic Changes in the DPRK.* Seoul: NKHR, 2013.

Clark, Donald. *Living Dangerously in Korea: The Western Experience, 1900–1950.* Norwalk, Conn.: EastBridge, 2003.

Cohen, Elizabeth F. "Neither Seen nor Heard: Children's Citizenship in Contemporary Democracies." *Citizenship Studies* 9, no. 2 (2005).

Cohen, Roberta. "Admitting North Korean Refugees to the United States." Brookings, September 20, 2011. https://www.brookings.edu/opinions/admitting-north-korean-refugees-to-the-united-states-obstacles-and-opportunities/.

Collins, Robert. *Marked for Life: Songbun, North Korea's Social Classification System.* Washington, D.C.: Committee for Human Rights in North Korea, 2012. https://www.hrnk.org/uploads/pdfs/HRNK_Songbun_Web.pdf.

——. *Pyongyang Republic: North Korea's Capital of Human Rights Denial.* Washington, D.C.: Committee for Human Rights in North Korea, 2016.

Collins, Robert, and Amanda Mortwedt Oh. *From Cradle to Grave: The Path of North Korean Innocents.* Washington, D.C.: Committee for Human Rights in North Korea, 2017. https://www.hrnk.org/uploads/pdfs/Collins_Cradle_to_Grave_WEB_FINALFINAL.pdf.

Connelly, Steve, and John Pilger, dirs. *Breaking the Silence: Truth and Lies in the War on Terror.* TV documentary. Australia: Carlton Television, 2003.

Coundouriotis, Eleni. "'You only have your word': Rape and Testimony." *Human Rights Quarterly* 35, no. 2 (May 2013): 365–85.

Crawford, Neta C. "The Passion of World Politics: Propositions on Emotion and Emotional Relationships." *International Security* 24, no. 4 (Spring 2000): 116–56.

Criminal Law of the Democratic People's Republic of Korea, trans. Sang hyup Lee, Hyeong Su Park, Kyung Eun Ha, Markus Simpson Bell, Lillian Lee, and Andrew Wolman. Seoul: Citizens' Alliance for North Korean Human Rights, 2009. https://www.hrnk.org/uploads/pdfs/The%20Criminal%20Law%20of%20the%20Democratic%20Republic%20of%20Korea_2009_%20(1).pdf.

Crisis Group International. "Perilous Journeys: The Plight of North Koreans in China and Beyond." *Crisis Group Asia Report No. 122,* October 26, 2006. https://web.archive.org/web/20070927012303/http://www.nautilus.org/fora/security/0694IGC.pdf.

Cubilié, Anne. *Women Witnessing Terror: Testimony and the Cultural Politics of Human Rights.* New York: Fordham University Press, 2005.

Cumings, Bruce. *Korea's Place in the Sun: A Modern History.* New York: Norton, 2005.

——. *The Korean War: A History.* New York: Modern Library, 2010.

D'Sousa, Francis. "Democracy as a Cure for Famine." *Journal of Peace Research* 31, no. 4 (1994): 369–73.

Database Center for North Korean Human Rights (NKDB). "2010 North Korean Defectors' Economic Activity" [Pukhani taljumin kyunjae hwaldong donghyang: chiop, silop, soduk]. Seoul: NKDB, 2010.

——. *White Paper on North Korean Human Rights 2016.* Seoul: NKDB, October 10, 2016. http://www.nkdb.org/en/library/Books_list.php.

David-West, Alzo. "Archetypal Themes in North Korean Literature: Working Notes on Problems and Possibilities." *Jung Journal: Culture & Psyche* 5, no. 1 (2011): 65–80.

de Botton, Alain. *Status Anxiety.* New York: Vintage, 2004.

De Waal, Alex. "Famine and Human Rights." *Development in Practice* 1, no. 2 (1991): 77–83.

Delaunay, Sophie. "North Korea: The Humanitarian Situation and Refugees." MSF Testimony Delivered to the House Committee on International Relations Subcommittee on East Asia and the Pacific in Washington, D.C., May 1, 2002. https://www.doctorswithoutborders.org/what-we-do/news-stories/research/north-korea-humanitarian-situation-and-refugees.

Demick, Barbara. "Rescue Yields Repercussions for South Korea." *Los Angeles Times,* August 28, 2004. http://articles.latimes.com/2004/aug/28/world/fg-defect28.

Devalpo, Alain. "North Korean Slaves." *Le Monde Diplomatique*, April 8, 2006. https://mondediplo.com/2006/04/08koreanworkers.

Devereux, Stephen, ed. *The New Famines: Why Famines Persist in an Era of Globalization* Routledge Studies in Development Economics. New York: Routledge, 2007.

——. *Theories of Famine: From Malthus to Sen*. Hemel Hempstead, U.K.: Harvester Wheatsheaf, 1993.

Di Martino, Kristen. "China: Ensuring Equal Access to Education and Health Care for Children of Internal Migrants." In *Children Without a State: A Global Human Rights Challenge*, ed. Jacqueline Bhabha, 279–305. Cambridge, Mass.: MIT Press, 2011.

Dietz, Bob. "Signs of Change in North Korea." Committee to Project Journalists, May 17, 2012. https://www.cpj.org/blog/2012/05/signs-of-change-in-north-korea.php.

Dirks, Robert. "Social Responses During Severe Food Shortages and Famine [and Comments and Reply]." *Current Anthropology* 21, no. 1 (February 1980): 21–44.

Dolar, Mladen. *A Voice and Nothing More*. Cambridge, Mass.: MIT Press, 2006.

DPRK Association for Human Rights Studies. "Full Text of the Report of the DPRK Association for Human Rights Studies." September 13, 2014. https://www.ncnk.org/resources/publications/Report_of_the_DPRK_Association_for_Human_Rights_Studies.pdf.

Dyson, Tim, and Cormac O Gráda, eds. *Famine Demography: Perspectives from the Past and Present*. Oxford: Oxford University Press, 2002.

Dzerzhinsky, Felixius. "North Korea on Human Rights, UN 150921." YouTube video, 4:47, September 21, 2015. https://www.youtube.com/watch?v=WpbXvlkwcnk.

Eide, Wenche Barth, and Uwe Kracht, eds. *Food and Human Rights in Development*. Vol. 1, *Legal and Institutional Dimensions and Selected Topics*. Oxford: Intersentia, 2005.

Eltagouri, Marwa. "What We've Learned About the North Korean Soldier Whose Daring Escape Was Caught on Video." *Washington Post*, November 24, 2017. https://www.washingtonpost.com/news/worldviews/wp/2017/11/24/what-weve-learned-about-the-north-korean-soldier-whose-daring-escape-was-caught-on-video/?utm_term=.f834797118eb.

Eremenko, Alexey. "Решения, принятые на заседании Правительства 16 октября 2014 года" [Decisions taken at the government meeting on October 16, 2014]. *Moscow Times*, October 17, 2014. http://government.ru/news/15262/.

——. "Russia Moves to Send North Korean Refugees Back Home to Uncertain Fate." *Moscow Times*, November 4, 2014. http://www.themoscowtimes.com/news/article/russia-movesto-send-north-korean-refugees-back-home-to-uncertain-fate/511179.html.

Fahy, Sandra. "DPRK 8 o'Clock News November 25, 2014." YouTube video, 3:06, April 4, 2018. https://www.youtube.com/watch?v=VAHZH5HX4jU.

——. *Marching Through Suffering: Loss and Survival in North Korea*. New York: Columbia University Press, 2015.

Feller, Erika, Volker Türk, and Frances Nicholson. *Refugee Protection in International Law: UNHCR's Global Consultations on International Protection*. Cambridge: Cambridge University Press, 2003.

Fifield, Anna. "Life Under Kim Jong Un: Recent North Korean Escapees Relate How the Secretive Country Has Changed Under the 'Great Successor.'" *Washington Post*, November 17, 2017. https://www.washingtonpost.com/graphics/2017/world/north-korea-defectors/?utm_term=.4da9ebbb9534.

Flake, L. Gordon, and Scott Snyder. *Paved with Good Intentions: The NGO Experience in North Korea*. Westport, Conn.: Praeger Publishers, 2003.

Food and Agriculture Organization of the United Nations. *The Right to Food: Voluntary Guidelines to Support the Progressive Realization of the Right to Adequate Food in the Context of National Food Security*. Adopted November 2004. Rome: FAO of the UN, 2005. http://www.fao.org/3/a-y7937e.pdf.

Ford, Matt. "Is North Korea Right About U.S. Human-Rights Abuses?" *Atlantic*, May 4, 2014. https://www.theatlantic.com/international/archive/2014/05/is-north-korea-right-about-us-human-rights-abuses/361589/.

Foucault, Michel. *Discipline and Punish: The Birth of the Prison*. Trans. Alan Sheridan. London: Penguin, 1977.

Frank, Rüdiger. "The Political Economy of North Korean Arts." In *Exploring North Korean Arts*, ed. Frank Rüdiger, 9–30. Wien: Universität Wien, 2011.

Friedman, Uri. "Coming of Age in North Korea: A Man Who Served the Regime Recounts His Efforts to Bring It Down." *Atlantic*, August 26, 2016. https://www.theatlantic.com/international/archive/2016/08/north-korea-defector-jung/496082/.

Furet, Francois. *The Passing of an Illusion: The Idea of Communism in the Twentieth Century*. Trans. Deborah Furet. Chicago: University of Chicago Press, 1999.

Gause, Ken E. "Coercion, Control, Surveillance, and Punishment: An Examination of the North Korean Police State." Committee for Human Rights in North Korea, 2012. https://www.hrnk.org/uploads/pdfs/HRNK_Ken-Gause_Web.pdf.

Gearin, Daniel. "Chinese Infrastructure and Natural Resources Investments in North Korea." U.S.-China Economic and Security Review Commission, Staff Backgrounder report, October 20, 2010. https://www.uscc.gov/sites/default/files/Research/ChineseInfrastructureandNaturalResourcesInvestmentsinNorthKorea.pdf.

George, Susan. *How the Other Half Dies: The Real Reasons for World Hunger*. Middlesex: Penguin, 1977.

Giddens, Anthony. *The Consequences of Modernity*. Cambridge, U.K.: Polity, 1990.

Go, Myong-Hyun, and Ben Forney. "Kidnapping as Foreign Policy: North Korea's History of State Sponsored Abductions." *Asan Institute for Policy Studies*, April 11, 2018.

Goedde, Patricia. "Law 'of our own style': The Evolution and Challenges of the North Korean Legal System." *Fordham International Law Journal* 27, no. 4 (2003): 1265–88.

Grant, Sarah. "Watch John Oliver Break Down Trump's Three Dangerous Manipulation Tactics." *Rolling Stone*, November 13, 2017. https://www.rollingstone.com/tv/news/john-oliver-breaks-down-trumps-dangerous-speaking-tactics-w511598.

Granthan-McGregor, Sally. "A Review of Existing Studies of the Effect of Severe Malnutrition on Mental Development." *Journal of Nutrition* 125, no. 8 (August 1995): 2233S–38S.

Green, Chris. "Wrapped in a Fog: On the DPRK Constitution and the Ten Principles." In *Change and Continuity in North Korean Politics*, ed. Adam Cathcart, Robert Winstanley-Chesters, and Christopher K. Green, 23–38. New York: Routledge, 2017.

Greenhill, Kelly M. *Weapons of Mass Migration: Forced Displacement, Coercion, and Foreign Policy*. Cornell Studies in Security Affairs. Ithaca, N.Y.: Cornell University Press, 2010.

Gregory, Sam. "Cameras Everywhere: Ubiquitous Video Documentation of Human Rights, New Forms of Video Advocacy, and Considerations of Safety, Security, Dignity and Consent." *Journal of Human Rights Practice* 2, no. 2 (2010): 191–207. https://doi.org/10.1093/jhuman/huq002.

Greitens, Sheena Chestnut. "Authoritarianism Online: What Can We Learn from Internet Data in Nondemocracies?" *PS: Political Science & Politics* 46, no. 2 (2013): 262–70.

——. *Illicit: North Korea's Evolving Operations to Earn Hard Currency*. Washington, D.C.: Committee for Human Rights in North Korea, 2014. https://www.hrnk.org/uploads/pdfs/SCG-FINAL-FINAL.pdf.

Griffiths, James. "How the Seizure of a US Spy Ship by North Korea Nearly Sparked Nuclear War." *CNN*, January 21, 2018. https://edition.cnn.com/2018/01/20/asia/north-korea-uss-pueblo-intl/index.html.

Gyupchanova, Teodora. "Labor and Human Rights Conditions of North Korean Workers Dispatched Overseas: A Look at the DPRK Exploitative Practices in Russia, Poland, and Mongolia." *Cornell International Law Journal* 51 (2018): 183–217.

Haddad, Emma. "The Refugee: The Individual Between Sovereigns." *Global Society* 17, no. 3 (2003).

Haddad, Lawrence, Eileen Kennedy, and Joan Sullivan. "Choice of Indicators for Food Security and Nutrition Monitoring." *Food Policy* 19, no. 3 (1994): 329–43.

Hafner-Burton, Emilie M. "Sticks and Stones: Naming and Shaming the Human Rights Enforcement Problem." *International Organization* 62 (Fall 2008): 689–716.

Haggard, Stephan. "Detainee Update: Otto Warmbier." PIIE, *North Korea: Witness to Transformation* (blog), March 8, 2016. https://piie.com/blogs/north-korea-witness-trans formation/detainee-update-otto-warmbier.

——. "Mike Chinoy on Merrill Newman." PIIE, *North Korea: Witness to Transformation* (blog), December 17, 2014. https://piie.com/blogs/north-korea-witness-transformation /mike-chinoy-merrill-newman.

Haggard, Stephan, and Marcus Noland. *Famine in North Korea: Markets, Aid, and Reform.* New York: Columbia University Press, 2007.

——, eds. *The North Korean Refugee Crisis: Human Rights and International Response.* Washington, D.C.: U.S. Committee for Human Rights in North Korea, 2006. https:// www.hrnk.org/uploads/pdfs/The_North_Korean_Refugee_Crisis.pdf.

——. "The North Korean Refugees as a Human Rights Issue." In *The North Korean Refugee Crisis: Human Rights and International Responses*, ed. Stephan Haggard and Marcus Noland. Washington, D.C.: U.S. Committee for Human Rights in North Korea, 2006.

——. "Repression and Punishment in North Korea: Survey Evidence of Prison Camp Experiences." *East-West Center Working Papers: Politics, Governance, and Security Series*, no. 20, October 2009. https://www.eastwestcenter.org/system/tdf/private/pswp020.pdf ?file=1&type=node&id=32365.

Han, Dong-ho, Soo Kim, Kyu Lee, Keum Lee, and Jeong Cho. *White Paper on Human Rights in North Korea.* Seoul: Korea Institute for National Unification, 2014. http://www .kinu.or.kr/pyxis-api/1/digital-files/a55edee1-5640-41b9-845d-89fd3dfc9509.

Hassig, Ralph C., and Kongdan Oh. *The Hidden People of North Korea: Everyday Life in the Hermit Kingdom.* Lanham, Md.: Rowman & Littlefield, 2009.

Henley, Jon. "Meet Srdja Popovic, the Secret Architect of Global Revolution." *Guardian*, March 8, 2015. https://www.theguardian.com/world/2015/mar/08/srdja-popovic-revolution -serbian-activist-protest.

Herman, Judith. *Trauma and Recovery: The Aftermath of Violence—from Domestic Abuse to Political Terror.* New York: Basic Books, 1997.

Higgins, Andrew. "In Siberia's Last Gulag." *Independent*, June 26, 1994. http://www .independent.co.uk/arts-entertainment/in-siberias-last-gulag-conditions-in-north -koreas-russian-logging-camps-originally-built-for-1425245.html.

Holmes, Oliver. "Kim Jong-nam's Body Targeted in Morgue Break-In, Say Police." *Guardian*, February 22, 2017. https://www.theguardian.com/world/2017/feb/22/kim-jong-nams-body -targeted-in-morgue-break-in.

Holmes, Oliver, Tom Phillips, and Agencies. "Kim Jong-nam Killed by VX Nerve Agent, a Chemical Weapon, Say Malaysian Police." *Guardian*, February 24, 2017. https://www .theguardian.com/world/2017/feb/24/kim-jong-nam-north-korea-killed-chemical -weapon-nerve-agent-mass-destruction-malaysian-police.

Holt-Gimenez, Eric, and Loren Peabody. "From Food Rebellions to Food Sovereignty: Urgent Call to Fix a Broken Food System." *Institute for Food and Development Policy*,

May 16, 2008. https://international.uiowa.edu/sites/international.uiowa.edu/files/file_uploads/bgrspring2008-FoodRebellionstoFoodSovereignty.pdf.

Hong, Albert. "Tanzania Shutters Two North Korean Medical Clinics." *Radio Free Asia*, April 19, 2016. http://www.rfa.org/english/news/korea/tanzania-shutters-two-04192016 143509.html.

Hong Soon-Do. "50,000–200,000 N. Korean Defectors Estimated to Be Residing in China." *Huffington Post*, June 7, 2016.

Horst, Heather A., and Daniel Miller. *The Cell Phone: An Anthropology of Communication.* Oxford: Berg, 2006.

Hotham, Oliver. "Sandra Fahy Clip—NK News." YouTube video. 0:59. September 14, 2016. https://www.youtube.com/watch?v=Jqcjv7wcajQ.

——. "Work Visas for North Koreans Going to China up 17.2%." *NK News*, April 15, 2014. http://www.nknews.org/2014/01/work-visas-for-north-koreans-going-to-china -up-17-2/.

Hovy, Bela. "Human Rights and Citizenship: The Need for Better Data and What to Do About It." In *Children Without a State: A Global Human Rights Challenge*, ed. Jacqueline Bhabha, 89–106. Cambridge, Mass.: MIT Press, 2011.

Howard-Hassmann, Rhoda E. *State Food Crimes.* Cambridge: Cambridge University Press, 2016.

Hu, Elise. "North Korean Defector: Information Flow Will Help Bring Down Kim Jong Un." *NPR*, January 26, 2017. http://www.npr.org/sections/parallels/2017/01/26/511745886 /north-korean-defector-information-flow-will-help-bring-down-kim-jong-un.

Human Rights Committee. "CCPR General Comment No. 28: Article 3 (The Equality of Rights Between Men and Women)." CCPR/C/21/Rev.1/Add.10. https://www.refworld .org/docid/45139c9b4.html.

——. "Concluding Observations of the Human Rights Committee: Nigeria." CCPR/C/79 /Add.65, July 24, 1996. http://hrlibrary.umn.edu/hrcommittee/57nig4.htm.

Human Rights Council. "Promotion and Protection of All Human Rights, Civil, Political, Economic, Social and Cultural Rights, Including the Right to Development." A/HRC/7/3, January 15, 2008. https://documents-dds-ny.un.org/doc/UNDOC/GEN/G08 /101/61/PDF/G0810161.pdf?OpenElement.

——. "Report of the Special Rapporteur on Extrajudicial, Summary or Arbitrary Executions, Philip Alston." A/HRC/14/24, May 20, 2010. https://www2.ohchr.org/english/bod ies/hrcouncil/docs/14session/A.HRC.14.24.Add6.pdf.

——. "Report of the Special Rapporteur on the Situation of Human Rights in the Democratic People's Republic of Korea, Marzuki Darusman." A/HRC/22/57, February 1, 2013. https://www.ohchr.org/Documents/HRBodies/HRCouncil/RegularSession/Session22 /A.HRC.22.57_English.pdf.

——. "Special Rapporteurs on Torture and Other Cruel, Inhuman and Degrading Treatment." A/HRC/22/53, February 1, 2013. https://www.ohchr.org/Documents/HRBodies /HRCouncil/RegularSession/Session22/A.HRC.22.53_English.pdf.

——. "UNHRC: Significant Resolution Reaffirming Human Rights Online Adopted. ORAL REVISIONS of 30 June." A/HRC/32/L.20, June 27, 2016. https://www.article19.org/data /files/Internet_Statement_Adopted.pdf.

Human Rights Watch. "Ad Hoc and Inadequate: Thailand's Treatment of Refugees and Asylum Seekers." September 12, 2012. https://www.hrw.org/report/2012/09/12/ad-hoc -and-inadequate/thailands-treatment-refugees-and-asylum-seekers.

——. "Appendix B: Letter from Chinese Ministry of Foreign Affairs to Foreign Embassies, May 31, 2002." https://www.hrw.org/reports/2002/northkorea/norkor1102-06.htm.

——. "The Invisible Exodus: North Koreans in the People's Republic of China." *Human Rights Watch* 14, no. 8 (November 2002). https://www.hrw.org/reports/2002/northkorea /norkor1102.pdf.

——. "UN: North Korea Exploiting Children," February 8, 2017. https://www.hrw.org/news /2017/02/08/un-north-korea-exploiting-children.

——. "War in Iraq: Not a Humanitarian Intervention." January 25, 2004. https://www.hrw .org/news/2004/01/25/war-iraq-not-humanitarian-intervention.

Hunter, Helen-Louise. *Kim Il-Song's North Korea.* Westport, Conn.: Praeger, 1999.

Institute of North Korean Studies. *Comprehensive Survey 1945–1982.* Seoul: Institute of North Korean Studies, 1983.

International Federation for Human Rights (FIDH). *The Death Penalty in North Korea: In the Machinery of a Totalitarian State.* Paris: FIDH, May 2013. https://www.fidh.org/IMG /pdf/en-report-northkorea-high-resolution.pdf.

Ja Song Nam. "Letter Dated 15 March 2014 from the Permanent Representative of the Democratic People's Republic of Korea to the United Nations Addressed to the President of the Security Council," March 17, 2014. United Nations Security Council, S/2014/194.

Jang Il Hun. "Ambassador Jang Il Hun on Human Rights in North Korea." *Council on Foreign Relations,* October 20, 2014. http://www.cfr.org/north-korea/ambassador-jang-il -hun-human-rights-north-korea/p35758.

Jang Jin-Sung. *Dear Leader.* Trans. Shirley Lee. London: Ebury, 2014.

——. "The Market Shall Set North Korea Free." *New York Times,* April 26, 2013. http://www .nytimes.com/2013/04/27/opinion/global/The-Market-Shall-Set-North-Korea-Free.html.

Jenkins, Charles Robert. *The Reluctant Communist: My Desertion, Court-Martial, and Forty-Year Imprisonment in North Korea,* with Jim Frederick. Berkeley: University of California Press, 2008.

Jenkins, Mark. "A Korean Celebrity Couple Kidnapped by Kim Jong Il: 'The Lovers and the Despot'." *NPR,* September 22, 2016. https://www.npr.org/2016/09/22/494908429/a -korean-celebrity-couple-kidnapped-by-kim-jong-il-the-lovers-and-the-despot.

Jeon, Woo-Teak, Shi-Eun Yu, Young-A Cho, and Jin-Sup Eom. "Traumatic Experiences and Mental Health of North Korean Refugees in South Korea." *Psychiatry Investigation* 5, no. 4 (2008): 213–20. https://dx.doi.org/10.4306%2Fpi.2008.5.4.213.

Johnston, Eric. "The North Korea Abduction Issue and Its Effect on Japanese Domestic Politics." JPRI Working Paper No. 101, June 2004. http://www.jpri.org/publications/work ingpapers/wp101.html.

Jolley, Mary Ann. "The Strange Tale of Yeonmi Park." *Diplomat,* December 20, 2014. https:// thediplomat.com/2014/12/the-strange-tale-of-yeonmi-park/.

Joo, Hyung-Min. "Hidden Transcripts in Marketplaces: Politicized Discourses in the North Korean Shadow Economy." *Pacific Review* 27, no. 1 (2014): 49–71.

Jowett, Garth S., and Victoria O'Donnell. *Propaganda and Persuasion.* 2nd ed. Newbury Park, Calif.: Sage, 1992.

Kakegawa, Tomiko. "The Press and Public Opinion in Japan 1931–1941." In *Pearl Harbor as History: Japanese-American Relations 1931–1941,* ed. Dorothy Borg, Shumpei Okamoto, and Dale K. A. Finlayson, 533–49. New York: Columbia University Press, 1973.

Kang Chol-Hwan, and Pierre Rigoulot. *The Aquariums of Pyongyang: Ten Years in a North Korean Gulag,* trans. Yair Reiner. New York: Basic Books, 2001.

Kang Jin-kyu. "Pyongyang's Flying Doctors Pull in $15M a Year: NIS." *Korea Joongang Daily,* November 25, 2015. http://koreajoongangdaily.joins.com/news/article/Article .aspx?aid=3011968.

Kang Mi-jin. "North Korean 'Executed for Communicating with the Outside World.'" *Guardian*, May 23, 2014. http://www.theguardian.com/world/2014/may/23/north-korean-executed-for-communicating-with-outside-world.

Katz, James E., and Mark Aakhus. *Perpetual Contact: Mobile Communication, Private Talk, Public Performance*. Cambridge: Cambridge University Press, 2002.

KCNA Watch. "Open Questionnaire of DPRK Institute of International Studies." *Rodong Sinmun*, August 12, 2016. https://kcnawatch.co/newstream/1530454241-789560501/open-questionnaire-of-dprk-institute-of-international-studies/.

Kent, George. *Freedom from Want: The Human Rights to Adequate Food*. Washington, D.C.: Georgetown University Press, 2005.

Kern, Holger Lutz, and Jens Hainmueller. "Opium for the Masses: How Foreign Media Can Stabilize Authoritarian Regimes." *Political Analysis* 17, no. 4 (2009): 377–99. https://doi.org/10.1093/pan/mpp017.

KH Digital 2. "N. Korea Sends Letter to UN Chief Demanding Repatriation of Women 'Abducted' by S. Korea." *Korea Herald*, January 31, 2017. http://www.koreaherald.com/view.php?ud=20170131000914.

Kim Dae-hyon. "NK State Security Department Data on Physical Data of 2,100,000 Pyongyang Residents." *Weekly Chosun Magazine*, October 24, 2011. http://weekly.chosun.com/client/news/viw.asp?nNewsNumb=002177100002&ctcd=C)1.

Kim Hyun Hee. *Tears of My Soul*. New York: Morrow, 1993.

Kim Il Sung. "On the Establishment of the Workers' Party of North Korea and the Question of Founding the Workers' Party of South Korea," September 1946. In *Kim Il Sung: Selected Works*, 1:102–20. Marxists Internet Archive. https://www.marxists.org/archive/kim-il-sung/1946/09/26.htm.

Kim, Immanuel. "Problems with Institutionalizing the April 15 Literary Production Unit." *Korea Journal* 56, no. 1 (Spring 2016): 140–64.

Kim In Ryong. "Kim In Ryong (DPRK) on Human Rights—Press Conference (13 December 2016)." UN Web TV video, 25:49. http://webtv.un.org/watch/kim-in-ryong-dprk-on-human-rights-press-conference-13-december-2016/5246257589001#full-text.

——. "Kim In Ryong (DPRK) Press Conference (15 November 2016)." UN Web TV, 23:59. http://webtv.un.org/watch/kim-in-ryong-dprk-press-conference-15-november-2016/5211267770001.

Kim, Jeong Eun. "Nutritional State of Children in the Democratic People's Republic of Korea (DPRK): Based on the DPRK Final Report of the National Nutrition Survey 2012." *Pediatric Gastroenterology, Hepatology & Nutrition* 17, no. 3 (2014): 135–39.

Kim, Jong-il. *The Cinema and Directing*. Pyongyang: Foreign Languages Publishing House, 1987. http://www.korea-dpr.info/lib/209.pdf.

——. *On the Art of Cinema*. Pyongyang: Foreign Language Publishing House, 1989.

——. *On Strengthening Socialist Lawful Life*. Pyongyang: Korean Workers' Party Publishers, 1989.

——. "Socialism Is Science." *Rodong Shinmun*, November 4, 1994.

Kim, Joseph. *Under the Same Sky: From Starvation in North Korea to Salvation in America*, with Stephan Talty. New York: Houghton Mifflin Harcourt, 2015.

Kim Sang-son and Ri Song-hi. *Resident Registration Project Reference Manual*, ed. Ri Pang-sun. Pyongyang: DPRK, 1993.

Kim, Sarah. "North Orders Terror Strikes on South Koreans." *Korea JoongAng Daily*, July 27, 2016. http://koreajoongangdaily.joins.com/news/article/article.aspx?aid=3021812.

Kim, Seong Hwan. "Thae Yong Ho Believes Outside Information Will Topple Regime." *Daily NK*, December 29, 2016. http://www.dailynk.com/english/read.php?cataId=nk 00100&num=14280.

Kim, Seong Hwan, and Min Kwon Bae. "North Korean Website Reports on Self-Criticism Sessions Following New Year's Address." *Daily NK*, January 19, 2017. http://www .dailynk.com/english/read.php?cataId=nk01700&num=14321.

Kim Soo-Am. "Conceptions of Democracy and Human Rights in the Democratic People's Republic of Korea." KINU: Korea Institute for National Unification, 2008.

——. "The North Korean Penal Code, Criminal Procedures, and Their Actual Applications." Korea Institute for National Unification Studies Series 06-01, 2006.

Kim Suk-Young. *Illusive Utopia: Theatre, Film and Everyday Performance in North Korea.* Ann Arbor: University of Michigan Press, 2010.

Kim, Y. "North Korea on Human Rights, UN 150921." YouTube video, 4:47. September 15, 2015. https://www.youtube.com/watch?v=WpbXvlkwcnk.

Kim Yong and Kim Suk-Young. *The Long Road Home: Testimony of a North Korean Camp Survivor.* New York: Columbia University Press, 2009.

Kim, Yonho. "Cell Phones in North Korea." *Voice of America*, 2014. https://38north.org/wp -content/uploads/2014/03/Kim-Yonho-Cell-Phones-in-North-Korea.pdf.

Kirby, Michael. Foreword to *The United Nations Universal Periodic Review and the DPRK: Monitoring of North Korea's Implementation of Its Recommendations.* Seoul: NKDB, 2017.

Kirby, Michael, and Kim Song. "Epic Exchange Between Justice Kirby and DPRK Councillor Kim Song." Michaelkirby.com, February 2016. http://www.michaelkirby.com.au /content/epic-exchange-between-justice-kirby-and-dprk-councillor-kim-song-1.

Korean Bar Association. *2012 White Paper on Human Rights in North Korea.* Seoul: Korean Bar Association, 2013.

Kretchun, Nat, and Jane Kim. "A Quiet Opening: North Koreans in a Changing Media Environment." *InterMedia*, May 2012. http://www.intermedia.org/wp-content/uploads /2013/05/A_Quiet_Opening_FINAL_InterMedia.pdf.

Kretchun, Nat, Catherine Lee, and Seamus Tuohy. "Compromising Connectivity: Information Dynamics Between the State and Society in a Digitizing North Korea." *Inter Media*, 2017. http://www.intermedia.org/wp-content/uploads/2017/02/Compromising-Con nectivity-Final-Report_Soft-Copy.pdf.

Křivka, Vladimír. "Šít a žít ve jménu vůdce." *Týden.cz* (n.d.). http://t.tyden.cz/tema/sit-a-zit -ve-jmenu-vudce_2245.html.

Kunreuther, Laura. "Technologies of the Voice: FM Radio, Telephone, and the Nepali Diaspora in Kathmandu." *Cultural Anthropology* 21, no. 3 (2006): 323–53.

Kurlantzick, Joshua, and Jana Mason. "North Korean Refugees: The Chinese Dimension." In *The North Korean Refugee Crisis: Human Rights and International Response*, ed. Stephan Haggard and Marcus Noland, 34–52. Washington, D.C.: U.S. Committee for Human Rights in North Korea, 2006.

Kwon Hyo-jin. "North Korea Calls Anti-Government Leaflet Drop 'Grave Provocation.'" *Guardian*, September 25, 2014. http://www.theguardian.com/world/2014/sep/25/north -korea-condemns-anti-government-leaflets.

Kwon Hyo-jin and Kang Mi-jin. "North Korea Releases Video of Defectors Forced to Return." *Guardian*, December 11, 2014. https://www.theguardian.com/world/2014/dec /11/north-korea-releases-video-defectors-forced-return.

Landau, Emily B. "A Nuclear Crisis in Search of a Model: Lessons from Iraq, North Korea, Libya, and Syria." *INSS Insight 491*, December 2, 2013. http://www.inss.org.il/publication/a -nuclear-crisis-in-search-of-a-model-lessons-from-iraq-north-korea-libya-and-syria/.

Lankov, Andrei. *Crisis in North Korea: The Failure of De-Stalinization*. Honolulu: University of Hawai`i Press, 2005.

——. *From Stalin to Kim Il-Sung: The Formation of North Korea, 1945–1960*. New Brunswick, N.J.: Rutgers University Press, 2002.

——. *North of the DMZ: Essays on Daily Life in North Korea*. Jefferson, N.C.: McFarland, 2007.

——. "North Korean Refugees in Northeast China." *Asian Survey* 44, no. 6 (November/December 2004): 856–73.

——. *The Real North Korea: Life and Politics in the Failed Stalinist Utopia*. Oxford: Oxford University Press, 2014.

——. "Why Increasing Numbers of Senior Officials Are Fleeing North Korea." *NK News.org*, August 24, 2016. https://www.nknews.org/2016/08/why-increasing-numbers-of-senior-officials-are-fleeing-north-korea/.

Lankov, Andrei Nikolaevich, In-ok Kwak, and Choong-Bin Cho. "The Organizational Life: Daily Surveillance and Daily Resistance in North Korea." *Journal of East Asian Studies* 12, no. 2 (2012): 193–214.

Lansdown, Gerison. "Children's Welfare and Children's Rights." In *Children in Society: Contemporary Theory, Policy and Practice*, ed. Pam Foley, Jeremy Roche, and Stan Tucker, 143–56. New York: Palgrave Macmillan, 2001.

Lautze, Sue. "The Famine in North Korea: Humanitarian Responses in Communist Nations." Feinstein International Famine Centre Working Paper, School of Nutrition Science and Policy, Tufts University, June 1997. http://repository.forcedmigration.org/show_metadata.jsp?pid=fmo:1744.

Lea-Henry, Jed. "Korea Now Podcast #10—Ben Young—'Friends in Strange Places—Cold War Allies,'" 2018. https://player.fm/series/the-korea-now-podcast/the-korea-now-podcast-10-ben-young-friends-in-strange-places-cold-war-allies.

——. "The Korea Now Podcast #21—Michael Kirby—'Human Rights in North Korea—Looking Back on the Commission of Inquiry.'" August 30, 2018. https://tunein.com/podcasts/Politics/The-Korea-Now-Podcast-p1106028/?topicId=123772327.

Lee, Ahlam. *North Korean Defectors in a New and Competitive Society: Issues and Challenges in Resettlement, Adjustment and the Learning Process*. Lanham, Md.: Lexington, 2016.

Lee, Christy. "UN Official: 'Time' to Talk Human Rights with North Korea." *Voice of America*, June 17, 2018. https://www.voanews.com/a/un-official-now-is-the-time-for-north-korea-human-rights/4441668.html.

Lee, Ji-Young. *China's Hegemony: Four Hundred Years of East Asian Domination*. New York: Columbia University Press, 2016.

Lee Jin-a. "Pastor Slain Near China N-Korea Border." *Korea Times*, May 2, 2016. http://www.koreatimes.co.kr/www/news/nation/2016/05/485_203854.html.

Lee, Jun Ha. *Reeducation Story* [Kyohwaso iyagi]. Seoul: Shidae Generation Publishing, 2008.

Lee, Kyo Duk, and Kyu Sup Chung. "Study of Disciplinary Problems in the North Korean Army." Study Series 12-01. Seoul: Korea Institute for National Unification, 2012. www.kinu.or.kr/upload/neoboard/DATA05/ra11-02.pdf.

Lee, Luke. "Internally Displaced Persons and Refugees: Toward a Legal Synthesis?" *Journal of Refugee Studies* 9, no. 1 (1996): 27–42.

Lee, Shin-Wha. "International Engagement in North Korea's Humanitarian Crisis: The Role of State and Non-State Actors." *East Asia: An International Quarterly* 20, no. 2 (Summer 2003): 74–93.

Lefort, Claude. *Communism and the Dilemmas of Democracy.* New York: Columbia University Press, 1999.

Lerner, Jennifer S., and Dacher Keltner. "Fear, Anger, and Risk." *Journal of Personality and Social Psychology* 81, no. 1 (2001): 146–59. http://dx.doi.org/10.1037//O022-3514.81.1.146.

Lerner, Jennifer S., Roxana M. Gonzales, Deborah A. Small, and Baruch Fischhoff. "Effects of Fear and Anger on Perceived Risks of Terrorism: A National Field Experiment." *Psychological Science* 14, no. 2 (2003): 144–50. http://dx.doi.org/10.1111/1467-9280.01433.

Lindy, Jacob D., and Robert Jay Lifton. *Beyond Invisible Walls: The Psychological Legacy of Soviet Trauma.* London: Taylor and Francis, 2001.

Lipes, Joshua. "China Deports North Korean Workers Forced into Sex Trade." *Radio Free Asia,* June 12, 2014. http://www.rfa.org/english/news/korea/deportation-06122014162010.html.

——. "Exporting Fakes? North Korean Clinics Hawk Questionable Medical Care to Tanzania." *Radio Free Asia,* special investigation, 2015. http://www.rfa.org/english/news/special/nkinvestigation/tanzania.html.

Longworth, Karina. "Charlie Chaplin, 'the Peace-Monger.'" *Slate,* March 30, 2016. https://slate.com/culture/2016/03/charlie-chaplin-and-the-blacklist-and-the-making-of-monsieur-verdoux.html.

Lorde, Audre. "The Master's Tools Will Never Dismantle the Master's House." In *This Bridge Called My Back: Writings by Radical Women of Color,* ed. Cherríe Moraga and Gloria Anzaldúa, 94–97. New York: Kitchen Table Press, 1983.

Ma, Zhongdong., and Donglin Zeng. "Population and Internal Migration in North Korea Since 2000." *Eurasian Geography and Economics* 56, no. 4 (2015): 446–68.

MacDonald, Hamish. "Equatorial Guinea Calls for Suspension of North Korean Business Dealings: MFA." *NKNews.org,* January 25, 2018. https://www.nknews.org/2018/01/equatorial-guinea-bringing-an-end-to-north-korean-business-dealings-mfa/.

Malthus, Robert. *An Essay on the Principle of Population as It Affects the Future Improvement of Society, with Remarks on the Speculations of Mr. Goodwin, M. Condorcet and Other Writers.* London: J. Johnson in St Paul's Church-yard, 1798.

Mansourov, Alexandre. "North Korea: The Dramatic Fall of Jang Song Thaek," *38 North,* December 9, 2013. http://38north.org/2013/12/amansourov120913/.

——. "North Korea on the Cusp of Digital Transformation." *Nautilus Institute Special Report,* October 2011. http://nautilus.org/wp-content/uploads/2011/12/DPRK_Digital_Transformation.pdf.

Margesson, Rhoda, Emma Chanlett-Avery, and Andorra Bruno. *North Korean Refugees in China and Human Rights Issues: International Response and U.S Policy Options.* CRS Report for Congress RL34189. Washington, D.C.: Congressional Research Service, 2007.

McCurry, Justin. "The Defector Who Wants to Go Back to North Korea." *Guardian,* April 22, 2014. https://www.theguardian.com/world/2014/apr/22/defector-wants-to-go-back-north-korea.

——. "Fears for North Korean Refugees Who May 'Face Death' if Returned by China." *Guardian,* November 25, 2015. https://www.theguardian.com/world/2015/nov/25/fears-for-north-korean-refugees-who-may-face-death-if-returned-by-china.

——. "The Intriguing Deaths of Two North Korean Doctors in Cambodia." *Guardian,* January 5, 2016. https://www.theguardian.com/world/2016/jan/05/two-north-korean-doctors-die-cambodia-intrigue.

——. "North Korea Claims Propaganda Win After Exiled Woman Returns." *Guardian,* June 29, 2012. https://www.theguardian.com/world/2012/jun/29/north-korea-defector-returns-south.

——. "North Korea Executes Officials with Anti-Aircraft Gun in New Purge—Report." *Guardian*, August 30, 2016. https://www.theguardian.com/world/2016/aug/30/north -korea-reportedly-executes-officials-anti-aircraft-gun-purge.

McCurry, Justin, and agencies in Seoul. "North Korea Defence Chief Reportedly Executed with Anti-Aircraft Gun." *Guardian*, May 13, 2016. https://www.theguardian.com/world /2015/may/13/north-korean-defence-minister-executed-by-anti-aircaft-gun-report.

McDermott, Rose. "Experimenting with Emotions." In *Emotions, Politics and War*, ed. Linda Åhäll and Thomas Gregory, 100–111. London: Routledge, 2015.

McEachern, Patrick. *Inside the Red Box: North Korea's Post-Totalitarian Politics*. New York: Columbia University Press, 2010.

——. "North Korea's Internal Politics and U.S. Foreign Policy." In *Origins of North Korea's Juche: Colonialism, War, and Development*, ed. Chae-Jong So and Jae-Jung Suh, 145–162. Lanham, Md.: Lexington Books, 2013.

McPherson, Poppy. "The Curious Case of North Korea's Overseas Doctors." *Diplomat*, April 10, 2015. http://thediplomat.com/2015/04/the-curious-case-of-north-koreas-overseas -doctors/.

Meintjes, Shelia. "South Africa's Truth and Reconciliation Commission and Gender Justice." Gunda Werner Institute: Feminism and Gender Democracy, March 12, 2012. https:// www.gwi-boell.de/en/2012/03/12/south-africa%E2%80%99s-truth-and-reconciliation -commission-and-gender-justice.

Mendez, M. S., and L. S. Adair. "Severity and Timing of Stunting in the First Two Years of Life and Affect Performance on Cognitive Tests in Late Childhood." *Journal of Nutrition* 129 (1999): 1555–62.

MilitaryNotes. "North Korea: The Most Daring Escape Captured on Camera." YouTube video, 8:07. November 22, 2017. https://www.youtube.com/watch?v=bYKNJ--GHGU.

Mills, Michael J., Owen B. Toon, Julia-Lee Taylor, and Alan Robock. "Multidecadal Global Cooling and Unprecedented Ozone Loss Following a Regional Nuclear Conflict." *Earth's Future* 2, no. 4 (2014): 161–76. https://agupubs.onlinelibrary.wiley.com/doi/abs /10.1002/2013EF000205.

Ministry of Unification, Institute for Unification Education. *Understanding North Korea: 2014*. Seoul: Ministry of Unification, 2014.

Moore, Malcolm. "China Defends Policy of Sending Back North Korean Defectors." *Daily Telegraph*, February 19, 2014.

Morton, David. "Steep Learning Curves in the DPRK." In *Humanitarian Diplomacy: Practitioners and Their Craft*, ed. Larry Minear and Hazel Smith, 194–214. New York: United Nations University Press, 2007.

Mühlhahn, Klaus. "The Dark Side of Globalization: The Concentration Camps in Republic of China in Global Perspective." *World History Connected* 6, no. 1 (2009). http://world historyconnected.press.illinois.edu/6.1/muhlhahn.html.

Myers, Brian Reynolds. *The Cleanest Race: How North Koreans See Themselves and Why It Matters*. New York: Melville House, 2010.

——. "Knocking on the Great Gate: The 'Strong and Prosperous Country' Campaign in North Korean Propaganda." In *Exploring North Korean Arts*, ed. Rüdiger Frank. Wien: University of Vienna Press, 2011.

——. *North Korea's Juche Myth*. Busan, ROK: Sthele Press, 2015.

Myhrvold-Hanssen, Thomas L. "Democracy, News Media, and Famine Prevention: Amartya Sen and the Bihar Famine of 1966–67." Unpublished manuscript, June 2003. https://www.sas.upenn.edu/~dludden/BIHAR1967counterSen.pdf.

Nathwani, Niraj. *Rethinking Refugee Law*. Boston: Martinus Nijoff Publishers, 2003.

Natsios, Andrew. "North Korea's Chronic Food Problem." In *Troubled Transition: North Korea's Politics, Economy, and External Relations*, ed. Sang-Hun Choe, Gi-Wook Shin, and David Straub, 126–27. Stanford, Calif.: Shorenstein Asia-Pacific Research Center, September 2013.

——. "The Politics of Famine in North Korea." United States Institute of Peace, August 2, 1999. https://www.usip.org/publications/1999/08/politics-famine-north-korea.

Noland, Marcus. "Famine and Reform in North Korea WP 03-5." *Institute for International Economics*, 2003. https://piie.com/publications/wp/03-5.pdf.

——. "Rust Buckets of the World Unite! You Don't Want to Be a North Korean Sailor." PIIE, *North Korea: Witness to Transformation* (blog), June 20, 2016. https://piie.com/blogs/north-korea-witness-transformation/rust-buckets-world-unite.

Noland, Marcus, and Stephan M. Haggard. "Reform from Below: Behavioral and Institutional Change in North Korea." *Journal of Economic Behavior & Organization* 73, no. 2 (February 2010): 133–52. https://doi.org/10.1016/j.jebo.2009.09.009.

North Korea Freedom Coalition. "2013 Update 'The List' of North Korean Refugees and Humanitarian Workers Seized by Chinese Authorities." N.d. http://www.nkfreedom.org/UploadedDocuments/2013.12.10_THE_LIST_ENGLISH.pdf.

North Korean Human Rights Archives. *White Paper on North Korean Human Rights*. Seoul: NKDB, 2008. Database Center for North Korean Human Rights. http://www.nkdb.org/en/library/Books_list.php.

O'Neill, Onora. "Children's Rights and Children's Lives." *Ethnics* 98, no. 3 (1988).

Oh, Kongdan, and Ralph C. Hassig. *Through the Looking Glass*. Washington, D.C.: Brookings Institution Press, 2000.

——. *The Hidden People of North Korea: Everyday Life in the Hermit Kingdom*. Lanham, Md.: Rowman and Littlefield, 2015.

Onishi, Norimitsu. "South Brings Capitalism, Well Isolated, to North Korea." *New York Times*, July 18, 2006.

Pak, Sun Young, Daniel Schwekendiek, and Hee Kyoung Kim. "Height and Living Standards in North Korea, 1930s–1980s." *Economic History Review* 64 (2011): 142–58.

Pan Xiaoling. "Precious Pyongyang's Household Registration." *Southern Weekly*, 2011.

Park, Chan Hong. "Conditions of Labor and Human Rights: North Korean Overseas Laborers in Russia." Seoul: NKDB, 2016.

Park, Yeonmi. *In Order to Live: A North Korean Girl's Journey to Freedom*, with Maryanne Vollers. New York: Penguin, 2015.

Paterson, Alexander. *Paterson on Prisons: Being the Collected Papers of Sir Alexander Paterson*, ed. S. K. Ruck. London: F. Muller, 1951.

Paviour, Ben, and Kuch Naren. "North Korean Attackers Sent to Cambodia, Paper Reports." *Cambodia Daily*, July 28, 2016. https://www.cambodiadaily.com/news/north-korean-attackers-sent-to-cambodia-paper-reports-115985/.

Penny, Mary E. "Severe Acute Malnutrition: Pathophysiology, Clinical Consequences, and Treatment." In *Nutrition in Pediatrics: Basic Science, Clinical Applications*, 5th ed., ed. Christopher Duggan, John B. Watkins, Berthold Koletzko, and W. Allan Walker, 496–557. Shelton, Conn.: People's Medical, 2016.

Perlez, Jane. "Fearing the Worst, China Plans Refugee Camps on North Korean Border." *New York Times*, December 11, 2017. https://www.nytimes.com/2017/12/11/world/asia/china-north-korea-border.html.

——. "Merrill Newman, U.S. Veteran Who Was Held in North Korea, Tells His Story." *New York Times*, December 11, 2014. http://www.nytimes.com/2014/12/12/world/asia/merrill-newman-us-veteran-who-was-held-in-north-korea-tells-his-story.html.

Person, James F. "We Need Help from Outside: North Korean Opposition Movement of 1956." Wilson Center Cold War International History Project, Working Paper #52, August 2006. https://www.wilsoncenter.org/sites/default/files/WP52.pdf.

Pottier, Johan. *Re-Imagining Rwanda: Conflict, Survival and Disinformation in the Late Twentieth Century.* Cambridge: Cambridge University Press, 2002.

Power, John. "North Korean Defectors and Their Skeptics." *Diplomat*, October 29, 2014. https://thediplomat.com/2014/10/north-korea-defectors-and-their-skeptics/.

Power, Samantha. "Remarks at a Panel Discussion on Human Rights Abuses in North Korea, 'Victims' Voices: A Conversation on North Korean Human Rights.'" April 30, 2015. http://webtv.un.org/watch/victims'-voices-a-conversation-on-north-korean-human-rights/4207187028001.

Ra Jong-yil. *Jang Song-Taek-ui gil* [The road of Jang Song Taek]. Seoul: Ama, 2016.

Rafael, Vincente L. "The Cell Phone and the Crowd: Messianic Politics in the Contemporary Philippines." *Public Culture* 15, no. 3 (2003): 399–425.

Refugees International. "Acts of Betrayal: The Challenge of Protecting North Koreans in China." Relief Web, May 12, 2005. https://reliefweb.int/report/democratic-peoples-republic-korea/acts-betrayal-challenge-protecting-north-koreans-china-0.

Reuters. "North Korea Human Rights Remain Dire After Year of Work." *VOA, East Asia*, January 11, 2019. https://www.voanews.com/a/north-korea-human-rights-remain-dire/4738466.html.

——. "North Korea Sentences South Korean Reporters to Death over Review of Book About Country," September 1, 2017. https://www.reuters.com/article/us-northkorea-southkorea-media-threat/north-korea-sentences-south-korean-reporters-to-death-over-review-of-book-about-country-idUSKCN1BB2J0.

——. "Trump and Kim's Joint Statement," June 12, 2018. https://www.reuters.com/article/us-northkorea-usa-agreement-text/trump-and-kims-joint-statement-idUSKBN1J80IU.

Ri Song Chol. "Statement Made by Mr. Ri Song Chol, Counsellor of the Permanent Mission of the Democratic People's Republic of Korea (DPRK) to the United Nations at the 'Panel Discussion' Organized by the US and South Korea on 30 April 2015." Press Release, No. 11/04/15, April 30, 2015. https://www.scribd.com/doc/263669008/North-Korea-Speech-at-UN-Event-US-Said-Turn-Off-the-Mic-So-Here.

Ri Su Yong. "North Korean Foreign Minister at UN General Assembly (English)." YouTube video, 17:02. September 27, 2014. https://www.youtube.com/watch?v=Ys56r7IleWY.

Richards, Paul. *Coping with Hunger: Hazard and Experiment in an African Rice-Farming System.* London: Allen and Unwin, 1983.

Rilke, Rainer Maria. *Duino Elegies and the Sonnets to Orpheus.* Trans. and ed., Stephen Mitchell. Vintage International Series. New York: Knopf Doubleday, 2005.

Rinna, Anthony W. "Ulan Bator's Small Country Diplomacy: The Case of North Korea." *SINO-NK*, June 22, 2015. http://sinonk.com/2015/06/22/ulan-bators-small-country-diplomacy-the-case-of-north-korea/.

Ripley, Will. "North Korea Defends Human Rights Record." *CNN*, June 30, 2015. https://edition.cnn.com/videos/world/2015/06/30/north-korea-denies-abuses-pkg-ripley.cnn.

Risse, Thomas, Steve C. Ropp, and Kathryn Sikkink, eds. *The Persistent Power of Human Rights: From Commitment to Compliance.* Cambridge: Cambridge University Press, 2013.

——, eds. *The Power of Human Rights: International Norms and Domestic Change.* Cambridge: Cambridge University Press, 1999.

Robinson, Courtland. "Famine in Slow Motion: A Case Study of Internal Displacement in the Democratic People's Republic of Korea." *Refugee Survey Quarterly* 19, no. 2 (2000): 121–22.

Rothwell, James. "North Korean Defector Returns Home After 16 Years and Rips Up Her Memoirs on Camera." *Telegraph*, January 21, 2016. http://www.telegraph.co.uk/news /worldnews/asia/northkorea/12112246/North-Korean-defector-returns-home-after-16 -years-and-rips-up-her-memoirs-on-camera.html.

Ryall, Julian. "Polish Firms Employing North Korean 'Slave Labourers' Benefit from EU Aid." *Telegraph*, May 31, 2016. http://www.telegraph.co.uk/news/2016/05/31/polish-firms -employing-north-korean-slave-labourers-benefit-from/.

Ryu, Hyun-Jung. "A Study on North Korea's Dual Network of Mobil Telecommunications System Using Actor-Network Theory" [in Korean]. M.A. thesis, University of North Korean Studies, 2012.

Samuels, Richard J. "Kidnapping Politics in East Asia." *Journal of East Asian Studies* 10, no. 3 (2010): 363–95.

Sang-Hun Choe, Gi-Wook Shin, and David Straub, eds. *Troubled Transition: North Korea's Politics, Economy, and External Relations*. Stanford, Calif.: Shorenstein Asia-Pacific Research Center, September 2013.

Scanlon, Charles. "North Korea's Resort Seizure Ends Project of Hope." *BBC News*, August 22, 2011.

Scarlatoiu, Greg. "The Rime of the Juche Mariner: North Korean Sailors and Fishermen Dispatched Overseas Through Montevideo, Uruguay." *HRNK Insider*, June 22, 2016. http://www.hrnkinsider.org/2016/06/the-rime-of-juche-mariner-north-korean.html.

Scarlatoiu, Greg, and Joseph Bermudez Jr. "Unusual Activity at the Kanggon Military Training Area in North Korea: Evidence of Execution by Anti-Aircraft Machine Guns?" Committee for Human Rights in North Korea, *HRNK Insider*, April 29, 2015. http:// www.hrnkinsider.org/2015/04/unusual-activity-at-kanggon-military.html.

Scarry, Elaine. *The Body in Pain: The Making and Unmaking of the World*. New York: Oxford University Press, 1985.

Scheper-Hughes, Nancy. *Death Without Weeping: The Violence of Everyday Life in Brazil*. Berkeley: University of California Press, 1989.

Schloms, Michael. *North Korea and the Timeless Dilemma of Aid: A Study of Humanitarian Action in Famines*. Berlin: Lit Verlag Münster, 2004.

Schwekendiek, Daniel. *A Socioeconomic History of North Korea*. Jefferson, N.C.: McFarland, 2011.

Sekula, Allan. "On the Invention of Photographic Meaning." In *Thinking Photography*, ed. Victor Burgin, 84–109. London: Palgrave Macmillan, 1982.

Sen, Amartya. "Democracy as a Universal Value." *Journal of Democracy* 10, no. 3 (1999): 3–17.

——. *Development as Freedom*. Oxford: Oxford University Press, 1999.

——. "Famines as Failures of Exchange Entitlements." *Economic and Political Weekly* 14, nos. 31–33 (1976): 1273–80.

——. *Poverty and Famines: An Essay on Entitlement and Deprivation*. Oxford: Clarendon Press, 1981.

Sen, Amartya, and Jean Drèze, Jean. *The Amartya Sen & Jean Drèze Omnibus: Comprising Poverty and Famines, Hunger and Public Action; India: Economic Development and Social Opportunity*. Oxford: Oxford University Press, 1999.

Seymour, James D. "China: Background Paper on the Situation of North Koreans in China." Commissioned by the United Nations High Commissioner for Refugees, Protection Information Section, January 2005. http://nautilus.org/wp-content/uploads /2011/12/0527A_Seymour.pdf.

Shen, Zhihua, and Yafeng Xia. "Contested Border: A Historical Investigation into the Sino-Korean Border Issue, 1950–1964." *Asian Perspective* 37, no. 1 (January–March 2013).

Shin Chang-Hoon, and Myong-Hyun Go. "Beyond the UN COI Report on Human Rights in North Korea." Asian Institute for Policy Studies, November 3, 2014. http://en.asaninst .org/contents/asan-report-beyond-the-coi-dprk-human-rights-report/.

Shin Dong Hyuk. "Commission of Inquiry on Human Rights in the DPRK—Seoul Public Hearing Day 1 (pm) 20 August." UN Web TV, 3:47:02. August 20, 2013. http://webtv.un .org/search/commission-of-inquiry-on-human-rights-in-the-dprk-seoul-public -hearing-day-1-pm-20-august/2668611257001?term=%EA%B3%B5%EC%B2%AD%ED %9A%8C.

Shin, Gi-wook. Ethnic Nationalism in Korea: Genealogy, Politics, and Legacy. Stanford, Calif.: Stanford University Press, 2006.

Shin Junshik. "North Korean People's Speech Shortening" [in Korean]. New Focus, December 18, 2014. http://www.newfocus.co.kr/client/news/viw.asp?cate=M1004&nNewsNumb =20141215201.

Shin, Young Jeon. "The Characteristics of Korea's Eugenic Movement in the Colonial Period Represented in the Bulletin, Woosaeng." Korea Journal of Medical History 15, no. 2 (2006): 133–55.

Slim, Hugo. "Positioning Humanitarianism in War: Principles of Neutrality, Impartiality and Solidarity." Paper presented to the Aspects of Peacekeeping Conference, Royal Military Academy, Sandhurst, U.K., January 1, 1997. http://repository.forcedmigration.org /show_metadata.jsp?pid=fmo:2232.

Smith, Hazel. Introduction to Explaining North Korean Migration to China: E-Dossier #11. Woodrow Wilson International Center for Scholars. North Korea International Documentation Project e-Dossier #11, September 2012. https://www.wilsoncenter.org/sites /default/files/NKIDP_eDossier_11_Explaining_North_Korean_Migration_to_China _1.pdf.

——. North Korea: Markets and Military Rule. Cambridge: Cambridge University Press, 2015.

Solzhenitsyn, Aleksandr I. The Gulag Archipelago 1918–1956: An Experiment in Literary Investigation. New York: HarperCollins, 2002.

Song, Jiyoung. "The Complexity of North Korean Migration." Asia Pacific Memo, no. 229 (June 6, 2013). http://apm.iar.ubc.ca/the-complexity-of-north-korean-migration/.

——. Human Rights Discourse in North Korea: Post-Colonial, Marxist and Confucian Perspectives. New York: Routledge, 2014.

——. "Why Do North Korean Defector Testimonies so Often Fall Apart?" Guardian, October 13, 2015.

Sorokin, Pitirim. Hunger as a Factor in Human Affairs. Gainesville: University Presses of Florida, 1975.

Soukhorukov, Sergey. "I Escaped North Korea After Famine, Violence." Sunday Telegraph, August 8, 2007. http://web.archive.org/web/20070815123438/http://www.telegraph.co .uk/news/main.jhtml?xml=/news/2007/08/05/wnkor105.xml.

Stahler, Kevin. "New Research on Cell Phone Use in North Korea." North Korea: Witness to Transformation (blog), March 7, 2014. http://blogs.piie.com/nk/?p=12941.

Stanton, Joshua. "Guild of Liars, Part 2: North Korean Refugees Expose the Lies of the National Lawyers' Guild." One Free Korea (blog), September 30, 2006. https://freekorea .us/2006/09/30/guild-of-liars-part-2-north-korean-refugees-expose-the-lies-of-the -national-lawyers-guild/.

Steinhoff, Patricia G. "Kidnapped Japanese in North Korea: The New Left Connection." Journal of Japanese Studies 30, no. 1 (Winter 2004): 123–42.

StimmeKoreas. "North Korean Defectors Return After 4 Years in South Korea!" YouTube video, 3:20. November 9, 2012. https://www.youtube.com/watch?v=x139pGGR_40.

——. "North Korean Restaurant Workers Abducted by South Korea! [English]." YouTube video, 8:01. April 29, 2016. https://www.youtube.com/watch?v=IAkXVO24ZXw.

Strawiński, Paweł. "Niewolnicy Kima znad Wisły." *Onet.biznes*, June 15, 2016. http://biznes .onet.pl/praca/prawo-pracy/pracownicy-z-korei-polnicnej-w-polsce-niewolnicy-kima -znad-wisly/yb51zf.

Stueck, William. *The Korean War: An International History*. Princeton, N.J.: Princeton University Press, 1997.

Suh, Dae-Sook. *Kim Il Sung: The North Korean Leader*. New York: Columbia University Press, 1988.

Szalontai, Balazs. *Kim Il Sung in the Khrushchev Era: Soviet-DPRK Relations and the Roots of North Korean Despotism, 1953–1964*. Stanford, Calif.: Stanford University Press, 2005.

Taylor, Mi Ae, and Mark E. Manyin. "Non-Governmental Organizations' Activities in North Korea." Congressional Research Service, March 25, 2011. https://fas.org/sgp/crs /row/R41749.pdf.

Tenhunen, Sirpa. "Mobile Technology in the Village: ICTs, Culture, and Social Logistics in India." *Journal of the Royal Anthropological Institute* 14 (2008): 515–34.

Terry, Fiona. "Feeding the Dictator: Special Report: Korea." *Guardian*, August 6, 2001. http://www.guardian.co.uk/world/2001/aug/06/famine.comment.

Thae Yong Ho. Keynote address at the Center for Strategic and International Studies conference Beyond Nuclear Diplomacy: A Regime Insider's Look at North Korea. Washington, D.C., October 31, 2017. https://csis-prod.s3.amazonaws.com/s3fs-public/event /171001_Beyond_Nuclear_Diplomacy_transcript.pdf?jJogSGaZruUOmarE1J4.XUfWF 9B4.vwm.

——. "Testimony of Minister Thae Yong-Ho, House Committee on Foreign Affairs." November 1, 2017. https://docs.house.gov/meetings/FA/FA00/20171101/106577/HHRG -115-FA00-Wstate-Yong-hoT-20171101.pdf.

Todorov, Tzvetan. *Hope and Memory: Reflections on the Twentieth Century*. Trans. David Bellows. London: Atlantic Books, 2003.

United Nations. "General Assembly Resolution 1991 (XVIII)." December 17, 1963. http:// www.un.org/en/ga/search/view_doc.asp?symbol=A/RES/1991(XVIII).

——. "No. 14668 Multilateral International Covenant on Civil and Political Rights, Adopted by the General Assembly of the United Nations on 19 December 1966." *United Nations Treaty Series*, vol. 999, no. I-14668. https://treaties.un.org/doc/publication/unts /volume%20999/volume-999-i-14668-english.pdf.

——. Universal Declaration of Human Rights. December 10, 1948. http://www.un.org/en /universal-declaration-human-rights/.

United Nations General Assembly. "International Covenant on Civil and Political Rights." December 19, 1966. http://www.ohchr.org/EN/ProfessionalInterest/Pages/CCPR.aspx.

——. "Report of the DPRK Association for Human Rights Studies Submitted to the United Nations General Assembly Security Council." September 15, 2014, A/69/383–S/2014/668. https://undocs.org/A/69/383.

——. "Report of the Special Rapporteur on the Situation on Human Rights in the Democratic People's Republic of Korea." September 8, 2015, UN Doc. A/70/362. http://undocs .org/A/70/362.

United Nations Human Rights Council (UNHRC). *Commission of Inquiry on Human Rights in the Democratic People's Republic of Korea*, February 7, 2014. https://www .ohchr.org/Documents/HRBodies/HRCouncil/CoIDPRK/Report/A.HRC.25.CRP.1 _ENG.doc.

United Nations Human Rights Office of the High Commissioner (OHCHR). "End of Mission Statement by the United Nations Special Rapporteur on the Rights of Persons with

Disabilities, Ms. Catalina Devandas-Aguilar, on Her Visit to the DPRK, Delivered at the Taedonggang Diplomatic Club, Pyongyang." May 8, 2017. https://www.ohchr.org /EN/NewsEvents/Pages/DisplayNews.aspx?NewsID=21610&LangID=E.

——. "International Covenant on Civil and Political Rights. Adopted and opened for signature, ratification and accession by General Assembly resolution 2200A (XXI) of 16 December 1966, entry into force 23 March 1976, in accordance with Article 49." http:// www.ohchr.org/EN/ProfessionalInterest/Pages/CCPR.aspx.

United Nations Security Council. "Report of the Panel of Experts Established Pursuant to Resolution 1874 (2009)." March 5, 2018. S/2018/171. https://www.securitycouncilreport .org/atf/cf/%7B65BFCF9B-6D27-4E9C-8CD3-CF6E4FF96FF9%7D/s_2018_171.pdf.

——. Resolution 1718, Non-proliferation/Democratic People's Republic of Korea. S/RES/1718. October 14, 2006. http://unscr.com/en/resolutions/1718.

——. Resolution 2321 (2016). S/RES/2321. November 30, 2016. http://undocs.org/S/RES /2321(2016).

——. Resolution 2371 (2017). S/RES/2371. August 5, 2017. http://unscr.com/en/resolutions /2371.

——. "The Situation in the Democratic People's Republic of North Korea." S/PV.7830, December 9, 2016. http://www.securitycouncilreport.org/atf/cf/%7B65BFCF9B-6D27 -4E9C-8CD3-CF6E4FF96FF9%7D/s_pv_7830.pdf.

——. "United Nations ESCOR Sub-Committee on Prevention of Discrimination and Protection of Minorities, 49th Session." UN Doc. E/CN.4/Sub.2/1997/50 (1997).

"Uriminjokkkiri vs t'albukcha pakyŏnmi ch'uaksangŭl tashigŭm p'ahech'yŏ ponda" [Our People vs. Defector Yeonmi Park, Digging up the Beast Again]. *Cihiribey Japene*, March 23, 2016. YouTube video, 45:18. https://www.youtube.com/watch?v=__sIBm8eH3A.

U.S. Department of State. *Armistice in Korea: Selected Statements and Documents.* Washington, D.C.: Government Printing Office, 1953.

——. *Trafficking in Persons Report 2009.* Washington, D.C.: U.S. Department of State, 2009. http://www.state.gov/documents/organization/123357.pdf.

——. *Trafficking in Persons Report 2016.* Washington, D.C.: Government Publishing Office, June 2016. https://www.state.gov/documents/organization/258876.pdf.

Vollers, Maryanne. "The Woman Who Faces the Wrath of North Korea." *Guardian.* March 15, 2015. http://www.theguardian.com/world/2015/mar/15/park-yeon-mi-north -korea-defector.

Walker, Susan, Sally Grantham-McGregor, Christine A. Powell, and Susan M. Chang. "Effects of Growth Restriction in Early Childhood on Growth, IQ, and Cognition at Age 11 to 12 Years and the Benefits of Nutritional Supplementation and Psychosocial Stimulation." *Journal of Pediatrics* 137 (2000): 36–41. http://dx.doi.org/10.1067/mpd .2000.106227.

Weatherly, Robert, and Song Jiyoung. "The Evolution of Human Rights Thinking in North Korea." *Journal of Communist Studies and Transition Politics* 24, no. 2 (June 2008): 272– 96. https://doi.org/10.1080/13523270802003111.

Wedeen, Lisa. "Ideology and Humor in Dark Times: Notes from Syria." *Critical Inquiry* 39 (Summer 2013): 841–73. https://misr.mak.ac.ug/sites/default/files/events/CRITICAL%20 INQUIRY,%20final%20copy.pdf.

Weiss, Rabbi Abner. "Autopsies and Jewish Law: An Orthodox Perspective." *My Jewish Learning*, n.d. https://www.myjewishlearning.com/article/autopsies-and-jewish -law/.

Williams, Brad, and Erik Mobrand. "Explaining Divergent Responses to the North Korean Abductions Issue in Japan and South Korea." *Journal of Asian Studies* 69, no. 2 (May 2010): 507–36.

Williams, Jennifer, "Read the Full Transcript of Trump's North Korea Summit Press Conference." *Vox*, June 12, 2018. https://www.vox.com/world/2018/6/12/17452624/trump-kim-summit-transcript-press-conference-full-text.

Williams, Martyn. "DPRK Again Second-to-Last in Press Freedom Ranking." *North Korea Tech*, April 20, 2016. http://www.northkoreatech.org/2016/04/20/dprk-second-last-press-freedom-ranking/.

——. "DPRK Organizations Called out for Censorship." *North Korea Tech*, March 13, 2014. https://www.northkoreatech.org/2014/03/13/dprk-organizations-called-out-for-censorship/.

——. "DPRK UN Ambassador Takes Questions, Gives Advice." *North Korea Tech*, January 26, 2014. http://www.northkoreatech.org/2014/01/26/dprk-un-ambassador-takes-questions-gives-advice/.

——. "More on UN Meeting, Silencing of DPRK Microphone." *North Korean Tech*, May 2, 2015. http://www.northkoreatech.org/2015/05/02/more-on-un-meeting-silencing-of-dprk-microphone/.

——. "Victims' Voices: A Conversation on North Korean Human Rights." YouTube video, 1:32:19, May 1, 2015. https://www.youtube.com/watch?v=2V-TPBXB-F8.

Windrem, Robert, Ken Dilanian, and Abigail Williams. "North Korea Has a History of Assassination Attempts on Foreign Soil." *NBC News*, November 21, 2017. https://www.nbcnews.com/news/north-korea/north-korea-has-history-assassination-attempts-foreign-soil-n823016.

Winick, M., K. K. Meyer, and R. C. Harris. "Malnutrition and Environmental Enrichment by Early Adoption." *Science* 190 (1975): 1173–75.

Woo Seongji. "North Korea's Food Crisis." *Korea Focus*, May–June (2004): 63–80.

World Food Programme. "Emergency Operation Democratic People's Republic of Korea: 10757.0—Emergency Assistance to Population Groups Affected by Floods and Rising Food and Fuel Prices." N.d. https://one.wfp.org/operations/current_operations/project_docs/107570.pdf.

World Food Summit. "Part 1: Issues and Concepts for Protecting and Promoting Good Nutrition in Crisis Situations." Food and Agriculture Organization of the United Nations, n.d. http://www.fao.org/docrep/008/y5815e/y5815e05.htm.

Yi Han-yong. *Kim Jong-il's Royal Family*. Seoul: Sidae Jeongsin, 2005.

Yun, Jenna Yoojin. "30,000 North Korean Children Living in Limbo in China." *Guardian*, February 5, 2016. https://www.theguardian.com/world/2016/feb/05/north-koreas-stateless-children.

Yoon, Mina. "When a Goat and Pig Decided to Join the North Korean Army." *NK News*, November 13, 2013. https://www.nknews.org/2013/11/when-a-goat-and-pig-decided-to-join-the-north-korean-army/.

Yoon Yeo-sang, Chung Jai-ho, and An Hyunmin. *2016 White Paper on Religious Freedom in North Korea*. Seoul: NKDB, January 4, 2017. http://www.nkdb.org/en/library/Books_list.php.

Yoon Yeo-sang and Lee Seung-Ju. "Human Rights and North Korea's Overseas Laborers: Dilemmas and Policy Challenges." Seoul: NKDB, May 8, 2015.

——. "North Korea's Export Laborer's Status and Human Rights Situation." Seoul: NKDB, January 2015.

Yoon Yeo-sang, Jae-eun Lee, and Sun-young Han. *Political Prison Camps in North Korea Today*. Seoul: NKDB, 2011.

Young, Benjamin. "A Revolutionary State: North Korea's Support of Non-State Actors, Past Policies and Future Issues." Korea Economic Institute of America, *On Korea* Academic

Paper Series, October 5, 2017. http://www.keia.org/sites/default/files/publications/kei _aps_young_final.pdf.

Zhu, Lijiang. "The Hukou System of the People's Republic of China: A Critical Appraisal Under International Standards of Internal Movement and Residence." *Chinese Journal of International Law* 2 (2003): 519–66.

Zur, Dafna. *Figuring Korean Futures: Children's Literature in Modern Korea*. Stanford, Calif.: Stanford University Press, 2017.

——. "The Korean War in Children's Picture Books of the DPRK." In *Exploring North Korean Arts*. Wien: University of Vienna Press, 2011.

——. "Let's Go to the Moon: Science Fiction in the North Korean Children's Magazine Adong Munhak, 1956–1965." *Journal of Asian Studies*, May 2014, 1–25.

INDEX

CONTEMPORARY ASIA IN THE WORLD

David C. Kang and Victor D. Cha, Editors